HEMINGWAY'S

FETISHISM

SUNY Series in Psychoanalysis and Culture
Henry Sussman, Editor

HEMINGWAY'S FETISHISM

Psychoanalysis and the Mirror of Manhood

Carl P. Eby

STATE UNIVERSITY OF NEW YORK PRESS

Published by

State University of New York Press, Albany

© 1999 State University of New York

All rights reserved

Printed in the United States of America

Cover photo: Hemingway in Africa, 1953. (John F. Kennedy Library, courtesy *Look* and Earl Theisen).

For information, address State University of New York Press, State Unviersity Plaza, Albany, N.Y., 12246

Production by Diana Ganeles
Marketing by Fran Keneston

Library of Congress Cataloging-in-Publication Data

Eby, Carl P.
    Hemingway's fetishism : psychoanalysis and the mirror of
manhood / Carl P. Eby.
        p.   cm. — (SUNY series in psychoanalysis and culture.)
    ISBN 0-7914-4003-6 (HC : acid-free paper). —
    ISBN 0-7914-4004-4
(PB : acid-free paper)
    1. Hemingway, Ernest, 1899–1961—Knowledge—Psychology.
2. Psychoanalysis and literature—United States—History—20th
century.   3. Psychological fiction, American—History and criticism.
4. Authors, American—20th century—Psychology.   5. Hemingway, Ernest, 1899–1961—Psychology.   6. Gender identity in literature.   7. Masculinity in literature.   8. Fetishism in literature.
9. Men in literature.   I. Title.   II. Series.
PS3515.E37Z5858   1999
813'.52—dc21   98-6223
                                                         CIP

10 9 8 7 6 5 4 3 2 1

For Linda

Contents

Illustrations

Acknowledgments

I am deeply grateful to the many friends who made this book possible. First, I would like to thank my dissertation director, Peter Hays, for his guidance, wisdom, and friendship. Next, I would like to thank all of those friends who read portions of my book in manuscript form and who offered me insights and crucial support: Susan Beegel, Jeffrey Berman, Kay Blacker, Gerry Brenner, Jaqcueline Vaught Brogan, Alan Elms, Sandra M. Gilbert, Michael J. Hoffman, Toni Knott, Peter Loewenberg, Erik Nakjavani, Daniel Rancour-Laferrire, and Kathy Willingham. Special mention must go to Kay for lending me a clinician's eye, to Alan for introducing me to the marcel wave, and to Daniel for his volume *Signs of the Flesh* which I found extremely valuable.

For generous financial support which made it possible for me to study Hemingway's manuscripts, I would like to thank the John F. Kennedy Library Foundation. I am particularly indebted to Stephen Plotkin, curator of the Hemingway Collection, for assistance beyond the call of duty. I am grateful to the Hemingway Foundation and Society both for permission to publish material from Hemingway's previously unpublished letters and for a fellowship that allowed me to attend an international conference to exchange ideas with like-minded scholars. I would like to thank the Humanities Institute at the University of California, Davis, for funding a research cluster, "Contemporary Psychoanalysis Across the Disciplines," and I am indebted to members of that research cluster for their help with my project. I am, likewise, indebted to the members of the University of California Interdisciplinary Psychoanalytic Consortium, both for their financial support and for their insights. And I am deeply grateful to the Robert J. Stoller Foundation and to Sybil Stoller for financial and symbolic support. The work of Robert Stoller is the foundation upon which this book has been built.

I want to thank my friends for remaining my friends when I could speak about little else but this book for the past five years. And, lastly, I would like to thank my wife and my family for the daily support and understanding that made this book possible.

Grateful acknowledgment is made to the following for permission to reprint previously published material:

From "The Evolution of a Shoe Fetish" by James W. Hamilton. Copyright ©1977 by James W. Hamilton. Reprinted by permission of the author.

From "Four Cases of Autocastration" by K. H. Blacker and Normund Wong. Copyright ©1963 American Medical Association. Reprinted by permission.

From "From the Analysis of a Transvestite" by Mervin Glasser. Copyright ©1979 by Mervin Glasser. Reprinted by permission of the author.

From "The Mother's Contribution to Infantile Transvestic Behavior" by Robert Stoller, and "Notes on the Analysis of the Sexual Perversions" by W. H. Gillespie. Copyright ©1966 and ©1940 Institute of Psycho-Analysis. Reprinted by permission.

From "The Object in Fetishism, Homeovestism and Transvestism" by George Zavitzianos. Copyright ©1977 by George Zavitzianos. Reprinted by permission of Sylvia Zavitzianos.

From AT THE HEMINGWAYS by Marcelline Hemingway Sanford. Reprinted by permission of the Sanford family.

From ERNEST HEMINGWAY: A LIFE STORY by Carlos Barker. Copyright ©1969 by Carlos Baker and Mary Hemingway. Reprinted by permission of Scribner, a Division of Simon and Schuster, and HarperCollins Publishers Ltd.

From HEMINGWAY by Kenneth Lynn. Copyright ©1987 by Kenneth S. Lynn. Reprinted by permission of Harvard University Press.

From HOW IT WAS by Mary Welsh Hemingway. Copyright ©1976 by Mary Welsh Hemingway. Reprinted by permission of Alfred A. Knopf Inc.

From OBSERVING THE EROTIC IMAGINATION by Robert Stoller. Copyright ©1985 by Yale University Press. Reprinted by permission.

From SEXUAL VARIATIONS: FETISHISM, SADO-MASOCHISM, AND TRANSVESTISM by Chris C. Gosselin and Glenn Wilson. Copyright ©1980 by Faber & Faber. Reprinted by permission.

Canada for all of Hemingway's previously published works, ©Hemingway Foreign Rights Trust. Reprinted by permission.

I would like to thank *The Hemingway Review* for permission to reprint a much-expanded version of "'Come Back to the Beach Ag'in, David Honey!': Hemingway's Fetishization of Race in *The Garden of Eden Manuscript*."

An earlier version of "Rabbit Stew and Blowing Dorothy's Bridges" first appeared in *Literature and Psychoanalysis: Proceedings of the Thirteenth International Conference on Literature and Psychoanalysis, Boston, July 1996*. I would like to thank the Instituto Superior de Psicologia Aplicada in Lisbon, Portugal, for the permission to reproduce this material.

A shorter version of the first three sections of chapter 6 first appeared as an essay entitled "Hemingway and the Mirror of Manhood: Fetishism, Transvestism, Homeovestism, and Perverse *Méconnaissance*." I would like to thank *Arizona Quarterly* for permission to reproduce this material.

Abbreviations

ART   *Across the River and Into the Trees*

CSS   *The Complete Short Stories of Ernest Hemingway.* Finca Vigía Edition.

DIA   *Death in the Afternoon*

FTA   *A Farewell to Arms*

FWBT   *For Whom the Bell Tolls*

GE   *The Garden of Eden*

IITS   *Islands in the Stream*

MF   *A Moveable Feast*

SAR   *The Sun Also Rises*

SL   *Selected Letters: 1917–1961*

SS   *The Short Stories of Ernest Hemingway*

THHN   *To Have and Have Not*

Introduction:
A Short Apologia

> But all these guys have theories and try to fit you into
> the theory. Malcolm [Cowley] thot I was like him be-
> cause my father was a Dr. and I went to Michigan
> when I was 2 weeks old where they had Hemlock trees.
> P. Young: It's all trauma. Sure plenty of trauma in
> 1918 but symptoms absent by 1928. . . . Carlos Baker
> really baffles me. Do you suppose he can con himself
> into thinking I would put a symbol into anything on
> purpose. It's hard enough just to make a paragraph.
> What sort of symbol is Debba, my Wakamba fiancée?
> She must be a dark symbol. N'gui my rough bad
> brother. He must be a very dark symbol indeed.
>
> —Hemingway, Letter to Harvey Breit (1956)

Yes, I too have a theory about Hemingway. And no doubt, were
he alive today, he would not be pleased. He not only despised all
theories about his work, but—partly for reasons which will become clear in the course of my study—psychoanalytic theories
in particular always seemed to chafe an especially tender nerve.
Thus, in 1952 he complained to Wallace Meyer, "Criticism is getting all mixed up with a combination of the Junior F.B.I.-men,
discards from Freud and Jung and a sort of Columnist peephole
and missing laundry list school. . . . Every young English professor sees gold in them dirty sheets now. Imagine what they can
do with the soiled sheets of four legal beds by the same writer
and you can see why their tongues are slavering. . ." (*SL* 751).
Given the psychoanalytic reading of his life and work that follows, Hemingway would clearly count me among the "Junior
F.B.I.-men." I must, however, begin by pleading innocent to the
charge of trying to *reduce* his work to my theory.

1

I would be the first to say that my theory ignores innumerable extremely significant issues in Hemingway's work. I would also be among the last to say that the most important thing about his fiction is the psychosexuality underpinning so much of it. Hemingway's position in American literature surely owes more to his contribution as a literary stylist and technical innovator than it does to his expression of psychosexual issues—even though his expression of these issues contributed heavily both to the emotional impact of his fiction and to the process by which he became an icon of American masculinity. Some critics will inevitably complain that such terms as *narcissism, fetishism,* and *transvestism* are simply too crude for the complexity of the love relationships presented in Hemingway's fiction. This complaint, however, seems predicated upon the myth of a potentially "complete" or "totalizing" response to the text—a myth to which I do not subscribe. Such terms—which really are not so very crude when they are fully understood—*appear* crude only when the love relationships are *reduced* to them. Put simply, I make no attempt to describe the love relationships in their totality, and I stress the psychosexuality at work in these relationships not because I think it is their "essence," but because I think this *aspect* of these relationships has far-reaching ramifications for our understanding of *all* of Hemingway's fiction. Thus, while I freely admit that my theory offers only a partial explanation of Hemingway's work, I would also argue that, provided the logical principle of noncontradiction remains unviolated, the merits of a theory should be measured by what it *can* explain, not by what it cannot. And I believe my theory explains a good deal—even those "dark symbols," Debba and N'gui.

Elucidating Hemingway's psychosexuality is much more than a matter of spinning gold from dirty linen. It has grown increasingly apparent in the last few years that an appreciation for Hemingway's psychosexual concerns is not only essential for understanding his own or his characters' unconscious motivations; it is also essential for understanding his *subject matter* insofar as human sexuality and gender identity remained major concerns throughout his career. A coherent psychoanalytic understanding of this territory, then, has much to offer. Critics, of course, have speculated for years about such traditional psychoanalytic concerns as Hemingway's gender instability, narcissism, erotic attachment to hair, latent homosexuality, castration anxiety, and Oedipus complex—not to mention such related is-

sues as his construction of masculinity, his divided attitude toward women, his eroticization of race, and his passion for secret-keeping. Yet each of these issues has almost invariably been
treated in isolation, or at best as part of a network with one or
two other themes. Rather than presenting yet another psychoanalytic reading that reduces Hemingway's psychosexuality to
any one or two of these terms, my goal is to unite these various
disparate observations into a coherent theory and dynamic
model of Hemingway's psychosexuality. Moreover, as I develop
my theory, I hope to demonstrate how it can be used to clarify
thematic, symbolic, and structural concerns that are of tremendous importance to any understanding of Hemingway's fiction.

For the past two decades, Hemingway criticism has been
dominated by a reconsideration of the role of gender in his
work. Ever since Aaron Latham's "A Farewell to Machismo" appeared in *The New York Times* in 1977, it has become increasingly clear that Hemingway's reign as the hairy-chested icon of
American masculinity is coming to an end. To be sure, this
message hasn't yet filtered down to the general reading public.
In the popular imagination, Ernest the monovocally masculine
bullfight aficionado, boxer, hunter, deep-sea fisherman, and
pitchman for Ballantine Ale and khaki pants still looms over
the American literary horizon like a testosterone-crazed colos-
sus. Neither has the message filtered down to many academic
English departments, where opinions like those expressed
by Judith Fetterley in *The Resisting Reader* (1978) (i.e., that
Hemingway was merely a male-chauvinist-pig) are as often as
not still in vogue. Yet, in the wake of such publications as Kenneth Lynn's biography of Hemingway (1987), Mark Spilka's
Hemingway's Quarrel with Androgyny (1990), Peter Messent's
Hemingway (1992), and Nancy Comley and Robert Scholes'
Hemingway's Genders (1994), it has become obvious to most
serious Hemingway scholars (if it wasn't already) that, in Peter
Messent's words, "any remaining attempt to consign the author
automatically and simply to the 'cult of masculinity' . . . [is]
misguided in the extreme" (2). If a few serious Hemingway
scholars remain holdouts, unconvinced or unwilling to accept
the still emerging figure that Comley and Scholes call *el nuevo
Hemingway*, my study is unlikely to make new converts—nor
does it aim to. Rather, I think it is safe to say that Papa has
now been demythologized for almost all the serious Hemingway
scholars who are willing to have him so.

This is not to say, however, that further demythologization of Hemingway is entirely without merit. Insofar as Hemingway was, and in some quarters still is, an icon of American masculinity, any revelation about the process by which he constructed his personal masculinity—and femininity—suggests something about how a multitude of men in our culture may have done the same. However, I urge caution here. The psychoanalytic portrait that I paint of Hemingway is highly individual, not a transpersonal matter of cultural archetypes, and if the ideal of the "Hemingway man" struck a chord with many American men, it did so, I think, in part because many of his *personal* concerns reflected, in an exaggerated form, wider *cultural* concerns of his day.

I must also stress that the demythologization of Hemingway should not be confused with a "trashing" of the author, an accusation occasionally made by some of his more idolizing critics. True, most of us take a Twelfth-Night pleasure in seeing the world turned upside down, and if in this postmodern era we tire of hearing that the Emperor wears no clothes, our ears nevertheless always prick at the suggestion that he was fond of wearing *women's* clothes. Yet the "skirting of the Hemingway legend," as John Raeburn calls it, is not simply an exercise in critical prurience or *Schadenfreude*. Comley and Scholes may tell us that "the Hemingway [we] were taught about in high school is dead" (146), yet it is virtually axiomatic that mythical figures don't die easily. In fact, absent the periodic stake through the heart, they have an uncanny knack for rising from the dead only stronger than ever. Yet the Hemingway myth must be dismantled if we are to study the man behind it—or his work. Moreover, this man was far more fascinating and complex than the myth would ever suggest, and an appreciation of this complexity can only enhance our appreciation of his truly remarkable art.

Of course, there have always been critics, like Leslie Fiedler, who responded to what they perceived as Hemingway's hypermasculine world of boxing, bullfighting, and hunting with a skeptical "methinks he protests too much." As early as 1933, Max Eastman, in his famous article "Bull in the Afternoon"—the article that subsequently led to an infamous wrestling match between Eastman and Hemingway on the floor of Max Perkins's office—accused Hemingway of inventing a "literary style . . . of wearing false hair on the chest" and observed that it was a "commonplace that Hemingway lacks the serene confidence that he *is* a full-sized man" (96).[1] Yet even this skeptical approach to Hemingway, by stressing his "hypermasculinity," worked hand in glove with the traditional masculine myth which ignored the complex exploration of gender issues throughout Hemingway's work and marginalized such stories as "The Sea Change," "The Mother of a Queen," and "A Simple Enquiry"—stories which now are recognized as being an integral part of Hemingway's work. To make these stories *central* to his work would perhaps be as misguided as ignoring them, since they are generally not his best work, but we do need a theory which gives them a place—which allows them to be inflected by the other stories and which tells us how they inflect other stories. The appearance of *The Garden of Eden*, even in the bowdlerized edition published by Scribner's in 1986, has made the need for such a theory keenly felt. The publication of this posthumous novel—even more than the general shift in academic critical taste in the last two decades—has made gender issues in Hemingway's work virtually impossible to ignore. Or, rather, to ignore them entirely is no longer simply a reflection of other critical interests; it is an act of denial.

It should, therefore, be no mystery that I date the new focus in Hemingway studies to the appearance of Latham's article, the impetus for which had been provided by a mere glimpse of *The Garden of Eden* manuscripts as they were being transported to their current home at the John F. Kennedy Library. (Latham explains that he was allowed to see only the "first few chapters and the last chapter—and to browse through the rest of the manuscript" [55].) In this brief glimpse, Latham could see Hemingway's fascination with sexual "twinning," "androgynous" lovemaking, sexual metamorphoses, and male and female homosexuality. Moreover, Latham realized that "Ernest Hemingway's fascination with the Janus faces of sexuality was somehow intertwined with his fascination with hair" (90), and he correctly associated these then apparently "un-Hemingway-esque" themes with what he knew of Ernest's childhood in girl's clothing and with Hemingway's unusual behavior as an adult during his 1953 trip to Africa. These are among the most prominent of the themes which will preoccupy me throughout my study, and I hope to demonstrate—in detail and with solid new evidence—how they fit like pieces into a puzzle, or like cogs into the desiring machine of Hemingway's psyche.

I do not pretend to be the first to formulate a theory uniting these themes. Most notably, Mark Spilka and Nancy Comley and

Robert Scholes have been there before me, and I do not aim
to supplant their theories with my own. In fact, their books were
invaluable to my study. Obviously, Hemingway *did* employ the
cultural codes that Comley and Scholes describe. Just as
clearly, Hemingway was influenced by his childhood reading and
by the competing male and female Victorian models of masculinity promulgated by his parents and described so well by Spilka.
Moreover, Ernest's experience of being twinned with his older
sister, Marcelline, will be as important to my study as it was to
Spilka's—perhaps more so. Yet I also see my work as a corrective
for some significant failings of these works.

Comley and Scholes's observations are astute but seem
strangely untheorized and untheorizable. They reasonably claim
that "it makes sense to see a writer's life and work as a network
of codes that are cultural in origin but subject to selection, rejection, and modification by individuals" (4), but there seems to
be no mechanism for explaining the *process* of selection, rejection, and modification, nor does there seem to be any room for
entirely *personal*, non-cultural, codes. By defining *gender* as "a
system of sexual differentiation that is partly biological and
partly cultural" (ix), Comley and Scholes neglect the fact that
gender is also a *personal* construct. As Nancy Chodorow has recently reminded us, "Each person's sense of gender . . . is an in-
extricable fusion or melding of personally created . . . and
cultural meaning" (517). Psychoanalytic theory, which Comley
and Scholes wrongly eschew in deference to their laudable distaste for reductivism, provides a corrective for these problems,
as I hope to demonstrate in the reinterpretations that I will offer
of Hemingway passages which have also been analyzed in their
book. In each instance, my work does not contradict their interpretation, but it does clarify how each passage fits into a larger,
more theorizable, pattern in Hemingway's life and work.

Spilka's work, on the other hand, is plagued by the vague-
ness of his key term, "androgyny," which he defines simply as "a
mixture or exchange of traditionally male and female traits,
roles, activities, and sexual positions" (4). My theory complicates
and clarifies this notion of androgyny considerably. In doing so,
among other things, it allows us to discover the subtler workings
of Hemingway's gender concerns; it allows us to understand why
these concerns evolved and remained so entrenched; it allows
us to understand how Hemingway's favorite psychosexual symbols function in his work; and it de-sentimentalizes Heming-

way's attitude toward the eroticized fusion of his male and female characters.

To elaborate a thorough model of Hemingway's psychosexuality, I must inevitably employ some psychoanalytic jargon, but
as Marianne Moore would say, "These things are important not
because a // high-sounding interpretation can be put upon
them but because / they are / useful." The goal of my study is
not to "diagnose" Hemingway as if he were a patient, yet I must
first do exactly this to construct a useful theoretical framework
which can then be put to *use*.

Some will surely object that to "diagnose" Hemingway one
would have to have him "on the couch" and have access to his
free associations. And to be sure, I do not mean to equate literature, a product of conscious artistry, with dreams or free associations. (Five of Hemingway's actual dreams, however, *will* figure
in my analysis.) Yet I have always felt that Hemingway's unconscious fantasies were unusually close to the "surface" of his fiction—an opinion that should hardly surprise anyone familiar
with *The Garden of Eden*. (This quality of his fiction, in fact, is
intimately tied to his fetishism. We will eventually see that,
within an unconscious split-off portion of Hemingway's psyche,
portions of the ego and id remained in unbroken contact.[2]) Kenneth Johnston and others have noted the similarity between
Hemingway's iceberg principle, with its distinction between the
manifest and latent content of a story, and Freud's model of
conscious and unconscious thought. Hemingway was also fond
of calling his typewriter his "therapist"—a joke, admittedly,
which nevertheless invites us to imagine his work as the tran-
scripts of analytic "sessions." Hemingway, of course, was a
meticulous and very conscious prose stylist, but when I find patterns of association compulsively repeated not only throughout
his fiction, but throughout his letters and everyday life, I feel
justified in suspecting that these patterns were not determined
solely, or even primarily, by conscious artistry.

I realize that it is not as fashionable as it once was to psy-
choanalyze artists while analyzing their art, but this is simply
unavoidable in any thorough consideration of fetishism. Insofar
as we are concerned with *sexual fetishes*—as opposed to Marx-
ist "commodity fetishes" or the "anthropological fetishes" of
"primitive" religion (and it is important not to confuse and conflate such disparate phenomena)[3]—*there simply is no fetish without a fetishist*. For most of us, a shoe is something to be worn on

a foot, not a tool to aid masturbation; we might spend considerable time having our hair done, but we don't derive almost unbearable sexual excitement from cutting or dyeing our partners' hair. Items like shoes or hair only become genuine sexual fetishes when *someone* treats them as a fetish within the context of an intricate, enduring, compulsive, and highly personal psychodynamic. No doubt, as Freud claimed, an *element* of fetishism probably appears in everyone's sexuality—for instance in the form of a gentlemanly preference for blondes. Millions of people pay far too much attention to shoes and to hair, and this attention must often, if not always, partake of an element of erotic desire. This is the legacy of our infantile polymorphous perversity, a legacy which gives us some degree of erotic freedom. But not every eroticized object is a genuine sexual fetish, and such fleeting desires are a far cry from an organized adult perversion.

Perversion? The word makes us squirm. It seems so judgmental. Aren't we beyond it? Isn't it more enlightened to speak of mere *differences*?

I don't mean to be judgmental, although I might not be able to avoid it entirely. "Perversion" is the standard psychoanalytic term for an organized psychology, with its own characteristic defenses and mode of object relations, distinct from other organized psychologies such as the neuroses and psychoses. (Which isn't to say that perverse, neurotic, and/or psychotic organizations can't coexist within the same individual in different aspects of the psyche.) Perversion is *not* best defined as a "deviation" from some transcendental sexual "norm." To be sure, Freud at first defined it as a "deviation" in the choice of a sexual object or aim, and uncommon sexual practices are a hallmark of the male perversions (though not necessarily of the female perversions).[4] Yet if Freud taught us anything, it was that there is no such thing as "normal" a priori sexuality. Even if one *could* define such a (presumably heterosexual) "norm," one could imagine innumerable forms of sexual "deviation" that would not be organized perversions. Homosexuality, for instance, should not be considered a perversion. As Robert Stoller points out, homosexuality is a form of object choice (the selection of a partner of the same sex) and not a "condition" any more than heterosexuality is a "condition." There are, Stoller suspects, as many types of homosexuality as there are types of heterosexuality—some of which are perverse, some of which are not.[5] Perversion

is more usefully defined as a psychological strategy characterized by a certain set of concerns, a specific mode of object relations, and a characteristic set of defenses. Typically, it involves
the deployment of infantile gender stereotypes in a never-ending
attempt to regulate identity and negotiate a self-cure through
the undoing of infantile sexual trauma. Perverse sexuality—the
most obvious symptom of the male perversions—is compulsive
and fixated and largely devoid of erotic freedom. Thus, a perversion is not best defined by any sexual act but, rather, by the *significance* of the act to the person performing it.[6]

In the wake of Foucault's critique of the coercive power of
the social norms inherent in the psychological diagnosis of
"aberrant" sexuality, there has been a trend to replace the
power-laden term *perversion* with the more judgment-neutral
term *paraphilia*. However, the *Diagnostic and Statistical Manual
of Mental Disorders* (*DSM-IV*) still defines *paraphilia* as a "disorder" (a *para* of the *philia*: a deviation in the object of one's erotic
attraction), and it is simply a euphemism for *perversion*. I prefer
the word *perversion* for two reasons. First, Hemingway used it
himself repeatedly, though perhaps reluctantly. In "The Sea
Change," when Phil's wife tries to explain her plans for a lesbian
affair, Phil bitterly attempts to quote Pope's "An Essay on Man":
"Vice is a monster of such fearful mien . . . that something or
other needs but to be seen." (The complete quote ironically pre-
figures his change of heart and eventual attraction to his wife's
affair: "Vice is a Monster of so frightful mien, / As, to be hated,
needs but to be seen; / Yet seen too oft, familiar with her Face,
/ We first endure, then pity, then embrace.") But Phil's wife complains, "Let's not say vice. . . . That's not very polite." So Phil corrects himself: "Perversion" (SS 399). His wife isn't very happy
with this word either, but Hemingway uses it again in *For Whom
the Bell Tolls*, again in the *Islands in the Stream* manuscript, and
again in *The Garden of Eden* when David Bourne complains of
his wife's effusive reaction to her first lesbian experience: "Perversion's dull and old fashioned. I didn't know people like us still
kept up on it" (120).

My second reason for favoring the term *perversion* is that
the perversions are structured *by the perverse subject* precisely
in a simultaneously reifying and transgressive dialectic with
those coercive social norms which are comparatively elided by
the sanitized term *paraphilia*. In this spirit, Stoller argues that
we should reserve the term perversion "*because* of its nasty con-

notations. *Perversion* is a sturdy word, throbbing with assump-
tions, while *paraphilia* is a wet noodle. In trying to say nothing,
it says nothing. It is not only neutral; it is neutered, pithed. It
does not contain the quality I believe the person we would call
perverse finds essential. That quality is the sense of sin, or sinning" (*Observing* 6). Of course, as Stoller quickly acknowledges,
a belief in sin is unscientific; yet he points out that it is equally
"unscientific to believe that people do not believe in sin," and
that *belief* is essential to the structure of the perversions. For
Stoller, any sexual "activity is perverse . . . if the erotic excitement depends on one's feeling that one is sinning" (7). Thus, in
The Garden of Eden manuscript, when Barbara Sheldon first
hatches her plans to cut her husband's hair just like her own,
she urges him: "Let's think of something fun to do that we've
never done that will be secret and wicked. . ." (K422.1 3.1).[7] That
Nick and Barbara find "wickedness" in such apparently innocuous games, of course, testifies to the very Edenic innocence they
must lose. But more than this, it testifies as well to the perverse
nature of their desire.

     At first glance, a fetish might not look very interesting. After
all, why should we care if someone gets turned on by polishing
shoes or cutting hair? But a genuine sexual fetish is much more
than a casually eroticized object; it is not a mere toy chosen
lightly in freewheeling sex play. The fetish—usually a non-genital body part or item of clothing with bodily attributes—is an
obligatory prop in a highly compulsive, fixated, and ritualized
sexuality. Without it, sexual gratification for the fetishist is
nearly impossible.[8] It is nothing less than the linchpin of the
fetishist's psychosexuality, a radically overdetermined object
linked to every aspect of the fetishist's infantile sexuality, and a
vital tool in the fetishist's regulation of his personal identity.[9] In
the words of Robert Stoller, "a fetish is a story masquerading as
an object" (*Observing* 155); it is the key to an entire realm of interrelated ideas, feelings, and attitudes that Mervin Glasser calls
the fetishist's "core complex." As I hope to demonstrate in my
first chapter, Hemingway's fetish always appears in his fiction
with a retinue of attendant fantasies, themes, and symbols that
are among the most prominent and important in his *oeuvre*.
These are the ambassadors of his core complex to the realm of
fantasy. To define what I will call Hemingway's "field of fetishistic fantasy" I will have to retrace some territory that will be all
too familiar to many Hemingway scholars, but this first chapter

should provide readers with a necessary point of reference for further discussion. For as the rest of the book unfolds, my goal will be to use an analysis of the fetish to unlock the meaning of Hemingway's entire field of fetishistic fantasy.

I will only begin to elaborate a theory of fetishism in my second chapter. Using Freud's seminal work on fetishism, which remains the foundation for all later psychoanalytic considerations of the subject, I will explain why Hemingway favored wives and female characters with "boyishly" cut hair and why violent haircuts and scalpings are so common throughout his work. As my explanation of the Freudian model of fetishism unfolds, I will also be able to explain such disparate phenomena as the voice changes that accompany sexual excitement throughout Hemingway's fiction, the prominence of castration and amputation as themes in his work, and the recurrent appearance of "phallic women" in Hemingway's texts.

My third chapter reexamines Hemingway's childhood to explain why *he* became a fetishist and why *hair* became his fetish. Using the theoretical and clinical insights of Phyllis Greenacre and Robert Stoller, I will demonstrate that the origins of Hemingway's fetishism lay in an extended preoedipal trauma associated with his unusual handling by a mother who identified with her son so intensely that she christened him with a version of her stage name ("Ernestine") and dressed him in baby clothes that had once been her own. Still more critical to the development of Hemingway's fetishism was his mother's insistence on raising him as the "identical," "same-sex" "twin" of a sister who, in fact, was a year older. This may sound like well-trodden territory to those readers familiar with recent studies of Hemingway by Lynn and by Spilka, but my chapter aims to complicate and clarify these earlier studies by placing them for the first time on solid theoretical footing. The final section of the chapter will begin to explore the linguistic associations through which Hemingway's fetishism found expression. An analysis of one of Hemingway's key fetish *words* will reveal why Robert Jordan selects such a horribly inappropriate nickname for Maria in *For Whom the Bell Tolls*, and it will begin to expose the role played by aggression in the perversions.

Having established the linguistic nature of fetishistic associations, my fourth chapter will use an analysis of Hemingway's lifelong fascination with cats—a fascination particularly significant in *Islands in the Stream* and "Cat in the Rain"—to illuminate the relation between the fetishism and loss. I will suggest that the key to understanding this relation resides in the further relation between the fetish and the infantile possession that D. W. Winnicott calls the transitional object—the child's first not-me possession used during the process of separation and individuation from the maternal body. Traces of the transitional object persist in the fetish, illuminating Hemingway's fascination with sweaters and revealing a maternal presence behind that most phallic of objects, the fetish. In the final section of the chapter I hope to demonstrate how this understanding of the relation between fetishism and loss can help us to understand one of Hemingway's masterpieces, "Soldier's Home."

In each chapter, I take a significant problem in Hemingway's fiction as an invitation to probe more deeply into the nature and significance of his fetishism. Thus my theoretical speculations are always grounded in specific examples, and my attention to theory is always in the service of interpreting the fiction. In chapter 5, I try to explain why Catherine Bourne, in *The Garden of Eden*, becomes obsessed with changing her *race* when she changes her hairstyles and gender. By tracing Hemingway's fetishization of racial otherness, I reveal how Hemingway used the fetish to negotiate between masculinity and femininity, between latent homosexuality and heterosexuality, as well as between a narcissistic desire for merger and a concomitant need to objectify the *other* entirely. I demonstrate how Hemingway's fetish retained a linguistic tie to his sister Marcelline, and I reveal more fully how fetishism was related to the theme of "androgyny" in his work. Perhaps most surprisingly, this chapter offers solid, previously unpublished, evidence that Hemingway's fetishism occasionally manifested itself through transvestic behavior—a common occurrence in fetishism, but something hardly expected of America's erstwhile icon of literary machismo. Much as Catherine Bourne uses the fetish to facilitate her transformation into the "boy," "Peter," while cutting and dyeing her husband's hair to transform him into the "lovely girl," "Catherine," Hemingway and his fourth wife, Mary, engaged in similar fetishistic and transvestic games while on safari in Africa in 1953. On safari, Hemingway "went native," took up spear hunting, shaved his head like a Masai girl, developed an intense desire to pierce his ears, and obsessively cut and dyed Mary's hair. Moreover, he happily described his wife as a "boy" and himself as her "girl," calling her "Peter" and calling himself "Kathrin." My goal in exploring this

territory isn't to "out" Ernest Hemingway; my aim, rather, is to illuminate a set of interrelated fantasies, themes, and symbols
that were vital to Hemingway's personal identity and which are
vital to any understanding of his art.

In chapter 6, I offer further solid and previously unpublished evidence of Hemingway's transvestic behavior in order to
illuminate the significance of a bisexual split in his ego. In a remarkable series of 1947 letters to Mary Hemingway, Ernest ob-
sesses for pages about Mary's hair and describes dyeing his own
hair "as red as a French polished copper pot or a newly minted
penny." More to the point, he calls Mary "Peter" and aligns himself with a mysterious "Catherine"—Mary's girl—who appears in
the night. The shades of *The Garden of Eden* are impossible to
deny, but more importantly, a recognition of the split in Hemingway's ego demands a rethinking of traditional critiques of his
female characters, for on some level these women represented
an integral part of himself. Hemingway's characters, male and
female, often encounter the split in their identities while wearing
the fetish before mirrors, and the fourth section of this chapter
addresses the significance of this theme in Hemingway's work.
Drawing on the psychoanalytic work of George Zavitzianos, I use
the concept of *homeovestism*, a sort of "male male impersonation," to explain why Frederic Henry, in *A Farewell to Arms*,
feels like an impostor when regarding his own bearded face in
the mirror. In the final section of the chapter, I use Hemingway's
fascination with George Armstrong Custer, particularly in *Across
the River and Into the Trees* and *For Whom the Bell Tolls*, to further illuminate this sensation of imposture. Drawing upon the
theoretical work of Joyce McDougall, I try to explicate how Hemingway constructed his masculinity both in opposition to his
femininity and in relation to a paternal imago that was radically
split between a denigrated imaginary father and an idealized,
but unattainable, symbolic father.

In my final chapter, using *The Garden of Eden* and some
material sliced out of the manuscript to *Islands in the Stream*, I
address the vexed issue of the relation between perversion,
pornography, and creativity. This chapter, more than any other,
explicates the function of the "perverse scenario" in Hemingway's fiction, demonstrating how perversion transforms trauma
into triumph. Here I will argue that the perverse scenario was
paradoxically both fundamental to Hemingway's creativity and
yet the *least* creative element in his art.

The Core Complex and the Field
of Fetishistic Fantasy

Following the Fetish

> Everybody has strange things that mean things to
> them and we have to understand them.
>
> —*The Garden of Eden* Manuscript

> No other variation of the sexual instinct that borders
> on the pathological can lay so much claim to our inter-
> est as this one, such is the peculiarity of the phenom-
> ena to which it gives rise.
>
> —Freud on fetishism in *Three Essays on Sexuality*

An entire book devoted to Hemingway's fetishism? What could possibly be so interesting and important about a mere quirk of a great author's sex life?

Such doubts are understandable, and they would be entirely reasonable if fetishism *were* a mere quirk of the fetishist's bedroom behavior. But there is much more to a fetish than first meets the eye. No mere erotic quirk, the fetish is not only an obligatory prop in a highly compulsive, fixated, and ritualized sexuality, it is simply the most obvious manifestation of a highly complex psychology, and it is the key to an entire realm of inter-related ideas, feelings, and attitudes that Mervin Glasser calls the fetishist's "core complex." This core complex is fundamental to Hemingway's fiction and finds expression through a set of re-current, and highly personal, fantasies, themes, and symbols that are among the most prominent and important in Heming-way's art. The point of following the fetish is not to dwell on the kinkiness of famous men, but rather to unlock the meaning of this entire field of fetishistic fantasy.

For the fetishist, the fetish is more than a sex toy; it "is an essential feature of his psychic stability, and much of his life revolves around it" (McDougall 54). Barbara Sheldon, in a subplot excised from the published version of *The Garden of Eden*, testifies to this aspect of the perversions and seems to speak for her creator when she admits that her fetishistic fantasies have taken possession of her and now "own" her entirely (K422.1 5.5.7). Likewise, in the published version of the novel, after Catherine Bourne first uses her fetishized hair to transvestically switch "sexes" with David, she asks her husband if he now thinks she's "wicked." "Of course not," he replies, but he wonders how long she has been thinking about such transformations. "Not all the time," she replies. "But quite a lot" (17). Catherine's fetishistic games soon dominate her life, and she repeatedly insists that they are not a matter of choice. She *has* to do these things and is powerless to do otherwise. Such fixity and compulsion are a hallmark of the psychoanalytic perversions, and we will eventually see that Ernest Hemingway was moved by precisely the same spirit.

As Sylvia Payne has observed, "A study of what the fetish means to the fetishist reveals that . . . every component of the infantile sexual instinct has some connection with the fetish object, so that this object is associated with all the repressed infantile sexual experiences" (166). It is this radical overdetermination of the fetish that makes it such a fascinating object of study and such a vital tool in the fetishist's regulation of his personal identity. Thanks to this overdetermination, Hemingway could use his fetish as an "all-purpose tool" to negotiate between identification and object choice, between love and aggression, between merger and separation, between narcissistic and oedipal desire, between heterosexuality and homosexuality, and between masculinity and femininity. The fetish was also a tool for negotiating transvestic and homeovestic behavior, and it was a monument to, and a tool for mending, a bisexual split in Hemingway's ego which both led to and was reinforced by his fetishism. Most importantly for Hemingway's readers, the overdetermined trajectory of the fetish object becomes a psychosexual thread uniting Hemingway's most ubiquitous themes and most insistent imagery.

Of course this very overdetermination has its disadvantages, too. Writing of Nick and Barbara Sheldon's tonsorial experiments in *The Garden of Eden* manuscript, Hemingway's fictional writer, David Bourne, momentarily dismisses the topic as "banal enough," but he soon reconsiders, inventing a fine definition of overdetermination in the process: "It is all very well for you to write simply and the simpler the better. But do not start thinking so damned simply. *Know how complicated it is and then state it simply*" (my emphasis, K422.1 4.3.1).[1] I only wish I could do the same, but the artist, alone, can enjoy this simplicity of expression.

While the overdetermination of the fetish object allows the artist to express psychological complexity with an exquisite economy and clarity, it falls to the critic to unpack this complexity for those who would try not just to feel, but to understand it and, through understanding it, to feel it all the more fully.[2] I fear being taken for Emily Dickinson's bloody-fingered ornithologist who would split the lark to find its song; yet to use a different analogy, while *Gray's Anatomy* certainly lacks the beauty and complexity of the human body, anatomy nevertheless remains an essential field of study for anyone who would claim to understand the body's full complexity and beauty. Symbols, as invitations to interpretation, are always more meaningful and economical than any interpretation we can give them, but interpret them we must if we are to appreciate their richness. This is particularly the case with the fetish object. Its very richness and its connection to every aspect of Hemingway's psychosexuality hinder any attempt to explore it in a linear fashion and render almost anything said about it only partially satisfactory even from the limited position of psychoanalytic understanding, but this overdetermination also makes it a key generator of meaning within Hemingway's texts. Fetishistic overdetermination lurks like a land mine just beneath the surface of Hemingway's fictional icebergs, explosively destabilizing simplistic conceptions of gender identity, of the ego, of desire, and of homo- and heterosexuality. Like the munitions experts who clean up after a bomb, we can understand the fetishistic mechanism only by painstakingly examining the composition and trajectory of its innumerable shards.

Some readers probably suspect that too much has been written about Hemingway's fetishism already. After all, nearly thirty years ago Carlos Baker recognized that Hemingway's obsession with hair was "a special psychic quirk" worthy of a few paragraphs in his classic biography (646), and every major Hemingway biographer since then has given the topic at least cursory attention. James Mellow notes that Hemingway "had a lifelong erotic fascination with women's hair" (73). Jeffrey Meyers devotes a fine four-page subchapter to Hemingway's "hair fetishism" (437), though he never develops the matter any further than enumerating the most obvious examples of it. Michael Reynolds notes that hair was "a fetish present in [Hemingway's] fiction and private life" (*Young Hemingway* 120). And Kenneth Lynn devotes a considerable portion of his biography to Hemingway's obsession with hair. For some reason Lynn scrupulously avoids using the word "fetish," but he rightly ties Hemingway's obsession with hair to his childhood experience of being cross-dressed by a mother who alternately thought of him as a boy and a girl, and who "twinned" him with his older sister, Marcelline. Yet Lynn never explores the deeper implications of Hemingway's fetishism, and consequently the answers he arrives at, while not strictly incorrect, are far too simple.

Two critical studies, Comley and Scholes's *Hemingway's Genders* and Spilka's *Hemingway's Quarrel with Androgyny*, have recently tried to develop the critical implications of Ernest's erotic fascination with hair, but both books are overtly hostile to psychoanalysis. Spilka, who has explored Hemingway's tonsorial fixation at greatest length, uses the term "fetishism" (281), and is certainly on track when he claims that "hair was for Hemingway the public expression of his own private obsession with androgyny. . ." (291), but he never explores fetishism in its Freudian or post-Freudian sense, in spite of the fact that fetishism is perhaps one of the most interesting and well-understood areas of psychoanalytic theory. Like Lynn, Spilka sees Hemingway's taste for lovers with matching hair largely as a simple re-enactment of his twin-like relationship with Marcelline and as an attempt to come to terms with the more traditionally "feminine" aspects of himself, an interpretation which isn't entirely off-base, but which fails to unearth the riches of the fetish object's significance. So while many words have already been devoted to Hemingway's fetishism, curiously none of them have been written by anyone who knows anything about the subject of fetishism.

Yet since so many Hemingway scholars can agree on a "symptom," the value of any psychoanalytic approach to Hemingway should stand or fall by what it can tell us about this symptom and its importance to Hemingway's work. Much more than a translation of Lynn's and Spilka's observations into psychoanalytic jargon, a psychoanalytic reading of Hemingway's fetishism will develop a more theorizable approach to Hemingway's connection between tonsorial experiments and transvestic transformations. It will, likewise, develop a theorizable thread uniting major themes and images in Hemingway's fiction. It will reveal what is at stake in Hemingway's explorations of gender. It will clarify the connection between Hemingway's overt male homophobia and his elements of latent homosexuality. It will connect Hemingway's fetishism with previous oedipal readings of his work. It will allow us to see the influence of Hemingway's psychosexual concerns in subtle places that would otherwise be overlooked. It will suggest how these concerns express themselves in the *structure* of Hemingway's work, not just in the iceberg principle, but in the insistent doubling and dividing of characters that so typifies his later fiction. In short, if the value of a psychoanalytic reading will stand or fall according to what it can tell us about Hemingway's fetishism and its significance, I feel quite comfortable that stand it will.

Given my acknowledgment that Hemingway's erotic fascination with hair is well-recognized, the compilation of evidence that I will offer in support of this fact in the next section may initially strike some as unnecessary. My reasons for cataloging it, however, are threefold. First, I want to convey just how obsessive this topic was for Hemingway, and here there is no substitute for letting the author speak for himself. Second, I want to explore a few of the effects that this obsession produces on us as readers. Third, my unique approach to Hemingway's fetishism will influence my selection of evidence; my point is not simply that Hemingway fetishized hair, but rather that this fetish is linked to an entire field of fantasy within Hemingway's work. The evidence I offer will begin to define this field of fantasy for us and will serve as touchstones for subsequent analyses.

"Our Things"

No decent girls had ever had their hair cut short like that in this part of the country and even in Paris it was rare and strange and could be beautiful or could be very bad. It could mean too much or it could only mean showing the beautiful shape of a head that could never be shown as well.

—*The Garden of Eden*

From the hospital bed where she lies dying at the end of *A Farewell to Arms*, Catherine Barkley implores Frederic Henry, "You won't do our things with another girl, or say the same things, will you?" (331). Grief-stricken, Frederic swears that he never will, and when the novel ends a few pages later with his failed attempt to say good-bye to a body that now seems as cold as a statue, Frederic's eternal faithfulness is assured. Like the bold lover frozen on Keats's Grecian urn, Frederic, except in his role as the implied author of the novel, simply *has* no future; true to his promise to his dying love, he never has another girl.

Yet, somehow, Catherine's fears may indeed be justified. Insofar as Frederic partakes of those qualities that unify almost all of Hemingway's male protagonists—qualities which emanate primarily from an element of himself that Hemingway projected into most of his heroes—insofar as *part* of Frederic *does* live again in Jake Barnes, Robert Jordan, Richard Cantwell, Thomas Hudson, and David Bourne, he seems to be less than faithful to his promise. Yet if Frederic, or a part of him, lives again in Hemingway's other novels, perhaps Catherine didn't really die that rainy evening in Switzerland—at least not entirely.

Just exactly what "our things" *are* isn't entirely clear from the text, but they seem to involve the tonsorial experiments and almost mystical union that preoccupy Catherine and Frederic during the alpine idyll in the final chapters of the novel. Nowhere are these "things" clearer than during Catherine's after-lunch conversation with Frederic a few days before Christmas. In playful, loving banter, Catherine suggests that Frederic grow a beard, which he agrees to do. Then, after telling Frederic that she wishes she had slept with all of his past lovers and even wishes she had had gonorrhea so she could be exactly like him, "Cat" proposes another way to achieve this mystical fusion of identities:

> "Darling, why don't you let your hair grow?"
> "How grow?"
> "Just grow a little longer."
> "It's long enough now."
> "No, let it grow a little longer and I could cut mine and we'd be just alike only one of us blonde and one of us dark."
> "I wouldn't let you cut yours."
> "It would be fun. I'm tired of it. It's an awful nuisance in the bed at night."
> "I like it."

"Wouldn't you like it short?"
"I might. I like it the way it is."
"It might be nice short. Then we'd both be alike. Oh, darling, I want you so much I want to be you too."
"You are. We're the same one."
"I know it. At night we are."
"The nights are grand."
"I want us to be all mixed up. I don't want you to go away.
. . . You go if you want to. But hurry right back. Why, darling, I don't live at all when I'm not with you." (299–300)

With an irony that becomes clear only with Catherine's death, Frederic promises that he "won't ever go away." "I'm no good when you're not there," he tells her. "I haven't any life at all any more" (300). He then asks if Catherine wants him to continue with the beard, in spite of her desire to be exactly like him. "Go on," she replies. "Grow it. It will be exciting" (300).

There is something magical in the two lovers who can talk endlessly about the length of their hair while a war of almost apocalyptic proportions rages all around them—even if it seems a little odd that they find such matters so "exciting." The final book of the novel, up until the stillbirth and Catherine's death, takes place in a sylvan, snowbound dreamtime with only the slightest hints of the horrors beyond their little world. In fact, when Catherine and Frederic first arrive in neutral Switzerland, they both fear that, like Peyton Farquhar's escape from Union soldiers in Ambrose Bierce's classic story "An Occurrence at Owl Creek Bridge," their own escape from the war is merely a dream and they are liable to wake up at any moment and find themselves driving Frederic back to the *stazione* in Milan. In Bierce's tale, Farquhar's miraculous dream-escape downriver into the waiting arms of his wife initially seduces inattentive readers only to shock them all the more profoundly when it is revealed as an illusion by the snap of Farquhar's neck and the swaying of his body beneath Owl Creek Bridge. Likewise, the dreamlike peace in the final chapters of Hemingway's novel, coming as it does after the horrors of the retreat from Caporetto with Frederic's Farquhar-like escape from murderous battle police and plunge into the swollen Piave, lulls the unsuspecting reader into the complacent illusion that a "separate peace" is possible, that death and the harsh world can be escaped—an illusion which by contrast renders the ultimate death of Catherine and her child absolutely shattering. Even the attentive reader, who discovers the theme of stillbirth in the novel's first chapter with the men marching with ammunition bulging under their capes "as though they were six months gone with child" and who therefore expects an unhappy end to Catherine's pregnancy, cannot help but feel the contrast between the idyll in Switzerland and tragic loss of the novel's final pages (4). Likewise, the erotic fusion of Catherine and Frederic into a single symbiotic identity, each symbolically incapable of functioning without the other, makes Frederic's loss at the end of the novel all the more tragic. This fusion, moreover, is achieved largely though the sharing of fantasy-laden secrets and erotic activities—the "our things" of Catherine's plea.

The keeping and sharing of secrets was one of Hemingway's favorite tools for forging intense bonds between his fictional characters and between himself and his wives. We see it at work, for instance, in the relationship between Jake and Montoya in *The Sun Also Rises*:

> [Montoya] always smiled as though bull-fighting were a very special secret between the two of us; a rather shocking but really very deep secret that we knew about. He always smiled as though there were something lewd about the secret to outsiders, but that it was something that we understood. It would not do to expose it to people who would not understand. (131)

(Jake, of course, betrays this secret by introducing the *corrida* to the likes of Cohn and Mike, an act which mirrors the betrayal of Montoya implicit in his role as matchmaker between Brett and Romero after having promised Montoya to protect the young matador from predatory foreign women. As in *A Farewell to Arms*, the intensity of the bond accentuates the loss implied by its dissolution.) In *Across the River and Into the Trees*, we find this same sort of secret-sharing in the bond between Cantwell and the *Maitre d'Hotel* of the Gritti who invent the fictitious secret society "*El Ordine Militar, Nobile y Espirituoso de los Caballeros de Brusadelli*" (56).[3] The secret—whose contents by nature tend to be "either something highly prized or something shameful which must be hidden," or a combination of *both*—works its magic by delineating a contrast between a world of "outsiders" and a very select community of those "in the know." As Phyllis Greenacre notes, "If it is shared, then its joint owners must be held together by some special and primitive ritual bond, or the secret is in danger of becoming only common property" (190).

A sort of secret-sharing not entirely unlike this was a mainstay of Hemingway's art. Thematically, Hemingway loved to share "secrets" with his readers—literary gossip, special drink recipes, hints about where to travel, what wines to order, how to fish and hunt properly, how to enjoy a bullfight or boxing match, how to blow a bridge. When Robert Jordan ponders the knowledge of clandestine Spanish Republican politics that constitutes his status as an "insider" at Gaylord's, Hemingway transforms his readers into "insiders" by proxy (*FWBT* 229). Likewise, when Hemingway describes the ignorant "Biarritz crowd" in *The Sun Also Rises*, he elicits our indignation at their stupidity in failing to appreciate Romero's bravery or technique in fighting a color-blind bull, deftly baiting the animal with his body, then switching to the cape. "What's he afraid of the bull for? The bull's so dumb he only goes after the cloth," one asks. And with what can now appear to us only as utter idiocy, his companion replies, "He's just a young bull-fighter. He hasn't learned it yet" (218). Skillfully, Hemingway paints the Biarritz crowd as a hopeless bunch of "outsiders," and we, who may not have known a jot about bullfighting before picking up his novel, are invited to sit in judgment above them as privileged "insiders." Thus in *The Garden of Eden* manuscript, when David Bourne speaks of a "*mystère*" at the heart of his work and claims that he cares about the opinions of only those few readers who know what he is writing about or who at least know about writing, he seems to be speaking for Hemingway, defining a select community of ideal readers—a happy few amongst whom we inevitably must number ourselves (K422.1 37.20.4th insert).[4]

Stylistically, a sort of secret-sharing is implied by Hemingway's fondness for using pronouns or definite articles without clear referents, and, structurally, secret-sharing lies at the heart of Hemingway's "iceberg principle"—his contention that the emotional movement of his stories is determined by the weightier content which lurks beneath the surface of the text: "If a writer of prose knows enough about what he is writing about he may omit things that he knows and the reader, if the writer is writing truly enough, will have a feeling of those things as strongly as though the writer had stated them" (*DIA* 192). Thus Hemingway's implied ideal reader knows, or feels, that the unnamed operation in "Hills Like White Elephants" is an abortion and that Nick in "Big Two-Hearted River" has just returned from the First World War even though these things are never explicitly stated in the texts. The reader is moved by a sense of mystery and a sort of epistemophilia, an "urge to know." Hemingway, by contrast, assumes the mantle of "the one who knows." As a , highly conscious artist, Hemingway understood that the subtle sharing of these "secrets" brings his ideal reader into an unusually intimate relation with the text and its implied author.

As the "our things" of *A Farewell to Arms* imply, however, secret-sharing, with its implied distinction between a ritually or primitively-bonded "us" and an alienated "them," also formed a mainstay of Hemingway's erotic imagination. But while Cantwell allows Renata to join "*El Ordine*" and Jake successfully initiates Brett to the bullfight, the secrets shared by Hemingway's fictional lovers and the secrets he shared with his wives were generally of another sort.[5] Hemingway shared identical fetishistically-invested pet names with all of his wives, and in his relationships with Hadley and Pauline, both of whom at times sported boyish haircuts nearly identical to his own, he spoke repeatedly about his lover and himself being the "same guy."[6] In letters to Pauline, Hemingway writes of a feeling of "us against the world"—a phrase we find mirrored in *The Garden of Eden* when Catherine uses her fetishistic experiments with haircutting and suntanning to take herself and David "further away from other people," telling her husband, "We're us against all the others" (*SL* 221; *GE* 30; 37). But while the women in Hemingway's life and fiction changed, the fantasies and secrets uniting lovers almost never did. There is a remarkable uniformity to the "secrets, taboos, and delights" that Hemingway shared with Hadley in the '20s, the "secrets" and "tribal rules" that David Bourne shares with Catherine and Marita in *The Garden of Eden*, the "jollities and secrecies" that Ernest shared with his fourth wife, Mary, in the late '40s, and the "our things" of Frederic and Catherine in *A Farewell to Arms*.[7]

As Freud and Greenacre have suggested—and, indeed, as Hemingway's life and fiction also suggest—there is an intimate connection between fetishism and "secret-keeping."[8] Thus, in *The Garden of Eden* manuscript, when Barbara Sheldon first dreams up her erotic games, she proposes to Nick, "Let's think of something fun to do that we've never done that will be secret and wicked. . . ," and when she smiles at David Bourne in a Paris restaurant, she does so because she has already seen him in a barbershop and regards him as "a co-conspirator." Barbara defines her "conspiracy," then, as a fetishistic and transvestic obsession with hair—and no wonder. The fetish *is* a sort of secret shared between lovers, highly prized but sometimes also invoking an element of shame. Even though, as we shall see, fetishism can indicate a deeply riven ego-structure and can be tied indirectly to tremendous anxiety in the fetishist's life, it is almost never the presenting "symptom" in a clinical setting.[9] Rather than regarding the fetish as a symptom, the fetishist feels that he enjoys an "advantage" in his erotic life. "The meaning of the fetish is not known to other people, so the fetish is not withheld from him: it is easily accessible and he can readily obtain the sexual satisfaction attached to it" (Freud, *SE* XXI, 154). It is the consistency of this fetishistic secret and the *field of fantasy surrounding it*—a field of fantasy involving an insistence upon "first loves" and a sensation that the protagonist is somehow haunted by his past—which lends an air of *déjà vu* to the romances in Hemingway's work. Like souls forever united in love and reincarnated into different bodies in some Saturday matinee vampire movie, Catherine Barkley and Frederic Henry *seem* to reappear throughout Hemingway's fiction in various guises. It is as if the idyll in the final chapters of *A Farewell to Arms* were not only a dream, but a recurrent one.

True, in *For Whom the Bell Tolls* Robert Jordan is an instructor of Spanish, not an architect like Frederic Henry (not that Frederic's status as an architect is in any way convincing or important to *Farewell*)—but the two men seem to possess the same "erotic soul," albeit in different bodies under different circumstances. And while Maria, a young Spanish woman raped by the fascists and left with shorn hair, may have little in common with the English nurse Catherine Barkley, she does fantasize about nursing her wounded warrior: "When thou art wounded I will care for thee and dress thy wound and wash thee and feed thee—" (171). Moreover, she shares a remarkably similar taste for the erotic fusion of identities. "We will be as one animal of the forest and be so close that neither one can tell that one of us is one and not the other," she promises Jordan, asking him:

> "Can you not feel my heart be your heart?"
> "Yes. There is no difference."
> "Now, feel. I am thee and thou art me and all of one is the other. And I love thee, oh, I love thee so. Are we not truly one? Canst thou not feel it?"
> "Yes," he said. "It is true." (262)

If this merging of identities doesn't seem hauntingly familiar, Jordan's fantasies about what to do with Maria's cropped hair should certainly leave us with the eerie sensation that we've been here before. There is, however, an important difference. Identical haircuts are now proposed by the man in the relationship, not by some more safely dissociated half-crazy woman:

> "I have thought about thy hair," [Jordan] said. "And what we can do about it. You see it grows now all over thy head the same length like the fur of an animal and it is lovely to feel and I love it very much and it is beautiful and it flattens and rises like a wheatfield in the wind when I pass my hand over it."
> "Pass thy hand over it."
> He did and left his hand there and went on talking to her throat, as he felt his own throat swell. "But in Madrid I thought we could go together to the coiffeur's and they could cut it neatly on the sides and in the back as they cut mine and that way it would look better in the town while it is growing out."
> "I would look like thee," she said and held him close to her. "And then I would never want to change it." (345)

That Jordan's interest in Maria's hair involves more than a dispassionate concern for the latest trends in fashion should already be obvious, but the wave of fantasy that overtakes him when he begins to talk about Maria's hair reveals just how deeply he feels about these matters:

> Now the making believe was coming back in a great rush and he would take it all to him. It had him now, and again he surrendered and went on. "So it will hang straight to thy shoulders and curl at the ends as a wave of the sea curls, and it will be the color of ripe wheat and thy face the color of burnt gold and thine eyes the only color they could be with thy hair and thy skin, gold with the dark flecks in them, and I will push thy head back and look in thy eyes and hold thee tight against me—" (346).

An erotic pattern repeated once or twice might mean little enough, but the "erotic souls" of Frederic and Catherine are "reincarnated" once again, a bit more thoroughly disguised, in *Across the River and Into the Trees*. As if to make a specific point about this "reincarnation," Hemingway even has Colonel Cantwell, who like Jordan was in Spain for the Civil War, defecate on the very site where he, Frederic Henry, and Ernest Hemingway were all wounded at Fossalta di Piave in the First World War.[10] And while on the erotic front Cantwell never expresses any desire to cut Renata's long, beautiful, raven hair to match his own (perhaps because the fifty year-old author imagined his fifty year-old protagonist with his own thinning hair[11]), he does plainly fetishize her hair, and Renata knows it. When she combs her hair in front of the mirror, for instance, she offers to let Cantwell watch, and the authorial voice tells us, "She was not combing it for vanity, nor *to do to the Colonel what she knew it could and would do*" (my emphasis, 112). Moreover, in a dream of erotic fusion, Renata pleads with Cantwell, "I want to be like you. Can I be like you a little while tonight?" (142). Later, as they make love in a gondola, Renata's hair whipping about in the wind, she asks, "Don't you know how a woman feels?" "No," Cantwell replies. "Only what you tell me." Renata responds by doing something cryptic, which is apparently meant to give him a better idea, and then says, "Guess now" (154). The theme is picked up again a few pages later when Renata tells Cantwell, "Please hold me very tightly so we can be a part of each other for a little while."

> "We can try," the Colonel said.
> "Couldn't I be you?"
> "That's awfully complicated. We could try of course."
> "I'm you now," she said. (156)

In *To Have and Have Not*, Harry Morgan urges Marie to keep her bleached hair short, and in *Islands in the Stream*, Hemingway recreates his favorite erotic pattern even more obviously in Thomas Hudson's dream of his ex-wife—a dream which should shock us for the violence implicit in Hudson's "holstering" of his "gun" while reminding us of Frederic Henry's comparatively innocent pleasure at taking the pins out of Catherine Barkley's hair as she lies on top of him, letting her hair cascade over his face like a silken tent:

> Her hair hung down and lay heavy and silky on his eyes and on his cheeks and he turned his lips away from her searching ones and took the hair in his mouth and held it. Then with one hand he moistened the .357 Magnum and slipped it easily and sound asleep where it should be. Then he lay under her weight with her silken hair over his face like a curtain and moved slowly and rhythmically. (*IITS* 343-4)[12]

And once again, the hair fetish leads directly to a dream of erotic fusion. After Hudson asks his dream-wife, "Who's going to make love to who?" she replies with a question of her own, "Should I be you or you be me?"

> "You have first choice."
> "I'll be you."
> "I can't be you. But I can try."
> "It's fun. You try it. Don't try to save yourself at all. Try to lose everything and take everything too. . . . Are you doing it?"
> "Yes," he said. "It's wonderful. . . ."
> "Will you give up everything? Are you glad . . . that I come and be a devil in the night?"
> "Yes. I'm glad of everything and will you swing your hair across my face and give me your mouth please and hold me so tight it kills me?"
> "Of course. And you'll do it for me?" (344–5)

This recurrent fantasy takes a bizarre twist in Hemingway's long, unfinished, posthumous, short story, "The Last Good Country." Having killed a deer out of season, Nick Adams and his little sister, who insists on accompanying him, flee from game wardens to a "secret place" in one of the last remaining stands of virgin hemlock in the Michigan woods, a very old and "Indian" place which Nick had never shared with anyone else (*CSS* 515). Twelve year-old Littless, who accompanies her brother partly to keep him from being lonely, partly to keep him from killing someone, and partly out of a jealous need to keep him from running off with his pregnant Indian girlfriend, possesses fetishistic properties generally reserved for the adult love interests in Hemingway's work—"tanned dark brown" skin and "dark brown hair with yellow streaks in it from the sun" which Nick enjoys stroking (*CSS* 504). Early in the story, Littless, who "always wanted to be a boy anyway," proposes to make their escape easier by cutting her hair to look like a boy (*CSS* 505), and after Nick returns from fishing one day she has a "surprise" for him:

> "What did you do, you monkey?. . . ."
> "I cut it off," she said.
> "How?"
> "With a scissors. How did you think? . . . . Do I look like a
> boy?"

"Like a wild boy of Borneo. . . ."

"It's very exciting," she said. "Now I'm your sister but I'm a boy, too. Do you think it will change me into a boy?"

"No."

"I wish it would."

"You're crazy, Littless."

"Maybe I am." (CSS 531)

Nick offers to touch it up for her but likes her new haircut "very much" (CSS 531), and Littless, whom Nick calls "devil," then begins studying how to be a "boy" by taking her idolized brother as a template.

It may be tempting to discount any similarity between Littless's boyish haircut and the boyish cut that Brett Ashley refuses to grow out to look more "womanly" at the end of *The Sun Also Rises*. Littless's tonsorial preoccupations, in spite of the "excitement" she associates with them, probably seem more tomboyish than fetishistic. Yet it becomes more difficult to see her haircut as entirely childish and innocent in light of the story's glaringly incestuous undertones. Littless clearly substitutes in some ways for Nick's Indian girlfriend, Trudy, and we are told that she "and Nick loved each other and they did not love the others. They always thought of everyone else in the family as the others" (CSS 504). After Nick watches his little sister sleeping, noting that "it look[ed] as though someone had cut her hair off on a wooden block with an ax," Hemingway writes that Nick "loved his sister very much and she loved him too much. But, he thought, I guess those things straighten out" (CSS 535). And we see just how much straightening out is needed when Littless tells her brother that she plans to becomes his common-law wife someday. For obvious reasons, Nick can't agree to his sister's plan, but Littless isn't easily dissuaded: "I've got another scheme. We'll have a couple of children while I'm a minor. Then you'll have to marry me under the Unwritten Law" (CSS 537).

In spite of Hemingway's preoccupation with incest in this story, Mark Spilka calls Littless's talk "innocent prattle," and he has a point (270). No one, except perhaps Littless, really expects Nick and his sister to consummate their relationship, and such infatuations are a common part of childhood. But Spilka wrongly uses this "innocent prattle" to argue specifically against psychoanalysis. Our rush to note the story's "barely sublimated incest," he argues,

> suggests how unthinkingly we still operate under the post-
> Victorian, that is to say, Freudian, dispensation. We are so em-
> barrassed, apparently, by any genuine expression of affection,
> or any playful testing of limits, that we can only assign it to
> sentimentality or neurosis. . . . It is not the 'verge of incest' that
> Hemingway treads in this decidedly revealing story; it is the
> frontier of childhood affections, rather, which the completely
> open issue of incest helps to outline. (270)

No doubt the story *is* partly about tender childhood affections,
but Spilka's dichotomy is too easy, final, and ultimately mis-
leading. There is also a *perverse* (as opposed to *neurotic*) component to Nick's relationship with his sister which is simply not at
odds with the issue of these childhood affections.

As Hemingway realized in *A Moveable Feast*, "All things truly
wicked start from an innocence" (210), and in this story both
children know that their affections are no longer *entirely* innocent. In the manuscript Littless betrays an awareness of the social sanctions against incest when she asks, "It isn't dirty for a
brother and sister to love each other, is it?" (qtd. in Spilka 269).
And Nick, who is associated with "original sin," goes to the
wilderness in the first place because he is fleeing from *The Law*,
and as the story comes to its abrupt conclusion he is terribly
anxious about being caught.[13] It is this recognition of lost innocence which suggests why an escape to an Edenic garden cannot succeed. Nick and Littless may find the last patch of virgin
wilderness, an "Indian place," but in their minds at least they
can never escape "civilized" law; after the recognition of "original
sin" and "wickedness," a pre-sexual Edenic innocence can never
again be imagined from a position of such innocence and is
therefore constituted as always-already-lost. As much as the
loss of childhood freedom and the American wilderness, *this* is
the loss which haunts the story, much as it haunts Hemingway's posthumous novel *The Garden of Eden*.

If in "The Last Good Country" we smile at Littless's fantasy
that a haircut can magically transform her into a boy, making
her simultaneously Nick's *brother* and *sister*, and we don't take
her "craziness" very seriously, these things nevertheless take on
an entirely new dimension when we read this story against *The
Garden of Eden*. In this work, written at much the same time as
"The Last Good Country," Hemingway's fantasies about haircutting, hair dyeing, sexual transformation, and the erotic fusion of

identities reach their culmination and form nearly the entire
subject matter of the book.

Honeymooning in the South of France, the young lovers
David and Catherine Bourne—who look enough alike to be
brother and sister—exist at the beginning of the novel in a world
of continual orgiastic bliss with "only the happiness and loving
each other and then hunger and replenishing and starting over"
(14). With the rather odd aside that there was "no badness" after
he makes love to his wife, David is sitting in a café thinking that
"they could not be held tighter together than they were now,"
when Catherine walks through the door with the first of her
many tonsorial experiments and says "in her throaty voice,
'Hello darling'" (14).

> Her hair was cropped as short as a boy's. It was cut with no
> compromises. It was brushed back, heavy as always, but the
> sides were cut short and the ears that grew close to her head
> were clear and the tawny line of her hair was cropped close to
> her head. . . . She turned her head and lifted her breasts and
> said, 'Kiss me please.'"
>
> He kissed her and looked at her face and at her hair and
> he kissed her again.
>
> "Do you like it? Feel how smooth. Feel it in back," she said.
> He felt it in back. . . .
>
> "You see," she said. "That's the surprise. I'm a girl. But
> now I'm a boy too and I can do anything and anything and any-
> thing. (14–15)

Catherine knows her "surprise" is "dangerous," she explains,
but she tells David that they don't have "to go by everyone else's
rules. We're us." He isn't sure that the "surprise" is such a good
idea and clearly feels threatened, but Catherine knows her husband well: "You do like it. I can feel and I can tell. . . . It isn't
faked or phony. It's a true boy's haircut and not from any beauty
shop." When David asks who cut it, Catherine's reply is telling:

> "The coiffeur at Aigues Mortes. The one who cut your hair a
> week ago. You told him how you wanted yours cut then and I
> told him to cut mine just the same as yours. He was very nice
> and wasn't at all surprised. He wasn't worried at all. He said
> exactly like yours? And I said exactly. Doesn't it *do* anything to
> you, David?"
>
> "Yes," he said. (my emphasis, 15–16)

Just what it *does* to Catherine and David we find out that
night when they make love. David is holding Catherine's
breasts, "feeling the hard erect freshness between his fingers,"
when Catherine asks him to feel her "new surprise," her hair. A
bizarre metamorphosis then begins which brings David "closer"
to Catherine than he had ever imagined possible:

> He lay there and felt something and then her hand holding him
> and searching lower and he helped with his hands and lay
> back in the dark and did not think at all and only felt the
> weight and the strangeness inside and she said, "Now you can't
> tell who is who can you?"
>   "No."
>   "You are changing," she said. "Oh you are. You are. Yes
> you are and you're my girl Catherine. Will you change and be
> my girl and let me take you?"
>   "You're Catherine."
>   "No I'm Peter. You're my wonderful Catherine. You're my
> beautiful lovely Catherine. You were so good to change. Oh thank
> you, Catherine, so much. Please understand. Please know and
> understand. I'm going to make love to you forever." (17)

These fetishistic and transvestic adventures become more
and more obsessive for Catherine as the novel progresses, and
David's feelings about them become ever more divided. When
they cease to be merely "things of the night" and spill over into
the daylight with Catherine wandering through the Prado as a
"boy," David suffers from acute "remorse." But later, after Catherine gets him to cut and lighten his hair to match her own, he
stands in front of the mirror looking at himself and realizes that
he *likes* it:

> "So that's how it is," he said to himself. "You've done that to
> your hair and had it cut the same as your girl's and how do you
> feel?" He asked the mirror. "How do you feel? Say it."
>   "You like it," he said.
>   He looked in the mirror and it was someone else he saw
> but it was less strange now.
>   "All right. You like it," he said. "Now go through with the
> rest of it whatever it is and don't ever say anyone tempted you
> or that anyone bitched you." (84)

Soon after this in the heavily edited Scribner's version of the
novel a new girl appears on the scene, more compliant and lack-

ing Catherine's jealousy of David's work or Catherine's urge to be a boy. After a short *ménage à trois* where both share the new woman, Catherine burns David's stories, goes insane, and leaves her husband alone with the idolizing new girl, Marita. Hemingway's manuscript, however, suggests that he intended something quite different. In addition to an entire subplot about another couple, the Sheldons (based largely on Hemingway and Hadley), who live in Paris and *grow* their hair out identically, we find quite a different Marita. Here she simply becomes another Catherine. Like her mentor, she grows obsessed with cutting her hair, tanning her skin, and trying to be a boy. And she isn't so compliant. She wishes *she* had been the one to bleach David's hair. Most importantly, Hemingway's "provisional ending" to the novel concludes not with the union of David and Marita, but with David and Catherine together on the beach contemplating the ultimate fusion, or disintegration, of identities—a double suicide.

After this catalogue of lovers, it should hardly come as a surprise when I say that the possession of the fetish object provides a unifying link between all of the significant women in Hemingway's life and fiction.[14] Writing of Ernest's request that she bleach her hair as a present to him and of his "entrancement" with the results, Mary Hemingway notes in her memoir, *How It Was*: "Deeply rooted in his field of esthetics was some mystical devotion to blondness, the blonder the lovelier, I never learned why" (170). But Hemingway wasn't devoted simply to blonde hair. It could be blonde, red, raven black; it could be long or short. But it was *always* fetishized. Thus, in *Islands in the Stream*, when young Tom jokes that "the same girl" appears in all of the books by Mr. Davis (largely a Hemingway cognate), Tom may distance himself from the observation by saying he was only teasing, but Audrey—herself a representative of "that same girl" who in some measure appears in all of Mr. Hemingway's books—is savvy enough to say, "I thought it was a little bit accurate" (175).

Of course, Hemingway's female characters are *not* all identical. Surely the Indian girl, Prudy Boulton, differs from the sophisticated denizen of Montparnasse, Lady Brett Ashley. What does the wealthy Margot Macomber have in common with the vulnerable and violated Maria of *For Whom the Bell Tolls* or the working-class ex-prostitute, Marie Morgan? Yet there is an uncanny similarity as well. To claim along with Leslie Fiedler that there simply *are* no women in Hemingway's fiction would be un-just. Hemingway was clearly capable of feeling a profound sym-pathy with women. Thus, when Jake Barnes broods to himself in his Pamplona hotel room, "To hell with women, anyway," he follows this with the recognition that he had not been thinking about their side of the situation: "I thought I had paid for every-thing. Not like the woman pays and pays and pays" (*SAR* 148). In fact, Hemingway's profound identification with women—an identification *far* more profound and agonistic than has hitherto been realized—will be a major theme of this book. Yet, in part *because* of this very identification, Hemingway's women are al-ways infused with aspects of masculine desire and fantasy. And as we shall see, on some psychosexual level intimately tied to their possession of the fetish object, Hemingway's women, as Fiedler realized, aren't really women at all.

But why must all of Hemingway's heroines possess the fetish object? Phyllis Greenacre's rather clinical definition of fetishism begins to offer us some insight into this question, even though it begs questions of its own:

> Fetishism generally appears as a distortion of sexual behavior in which there is the obligatory use of some nongenital object as part of the sexual act and without which gratification cannot be obtained. The fetish usually must possess qualities repre-senting, in only slightly concealed form, body parts and body attributes. Articles of leather such as shoes, gloves, thongs; ar-ticles of clothing closely associated with the body, such as un-derwear; braids of hair and wigs—these all have the common fetishistic properties. Furthermore, the fetish must be some-thing that is visible, tangible, inanimate, invested with body odors, and not easily destructible. (301)

(One may wonder how indestructibility applies to hair, but Mary Hemingway told Carlos Baker that her husband's "interest in the sexual connotations of hair was all the greater because he thought it the one part of a woman's anatomy that could be changed for fun and without permanent damage" [qtd. in Baker 646].)

Simply put, Hemingway needed the fetish object to attain sexual gratification. Thus, he quite literally could not conceive of a lover or a romantic scene without its active presence. The con-nection between the fetish object and the act of sex is ubiquitous in Hemingway's work. Catherine Barkley complains that her long hair is a nuisance *in bed*, but Frederic loves to have it dangled above him as Catherine makes love to him from on top. Robert Jordan rubs Maria's cropped head while they make love, and she nuzzles up to him with it. In *To Have and Have Not*, Marie Morgan's newly bleached hair excites Harry so much that he insists that they go to a hotel immediately. In his fantasies, Thomas Hudson mouths his ex-wife's hair as they make love. And Catherine Bourne's fetishized hair seems to make virtually *anything* possible in bed.

Freud defined a fetishist, somewhat tautologically, as a man whose "object-choice was dominated by a fetish" (*SE* XXI 152), and the possession of the fetish is always a deciding factor in the selection of a love object in Hemingway's fiction. When we first meet Brett Ashley, for instance, we are told that she is "damned good-looking," with "a slipover jersey sweater and a tweed skirt, and her hair . . . brushed back like a boy's. She started all that" (*SAR* 22). When Frederic Henry meets Catherine Barkley, virtually the first words out of his mouth are "You have beautiful hair" (*FTA* 19). Likewise, the first thing that Robert Jordan notices about Maria is her cropped head, something admittedly difficult to miss, but its effect on him is curious and immediate—love at first sight:

> The girl stooped as she came out of the cave mouth . . . and Robert Jordan saw her face turned at an angle and at the same time saw the strange thing about her. . . . Her hair was the golden brown of a grain field that has been burned dark in the sun but it was cut all over her head so it was but little longer than the fur on a beaver pelt. She smiled in Robert Jordan's face and put her brown hand up and ran it over her head, flattening the hair which rose again as the hand passed. . . .
>
> "That is the way I comb it," she said to Robert Jordan and laughed. "Go ahead and eat. Don't stare at me. . . ."
>
> Every time Robert Jordan looked at her he could feel a thickness in his throat. (22)

Hemingway's fetishism dominated his real life object choice as well. Hadley almost immediately recognized the importance of her reddish auburn hair in first attracting Ernest, and in a June 1921 letter to him she wrote: "My hair is turning a nice shade of red it never looked before. I love to have you love my hair. I love yours. Love to pet it back from your forehead" (qtd. in Griffin

188). In February, soon after their courtship began, she had mailed Ernest a letter enclosing a mass of auburn hair: "For you, Ernesto Mio. . . . Had a big lot of it cut out a year ago to make the knot a manageable size . . . but this piece is for you. Kept it the length and size for you to shape it as you will. My hair is this color when I dry it in the sun. Put it in the sunshine and see" (qtd. in Griffin 160). According to Ernest's sister Marcelline, Hemingway's mother had always told him that this was the most beautiful color for hair. And the impression it made on him is obvious in an uncharacteristically exclamatory passage from a work of juvenilia entitled "The Current," written during his courtship of Hadley. In this piece, "Dorothy" clearly substitutes for Hadley, a figure whose devotion must be won by the boxer protagonist, Stuy.

> Her hair was the first thing about Dorothy that everyone noticed. It was the raw gold color of old country burnished copper kettles, and it held all of the firelight and occasionally flashed a little of it back. Her hair was wonderful! The rest of her was altogether adorable and Stuy looked at her appreciatively.
>
> "You always look wonderful, Do," he said as she sank into one of the deep leather chairs before the fire. He sat on the arm of her chair and looked down at her glorious hair! (qtd. in Griffin 201)

Hemingway's second wife, Pauline, lacked this beautiful hair color and Hemingway initially preferred her sister, Jinny (who happened to be lesbian); yet he *was* quite impressed with Pauline's chipmunk-fur coat, a simple displacement of the fetish. According to Kitty Cannell, after first meeting Pauline, Hemingway said that he'd like "to take [Jinny] out in her sister's coat" (qtd. in Baker 142). Pauline, however, quickly learned how to make her hair exciting for Ernest. Pictures from Schruns in 1926 show both Hadley and Pauline with boyish cuts not so unlike Ernest's. In July 1929 Pauline dyed her hair blonde as a birthday surprise for Ernest, and throughout the 1930s she continued to change her hair color and style frequently. In September 1934, for instance, Ernest described the color as a "fine South American white gold" (qtd. in Reynolds, *1930s* 184).[15]

With Hemingway's third wife, Martha Gellhorn, hair was a significant attraction as well. According to Hemingway's youngest son, Gregory: "Her hair was honey blonde then, cut shoulder

length, and she had a way of tossing it when she talked. . ." (41).
When Martha appears, only slightly disguised, as Dorothy
Bridges in Hemingway's play, *The Fifth Column*, the stage directions tell us that "her hair is very beautiful" (22), and Jeffrey
Meyers writes that in the early 40s "Martha cut her hair to resemble the fictional Maria and sought Hemingway's approval"
(435). One suspects, however, that the change may have been
Ernest's idea, not Martha's—particularly given her taunting attitude about it: "But Pussy darling, you like it, don't you?" she
reportedly asked him, to which he gruffly replied: "I've said it's
all right" (Meyers 377).

Hemingway was continually urging his last wife, Mary, to
play games with her hair. In 1945 he urged her to dye her hair
blonde, and then in a series of letters in 1947 he asked her to
dye it "smoky silver" or "red." In the winter of 1948, Mary, no
doubt at Ernest's instigation, was a platinum blonde, and on his
1953 trip to Africa Ernest speaks of "devoting a day to Miss
Mary's [bleached] Christmas haircut" (Mary Hemingway 370).
Slight changes in Mary's hair style, moreover, could have a powerful irrational effect on Hemingway. After a horrible fight with
Mary in the first months of their relationship, in which Hemingway had actually slapped her, he explained his actions as follows: "'You had your hair done yesterday, didn't you?'" When
Mary replied that she had, Hemingway *ir*rationalized, "'Some-
thing she did to your hair made you look mean and malicious.
She really changed the expression of your face. I didn't know
what it was last night. But that was it'" (Mary Hemingway 132).[16]
As if Mary could be expected to understand!

Insofar as I have merely documented Hemingway's obsessive
attachment to the erotic symbolism of hair, I have only covered
well-surveyed ground, but as I've suggested, a close reading of
my examples reveals an entire field of fetishistic fantasy that has
yet to be explained. Any thorough explanation of Hemingway's
fetishism should be able to tell us how it is related to the interest in lesbian love implied by Catherine Bourne's relationship
with Marita or by Catherine Barkley's desire to have slept with
Frederic's ex-girlfriends. It should as well clarify the sort of sublimated male homosexuality implied by Hemingway's attachment to "boyish" women or women with "boyish" haircuts. It
should tell us why Hemingway so often expressed his erotic attachment to hair as a need for the erotic fusion of identities and

Figure 1. Hadley and Pauline in Schruns, Austria, 1926. (John F. Kennedy Library)

Figure 2. Pauline Hemingway with a boyish haircut. (John F. Kennedy Library)

identically cut or dyed hair. It should explain why Hemingway was so fascinated by the contrast of dark and light hair, or light hair and dark skin. It should clarify why the hair fetish so often appears against a backdrop of loss and loneliness and why there is such a mixture of love and aggression in the treatment of Hemingway's heroines. It should reveal how hair fetishism relates to the castration anxiety implicit in Frederic's gonorrhea or Jake Barnes's war wound. It should explain Hemingway's ongoing interest in nurse-figures, "first loves," sisters, and incest. It should explain the similarities between Hemingway's adult lovers and the childhood affections of Nick and Littless. It should explain Hemingway's fascinations with "silken" hair, cats, furs, brown skin, and racial otherness. It should tell us why Hemingway's male and female characters often seem so confused as they stare at their new hairdos in the mirror. It should tell us why Hemingway's male characters regularly experience a swelling in their throat as they stare at their lover's hair. It should clarify the difference between the "things of the night" and the "things of the day" that so preoccupy David Bourne. It should reveal a relationship between Hemingway's fetishism and his taste for women with "hard, erect" breasts. It should illuminate why Hemingway returns to the name "Catherine" in his fiction and why "Catherine" becomes "Peter" in *The Garden of Eden*. It should help us to understand the "badness" or "remorse" that follows David and Catherine Bourne's erotic experiments. And it should help us to see how Catherine can think that tonsorial experiments can accomplish transvestic miracles.

Obviously, we cannot hope to arrive at answers to so many questions in the blink of an eye. In fact, defining the relationship between the fetish object and the field of fantasy surrounding it, which is even broader than I have as yet suggested, will occupy almost my entire study. We must begin, however, with an understanding of fetishism, and to achieve this we must turn first to Freud.

Freud, Fetishism, and Hemingway's Phallic Women

Choked by Desire

> "You aren't really a woman at all," Marita said.
> "I know it," Catherine said. "I've tried to explain it to David often enough. . . . I did try and broke myself to pieces in Madrid to be a girl and all it did was break me to pieces. . . . You're a girl and a boy both and you really are."
>
> —*The Garden of Eden*

Hemingway's fetishism often left him choked by desire. Insofar as it can be equated with a sort of "genuine desire," that is, fetishism often makes its presence felt in Hemingway's fiction by a swelling of the male protagonist's throat and a thickening of his voice. When Frederic Henry watches Catherine getting her hair cut and waved near the end of *A Farewell to Arms* he tells us, "My voice was a little thick from being excited" (292). Or when Robert Jordan first meets Maria with her tawny brown face and closely-cropped, golden brown hair in *For Whom the Bell Tolls*, "His throat [feels] too thick for him to trust himself to speak" (25). When Marie Morgan bleaches her hair in *To Have and Have Not*, she gets "an excited feeling all funny inside, sort of faint like" and notes that Harry's "voice was thick and funny when he said, 'Jesus, Marie, you're beautiful'" (259). In "The Sea Change," Phil tells his lover, a woman with "smooth golden brown" skin and short blonde hair, to go ahead and have a lesbian affair ostensibly against his own wishes, but "his voice sounded strange to him," indicating a not-so-secret desire to experience the relationship by proxy (SS 397). "'And when you come back,'" he adds, "'tell me all about it.' His voice sounded very strange. He did not recognize it" (400). In *Islands in the Stream*, when Thomas Hudson's ex-wife takes off her hat and shakes her hair loose, "hair that was the same silvery ripe-wheat color as always," Hudson's throat "aches" (306–7). After Catherine Bourne first transforms herself into "Peter" and her husband into "Catherine," in *The Garden of Eden* manuscript, David's voice feels "thick" (K422.1 1.22). And we see this characteristic thickening of the voice yet again in *Across the River and Into the Trees*. Over a meal at *Harry's* Bar in Venice, Cantwell and Renata discuss a portrait of Renata with her hair "twice as long as it has ever been," and the nineteen year-old Renata proposes that the fifty year-old Cantwell call her "daughter"; Cantwell objects that "that would be incest," but "his voice was thickened a little," suggesting that the incestuous undertones might not be entirely disagreeable (98).[1]

In reference only to *For Whom the Bell Tolls*, Kenneth Lynn has argued that to avoid almost certain censorship Hemingway substituted "sensations of swelling and feelings of thickness in Jordan's throat for what happens to his member when he strokes Maria's hair" (487). But while Lynn is probably right about the nature of the substitution, he cannot be right about the purpose behind it. The ubiquity of this substitution, and its presence in posthumous stories like "The Summer People," which Hemingway probably never intended to publish and in which he demonstrates very little inclination toward euphemism, imply that it was not so much a conscious artistic decision adopted to mollify censors so much as it was a substitution that Hemingway probably experienced physically himself and mistakenly considered entirely normal.[2] Yet if a swelling in the throat represents an erection, we are faced with an interesting problem: Why does Robert Jordan stare at *Maria's* throat as his own swells? Why is *Marie Morgan* "choked with excitement" after she bleaches her hair? And after Catherine cuts her hair at the beginning of *The Garden of Eden*, why is *she* the one with the "throaty voice"?

Faced with this problem, it would be easiest to claim that Lynn is simply wrong about the nature of the substitution and that the swelling of Robert Jordan's throat has nothing to do with what happens in his pants, but I think Lynn *is* right, and I think Freud's theory of fetishism can show us how. This theory begs a number of serious questions which we will eventually

have to answer, and it has been substantially modified and expanded by subsequent psychoanalytic theorists, but it is still
the foundation upon which the modern understanding of
fetishism has been built, and it remains the place to begin if one
wants to understand fetishism and the psychosexual aspects of
Hemingway's work.

As Freud explains in his essay on fetishism (1927), his work
with "a number of men whose object-choice was dominated by a
fetish" continually led him back to the same issue:

> In every instance, the meaning and the purpose of the fetish
> turned out, in analysis, to be the same. It revealed itself so nat-
> urally and seemed to me so compelling that I am prepared to
> expect the same solution in all cases of fetishism. When now I
> announce that the fetish is a substitute for the penis, I shall
> certainly create disappointment; so I hasten to add that it is
> not a substitute for any chance penis, but for a particular and
> quite special penis that had been extremely important in early
> childhood but had later been lost. That is to say it should nor-
> mally have been given up, but the fetish is precisely designed to
> preserve it from extinction. To put it more plainly: the fetish is
> a substitute for the woman's (the mother's) penis that the little
> boy once believed in and—for reasons familiar to us—does not
> want to give up. (*SE* XXI, 152–3)

Given this understanding of the fetish, we can now see why
Maria, Marie Morgan, and Catherine Bourne can indeed experience a swelling in the throat that is nonetheless phallic. *Their
hair is itself a symbolic "female phallus," and all of Hemingway's
fetishized women are phallic women*. Any additional phallic symbols in their possession are simply redundant and serve largely
to underscore the original equation.[3]

Women with phallic attributes—aside from the fetish object
itself, which makes *all* of them phallic—abound in Hemingway's
fiction. Margot Macomber totes her Mannlicher gun, Catherine
Barkley carries her swagger stick, and "husky-voiced" Pilar seldom speaks softly but does wield a "big spoon as authoritatively
as though it were a baton" (*FWBT* 391; 56).[4] A curiously androgynous and bisexual figure and one of Hemingway's most compelling female characters, Pilar, in the words of Comley and
Scholes, "is an interesting mixture of the older nurturing female
and the erotic wise woman, a creature whose sexuality transcends and threatens any comfortable division of the genders

into discreet opposites interested only in one another" (49). Yet, while her traditionally "masculine" qualities transcend in breadth and significance her phallic attributes, these attributes, nevertheless, must for the moment remain the focus of our attention since they are most integral to Pilar's position within the field of fetishistic fantasy. Moreover, all of Pilar's masculine qualities, overtly phallic or not, function within this field to confirm her possession of the phallus.

Like Littless in "The Last Good Country" who somehow manages to be both "brother" and "sister" to Nick, or like Catherine Bourne who claims to be simultaneously a "boy" and a "girl," Pilar straddles the traditional binary construction of sexuality and gender. Jordan's first impression of her stresses both her hair and her masculine bulk: "Robert Jordan saw a woman of about fifty almost as big as Pablo, almost as wide as she was tall, in black peasant skirt and waist, with heavy wool socks on heavy legs, black rope-soled shoes and a brown face like a model for a granite monument. She had big but nice looking hands and her curly black hair was twisted into a knot on her neck" (30). And Pilar is well aware of her own masculinity. As she explains at one point to Jordan, "I would have made a good man, but I am all woman. . ." (97). In a sense both man and woman, Pilar is a phallic woman—a status alluded to by her very name, one of great significance for Hemingway. "Pilar" was the secret nickname Pauline chose for herself during her adulterous romance with Hemingway, and Ernest later christened his fishing boat, *The Pilar*, in her honor. Thus Pilar's name aligns her with Hemingway's second wife, but it further aligns her with her namesake, *Nuestra Señora del Pilar* (Our Lady of the Pillar), who is mentioned in the text of *For Whom the Bell Tolls* and whose shrine, at Zaragoza in Spain, consists of an image of the Blessed Virgin on a pillar of porphyry.

In a common variation on the woman *with* a phallus, Hemingway, like some sort of anti-Pygmalion, often petrified his women, thus turning them into the phallus itself.[5] According to Carlos Baker, "When things were going well, [Hemingway] spoke of his wives in a standard phrase: they were happy, healthy, *hard as a rock*, and well-tanned" (my emphasis, x). Robert Jordan, in a moment of free-association, muses about registering at a hotel with Maria as "Doctor and Mrs. Living[-]stone," and at the end of *A Farewell to Arms*, Frederic Henry indirectly compares the body of his beloved to "a statue." Catherine Bourne and Barbara Sheldon, in *The Garden of Eden* manuscript, both derive their transvestic ideas from Rodin's statue, *The Metamorphoses of Ovid*, and Catherine speaks of becoming *like* this statue when she transforms herself into "Peter" ("rock") and her husband into "Catherine."[6] When Catherine waltzes into dinner one night in a white sharkskin dress that shows magnificently against her dark skin, David, with a nod to the Sodom and Gomorrah of the Bible and Proust, calls it her "pillar of salt suit" (K422.1 8.37). It would seem, then, that in spite of her impressive bulk, Pilar's name alone, not to mention her "granite" features and legs like columns, makes her into yet another of Hemingway's "statuesque" women. As a human pillar, Pilar *is* the phallus, but her association with the *Virgin* of the Pillar suggests that she also *has* it.

In "The Semiotic Virgin," a chapter from his book *Signs of the Flesh*, Daniel Rancour-Laferriere provides evidence that within a phallocentric signifying system (and the discourse of fetishism is nothing if not that) virgins are traditionally unconsciously regarded as phallic, since defloration is imagined as a symbolic "castration." "For a man, it is as if a virgin were another *man* (note that, in English, '*virgin*,' '*virile*,' and '*virago*' are etymologically related). Not until he has deflowered her has he 'made a woman out of her'" (Rancour-Laferriere 187).[7] Pilar's association with a shrine devoted to the Virgin on a pillar of stone, thus, makes her into an icon of the phallic woman in her maternal aspect.

Significantly, one of Pilar's most masculine attributes is her "deep voice," which we hear off-stage before she makes her first appearance in the novel (30). But while Pilar at times speaks with a "husky whisper" or "husky voice" suggestive of the throat-swelling elsewhere in his work (387; 391), Hemingway more often describes her voice as "booming." And while this may hardly seem sexy, this booming voice is nonetheless phallic. After symbolically unmanning Pablo by taking control of the guerrilla band, Pilar stands brandishing "the big wooden stirring spoon" that functions as the phallic insignia of her office and mocks her husband's assertion that in war as with bullfighting "within the danger there is the safety of knowing what chances to take" (54). "How many times have I heard matadors talk like that before a goring," she demands and launches into a tale which pointedly contrasts her own booming voice with the effeminate voice of Finito, her symbolically castrated former lover, a *matador de toros*:

"How often have I heard Finito say that it is all knowledge and
that the bull never gored the man; rather the man gored himself on the horn of the bull. Always do they talk that way in
their arrogance before a goring. Afterwards we visit them in the
clinic." Now she was mimicking a visit to a bedside, "'Hello, old
timer. Hello,'" she boomed. Then, "'*Buenas, Compadre*. How
goes it, Pilar?'" imitating the weak voice of the wounded bullfighter. "'How did this happen, Finito, *Chico*, how did this dirty
accident occur to thee?'" booming it out in her own voice. Then
talking weak and small, "'It is nothing, woman. Pilar, it is nothing. It shouldn't have happened. I killed him very well, you understand. Nobody could have killed him better. Then having
killed him exactly as I should and him absolutely dead, swaying on his legs, and ready to fall of his own weight, I walked
away from him with a certain amount of arrogance and much
style and from the back he throws me this horn between the
cheeks of my buttocks and it comes out of my liver.'" She com-
menced to laugh, dropping the imitation of the almost effeminate bullfighter's voice. . . . (55)

Stretched out passively on a bed, squeaking out his story with
an effeminate voice, Finito provides the perfect foil for the "true"
representative of masculinity—the phallic woman, Pilar. (Pilar
here embodies the aspect of the phallic women who assumes her
phallic attributes at the expense of her male partners. Thus,
even when we hear of him uninjured, Finito's voice is always described as "thin.")

Critics have often detected elements of Gertrude Stein or
Hemingway's mother in Hemingway's description of Pilar. Comley and Scholes, for instance, observe that Pilar's appearance
bears a more than casual resemblance to Hemingway's description of Stein in *A Moveable Feast*: "Miss Stein was very big but
not tall and heavily built like a peasant woman. She had beautiful eyes [like Pilar's "fine grey eyes"] and a strong German-Jew-
ish face . . . and she reminded me of a northern Italian peasant
woman with her clothes, her mobile face and lovely, thick alive
immigrant hair which she wore put up" (*MF* 14). Comely and
Scholes further note that "both Pilar and Stein are figures of ambiguous gender. . . . Both women were seen by Hemingway not
only as exemplars of different sexualities but as teachers of
these differences. Robert Jordan's ambivalent feelings about
Pilar resemble Hemingway's about Stein, to whom he was sexually attracted" (46). In a 1948 letter to W. G. Rogers, for instance,

Hemingway wrote, "I liked [Stein] better before she cut her hair and that was sort of a turning point in all sorts of things. She used to talk to me about homosexuality and how it was fine for women and no good for men and I used to listen and learn and I always wanted to fuck her and she knew it and it was a good healthy feeling and made more sense than some of the talk" (*SL* 650). A similar sexual tension colors Jordan's relationship with Pilar—and Pilar's relationship with Maria. (As Thomas Gould has demonstrated, the lesbian element of Pilar's nature is even stronger in the manuscript than in the published version of the novel.) Jordan respects Pilar's abilities as a storyteller, much as Hemingway respected Stein's, and Jordan explicitly evokes Stein when he excuses the odor of his onion sandwich: "'A rose is a rose is an onion,'" Jordan tells Agustín. "'An onion is an onion is an onion'. . . and, he thought, a stone is a stein is a rock is a boulder is a pebble"—the last chain of associations transmuting Stein into its German equivalent, stone, thereby giving her a place among Hemingway's "statuesque" phallic women (289).

Yet trying to distinguish between those elements of Stein and those of Grace Hall Hemingway in Pilar's character is no easy matter. Both Grace and Stein were talented, artistic, ambitious, full-bodied women. And as Kenneth Lynn notes, in Ernest's native Oak Park,

"Mrs. Stein" had been one of Ernest's nicknames for his mother [short for "Mrs. Hemingstein"]; in Paris, Miss Stein would become Grace's most encompassing replacement. Although the two women could not have been more different in some respects, the several similarities between them were significant.

To begin with, they were only twenty months apart in age. Both liked to dominate conversations, *and Gertrude spoke, as Grace did, in a contralto voice that commanded attention by its velvety loveliness as well as by its tone of assurance.* As for Gertrude's attachment to Alice Toklas, Hemingway may have thought of it as a bolder, Parisian variation on his mother's relationship with Ruth Arnold. (my emphasis, 168)

Grace's relationship with her voice student, become housekeeper, become companion, Ruth Arnold may very well have been entirely "innocent" sexually (and Michael Reynolds is comparatively sure that it was so), but it was suggestive enough to inspire Ernest's father to banish Ruth from the house, and, as Lynn reports, "there was gossip in certain quarters—which would be renewed in the later years of Grace's widowhood, when she and Ruth lived together in River Forest—that they were lovers" (100). Whatever the case, Hemingway later complained to one of his sons that Grace was "androgynous," an attitude which, however accurate or inaccurate, provides a further point of connection between Grace and Stein (Reynolds, "Hemingway's Home" 13). In a 1922 letter to Sherwood Anderson, Hemingway exclaimed, "Gertrude Stein and me are just like brothers" (*SL* 62), and, as Lynn explains, Hemingway's

> perception of her as double sexed was underscored by Gertrude's sense of herself. She subscribed to the notions put forth in a book called *Sex and Character* (1906), by Viennese psychologist Otto Weininger, who maintained that completely female women were devoid of imagination and that the only ones who possessed it were those who were part male. . . . He further argued that "the woman who attracts and is attracted by other women is herself half male." (169)

These ties between Grace and Stein certainly suggest the presence of a powerful oedipal current in Hemingway's attraction to the older writer. As Jeffrey Meyers notes, Hemingway probably felt that he could safely express such forbidden desires for Stein precisely because "he knew he could not actually sleep with a lesbian any more than he could sleep with his mother" (77). But leaving the oedipal on the side for the present, Ernest also clearly made an important fetishistic association between Grace and Stein. In 1922, soon after meeting the young Hemingway, Stein wrote enthusiastically to Sherwood Anderson, Hemingway "is a delightful fellow and I like his talk and I am teaching him to cut his wife's hair" (Stein 18). "Since arriving in Paris," Lynn explains, "Hadley had been wearing her hair in a bob, and because her husband wanted it to be even shorter, she too wanted it that way. Probably no other piece of advice that Hemingway received from Gertrude in the early months of their acquaintance served more effectively than this haircutting demonstration to make him think of her as 'family'" (170). Stein's barbering could only have reminded Ernest of the mother who had obsessively given him and his sister matching "boyish" or "girlish" haircuts in his youth. And as Spilka and Lynn both correctly argue, Grace's tonsorial experiments with her children and her pseudotwinning of Ernest with Marcelline played a crucial role in the development of her son's fetishism.

Memories of this lurk behind the figure of Pilar who "gives" Jordan a young girl with shorn hair who looks enough like him to be his "sister."

Given Hemingway's assertions about his mother's "androgyny" and his association of her with the obviously androgynous Stein, could it be that Hemingway derived the phallic properties of Pilar's booming voice—and the phallic properties of the "swollen throats" throughout his work—from his childhood impressions of the operatic voice of Grace Hall Hemingway, a professional voice instructor? In his essay, "The Phallic Representation of the Voice," Alvin Suslick relates the case of an actress who "in the service of a more general unconscious wish for a masculine identity" employed "a number of partial and total body-part representations of a phallic nature" (345), the most prominent of which was her voice:

> Two years before analysis, she developed acute herpetic vaginitis. Her voice changed, became high and squeaky, and she feared the loss of her career. She said the doctor told her that voice changes occurred with genital pain. She referred to episodes of voice blocking, or silent periods when she was unable to speak, as her impotence, which term was also used in describing her helpless feeling at being the passive person in intercourse. On stage when she blocked and could not speak her lines, it felt like her head or something was cut off. By contrast, in the same hour, she said, "The theater has replaced sex in my life. I get an exalted feeling on stage. When I deliver an emotionally charged speech, I get an almost climactic feeling. Afterwards there's a relaxed sense of fulfillment—what I think I should derive from the sex act." Her difficulties multiplied before a microphone. She got "mike fright"—lost breath control, stood stiff and straight, and her voice froze. On television with hidden microphones she could control her voice. . . . Following an episode of compulsive masturbation in which she used a shower hose, she dreamed: "My son kept wetting—so I took a knife and cut off his penis—it was gone—it wasn't bloody—just a small round hole. The doctor sewed it on, but it was only good for an ornament." In a second dream that night, "I was on stage, and couldn't speak my lines—I had lost my voice. . . ." Associations to her own childhood bed wetting confirmed her identification with the son. . . . Discussing a proposed hysterectomy, which she felt would masculinize her, she visualized herself as a shaft of marble which I was chipping away. The sound of her voice at that moment "was driving her crazy." (352)

Elsewhere, this patient explains her fascination with her own voice: "I become enamored and entranced listening to my voice on the stage. I have a mental picture of it in different settings. It's my tool" (351). Or: "My voice was well controlled last night. I played it like an instrument. I pictured my voice in my mind the way I wanted it, and hit it every time. It doesn't matter what I'm reading. As long as I'm exhibiting myself I enjoy it" (351). And in perhaps the most phallic example, "My voice gets sharp and bigger and bigger—not like a normal woman's voice. Sometimes at home it's so hard I can almost feel it" (354).[8] And just such a "hardening" of the voice occurs in *For Whom the Bell Tolls.* When through an interrogation Pilar tries to experience by proxy Jordan's and Maria's lovemaking, she takes on menacing, phallic, serpentine qualities—"There was a spreading . . . as a cobra's hood spreads"—Jordan's voice changes, and we are told twice that Pilar's voice becomes "*hard*" (173).

According to Mark Spilka, Grace Hall Hemingway identified strongly with the men in her family, particularly her son and her father, Ernest Hall. Grace named her first-born son after her father and "had taken Ernestine as her professional middle name when she began her short-lived opera career in New York in 1895" (Spilka 21), which suggests that she somehow tied her singing to a paternal identification. It's certainly possible that Grace, who was something of a tomboy in her youth, may have, like Suslick's patient, had on some level an "unconscious wish for a masculine identity," and she may well have regarded her voice, her exhibitionistic "tool" and means of economic empowerment, as phallic. If so, Ernest easily could have absorbed a subtle awareness of this in his youth. And even if Grace did not conceive of her own voice as phallic, there's no reason why Ernest should not have. If Ernest thought of his mother as phallic, as Freud's theory of fetishism would have us believe, why should he not have endowed one his mother's most impressive qualities with phallic significance?

Before enumerating and exploring more—and much more obvious—examples of phallic women in Hemingway's fiction, it would be better to address some of the questions that Freud's theory must surely have inspired by this point. Answers to these questions, however partial, will render the examples I will eventually offer both more plausible and far more intelligible.

First, if "the fetish is a substitute for the woman's (the mother's) penis that the little boy once believed in and . . . does not want to give up," one may well wonder why the little boy *ever* believed that women, or more specifically his *mother*, had a penis in the first place. In his essay "On the Sexual Theories of Children" (1908), Freud argues that little boys attribute "*to everyone, including females, the possession of a penis*, such as the boy knows from his own body" (Freud's emphasis, *SE* IX, 215). A little boy, he argues, simply cannot imagine *any*one without a part which is so important to himself. And as Freud elaborates in the work in which he first puts forth his theory of fetishism, *Leonardo da Vinci and a Memory of his Childhood* (1910), the little boy's inability to accept the lack of the penis in the *mother* is particularly acute since he feels that she so much resembles himself. Thus, he imagines everyone with a penis like his own, and "this preconception is so firmly planted in the youthful investigator," Freud explains, "that it is not destroyed even when he first observes the genitals of little girls. His perception tells him, it is true, that there is something different from what there is in him, but he is incapable of admitting to himself that the content of his perception is that he cannot find a penis in girls" (*SE* XI, 95). Thus, "When a small boy sees his little sister's genitals, what he says shows that his prejudice is already strong enough to falsify his perception. He does not comment on the absence of a penis, but *invariably* says, as though by way of consolation and to put things right: 'Her ---'s still quite small. But when she gets bigger it'll grow all right'" (*SE* IX, 216).[9]

With the phallocentrism for which he is so famous and so often vilified, Freud argues, for far less compelling reasons than apply specifically to little boys, that *all* children—boys and girls alike—"universally" hold the theory of the phallic mother, a fantasy, thus, intimately tied to penis-envy in little girls, who supposedly customarily feel deprived of the phallus by their mothers. And with his easy equation of the primitive mind and the primitive world, Freud finds evidence for this universality in the phallic attributes of such goddesses of antiquity as the Egyptian Mutt, Isis, and Hathor, or the Greek Aphrodite, the virgin who according to Hesiod sprang from the foam of Ouranos' cast-off genitals after his castration at the hands of Kronos. Indeed, Géza Róheim tells us, in his article "Aphrodite, Or the Woman with a Penis," that during her famous beauty contest with Athene and Hera, Aphrodite, one of whose titles was *Mandragoritis* ("she of the mandrake"), wore an irresistible cestus or girdle which concealed a mandrake, a symbolic phallus associ-

ated with witchcraft and overpowering sexual charms. Then
there is the *Venus Barbata of Cyprus*, described by Macrobius: a
statue of Aphrodite "bearded, but with female dress, with the
scepter and the signs of the male nature, and they think that
the same goddess is both male and female. Aristophanes calls
her Aphroditos" (qtd. in Farnell 628). Aphrodite's phallic, or androgynous, properties, however, are most evident in her merger
with the phallic Hermes "to form the unquestionably phallic figure Hermaphrodite, the protector of sexual intercourse" (Rancour-Laferriere, *Signs* 188). Freud acknowledges that the joining
of the male and female genitals symbolizes fertility and perfec-
tion in these goddesses, but "none of these considerations,"
Freud contends, "gives us an explanation of the puzzling psychological fact that the human imagination does not boggle at
endowing a figure which is intended to embody the essence of
the mother with a mark of male potency which is the opposite of
everything maternal" (*SE* XI, 94).

Of course, Freud's ideas about the origins and universality
of the fantasy of the phallic woman, with its implied primacy of
the phallus for both sexes, now appear debatable to say the
least.[10] While there is overwhelming evidence that penis-envy
(really *phallus* envy) does occur in many women (such as the actress with the phallic voice)—as does womb-envy and breast-
envy in many men—it is apparently hardly as common as Freud
thought. And in the wake of studies by Karen Horney, Helene
Deutsch, Ernest Jones, and Melanie Klein—not to mention more
recent feminist theorists—an acceptance of Freud's phallic primacy is hardly a *sine qua non* of psychoanalysis. Accordingly,
Freud's pupil, Ruth Mack Brunswick has argued that the fantasy of the phallic mother is not an a priori, but rather appears
"to insure the mother's possession of the penis, and as such
probably arises at the moment when the child becomes uncertain that the mother does indeed possess it. Previously . . . it
seems more than probable that the executive organ of the
mother is the breast; the idea of the penis is then projected back
upon the active mother after the importance of the phallus has
been recognized" (304).

More recent studies have complicated Brunswick's formulation considerably, but for the moment it should be more than
adequate. Furthermore, it has two great virtues. First, it hints at
a path by which a study of the fetish, the phallocentric object
par excellence, might eventually lead us *beyond* phallocentrism;

this is a path to which, in spite of the undeniable phallocentrism of *this* chapter, we will eventually return. Second, it forces two important questions: Why would the child want to "insure the mother's possession of the penis" anyway, and once this has been done, why would he (or very much less often, she) refuse to give up the imago that allows him to retain this illusion?

Freud's answer to both questions?: castration anxiety. Although, unlike Brunswick, Freud posits an (I would argue, unnecessary) a priori imago of the phallic mother that the child does not want to give up, he argues that the *fetishist's* imago of the phallic mother is a *regressive* one, designed, like Brunswick's, to insure the mother's possession of the phallus precisely after her possession of it has been called into doubt. Whether or not one accepts Freud's theory of phallic primacy, there can be little doubt that fetishism *is* a phallic position fixation, intimately tied to the phallic phase (traditionally given as three to five years of age) when the little boy's valuation of his penis (like the little girl's valuation of her clitoris), and fear for its safety, reaches its height.[11] And given the little boy's phallic stage construction of the anatomical distinction between the sexes—based solely on the presence or absence of the phallus, with no recognition of the female genitalia as such—to acknowledge the mother's lack of the phallus is to perceive her as "castrated."[12] This possibility, Freud explains, the little boy finds intolerable. "For if a woman [has] been castrated, then his own possession of a penis [is] in danger. . ." (*SE* XXI, 153). To escape his dilemma, the little boy disavows his "recognition" of female "castration" by endowing the mother with a symbolic substitute for her imaginary penis: the phallic fetish object.

Thus, Freud claims that "an investigation of fetishism is strongly recommended to anyone who still doubts the existence of the castration complex. . ." (*SE* XXI, 155).[13] Indeed, among adult fetishists, the construction of the anatomical distinction between the sexes parallels exactly that of the little boy in the phallic stage:

> The existence of an unusually severe castration complex is evident in many different ways, and is associated with two opposing views of the female genitals. These either are conceived of as degraded, dirty—and mutilated. . . ; or there is a latent illusion of the female possessing a penis. This illusion may be manifest, but is more often preconscious and is betrayed in various slips, dreams, and special attitudes. (Greenacre 302)

Hemingway's fiction betrays the illusion of the phallic woman precisely through such "slips, dreams, and special attitudes," but as an example of how strangely manifest such an illusion can be and how tenaciously it can be held by adults who really ought to know better, it is worth citing a case reported by George Devereux:

> A gynecological surgeon (!) of exceptional ability, who firmly believed that women had a penis, though his professional training and experience should have taught him differently[,] . . . clung to this—at first unconscious—idea so tenaciously, that his analyst had to show him periodically a text book of anatomy, so as to convince him, at least momentarily, that the female had no penis. The analysis revealed that the unconscious objective of this surgeon's gynecological operations was the discovery of the female phallus." (qtd. in Rancour-Laferriere, *Signs* 311)[14]

Freud's contention in his essay on fetishism that "probably no male human being is spared the fright of castration at the sight of a female genital" raises some troubling questions—not to mention ire. Needless to say, a little boy's castration anxiety and reluctance to relinquish the fantasy of the phallic woman are the result of his fantasies, wishes, and anxieties and are not the result of any insufficiency of the female genitalia. (As Louise Kaplan notes, Freud is less than clear about this.) Nevertheless, Freud's pronouncement points to an important intuition on his part (*SE* XXI, 154). Freud links castration not to the traditional paternal oedipal prohibition, but rather to an awareness and disavowal of sexual difference itself.[15] True, Freud eventually worked such thought into his oedipal model of castration, suggesting that a "recognition" of female "castration" makes paternal oedipal castration threats credible for little boys; yet it also points to a deeper awareness that fetishism was somehow tied to a *pre*oedipal castration threat—for an awareness of sexual difference must *precede* the triangular oedipal situation.[16] In this respect, Freud seemed to intuit the direction taken by later studies of fetishism. As Phyllis Greenacre, one of the most distinguished post-Freudian theorists of fetishism, notes: "It is now a common observation that fear of castration in boys and penis envy in girls occur earlier than used to be thought—i.e., well before the phallic [and oedipal] phase, quite commonly about the age of two. . . . It is exactly the peculiar quality of the castration complex that comes into florescence in the phallic phase—rather than originating in it, as Freud postulated. . ." (304–305). On the other hand, if *every* "male human being" suffers castration anxiety at the sight of the female genitals, we are faced with a difficult problem, which to his credit, Freud recognized: "Why some people become homosexual as a consequence of that impression, while others fend it off by creating a fetish, and the great majority surmount it, we are frankly unable to explain" (*SE* XXI, 154). Had he only followed his intimation of the preoedipal, Freud might have arrived at an answer to this problem, as we shall see in my next chapter.[17]

In the meantime, while analysts no longer look for the *origins* of fetishism in castration anxiety, "an unusually sharp castration complex is [still] generally agreed to be the *central organizing nucleus* in the structure of fetishism" (my emphasis, Roiphe & Galenson 192). And Hemingway's interest in, and concern about, castration is difficult to ignore.

Hemingway's Castrati Choir

> No one of his other wounds had ever done to him what the first big one did.
>
> —*Across the River and Into the Trees*

From the small Indian in *Torrents of Spring* who had both arms and both legs shot off at Ypres and who now has detachable leather limbs, to the lame husband in "Indian Camp," with his foot cut by an axe, who slits his own throat and may or may not be the father of the child born in the bunk beneath him, Hemingway's fiction offers us a veritable gallery of amputees and other symbolic castrati. Old Count Greffi's complaint in *A Farewell to Arms*, "Sometimes I am afraid I will break off a finger as one breaks a stick of chalk," emphasizes his fragility, but it may also hint at castration and geriatric impotence (261). And Count Greffi's imaginary condition should remind us of Colonel Cantwell's mangled hand in *Across the River*, a wound which testifies to his soldierly experience while also exercising a strange erotic attraction for Renata.[18] In "Snows of Kilimanjaro," Harry Walden's gangrenous leg plainly symbolizes the dry rot of his artistic soul, but "Hairy" also interprets his amputation as a symbolic castration, blaming it for the loss of his potency. As he

cruelly tells his wife, "The only thing I ever really liked to do with
you I can't do now"; with admirable composure, however, she assures him that the doctors will fix up his leg and they will soon
be able to make love again (*SS* 58).

Having said farewell to his arm, Harry Morgan, next to Jake
Barnes the most notable of Hemingway's amputees, is oddly insistent about his *cojones*. "There's worse things than lose an
arm," he tells himself. "You've got two arms and you've got two
of something else. And a man's still a man with one arm or with
one of those" (97). Bee-lips recognizes this as a touchy subject
with Morgan and presses it to his advantage. "I thought you had
cojones," he cajoles, to which Harry replies, "I got *cojones*. Don't
you worry about my *cojones* (109). Nevertheless, in bed with
Marie, Harry/Hairy feels a little awkward about his missing
arm: "Listen, do you mind the arm?" he asks. "Don't it make you
feel funny?" But Marie doesn't mind at all. "You're silly," she tells
him, adding a little strangely, "I *like* it" (my emphasis, 113).
(How do we understand Marie's response to her husband's amputation, which so resembles Renata's response to Cantwell's
hand in *Across the River*? In keeping with the phallic position
fixation of his male characters, Hemingway's female characters—products of male fantasy—often share a similar phallic position fixation with its attendant penis-envy; and the erotic
attraction to amputees, seen in Renata, Marie Morgan, or Brett
Ashley, is a classic sign of penis-envy.)[19]

Lead contralto in Hemingway's castrati choir, however, could
be none other than Jake Barnes. Although in *Torrents of Spring*
Hemingway parodied Sherwood Anderson's easy connection between World War I and cultural impotence (Yogi Johnson comically blames his impotence on the war, and the limbless Indian
excuses his game of billiards with elephantine wit: "Me not shoot
so good since the war" [109]), he realized nevertheless that Jake
Barnes' missing penis, shot off in the war, was the image that
the age demanded. In a sense, Jake's missing penis objectifies in
a horrifying way that enigmatic *something* lost by the "lost generation."[20] Like the impotence of T. S. Eliot's Fisher King, Jake's
wound speaks of a general cultural malaise associated with the
post-war period—an anxiety about the "sterility" of cultural life,
about personal alienation in the modern world, about the rising
sexual and social power of women, about a world of sexuality no
longer governed simply by the dictates of procreation. (Of
course, sexuality was never so-governed, but the recognition of

this fact seems to have been particularly intense during the '20s thanks to the rise of psychoanalysis and the increasing visibility of aggressive female sexuality and homosexuality.) Invoking a mythological motif more subtle than most of those at work in the literature of Eliot, Joyce, and Pound, Hemingway's Jake Barnes, like those autocastrating priests of Attis, is a devotee of the Great (Phallic) Mother in her "terrible" or "castrating" aspect: Brett Ashley, a Circean woman who assumes her phallic attributes at the expense of the men surrounding her.[21] But as F. Scott Fitzgerald also realized, Jake in some ways resembles "a man in a sort of moral chastity belt" as much as he does a man with his penis shot off—a fact which can perhaps best be explained by acknowledging Jake's semi-autobiographical status (qtd. in Bruccoli xii).

Accompanied by his wife, Hadley, on the 1925 trip to Pamplona that served as the inspiration for *The Sun Also Rises*, Hemingway could hardly indulge his passion for Duff Twysden, the most immediate model for Brett Ashley.[22] However, with the deletion of Hadley from the novel (she is mentioned early in the manuscript) and the creation of a passionate love between a character based on himself (Jake is called "Hem" and "Ernest" early in the manuscript) and a character based on Duff, castration offered itself as one, admittedly odd, explanation for Jake's inability to consummate this relationship. Of course, as a writer of fiction, Hemingway could as easily have *had* Jake and Brett consummate their relationship, but the novel's plot and emotional interest depends largely on the impossibility of their doing so. And, for Hemingway, this very impossibility was inherently castratory. As Jake explains in a deleted postscript from *The Sun Also Rises* manuscript: "The thing I would like to make my reader believe, however incredible, is that such a passion and such a longing could exist in me for Brett Ashley that I would sometimes feel that *it would tear me to pieces. . .*" (my emphasis, 618).

Yet if plenty of conscious, logical reasons suggest themselves for Jake's castration, it nonetheless also carried a psychosexual import that wasn't entirely lost on Jake's creator. While Jake eventually grew into a distinct character, different from the "Hem" or "Ernest" of the early pages of the manuscript, the connection between the author and his creation persisted and unsettled Hemingway. After all, it is highly unusual for a man to portray himself as castrated, even if the self-representation is much distorted and achieves a good deal of distance from its creator. Thus in 1951, worried that Philip Young was "writing a book which proves that I am all my heroes," Hemingway complained to Thomas Bledsoe,

> Every writer is in much of his work. But it is not as simple as all that. I could have told Mr. Young the whole genesis of *The Sun Also Rises* for example. It came from a personal experience in that when I had been wounded at one time there had been an infection from pieces of wool cloth being driven into the scrotum. Because of this I got to know other kids who had genito urinary wounds and I wondered what a man's life would have been like after that if his penis had been lost and his testicles and spermatic cord remained intact. I had known a boy that had happened to. So I took him and made him into a foreign correspondent in Paris and, inventing, tried to find out what his problems would be when he was in love with someone who was in love with him and there was nothing they could do about it.

In this somewhat disingenuous letter Hemingway insists, "My own wound had healed rapidly and well. . . ," and "I was not Jake Barnes" (*SL* 745). Yet in a 1952 letter to another early Hemingway critic, Charles Fenton, Hemingway was less successful at distancing himself from Jake:

> The man [Harold Loeb] who identifies himself as Cohn in *The Sun Also Rises* once said to me, "But why did you make me cry all the time?"
>   I said, "Listen, if that is you then the narrator must be me. Do you think that I had my prick shot off. . .? And I'll tell you a secret: you do cry an awful lot for a man." (*SL* 764)

Hemingway's explanation to Fenton can only remind us of Freud's famous joke about "the defense put forward by the man who was charged by one of his neighbors with having given him back a borrowed kettle in a damaged condition. The defendant asserted first, that he had given it back undamaged; secondly, that the kettle had a hole it when he borrowed it; and thirdly, that he had never borrowed a kettle from his neighbor at all" (*SE* IV, 120). Logically, "each one of the defenses is valid in itself, but taken together they exclude one another" (*SE* VIII, 62). There is, however, an unconscious logic to Hemingway's defense: Loeb both *was* and *was not* Cohn, and the relationship between Hemingway and Jake was much the same.

Hemingway's renditions of his own wounding at Fossalta di Piave on July 8, 1918, were notoriously prone to mutation and embellishment—so much so that a definitive account of this event can probably never be written—but clearly his penis was not shot off, nor is it even likely that wool was blown into his scrotum. James Nagel has recovered the uniform that Hemingway was wearing at the time of the explosion, and there are no holes in the pants above the knee. Thus it is all the more telling that Hemingway consistently constructed this experience as threateningly castratory. In 1950, he told A. E. Hotchner that he "had been nicked in the scrotum by a piece of shrapnel" during the war (Hotchner 48). And in a 1950 letter to Arthur Mizener rich with inventions which, like Hemingway's fictions, are more truthful than the truth, Hemingway not only endowed his old wounds with castratory significance but situated them squarely within a psychologically-laden family dynamic.

> I get sick of [Edmund] Bunny Wilson writing [in *The Wound and the Bow*] about some mysterious thing that changed or formed my life and then dismissing *For Whom the Bell Tolls* in a footnote. Why doesn't he say what the mysterious thing is? Could it be that my father shot himself? Could it be that I did not care, overly, for my mother? Could it be that *I have been shot twice through the scrotum* and through the right hand, left hand, right foot and left foot and through both knees and the head? (my emphasis, *SL* 694)[23]

Of course, Hemingway was *not* shot through his head or through his scrotum, but, in addition to over 220 shrapnel wounds, he *was shot twice: once in the foot and once in the knee.* (Villard and Nagel provide x-rays in *Hemingway in Love and War.*) The imaginary migration of these two magic bullets from the foot and knee to the genitals—which should remind us of Colonel Cantwell who likewise was wounded at Fossalta and whose hand has been "shot through twice" (*ART* 55)—forces us to recognize the depth of the affinity between Jake Barnes's castration and Hemingway's interpretations of his own wartime experience.

The fact that Hemingway associated Jake's castration with his own war wound and family romance suggests that the experience of being blown up, with the attendant threat to the genitals (no matter how skeptical we may be about the wounds to Ernest's scrotum), may have been the adult trauma which reactivated Hemingway's childhood fixations. Though rooted in childhood, fetishism seldom becomes manifest until young adulthood when it is often triggered by a trauma constituting a severe castration threat, and Hemingway's wounding in World War I bears all the markings of such a trauma.[24] At least I can find no evidence of Hemingway's fetishism before July 1918; there is, however, evidence of it soon afterward—on September 7, to be exact. Agnes von Kurowsky, the nurse Hemingway fell in love with soon after he arrived at the hospital in Milan, noted in her diary an incident involving one of her hairpins: "Lo'dy, Lo'dy, Goodness me—Mac found one of my yellow hairpins under Hemingway's pillow, & she & Mr. Lewis will never let me forget now. I think both Ernie & I got through it pretty well" (qtd. in Villard and Nagel 77).[25]

That Hemingway and Agnes actually consummated their relationship in the hospital, as do Frederic and Catherine in *A Farewell to Arms*, seems highly unlikely, but in her wartime letters Agnes writes of laying her head on a "nice hollow place" (probably Ernest's chest), and we can reasonably assume that Hemingway enjoyed playing with her hair when she did so (qtd. in Villard and Nagel 99). Of course, extrapolating from the fiction to Ernest's life is one of the classic temptations and pitfalls of Hemingway scholarship; yet Hemingway's liberal use of autobiography in the composition of his fiction, and his credo that a writer should write what he knows from experience, make the temptation at times too inviting and useful to pass up. Thus, given the entry about hairpins from Agnes's diary, I think it is safe to speculate that Frederic's memory of playing with Catherine's hair in *A Farewell to Arms* is based largely on Hemingway's experience with Agnes:

> I loved to take her hair down and she sat on the bed and kept very still, except suddenly she would dip down to kiss me while I was doing it, and I would take out the pins and lay them on the sheet and it would be loose and I would watch her while she kept very still and then take out the last two pins and it would all come down and she would drop her head and we would both be inside of it, and it was the feeling of inside a tent or behind a falls. (*FTA* 114)

As for the relation of Hemingway's wound to castration anxiety, Agnes recalled a little over half-a-century later that Hemingway had been "worried about his leg. He was afraid they'd amputate" (qtd. in Reynolds, "Agnes" 269). Agnes's memories, like Ernest's, were less than reliable; her World War I diaries and letters to Ernest, published in 1989, contradict her interviews from the 1970s consistently and quite significantly. Nevertheless there is little reason to doubt Ernest's fear of an amputation. Citing an interview with Ernest's fellow-convalescent, Henry Villard, Carlos Baker notes that "there had been some loose talk about possible amputation" (48).

The trauma objectified by Jake Barnes's wound, however, extended well beyond the explosion on the battlefield and the physical damage suffered by young Hemingway. The experience after his return to America of being rejected by his first adult love plunged Ernest into a despair which psychiatrists Irvin and Marilyn Yalom speculate may have been Hemingway's first recorded instance of clinical depression. According to Marcelline, Ernest was crushed. He ran a fever, took to bed, and for weeks thereafter was unable to think of anything else. Years later, he recalled, "I was hurt very badly; in the body, mind and spirit and also morally. . . . I was hurt bad all the way through and I was really spooked at the end" (qtd. in Meyers 48).

Given the tragic history of mental illness and suicide in his family, there can be little doubt that Hemingway had a genetic predisposition to the bipolar mood disorder which plagued him throughout his adult life.[26] A depressive episode at this point in his life, therefore, should hardly surprise us. In his young adulthood Hemingway was probably *cyclothymic*.[27] That is, he probably suffered from a condition in which periods of *hypomania* (mild mania) alternate with periods of not entirely debilitating depression. Like full-blown manic-depression (and fetishism, to which it is almost entirely unrelated etiologically), cyclothymia typically manifests itself in young adulthood. Yet there is also an intimate association between depression and *loss*, and even in those with genetic or chemically-induced predispositions to depression, the onset of a mood disorder can often be linked to a major loss. As William Styron explains in his moving account of his own struggle with clinical depression, heredity, chemistry, and behavior all play a role in the disease, "but certainly one psychological element has been established beyond a reasonable doubt, and that is the concept of loss. Loss in all of its manifestations is the touchstone of depression—in the progress of the disease and, most likely, in its origin" (56). We can't be certain that Hemingway's despair after the loss of Agnes was an instance of clinical depression, but it does seem likely, and he did experience periods of depression from that date forward with some regularity.[28]

Whatever the case, Hemingway seems to have associated the dissolution of his romance with Agnes with a sort of symbolic castration. In his brief fictional account of this affair in "A Very Short Story," the protagonist responds to the failure of his romance by anti-romantically contracting "gonorrhea from a sales girl . . . while riding in a taxicab through Lincoln Park" (SS 142).[29] (The loss of a "nurse" and a "first love," a loss linked to depression, must also have touched aspects of Hemingway's psyche that lay close to the core of his fetishism—even deeper than the fear of castration. These aspects of Hemingway's psyche, however, will be my subject in the next two chapters.)

Given the association of Hemingway's war wound with the amputation of Jake Barnes's penis, we should hardly be surprised to discover a pervasive threat of castration throughout *A Farewell to Arms*, the novel which re-imagines Hemingway's wounding at Fossalta most extensively. Once again, and quite understandably, the experience of being blown up presents the most obvious threat, but other castration threats abound—many of them intriguingly associated with the fetish. When Frederic tries to get a haircut in the hospital, for instance, the barber is unusually taciturn and his manner unsettles Frederic: "If he was crazy, the sooner I could get out from under his razor the better. Once I tried to get a good look at him. 'Beware,' he said. 'The razor is sharp'" (90). Later, when Frederic asks if the barber is crazy, the porter tells him, "'No, signorino. He made a mistake. He doesn't understand very well and he thought I said you were an Austrian soldier. . . . Ho ho ho,' the porter laughed. 'He was funny. One move from you he said and he would have—' he drew his forefinger across his throat" (91). And after Miss Van Campen accuses Frederic of producing jaundice with alcoholism, we again see the connection between castration and a violent cutting of the fetish object. Indignant at the accusation, Frederic asks, "'Miss Van Campen, . . . did you ever know a man who tried to disable himself by kicking himself in the scrotum?'"

> "I have known many men to escape the front through self-inflicted wounds."
> "That wasn't the question. I have seen self-inflicted wounds also. I asked you if you had ever known a man who

had tried to disable himself by kicking himself in the scrotum. Because that is the nearest sensation to jaundice and it is a sensation that I believe few women have experienced." (144)[30]

After Miss Van Campen storms out of the room, Miss Gage enters and demands, "What did you say to Van Campen? She was furious." Frederic explains, "'We were comparing sensations. I was going to suggest that she had never experienced childbirth——' 'You're a fool,'" Gage interrupts. "She's after your *scalp*" (my emphasis, 145). Thus, via Hemingway's fetishistic associations, we have floated from a direct threat to the *genitals* to a threat to Frederic's *scalp*—an association we find again in *For Whom the Bell Tolls*.

In this novel, set almost entirely in "*la cueva de los huevos perdidos*" (i.e., "the cave of the lost balls"), castration is a running joke—and a running threat (199).[31] Anselmo silently compares Pablo to a castrated boar, and Rafael repeatedly proposes blinding him. For his part, Pablo purposefully confuses the *Ingles* (who is really American) with a Scot and demands to know what Jordan wears beneath his kilts. "*Cojones*," Jordan replies, plainly implying Pablo's lack of them. Nevertheless, Pablo counters that Jordan lacks the *cojones* to assassinate him. This concern about *cojones*, of course, is entirely appropriate for a novel set in Spain, a country where *cojones* symbolize honor and courage and where men are notoriously boastful about their testicles. Such talk is simply the lingo of the land. Yet Hemingway's interest in castration in this novel runs deeper than this. Symbolically, the Fascists threaten to emasculate Spain. In the final pages, for instance, the Fascists shoot Fernando through the groin. Yet, as we see in the fate of El Sordo's band, decapitated after a hilltop defense modeled on Custer's Last Stand, the Fascist threat is once again expressed in terms of the fetish. The connection between *decapitation* (a classic castration symbol) and *scalping* is explicit: The Fascist leader thinks to himself that "taking the heads is barbarous. But proof and identification is necessary"—thus invoking the traditional rationale behind scalping. Then, thinking about his grandfather, an Indian fighter of old, Jordan tries to reassure himself: "What if they took the heads? Does that make any difference? None at all. The Indians always took the scalps when Grandfather was at Fort Kearny after the war" (336).[32]

Hemingway's work is absolutely full of strangely dangerous and violently castratory haircuts. Take, for instance, the fate of the inept bullfighter in "Chapter XI" of *In Our Time*:

> The crowd shouted all the time and threw pieces of bread down into the ring, then cushions and leather wine bottles, keeping up whistling and yelling. Finally the bull was too tired from so much bad sticking and folded his knees and lay down and one of the *cuadrilla* leaned out over his neck and killed him with the *puntillo*. The crowd came over the barrera and around the torero and *two men grabbed him and held him and someone cut off his pigtail and was waving it and a kid grabbed it and ran away with it*. Afterwards I saw him at the café. He was very short with a brown face and quite drunk and he said after all it has happened before like that. I am not really a good bull fighter. (my emphasis, SS 171)

The cutting of a bullfighter's *coleta*, the very symbol of his status as a *matador de toros* (at least before matadors began wearing artificial coletas pinned to their caps), represents a threat to his dignity, professional status, and manhood; yet given Hemingway's hair fetish, it also signifies castration.

Hemingway's bullfighting masterpiece, "The Undefeated," hinges precisely upon the cutting of a coleta. Recovering from a serious goring and well past his fighting prime, Manuel Garcia talks his friend Zurito into pic-ing for him one last time, with the proviso that he will cut his coleta and retire if he doesn't go over well. At the end of the story, after a fight of impressive bravery and much bad luck, Manuel lies on the operating table with Zurito looming above him, scissors in hand. Badly gored, Manuel is nevertheless at least as worried about his coleta as he is about dying:

> Zurito stood beside the table, bending over where the doctor was working. . . . One of the men in white smiled and handed Retana a pair of scissors. Retana gave them to Zurito. Zurito said something to Manuel. He could not hear it.
>
> To hell with this operating-table. He'd been on plenty of operating-tables before. He was not going to die. There would be a priest if he was going to die.
>
> Zurito was saying something to him. Holding up the scissors.
>
> That was it. They were going to cut off his coleta. They were going to cut off his pigtail.

> Manuel sat up on the operating-table. The doctor stepped
> back, angry. Someone grabbed him and held him.
> "You couldn't do a thing like that, Manos," he said. (SS 265)

"I was just joking," Zurito assures him as Manuel slips away
under the influence of the anesthetic. Manuel's refusal to give
up his coleta signifies his refusal to give up his dignity and pro-
fession, and it is precisely this which makes him "undefeated";
yet the equation of Manuel's manhood with his pigtail is telling
nonetheless.

One of Hemingway's first pieces for the *Toronto Star*, "Taking
a Chance for a Free Shave" (March 6, 1920), makes the connection between haircutting and castration almost transparently.
Prefiguring Frederic's haircut in *A Farewell to Arms* and Hemingway's later writing about bullfights, in what were it not for
the reverse chronology could only be considered a self-parody,
Hemingway playfully writes that "a visit to the barber college requires the cold, naked valor of the man who walks clear-eyed to
death" (*Dateline* 5). When the young reporter passes up the
soon-to-be graduates on the first floor, who charge five cents for
a shave and fifteen for a haircut, and mounts the stairs to the
room where the beginners offer their services for free, tension
fills the room:

> A hush fell over the shop. The young barbers looked at one an-
> other significantly. One made an expressive gesture with his
> forefinger across his throat.
> "He's going upstairs," said a barber in a hushed voice.
> "He's going upstairs," the other echoed him and they
> looked at one another.
> I went upstairs. (5)

(Hemingway obviously knew something about the artful use of
repetition long before he met Gertrude Stein.) Nervous, Hemingway makes small talk with a young red-haired barber, asking
how long the student has been at the college. And he isn't very
encouraged by the reply. Yet when he asks how long it will take
before the young barber can join the soon-to-be graduates
downstairs, he is even less encouraged:

> "Oh, I've been downstairs," he said lathering my face.
> "Why did you come back up here?" said I.
> "I had an accident," he said, going on with the lathering.

> Just then one of the non-workers came over and looked
> down at me.
> "Say, do you want to have your throat cut?" he inquired
> pleasantly.
> "No," said I.
> "Haw! Haw!" said the non-worker. (6)

We might be inclined to dismiss the repeated references to decapitation as something other than a castration threat. After all,
if a cigar can occasionally just be a cigar, then perhaps a decapitation can simply be a decapitation—but what happens next
seems to indicate otherwise:

> Just then I noticed that my barber had his left hand bandaged.
> "How did you do that?" I asked.
> "Darn near sliced off my thumb with the razor this morn-
> ing," he replied amiably. (6)

The mood is light, but the symbolic threat is clear.[33]
    We hear echoes of this early newspaper piece and the anxi-
eties behind it in "The Porter," a scene from an untitled and unfinished novel (circa 1927) published in the *Finca Vigía* collection
of Hemingway's stories. Here, George, a black Pullman Porter, de-
livers a disquisition on the martial art of razor-fighting to young,
white Jimmy. Drunk with liquor given to him by Jimmy's father
(a professional revolutionist and "champion drinker"), George
asks the boy, "Did you ever see a man cut with a razor?" When
wide-eyed Jimmy replies that he hasn't, George offers to demonstrate. Using a hair from Jimmy's head, George reveals the keen-
ness of his blade's edge. He then launches into an absurd cross
between shadow-boxing and Japanese *kendo*, whirling and duck-
ing, jabbing and slashing at the air. But after a moment he tires
and sits down. Sweating, he confesses to the boy,

> "The razor's a delusion," he said. "The razor's no defense. Any-
> body can cut you with a razor. If you're close enough to cut
> them they're bound to cut you. If you could have a pillow in
> your left hand you'd be all right. But where you going to get a
> pillow when you need a razor? *Who you going to cut in bed*? The
> razor's a delusion, Jimmy." (my emphasis, *CSS* 576)

The delusional path from Jimmy's sliced *hair* to the sort of cut
one might get in *bed* is swift and suggestive.[34]

Yet the most interesting example of the connection between haircutting and castration must be the subtle one underlying "God Rest You Merry, Gentlemen," Hemingway's relatively obscure short story about a guilt-ridden boy's grotesque autocastration with a razor on Christmas Day.[35] The compassionate Doc Fischer and the incompetent Doctor Wilcox (who always carries a copy of *The Young Doctor's Friend and Guide* in his pocket to compensate for his ignorance) are confronted on Christmas Eve by a hatless, "curly-haired" sixteen year-old seeking "eunuch-hood":

> "I want to be castrated," the boy said.
> "Why?" Doc Fischer asked.
> "I've prayed and I've done everything and nothing helps."
> "Helps what?"
> "That awful lust."
> "What awful lust?"
> "The way I get. The way I can't stop getting. I pray all night about it. . . . It's a sin against purity. It's a sin against our Lord and Saviour." (SS 394)

Impatient, Doctor Wilcox tells the boy, "You're just a goddamned fool" (in the manuscript he also tells the boy to go off and masturbate); Doc Fischer, however, kindly explains that lust is normal and healthy and that the boy certainly doesn't need to be castrated.

> "Then you won't do it?" the boy asked.
> "Do what?"
> "Castrate me."
> "Listen," Doc Fischer said. "No one will castrate you. There is nothing wrong with your body. . . . If you are religious remember that what you complain of is no sinful state but the means of consummating a sacrament." (395)

When the boy returns at one o'clock on Christmas morning he is bleeding to death after having sliced off his penis with a razor. It seems he didn't know the difference between medical and psychological castration, between the severing of the testicles and the amputation of the penis. Wilcox, the doctor on call, cannot find this emergency listed in *The Young Doctor's Friend and Guide*, and the failure may cost the boy his life.

Most obviously this is a story condemning sexual prudery as a measure of religiosity and defining compassion as the true meaning of Christianity. The boy's misplaced fundamentalism stands condemned as an essentially perverse (in the clinical *and* moral sense of the term) and pathological interpretation of religion; yet the story's other "Christian," Doctor Wilcox, who pointedly reminds Doc Fischer of his Jewishness—"*Our* Saviour? Ain't you a Jew?"—lacks the basic "Christian" compassion for the boy that we find in Doc Fischer. A slim blond Jew and "fisher of men," Fischer is a Christ figure. As Peter Hays points out, Fischer has ridden an ass, namely Wilcox, who complains, "I wish you wouldn't ride me. . . . There isn't any need to ride me" (*Limping* 395). Hays further notes that Fischer "heals men with his hands and has suffered for it" (73); and, like Christ, Fischer has visited hell, if not "to harrow, . . . to be harrowed" (Hays 75). Thus, when Wilcox tells Fischer to go to hell, he replies: "All in good time. If there is such a place I shall certainly visit it. I have even had a very small look into it. No more than a peek, really. I looked away almost at once" (396).

    The story, nevertheless, also clearly invites an oedipal interpretation. The boy, who fears he has sinned against God the Father, and who suffers guilt as a result of uncontrollable (fetishistic?) desires that he may recognize unconsciously as directed toward a maternal figure, goes to two doctors for ritual castration. (Fetishistic desire, like more traditional oedipal desire, occasionally provokes intense feelings of guilt. In "Fetishism: A Case Report," Henry Lihn describes a patient who resembles the boy of this story uncannily: "He . . . struggled with strong impulses to gouge out his eyeballs with his fingers, to cut himself, or to rip off his genitals" [351].) Significantly, Hemingway's father was a doctor, and what Carlos Baker reveals about punishment with fetishistically-invested instruments in the Hemingway household suggests an affinity to this story:

> In the regulation of the children the doctor was by far the stricter of the two. He was always so nervously busy that any signs of idleness or procrastination among his brood roused him to sharp words and sudden scoldings. He forbade all recreational activity on the Lord's Day. . . . Except in times of illness, attendance at church and Sunday school was compulsory. Major infractions of the rules were swiftly punished with a *razor strop* (*Grace employed a hairbrush*), followed by injunctions to kneel and ask God's forgiveness. (my emphasis, 9)

    In this story Hemingway may have bifurcated his doctor father into an idealized "good father" and a denigrated "bad father." (Such splitting is common among fetishists and is particularly evident in Hemingway's later work.) Yet, interestingly, the "good father," Doc Fischer, is portrayed as symbolically castrated himself. His name, originally "Fisher" in the manuscript, invokes Eliot's impotent Fisher King (Hays, *Limping* 72), and his Jewishness may also signify circumcision as a symbolic castration. Doctor Wilcox, on the other hand, whose ineptitude may cost the boy his life, bears undeniably, if none-too-impressive, phallic attributes; his name was originally "Cox" in the manuscript, and he carries a "*limp leather*" copy of *The Young Doctor's Friend* in his *pocket* (SS 393). Perhaps it is Doc Fischer's symbolic affinity to the boy which allows him to grant the would-be eunuch such sympathy; yet in wanting to be "pure," like Christ, the boy ends up imitating the castrated Christ-figure, Fischer.

When their gender status is challenged, Hemingway's male characters (Jake Barnes, Frederic Henry, Francis Macomber, Robert Jordan, and David Bourne all come to mind) will often attempt to identify with undeniably phallic men, but the desire of the boy in "God Rest You Merry, Gentlemen" indicates that he is *seeking* cross-gender identification. His quest forces us to recognize that a "castration complex" is exactly that, *complex*, not a simple matter of castration *anxiety*. The boy's behavior is, however, entirely consistent with aspects of fetishistic fantasy. Bak, Greenacre, Zavitzianos, and others have argued that the intensity of castration anxiety in fetishists is *partly* the result of a profound, but threatening, desire to identify with the phallic woman in her "*castrated*" aspect.[36] For the moment, this may simply seem paradoxical, but it should begin to make sense in the next section. In the meantime, we might begin to understand this cross-gender impulse if we pursue the relation between castration and fetishism in this story.

Hemingway's interest in castration in "God Rest You Merry, Gentlemen" could hardly be more obvious, but aside from the razor employed in the boy's autocastration, the text offers little overt evidence of Hemingway's hair fetishism. Yet it *is* there, lurking beneath the enigmatic opening lines of the story:

> In those days the distances were all very different, the dirt blew off the hills that now have been cut down, and Kansas City was very like Constantinople. (SS 392)

These lines, which have puzzled a number of critics, are striking for what Comley and Scholes call the "inappropriateness" and "farfetchedness" of their comparison (78). When in a 1922 dispatch from Constantinople for the *Toronto Star*, Hemingway describes the Golden Horn as looking "more like the Chicago River" than a site of myth and legend, the simile is simply deflating and anti-romantic in the best Hemingwayesque manner, but when the situation is reversed in "God Rest You," we wonder what in the world he means by comparing the mundane, gritty Kansas City of this story to "one of the most exotic and storied places in the world" (*Dateline* 228; Comley and Scholes 78). The very strangeness of this simile, moreover, is plainly intentional. The narrator, a reporter named Horace who hardly strikes one as a "man of the world" (he mistranslates the name of a French car, "Dans Argent," as "silver dance" or "silver dancer" and ironically takes pride in his "knowledge of a foreign language"), emphasizes this strangeness by adding to his initial comparison, "You may not believe this. No one believes this; but it is true" (392).

We might surmise that the immediate source of Horace's simile is an awful and perhaps unconscious pun. Horace has just come out of "Woolf Brothers' saloon where, on Christmas and Thanksgiving Day, a free *turkey* dinner was served," a fact he repeats to Doc Fischer a little later (my emphasis, *SS* 392). This wasn't the first time Hemingway used this pun. In one of his Greco-Turkish War dispatches from Constantinople to the *Toronto Star*, Hemingway writes that "Turkey is the national dish in Turkey. These birds live a strenuous life chasing grasshoppers over the sun-baked hills of Asia Minor and are about as tough as a racehorse" (*Dateline* 239). The significance of this pun in "God Rest You Merry, Gentlemen," however, is less than clear. Perhaps it stresses the role of unconscious associations in the genesis of this story, or perhaps it forges a link between the themes of charity (the free turkey) and castration, which for interesting reasons Hemingway associated with Turkey.

In their attempt to account for these troubling first lines, Comley and Scholes postulate that Hemingway, aware of the exalted position of eunuchs in Byzantine politics and society, consciously associated Constantinople, like the mutilated hills of Kansas City, with castration.

> The position of eunuchs in Byzantium was entirely different from that in the Arab countries or in Persia . . . for in Byzantium they often ran the government. In the sixth century, one of the greatest Byzantine generals was a eunuch. By the tenth

century, eunuchs in the imperial court took precedence over
non-eunuchs, and many of the most prominent men in both
the state and the Church were eunuchs. (Bullough 327; qtd. in
Comley and Scholes 80)

Indeed, as Comley and Scholes point out, Hemingway reveals an
awareness of the special status of Byzantine eunuchs in a
phrase from one of his attacks upon literary critics: "In the same
way the Eunuch's Trade Journal and House Organ of Stamboul,
Turkey gives little space and attention to the proprietors of the
Harems. It is a tender subject" (qtd. in Comley and Scholes 80).
No doubt, Comley and Scholes are correct about Hemingway's
conscious associations. But this isn't the entire story.

    Given his fetishization of hair—his furnishing of it with
phallic properties—it is surely significant that during his 1922
stay in Constantinople, Hemingway contracted head lice and
subsequently had to shave his head. For Hemingway, this signified a symbolic castration, which is perhaps why memories of
Constantinople trouble the gangrenous Harry Walden in "The
Snows of Kilimanjaro." And for Hemingway, to be castrated was
to be feminized. Thus, in "Snows," Harry's castration anxiety
and memories of Constantinople lead to a transvestic memory
concerning the unusual uniforms worn by the Greek elite forces,
the Evzones: "That was the day he'd first seen dead men wearing
white ballet skirts and upturned shoes with pompons on them.
The Turks had come steadily and lumpily and he had seen the
skirted men running and the officers shooting into them and
running then themselves. . ." (SS 66). According to Kenneth
Lynn, Hemingway, himself, saw no such thing. "The Turks had
driven the Greeks out of Anatolia in August, while he was still
on vacation in Germany, and the Greek infantrymen whom he
followed across Thrace in mid-October were dressed in surplus
U.S. Army uniforms. The dead soldiers in skirts had been described to him in Constantinople by a British captain. . ."
(181).[37] The fact that Hemingway decided to blend this story
with his own memories of Constantinople in "Snows" suggests,
therefore, that he saw a symbolic link between them.

    We shall have reason to return to Constantinople and its
fetishistic and transvestic significance for Hemingway when we
consider his fetishization of race in The Garden of Eden; until
then, suffice it to say that behind the tragic autocastration in
"God Rest You Merry, Gentlemen" lay an extremely personal and

fetishistically-invested castration threat. This threat, moreover, was intimately associated with a guilty desire—a desire for which castration was a means of satisfaction as much as it was a means of punishment.[38]

To Have or Have Not the Phallus

> You know no man ever looked at her that didn't have an erection. I don't know what women have but whatever it is I have it.
>
> —Barbara Sheldon to David Bourne
> *The Garden of Eden* Manuscript

But if the adoption of a fetish is supposed to ward off castration anxiety by endowing women with an illusory "female phallus," and cut hair signifies castration, how do we make sense of Hemingway's seemingly paradoxical taste for women with *cut* hair? At one time or another, all of Hemingway's wives sported short, "boyish" haircuts. Brett Ashley wears "her hair brushed back like a boy's." And Jake tells us, "She started all that" (*SAR* 22). Likewise, Catherine Barkley tells Frederic that she wants to cut her hair after "young Catherine" is born (*FTA* 304). Harry Morgan cajoles Marie into keeping her bleached hair short in *To Have and Have Not*, and Maria's hair, in *For Whom the Bell Tolls*, is "but little longer than the fur on a beaver pelt" (22). As her gender identity becomes ever more unhinged in *The Garden of Eden*, Catherine Bourne's skin grows ever darker and her hair gets ever shorter and lighter—a pattern which, minus the bleach, is repeated by the dark-haired Marita of the manuscript. Thus, of the many romantic heroines in Hemingway's novels, only Renata can keep her long, luxuriant locks intact, but even here, Renata's portrait of herself with her hair "twice as long as it has even been" establishes her current long hair as comparatively "cut" and may overcompensate for Hemingway's compulsion to play the coiffeur. Yet how can the fetish object be simultaneously "phallic" *and* "castrated"?

Because the imago of the phallic woman arises against the backdrop of the boy's doubt over whether or not the mother really has a penis—and this imago is preserved precisely to disavow the *recognition* that she does *not* have it—the phallic woman of fetishistic fantasy is always, in fact, a "phallic/cas-trated" woman. One attribute or the other may predominate at any given moment, but almost always both are present, fre-quently through ingenious compromise formations. Even with his theory of an a priori imago of the phallic mother, Freud rec-ognized this divided attitude in the fetishist:

> It is not true that, after the child has made his observation of the woman, he has preserved unaltered his belief that women have a phallus. He has retained that belief, but he has also given it up. In the conflict between the weight of the unwelcome perception and the force of his counter-wish, a compromise has been reached, as is only possible under the dominance of the unconscious laws of thought—the primary process. Yes, in his mind the woman has got a penis, in spite of everything; but this penis is no longer the same as it was before. Something else has taken its place, has been appointed its substitute, as it were, and now inherits the interest which was formerly di-rected to its predecessor. But this interest suffers an extraordi-nary increase as well, because the horror of castration has set up a memorial to itself in the creation of this substitute. . . . We can now see what the fetish achieves and what it is that main-tains it. It remains a token of triumph over the threat of castra-tion and a protection against it. (*SE* XXI, 154)

Fetishism, therefore, involves a double, or divided, attitude to-ward the female genitalia and sexual difference. It replaces the "missing" *imaginary* female *penis* with a *symbolic phallus*, thereby warding off castration anxiety and disavowing the anatomical distinction between the sexes by paradoxically erect-ing a hypercathected monument to both. That is, the very *sym-bolic* status of the female phallus cannot help but call attention to the *lack* of the female penis for which it substitutes.

According to Freud, this division in the fetishist's attitude toward feminine "castration" leads to nothing less than a "rift in the ego which never heals but which increases as time goes on" (*SE* XXIII 276). (We shall eventually see, however, that this rift is structured by an earlier splitting of the pre-fetishist's body image.) Such splitting, in fact, is a defining characteristic of the psychoanalytic "perversions," all of which involve a fascination of one sort or another with the phallic mother. Whereas the neu-rotic *represses* a part of the id in deference to reality (only to ex-perience the return of the repressed as a symptom), and the psychotic *repudiates* a portion of reality in service of the id (only to see it return from without in the form of a hallucination), the "pervert" through a process of *disavowal* holds contrary attitudes within the structure of the ego itself.[39] Based as it is upon primary process "logic," this split must exist within an unconscious portion of the ego, yet the presence of this rift in the ego explains why "perverse" fantasies tend to be more ego-syntonic than neurotic symptoms and, thus, more *pre*conscious than *un*conscious—characterized by *reticence* and *secrecy*, rather than by *resistance* and *repression.*[40] How else could Hemingway have written a book like *The Garden of Eden* that explores his erotic fantasies so overtly and in such detail? Hemingway was always more discerning and honest about himself in his fiction than he was in his daily life, and his artistic powers of perception were truly extraordinary, but the depth and candor of his erotic self-analysis simply would not have been possible if his fantasies were entirely, or even primarily, unconscious.

As Freud realized, the fetishist's divided attitude toward female "castration" often finds expression through the construction of the fetish object itself, which thereby takes on the status of a compromise formation:

> This was so in the case of a man whose fetish was an athletic support-belt which could also be worn as bathing drawers. This piece of clothing covered up the genitals entirely and concealed the distinction between them. Analysis showed that it signified that women were castrated and that they were not castrated; and it also allowed of the hypothesis that men were castrated, for all these possibilities could equally well be concealed under the belt. . . . A fetish of this sort, doubly derived from contrary ideas, is of course especially durable. (*SE* XXI, 156)[41]

In precisely this way, Hemingway favored coifs for his wives and romantic heroines that were both "boyish" and short—"phallic" and "castrated."[42] Thus, Brett Ashley's short "boyish" hair establishes her as one of the "chaps," a status confirmed by Romero's notion that growing it out would somehow make her more "womanly." Like Brett Ashley, Marie Morgan wears a *"man's* felt hat" over her short bleached-blonde hair (*THHN* 176), and the American wife in "Cat in the Rain" wears her hair cut short like a "boy's." In "The Strange Country," some abortive chapters from an early draft of *Islands in the Stream*, Roger and Helena wonder

Figure 3. Pauline Hemingway in Cojimar Harbor. (John F. Kennedy Library)

if a haircut will obscure Helena's gender identity. "If we lived by the ocean all the time," Helena tells Roger, "I'd have to get my hair cut."

> "No."
> "It looks nice. You'd be surprised.
> "I love it the way it is."
> "It's wonderful short for swimming."
> "Not for bed though."
> "I don't know," she said. "You'd still be able to tell I was a
> girl."
> "Do you think so?"
> "I'm almost sure. I could always remind you." (*CSS* 624)

And when Roger tells the silky-haired Helena that she is "the most beautiful girl [he's] ever seen and wonderful and strange as hell in bed," Helena wonders why he thinks she's so strange in bed. "I'm not an anatomist," Roger explains. "I'm just the guy that loves you" (*CSS* 630). Roger and Helena's jokes aside, Littless, whose hair in "The Last Good Country" looks as if it were chopped off with a castratory axe, dreams that her haircut actually *will* magically make a boy out of her. And with Catherine Bourne, in *The Garden of Eden*, such ideas cease to be the stuff that dreams are made of and enter the realm of hallucination. Through her tonsorial experiments, Catherine becomes convinced that she is "a girl and a boy both"—"phallic" and "castrated"—and, while the Marita of the Scribner's edition assures David, "I'm your girl. . . . Your girl. No matter what I'm always your girl," the Marita of the manuscript lacks any such certainty (192; 245).[43] Like Catherine, she becomes obsessed with cutting her hair and trying to become a sort of magical hermaphrodite.

Beyond the *construction* of the fetish object itself, the fetishist can also express his divided attitude toward feminine "castration" through his *treatment* of the fetish, whether in reality or in his imagination. Consider, for instance, the shoe fetishist cited in a case study by Hamilton. At age four or five, when he first became interested in shoes, he "would cut up those belonging to his playmates and then expect these girls to continue wearing them" (325). Freud's prime example of this sort of behavior, moreover, should ring some bells:

> To point out that [the fetishist] reveres his fetish is not the whole story; in many cases he treats it in a way which is obvi-

ously equivalent to a representation of castration. . . . Affection and hostility in the treatment of the fetish—which run parallel with the disavowal and the acknowledgment of castration—are mixed in unequal proportions in different cases, so that the one or the other is more clearly recognizable. We seem here to approach an understanding, even if a distant one, of the behavior of the "*coupeur de nattes*" [Freud's note: "A pervert who enjoys cutting off the hair of females"]. In him the need to carry out the castration which he disavows has come to the front. His action contains in itself the two mutually incompatible assertions: "the woman has still got a penis" and "my father has castrated the woman." (*SE* XXI, 157)[44]

Was Hemingway what Freud calls a "*coupeur de nattes*"? Some significant evidence suggests that he was. We might wonder, for instance, what prompted Gertrude Stein to teach Hemingway how to cut Hadley's hair. Was it a coincidence? A casual remark from the young writer about wishing he could do so? A direct request? Whatever the case, a number of Hemingway's letters to Mary from May 1947 reveal that he was still occasionally playing the coiffeur some twenty-five years after Stein's lesson. In one letter, Ernest urges Mary, who was visiting with her parents, to dye her hair smoky silver or red, but he also assures her that if she can't find the time to have her hair done in Chicago, "I can always look after [your] dear head with great pleasure and what skill [I] have acquired" (May 2, 1947, ©1998, Ernest Hemingway Foundation). In subsequent letters he discourses at length about dyeing techniques, reminds Mary that it has been twenty-two days since he applied the last coat of color to her hair, and repeats his entreaties and offers of assistance. Then there is the following passage from Mary Hemingway's safari journal, dated January 3, 1954: "We've had big business about my hair which we've bleached again and Papa cut very short then I cut across the front in idiot imitation of the local Kamba girls." Ernest clearly enjoyed himself; immediately after her account of this barbering, Mary noted in her journal, "Big lunch. . . big love. . . . Papa has been saying too many nice things—'My kitten-brother is the bravest, lovliest, most understanding and best kitten in and out of bed. . .'" (JFK Library, 229).

But if Hemingway was a *coupeur de nattes*, he was one of a subtle sort. The available evidence from his letters and his life indicate none of the manic urgency that might lead to the rape of a lock or to the sort of behavior exhibited by a patient of

Romm's who sought treatment for his fetishism only after his
wife objected to the inconvenience and danger of his cutting her
hair during the act of sex.

> The only way in which he could get a satisfactory orgasm was
> to cut his wife's hair during the forepleasure stage, or at times
> after intercourse had started. His wife at first submitted to
> these demands but she became more and more disturbed by
> the performance and by her subsequent ludicrous appearance.
> The patient was, moreover, compelled to have his own hair cut
> several times a week, and looked longingly into the windows of
> every barber shop he passed, hoping to see a woman having
> her hair cut. . . . He indulged almost daily in masturbation dur-
> ing which he fantas[ized] he was cutting a woman's hair.
> (Romm 140)

Yet Freud notes that the divided treatment of the fetish object
can be real *or* imaginary, and Hemingway's fiction leaves little
doubt that he was often a *coupeur de nattes* in his imagination.

In *For Whom the Bell Tolls*, Robert Jordan fantasizes about
visiting the coiffeur's with Maria, and Frederic Henry, in *A Farewell to Arms*, plainly derives vicarious erotic pleasure from
watching Catherine have her hair done:

> Catherine was still in the hairdresser's shop. The woman was
> waving her hair. I sat in the little booth and watched. *It was ex-
> citing to watch* and Catherine smiled and talked to me and *my
> voice was a little thick from being excited.* The tongs made a
> pleasant clicking sound and I could see Catherine in three mir-
> rors and it was pleasant and warm in the booth. Then the
> woman put up Catherine's hair, and Catherine looked in the
> mirror and changed it a little, taking out and putting in pins;
> then stood up. "I'm sorry to have taken such a long time."
>   "Monsieur was very interested. Were you not, monsieur?"
> the woman smiled.
>   "Yes," I said. (my emphasis, 292–3)

The emphasis in this passage is more on a *changing* of the hair
than a *cutting* of it; yet, for Hemingway, the two were symbolically analogous, changing being merely a less aggressive version
of cutting.[45] Thus, when Hemingway wrote a detailed barbershop scene in which Marie Morgan grows more and more excited
as her naturally dark hair is bleached lighter and lighter, he was
probably expressing, through the act of narration, the desire of
a *coupeur de nattes*.

That was the first time I ever made my hair blonde. . . . They were working on it all afternoon and it was naturally so dark they didn't want to do it and I was afraid I'd look terrible, but I kept telling them to see if they couldn't make it a little lighter, and the man would go over it with that orange wood stick with cotton on the end, dipping it in that bowl that had the stuff in it sort of smokey like the way it steamed sort of, and the comb; parting the strands with one end of the stick and the comb going over them and letting it dry and I was sitting there scared inside my chest of what I was having done and all I'd say was, just see if you can't make it a little lighter.

And finally he said, that's just as light as I can make it safely, Madame, and then he shampooed it, and put a wave in, and I was afraid to look even for fear it would be terrible, and he waved it parted on one side and high behind my ears with little tight curls in back, and it still wet I couldn't tell how it looked except it looked all changed and I looked strange to myself. And he put a net over it wet and put me under the dryer and all the time I was scared about it. And then when I came out from under the dryer he took the net off and the pins out and combed it and it was just like gold.

And I came out of the place and saw myself in the mirror and it shone so in the sun and was so soft and silky. . . , and I couldn't believe it was me and I was so excited I was choked with it. (258–259)

Hemingway's interest in *changing* hair helps to explain Cantwell's excitement at watching Renata comb her hair, or watching her hair blow in the wind. And in another long barbershop scene from *The Garden of Eden*, Hemingway symbolically aligns his male protagonist, and himself, with the master coiffeur, Monsieur Jean. When Jean, who happens to be "about David's age," asks for his advice about Catherine's hair, David replies that he doesn't belong to the *syndicate*; but Hemingway endows Jean with his own considerable knowledge of hair dyeing techniques and portrays him as an artist, not a union man: "The man was working like a sculptor, absorbed and serious. 'I thought about it all last night and this morning,' the coiffeur said. 'If you don't believe that, Monsieur, I understand. But this is as important to me as your métier is to you'" (80). Needless to say, Catherine finds all this dyeing and cutting of hair frightening but "terribly exciting" (K422.1 1.insert 18).

Yet if any scene from Hemingway's novels exemplifies the impulse of the *coupeur de nattes* it is the rape of Maria from *For Whom the Bell Tolls*. Having shot her parents against the wall of the village slaughterhouse, the fascists herded Maria and "a long line of girls and women" up the hill to the barbershop which stood across the square from City Hall (351). There, the barber, shot for belonging to a union, lay dead on the floor. As daughter of the town's liberal Mayor, Maria was pulled out of line first, shoved into a barber's chair, and pinned down. Remembering her grief and the horror, she tells Jordan:

> "At that time I wore my hair in two braids and as I watched in the mirror one of them lifted one of the braids and then pulled on it so it hurt me suddenly through my grief and then cut it off close to my head with a razor. And I saw myself with one braid and a slash where the other had been. Then he cut off the other braid but without pulling on it and the razor made a small cut on my ear and I saw blood come from it. Canst thou feel the scar with thy finger?" (351)

Jordan feels the scar but suggests that they skip this topic; yet Maria persists. She tells him how the fascists had struck her in the face with her braids, how they had tied them around her neck and then shoved them into her mouth to form a gag. Then they shaved her head: "first from the forehead all the way to the back of the neck and then across the top and then all over my head and close behind my ears and they held me so I could see into the glass of the barber's mirror all the time that they did this and I could not believe it as I saw it done and I cried and I cried but I could not look away from the horror that my face made with the mouth open and the braids tied in it and my head coming naked under the clippers" (352). Only after this was Maria dragged across the street to her father's office and raped. The rape of Maria represents nothing less than the fascist rape of "virgin Spain" itself—to borrow a phrase from the title of a Waldo Frank book that Hemingway loathed—and the rape of her locks vividly objectifies the theft of her girlish innocence. Thinking about the kindness and cruelty of the Spaniards and about his own inability to forgive the fascists for what they had done to Maria, Jordan muses, "Forgiveness has been exaggerated. Forgiveness is a Christian idea and Spain has never been a Christian country. It has always had its own special idol worship within the Church. *Otra Virgen más.* I suppose that was why they had to destroy the virgins of their enemies" (355). Yet Maria has not been destroyed. Somehow she has retained her innocence, and in some sense her "virginity," in spite of the rape.

She has never kissed a man before kissing Jordan and has to ask "Where do the noses go?" and she accepts Pilar's wisdom that "nothing is done to oneself that one does not accept" (71; 73). Her strength holds out hope for the Spanish people and establishes her in the best Hemingway tradition as beaten but heroically "undefeated."

The cutting of braids, with their vaguely phallic shape, however, is also *the* classic act of the *coupeur de nattes*, and the horrifying aggression of this act, as well as the fact that Maria is finally raped in the office of her dead father, suggests an obvious parallel with Freud's understanding of such behavior. Fenichel, for instance, writes of "the braid cutter" as a standard type of fetishist (*Psychoanalytic Theory* 354), and Havelock Ellis describes a "young man of good family" who developed an "impulse to cut off girls' braids": "He would gaze admiringly at the long tresses and then clip them off with great rapidity; he did this in some fifty cases before he was caught and imprisoned" (2.1.75). And to glimpse the sort of aggression at work in these acts, we need only return to Romm's hair-raising case study:

> [The patient] seemed to be very considerate, kind and generous toward his wife, but when cutting her hair he occasionally had the fantasy of gouging out pieces of her scalp. On one occasion he resented what he considered her dominance and asked if she would let him shave her head. When she refused, he thought how nice it would be if he could shave her head and his own and his hair would grow faster; in that way he could get ahead of her. As his compulsion to cut his wife's hair closer and closer to the scalp became more intense, he became more sensitive about her appearance and was angry that she was not ingenious in utilizing a hat or a bandanna to cover her head. She retorted that as long as he mutilated her he should be exposed to the embarrassment of her appearance. (142)[46]

Of course, the violence of Maria's rape functions primarily to expose the injustice and brutality of the war, a brutality engaged in by the Republicans and Nationalists alike. And within the novel's romantic dynamic, this savagery throws the tenderness of Jordan's love for Maria into stark relief. But the cutting of Maria's braids also functions as an outlet for Hemingway's displaced aggression, an aggression shared ever so subtly by Robert Jordan. The connection between the cutting of Maria's braids and castration couldn't be much clearer. As we have al-

ready seen, deflowering is traditionally constructed within a
phallocentric system as a "castration." Here, there is a cutting, a
symbolic spilling of blood, a "nakedness" beneath the hair, and
a scar. This scar, moreover, is particularly meaningful, since it
reminds us of another scar mentioned only a few pages earlier.
Maria tells Jordan the story of her rape in the first place because
she wants to explain to him why she is too sore to make love
that night. When she speculates that the soreness may be a lingering effect of the rape, Jordan consoles her, "That is nothing.
. . . Truly it is nothing. It is possible thou wert hurt once and
now there is a *scar* that makes a further hurting. Such a thing
is possible" (my emphasis, 343). Of course, the other possibility,
that Maria's soreness is the result of her earlier wild lovemaking
with Jordan, subtly aligns and contrasts her lover with her attackers. (Perhaps this covert identification with Maria's as-
sailants explains why one of the heroes of the novel's final
chapters is the barber-turned-soldier, Gomez, who guides An-
drés through Republican lines that prove to be almost as dangerous as those of the enemy.) Either way, by pairing the
scarring of Maria's genitals with the scar left by her haircut,
Hemingway plainly constructs the chopping of her hair as a castration. Yet, in keeping with the Janus-faced nature of the fetish,
even here Maria is not constructed as simply "castrated." Between Maria's mention of her soreness and the narrative of her
rape, Jordan launches into his speech about his plans for her
hair. He strokes her hair and talks "to her throat" as his own
throat swells, and after Maria tells Jordan the story of her rape,
she lies "stiff" in his arms (345; 353).

There are, of course, more obvious examples of phallic women
in Hemingway's work. Surely it's no accident that Catherine
Bourne chooses the name "Peter" for the transvestic alter ego that
surfaces in her nighttime games with David. In a fragment from
The Garden of Eden manuscript, Hemingway writes: "I'd never
known anyone named Peter that wasn't a prick" (misc. fragments
K422). In fact, all of the women in *The Garden of Eden* manuscript
are plainly phallic. Thus, when Barbara Sheldon tries to explain
her attraction to Catherine, she tells David: "*You know no man
ever looked at her that didn't have an erection. I don't know what
women have but whatever it is I have it*" (my emphasis, K422.1,
5.5.7). Or when Marita playfully offers to be David's girl disguised
as a young Cossack officer, the ensuing conversation about

Gogol's tale of the Cossacks, *Taras Bulba*, and Gautier's *Mademoiselle de Maupin*—both of which involve the sort of cross-dressing which is a staple of fetishistic and transvestic fantasy—reveals Marita's phallic nature. David describes Gautier's novel as "pleasant fancy writing to make excitements," not "dirty like pornography," just "what we do made into musical comedy," and he asks Marita if Gautier's novel gave her "*an erection.*" "Of course," she replies, "Didn't it you?" "Sure," says David. "That's why he wrote it. For himself and his friends. That's how all books that are just fun are written" (my emphasis, K422.1, 36.22).

But even in these most obvious cases, the phallic attributes of Hemingway's women are always bound up with their possession of the fetish object. In *A Farewell to Arms*, for instance, when Frederic first meets Catherine Barkley, his question about the phallic swagger stick she carries leads, via a route which by now should seem entirely predictable, to a conversation about her hair:

> "What's the stick?" I asked. Miss Barkley was quite tall. She wore what seemed to me to be a nurse's uniform, was blonde and had tawny skin and grey eyes. I thought she was very beautiful. *She was carrying a thin rattan stick like a toy riding-crop, bound in leather.*
> "It belonged to a boy who was killed last year."
> "I'm awfully sorry."
> "He was a very nice boy. He was going to marry me and he was killed in the Somme. . . . They sent me the little stick. His mother sent it to me. They returned it with his things." (my emphasis, 18–19)

Frederic asks if they had been engaged long and learns that they had been for eight years and had grown up together. "And why didn't you marry?" he asks. She had been a fool not to, Catherine replies, but for some reason she had thought "it would be bad for him." When she asks if Frederic has ever loved anyone, he answers, "No," and tries to change the subject by complimenting Catherine on her "beautiful hair." But the subject *doesn't* change:

> "Do you like it?"
> "Very Much."
> "I was going to cut it all off when he died. . . . I wanted to do something for him. You see I didn't care about the other

thing and he could have it all. He could have had anything he
wanted if I would have known. . . . I didn't know about anything then. I thought it would be worse for him. I thought perhaps he couldn't stand it and then of course he was killed and
that was the end of it." (19)

This passage is remarkable for a number of reasons associated with Hemingway's fetishism. Catherine's name itself, her
status as a "nurse" and a "first love," her "tawny" skin, and the
fact that she had grown up together with her fiancé and that his
mother had sent her the "little stick" are all significant facts
within Hemingway's field of fetishistic fantasy, and we shall have
reason to return to this passage repeatedly; but for the moment
I am interested in Catherine's possession of the "little stick" and
her quasi-economic impulse to pay for it by cutting her hair.

Why, we might wonder, did Catherine think marriage—and
sex—would be "bad" for her fiancé? What made her think that
he might not be able to "stand it"? Are we to understand that,
away at war, he would miss Catherine so much that he would be
miserable or even lose his mind? Perhaps. But there seems to be
another dimension to Catherine's thought. That the swagger
stick, "bound in leather," came from the boy both emphasizes its
phallic properties and aligns the boy's death with castration, a
familiar Freudian analogy.[47] Like Pilar, Brett Ashley, Margot Macomber, and Catherine Bourne, then, Catherine Barkley has assumed her phallic attributes at the expense of her man, and this
apparently weighs on her conscience after his death. Her willingness to give up her hair, even if she didn't follow through on
it, reveals her status as "phallic/castrated" and atones for both
her possession of the "little stick" and her earlier unwillingness
to give up her virginity, that "other thing" that she claims she
didn't care about. That is, since defloration, for Hemingway, signified castration, Catherine's refusal to get married before the
war represented a refusal to give up her phallic properties, and
her fantasy about her fiancé wandering into a hospital with
something "picturesque" like a "sabre cut" implies that she envied his phallus (20). Given such a "castrate or be castrated" dynamic, intercourse understandably could have been "bad" for
both Catherine and her fiancé.

The fact that Catherine's fiancé suffered the distinctly un-
picturesque fate of being "blown all to bits"—much like the fate
of Brett Ashley's wartime "true love" who "kicked off with the

dysentery" (*SAR* 39)—drives home the horror of the First World War, which shocked so many of Hemingway's generation out of their romantic illusions about war and faith in patriotic rhetoric. It further establishes Catherine and the author as "disillusioned" realists—for realism and naturalism in American literature, and in Hemingway's work in particular, have traditionally founded their claims to honesty and verisimilitude in opposition to a sort of naive romanticism. (Of course, Catherine and Hemingway both try to escape this stance in Switzerland where each tries to create new romantic illusions, but Hemingway's conclusion leaves little doubt about the prospects for the success of such an endeavor.) The fate of Catherine's fiancé, however, also aligns him with Frederic, who is "blown up while . . . eating cheese" (63). Or, rather, Frederic's obvious status as a replacement for Catherine's fiancé—"Say, 'I've come back to Catherine in the night'" she importunes early in their relationship—foreshadows his fate on the battlefield, and perhaps in the bedroom (30). A more complete explication of this, however, will emerge only gradually from my study.

Biography, Post-Freudian Theory,
and Beyond the Phallus

Where Nothing Makes Any Difference:
Twinning and the Preoedipal Origins
of Hemingway's Fetishism

"It was fun seeing the fox."
"When he sleeps he wraps that tail around him to keep warm."
"It must be a lovely feeling."
"I always wanted to have a tail like that. Wouldn't it be fun if we had brushes like a fox?"
"It might be very difficult dressing."
"We'd have clothes made, or live in a country where it wouldn't make any difference."
"We live in a country where nothing makes any difference. Isn't it grand. . . ?"

—Catherine and Frederic, *A Farewell to Arms*

We were happy the way children are who have been separated and are together again. . . .

—*A Moveable Feast*

But why Hemingway? And why *hair*? If the fetish stands in for the "missing" imaginary female penis, we might expect that Hemingway would choose an object that approximates the phallic shape or which at least functions as a common symbol of the penis in other circumstances. However, while this may happen often enough, Freud explains, "it is certainly not a deciding factor" in the selection of a fetish object:

It seems rather that when the fetish is instituted some process occurs which reminds one of the stopping of memory in traumatic amnesia. As in this latter case, the subject's interest comes to a halt half-way, as it were; it is as though the last impression before the uncanny and traumatic one is retained as a fetish. Thus the foot or shoe owes its preference as a fetish— or part of it—to the circumstance that the inquisitive boy peered at the woman's genitals from below, from her legs up; fur and velvet [and we might as well add hair]—as has long been suspected—are a fixation of the sight of pubic hair, which should have been followed by the longed-for sight of the female member. . . . (*SE*, XXI 155)

Of course, as we have already seen, the very symbolic detachment of the fetish object from the penis, though always incomplete, is an important aspect of its function and significance. Nevertheless, as we have also seen, Hemingway's occasional attachment to pigtails and braids clearly reveals the fetish object's phallic symbolism—as does one of his childhood dreams. Hemingway's son Gregory recalls his father telling him that, as a boy, he had been scared by a recurrent nightmare about a "furry monster who would grow taller and taller every night and then, just as it was about to eat him, would jump over the fence" (qtd. in Lynn 501). But if, when he describes Maria's cropped hair as "but little longer than the fur on a *beaver* pelt," Hemingway lends support to Freud's idea that hair is chosen as a fetish object due to a traumatic fixation on the female pubic hair, we are nevertheless probably dealing with a later construction, or "screen memory," not a genuine memory of some initial trauma (*FWBT* 22).[1] As Freud acknowledged, fetish objects can be selected for reasons other than the one he describes, and—working primarily from the meticulously-kept baby books Grace Hall Hemingway made for her children and Marcelline Hemingway Sanford's account of her childhood with her famous brother—Mark Spilka and Kenneth Lynn have given us a pretty clear indication of Hemingway's reasons for choosing hair as an object.

Hair was a hypercathected object endowed with special properties in the household of Hemingway's youth, and Grace Hall Hemingway paid an unusual amount of attention to her children's barbering. Although her first-born children, Ernest and Marcelline, were born a year-and-a-half apart, Grace tried insofar as it was in her power to raise them as "twins," and hair

<u>was always an important signifier of this twinship</u>. In her well-kept baby books, filled with pictures of her "matching" children, Grace wrote of her toddlers, then three and four: "The two children were then always dressed alike, like two little girls" (qtd. in Lynn 41). "As for hairstyles, Grace sometimes wanted them to be identical and sometimes not," but while she eventually began dressing her children as "girls" in Oak Park and as "boys" during their summer vacations in Michigan, with but a few brief periods of respite she kept both children's hair long and "girlish" until Ernest was nearly seven years old (Lynn 41). Grace then gave both children "boyish" haircuts and recorded with a mixture of pride and regret on an envelope containing hair shearings, "Ernest Miller Hemingway, hair cut off Feb 15th 1906, he can never wear long hair again as he is $6\frac{1}{2}$ yrs and in school. My precious boy, a 'real' boy" (qtd. in Lynn 45). Whatever her pride in her son's new-found masculinity, this envelope nevertheless suggests, then, that *on some level* Grace thought of Ernest, until he was six-and-a-half years old, as something *other* than a "real" boy, and this identity for her was intimately bound up with the length of his hair.

Spilka and Lynn have both written fascinating chronicles of Ernest and Marcelline's pseudo-twinship, but Marcelline, herself, offers one of the best accounts of it in her memoir, *At the Hemingway's*:

> Mother often told me she had always wanted twins, and that though I was a little over a year older than Ernest . . . she was determined to have us be as much like twins as possible. When we were little, Ernest and I were dressed alike in various outfits, in Oak Park in gingham dresses and in little fluffy lace-tucked dresses with picture hats, and in overalls at the summer cottage on Walloon Lake. Later, we had a sort of compromise boy-girl costume: a high-necked type of 'Russian tunic,' a belted blouse worn over bloomers. I remember one set was made of gray flannel bloomers with gray plaid blouses to match. *We wore our hair exactly alike* in bangs in a square-cut Dutch bob. Ernest, in kindergarten, still had blond hair, while mine was always dark brown like my father's. . . .
>
> Mother admired blonds and people with all shades of red hair—she always hoped one of her children would be born with auburn hair, though there was no history of it in our family. But many of us grew up admiring red hair because Mother always pointed it out to us as the most beautiful hair in the world. Ernest's first wife, Hadley, had hair that color.

Figure 4. Ernest and Marcelline in matching checkered dresses, Waloon Lake, Michigan, date uncertain. (John F. Kennedy Library)

Figure 5. Ernest and Marcelline in matching checkered dresses, Waloon Lake, Michigan, date uncertain. (John F. Kennedy Library)

Mother continued with her plan of making us into twins even into our school life. I had an extra year of kindergarten while waiting for Ernest to be old enough so we could start first grade together when he became six. After kindergarten we played with small china tea sets just alike; we had dolls alike; and when Ernest was given a little air rifle, I had one too— Mother was doing her best to make us feel like twins by having everything alike. She encouraged us to play together, and to fish, hike and take trips to Horton Bay together in the summers as we were growing up. We were congenial and enjoyed doing things together, but being older and a girl, I matured faster than Ernest, and there were times, especially in school, when I would have liked to go ahead by myself. (my emphasis, Sanford 61–62)

Marcelline further reports that in the summer of 1906, when Ernest was seven years old, her mother "still wanted Ernest and me to look alike," so instead of overtly feminizing Ernest, she ignored her daughter's tears and entreaties and had Marcelline's "hair cut boy-fashion" (Sanford 109). Uncomfortable that fall with the way her hair was growing out unevenly, Marcelline, at the suggestion of a young friend, tried to even it out herself—with unfortunate results.[2] Marcelline's hair, trimmed almost to the top of her ears, horrified Grace so much that in spite of her daughter's pleas and tearful apologies she forced Marcelline to wear a baby bonnet to school until, after two humiliating weeks, the urging of Marcelline's second-grade teacher finally persuaded Grace to relent. The experience, understandably, proved so embarrassing for Marcelline that to escape her second-grade peers she was advanced to the third grade, a step above Ernest. This academic separation did not, however, stop Grace from trying to perpetuate her children's "twinship" in subtle ways right up through Ernest's high school years. Grace, for instance, held Marcelline back a year between the seventh and eighth grades so she could study music, and when she reentered school, she and Ernest were once again classmates. According to Lynn, Grace did everything she could to throw Ernest and Marcelline together during their high school years. She gave them "pairs of season tickets to the opera" and often refused to let Marcelline "go to parties with other boys, so that she could ask Ernest to escort his sister" (43).

Such brotherly duties may not appear very onerous, but they rankled Hemingway, nonetheless. Some forty years later,

Ernest still remembered—and resented—having to attend these dances with his "bitch sister Marcelline" (*SL* 671). Before marrying Mary Welsh in 1945 Hemingway offered her a highly fictionalized version of his high school years, complaining of his sister and mother: "When no boy invited her to a school prom, Marcelline and their mother maneuvered Ernest into taking her—his overbearing mother, who refused to cook for the family and bought fifty-dollar hats from Marshall Field's when his father's patients were not paying his fees. He had been disappointed by his father who allowed his mother to dominate him. . ." (Mary Hemingway 95). And in a 1949 letter to Malcolm Cowley, Hemingway wrote, "You know I never went to dances before my senior year in high school and what the fuck is high school and do you know I was not allowed to invite any girl to any of the school things until my sister Marcelline, who then was deservedly unpopular, had been invited? I could never ask my girls because you had to ask them well ahead and I had to wait until some jerk asked her maybe two days before the things. . ." (April 25, 1949, ©1998 Ernest Hemingway Foundation). That Grace Hemingway brought in most of the family income through her voice lessons, that the family (thanks to Grace's earnings) had a cook, and that Ernest's father, who indeed seems to have been dominated by his wife, enjoyed cooking himself are of little importance.[3] Reality isn't the issue; rather, the issue is Ernest's *perception* of reality. Throughout his adult life Ernest continued to invent and re-invent a fictional past for himself that, while often less than fair to both parents, was, like the best of his fiction, psychologically truer for him than reality.

Of course, the dressing of little boys in traditionally feminine garb was hardly uncommon at the turn of the century, and a number of Hemingway scholars have argued—usually in the process of critiquing Lynn's biography—that Ernest's boyhood experience of being dressed as a girl can hardly explain or even clarify his interest in or expression of sexuality and gender. If this experience alone accounted for Hemingway's gender insecurity and overcompensating hypermasculinity, we would expect to see the same or similar effects, for instance, in the works of Thomas Wolfe or Winston Churchill, who likewise wore dresses as infants. Logical as this may seem, however, this argument smells like a red herring and is hardly fair to Lynn's biography. Lynn, himself, devotes three well-researched pages of his biography to *fin-de-siècle* fashion for infants and notes:

> Most of the boys who were born in the United States in the
> final years of the nineteenth century and the first years of the
> twentieth wore dresses until they were old enough to walk.
> Only from that point onward did a clear majority wear clothes
> specially designed for boys. . . . Boys who were not taken out of
> girls' clothes after about a year generally wore blouses and
> bloomers or ankle-length dresses for another twelve to eighteen
> months. After the age of $2\frac{1}{2}$, however, most of these boys were
> also put into boys' clothes. Of the total number of little boys in
> the United States, no more than 10 or 15 percent were still
> kept in girls' clothes until they were four or five years old. (40)

Lynn, further, acknowledges the importance of the turn-of-the-
century fad for long-haired "feminine masculinity" in little boys
touched off by Frances Hodgson Burnett's *Little Lord Fauntleroy*.
(Spilka, however, offers a much more thorough and interesting
account of this fad.)

    It seems clear, then, that Lynn never really argues that the
mere experience of being cross-dressed as an infant led to Hemingway's gender insecurity and tendency to overcompensate
through masculine posing. On the other hand, Hemingway's son
Gregory, who describes his father as "kind, gentle, elemental in
his vastness, [and] tormented beyond endurance" (3), isn't at all
inclined to dismiss such theories. Trying to account for his father's boxing on Bimini in the '30s and his boastful challenge to
pay one hundred dollars to any native who could last three
rounds with him, Gregory can only say,

> Sure, it was Hemingway, the twentieth-century Byron, over-
> compensating for being dressed as a girl for the first two [actu-
> ally four-and-a-half] years of his life. Maybe he was protesting
> his virility too much. I can't forget the reaction of Marjorie Kin-
> nan Rawlings . . . who visited my father in Bimini. They got
> along wonderfully, but when she left she said to my brother
> Jack: "Why does a man with such great talent continually deny
> his sensitivity and overprotest his masculinity? He is so virile
> and so vast—why does he waste his time roughhousing with
> playboys, trying to catch the biggest fish, to bring that fish in
> the fastest, to drink the most? I know he loves to write, and
> why doesn't he spend more time at that?" Right on, Ms. Raw-
> lings, you're probably 90 percent correct! (31)

Nor was Gregory's father above applying such theories to others.
Writing about the Russian diplomat Tchitcherin in a dispatch

from the 1923 Lausanne Conference, Hemingway explained Tchitcherin's weakness for military posturing and uniforms in spite of his having never served as a soldier as the result of his having been "kept in dresses until he was twelve years old"—admittedly much longer than Ernest ever was (*Dateline* 259). But, for his part, Lynn never offers such a simple theory.

The argument implied by Lynn's biography rests, rather, on four far more unusual aspects of Hemingway's childhood. First, Grace continued to cross-dress her son far past the age of two and for much longer than was ever common in America. (Ernest wore alternating boyish and girlish costumes until he was four-and-a-half, and while there are no pictures of him in unmistakably feminine costumes later than this, he was still closely twinned with his sister, either in androgynous or boyish garb until he was seven.[4]) Second, Grace changed her son's appearance and the outward signs of his gender with an unusual and disorienting frequency. Third, Ernest's mother actually *thought* of him—at least at times—as something other than a "'real' boy," an attitude which Ernest, whatever his reluctance, could not help but absorb. Finally, Grace's insistence not only on twinning Ernest with Marcelline, but on pairing them always as *twins of the same sex*, was extraordinarily unusual and, I will argue, of pivotal importance in the etiology of Hemingway's fetishism.

The weakness of the argument implied by Lynn's biography and developed more thoroughly and explicitly by Spilka's book— i.e., that Grace's peculiar handling of her son left him so insecure about his gender identity that as an adult he repressed his tender, "feminine" side by adopting an overcompensating hyper-masculine pose while a continuing fascination with hair and twin-like lovers bespoke a sort of repetition compulsion based upon a return of the repressed—is not that Hemingway's childhood was insufficiently unusual to provoke such an effect, nor that such assertions are wrong; the weakness, rather, is in suggesting that the effects of Hemingway's childhood were this *simple*, for indeed they were not.

There is perhaps some psychological significance to the pattern Lynn describes of cross-dressing infant boys in turn-of-the-century America. According to Lynn, "After the age of two, the number of little boys who looked exactly like girls fell off to something like 5 percent, and there is some evidence that suggests that the percentage was considerably smaller" (40). While most current psychological theory suggests that the formation of gender identity is a never-ending process, what Robert Stoller calls "*core* gender identity"—"a conviction that the assignment of one's sex [is] anatomically, and ultimately psychologically, correct"—is generally "so firm that it is almost unalterable" by the age of two or three (*Presentations* 11).

> It has been found that the child perceives its own sexual identity at a very early stage (regardless of whether or not there is knowledge of differences in *genitalia*). Two-year-olds are quite opinionated (and usually correct) as to what sex they and other children are (Thompson 1975). As Daly and Wilson (1978, 254) say, "there can hardly be a surer way to provoke an outburst of childish indignation than to teasingly suggest the wrong gender identity." (Rancour-Laferriere, *Signs* 135)

One would expect, therefore, that with something more pronounced than mere "childish indignation," little boys would tend to rebel at being cross-dressed much past the age of two. And, for his part, Ernest certainly registered protests.

As Lynn notes, there is evidence that young Ernest, occasionally, relished the traditionally feminine aspects of his identity. "Among the photographs of his childhood he can be seen smiling at the camera with self-conscious delight as it catches him and Marcelline out for a stroll in their best dresses and fanciest hats, or contentedly at play with her in a let's-pretend tea for two" (Lynn 44). Ernest's mother further reported with pleasure that her son had taken to sewing on a pair of his father's pants. But he was far from comfortable with his "girlishness":

> The willingness with which the little boy played the part of his sister's sister was more than matched . . . by the vehemence with which he fought it. Even minor frustrations of his will to be a boy could cause him to slap his mother, and one day he symbolically shot her. She called him her Dutch dolly, as was her wont, but this time the feminine epithet triggered an outburst of sexual rage. "I not a Dutch dolly, I Pawnee Bill. Bang, I shoot Fweetee." He was also given to shooting Marcelline, who was supposed to "fall down dead" every time.
>
> That his mother was delighted to hear him say he was Pawnee Bill was typical of the baffling inconsistency of her behavior. Could it be that she really wanted him to be a boy after all? By sometimes dressing him in pants and a shirt, she tantalized him into thinking so. (Lynn 44)

Shifting him between "boyish" and "girlish" costumes and
continually playing with his appearance, Grace, in fact, sent
profoundly ambiguous and conflicting signals to her young son.
At times she clearly thought of him as a "girl." Beneath a picture
of the two-year-old Ernest in a white dress and frilly hat, for instance, Grace wrote the caption, "summer girl." Yet, "alongside a
series of photographs of Ernest in which he is dressed like a little girl in her Sunday best, she placed the quotation, 'A boy's a
boy for ah-that,'" and after Ernest's first visit to a barbershop, at
age two and four months, Grace responded "to the sight of her
shorn lamb by exclaiming, 'Such a man,' even though most of
the clothes in her son's closet were dresses" (Lynn 45). Clearly,
the vicissitudes in costume and, much more importantly, in his
mother's attitudes registered strongly with young Ernest. At
Christmas time in 1902, Grace reported that "he was quite fearful . . . as to whether Santa Claus would know if he was a boy,
because he wore just the same kind of clothes as [his] sister"
(qtd. in Lynn 45).

That Ernest, at age *three-and-a-half* (precisely when Stoller
tells us the child should have formed a relatively stable "core
gender identity"), wasn't sure if anyone really believed that he
was a boy suggests that on some level he may not have been *entirely* sure about this himself. Moreover, that he was suffering
from such doubts at precisely *this age* offers a compelling explanation for his fixation at the phallic position, for the phallic
stage normally takes hold at about the age of three. Thus,
Greenacre observes:

> It is noteworthy that the history of many fetishists shows
> marked disturbance with some evidences of *bisexual identifica-
> tion* becoming manifest at four or five years of age. *The phallic
> period, which should under ordinary circumstances be the time
> for the consolidation of the genital part of the body image, has
> become instead a period of increased anxiety and uncertainty re-
> garding the genital parts.* (my emphasis, 27)[5]

That is, during the phallic period in these children, an unstable
body-image and sense of gender identity grow into a particularly
fierce and tenacious castration anxiety ("anxiety regarding the
genital parts").

In an attempt to account for Grace's odd combination of
cross-dressing her son while simultaneously reveling in his
mannish displays, Mark Spilka speculates that—like so many

Victorian women novelists who, according to Elaine Showalter, lived out their unrealized ambitions and fantasies of what they would do if they were men through their male characters—Grace tried to live out her own desires vicariously through her son. It is certainly significant that the first dresses Grace put Ernest into had been *her own* as an infant. Moreover, she named him not only after her father, but after herself, "Ernestine" having been part of her professional stage name. Trying to save Grace from oft-leveled charges of "utter selfishness, a *grand-dame* manner, monstrous willfulness and self-delusion, frustrated careerism, and castrating Victorian momism"—epithets to which he grants this much truth: "like her gifted son, Grace was an extremely narcissistic personality, and with similar good cause" (25)—Spilka forces us to recognize the limited opportunities available for women in Victorian America and to acknowledge Grace's right to self-expression and to value her own personal and professional worth. "Thus," Spilka argues "what some male critics define as Victorian feminization of men in the genteel tradition seems more obviously a form of outward reaching among frustrated thinking women seeking participatory powers" (29). Yet, while we must understand Grace's motives to avoid demonizing her as Ernest later did, the fact remains that *using* an infant to satisfy one's own desires and fantasies, however legitimate, often has profoundly damaging and long-term consequences for the infant.[6] My point isn't to blame Grace—nor is it to credit her for helping to create psychological fixations in her son which contributed significantly to some of the greatest American literature of the twentieth century; both would be pointless. However, we must understand the etiology of Hemingway's fetishism if we are to understand both how it functioned and how it left traces of its origins throughout his work; to do this we have to understand Grace's powerful influence on her young son.

To Spilka's thesis, Lynn persuasively adds another dimension to Grace's motives, speculating that she twinned her children in response to lingering issues from her own childhood.

> Of the many other possible explanations, the most plausible is that Ernest's birth had aroused memories that were painful for her of her brother's birth. Ernest, after all, had arrived a year and half after Marcelline, just as Leicester had arrived two years after Grace. Leicester had promptly preempted his

parents' attention simply because he was a baby, and later had been given other privileges . . . simply because he was a boy. How much nicer it would have been for Grace if she and little Leicester had been twins of the same sex. How much nicer, correspondingly, it would be for Marcelline—her mother's surrogate—if she and little Ernest could be turned into twins. (40)

Yet, while Spilka and Lynn both offer persuasive explanations for Grace's behavior, there may also have been a more sinister element to her treatment of Ernest. In his essay, "The Mother's Contribution to Infantile Transvestic Behaviour," Robert Stoller claims that his five-year-old patient's "*transvestic behaviour was caused primarily by his mother's wishes*" (Stoller's emphasis, 384). That is, the little boy recognized and internalized his mother's desire for him to be feminine. After all, *clothes in and of themselves don't masculinize or feminize anyone; it is the significance of those clothes that has such power*, and that significance comes at first from outside—in Ernest's case from Grace. In the case of the mother of the transvestite boy, Stoller notes that "a second contribution to her son's crossdressing was her creating a merging of their identities so that each identified extensively with the other" (385). Stoller further argues that the boy's mother, who identified strongly with her own father, behaved as she did, in part, to negotiate the masculine aspects of her own bisexuality. "On the one hand, the boy was (the phallus) of her flesh, and on the other, he was clearly a male and no longer of her flesh. He was therefore both to be kept as a part of herself by identification and also treated as an object whom she would feminize. *He was his mother's feminized phallus*" (Stoller's emphasis, 390).[7] This association, thus, led her to encourage both the masculine (phallic) and feminine (self-reflective) development of her child.[8]

In Stoller's influential two-volume work, *Sex and Gender*, this observation becomes nothing less than a general principle: "Whatever the genetic, constitutional, or otherwise biological features that may in the future be discovered to contribute to the causes of transvestism, there is one consistent factor in the history of adult male transvestites. This is the mothers' need to feminize their little boys. These mothers have unusually strong envy of males which expresses itself in this rather subtle way" (1.183).[9] The mother of the transvestic male, Stoller claims, has an unconscious "need to damage her son" which expresses itself in behavior remarkably like Grace's toward Ernest: "In order to humiliate him, she makes a little 'girl' out of him *on occasion*. By 'on occasion' I mean that she lets him know that he is a boy (that is, the possessor of a penis and a member of the class 'male'), but she very specifically and precisely introduces occasions on which the child is to be like a girl; that is, when she dresses him in girl's clothes or otherwise expresses her wish that he be a girl" (Stoller's emphasis, 1.183).

Now, admittedly, fetishism and transvestism are hardly the same thing, but they *are* mirror-images of one another. That is, whereas the the fetishist needs to turn his partner into a phallic woman, the transvestite needs *to be* the phallic woman, if only to verify in his own reflection that such a thing exists. Thus, while the same could not be said for the reverse, all transvestites go through a stage of fetishism (although for many transvestites the fetishistic urge diminishes with time).[10] Moreover, as Louise Kaplan observes, "in most cases that start out looking like a pure fetishistic perversion . . . the border between fetishism and transvestism [becomes] barely distinguishable" (161). Even behavioral psychologists with a skepticism for psychoanalysis admit that, for reasons which they cannot fathom, transvestism and fetishism occur in tandem with remarkable frequency. According to learning theorists Gosselin and Wilson, who base their findings on a rather trusting "fantasy questionnaire" and who speculate that the fetish is a stimulus response to some accident of childhood conditioning, nearly sixty percent of transvestites are fetishists (152). One could only expect that with analytic scrutiny they would have discovered that *all* of the transvestites in their control group either once were or were still fetishists. Analytic scrutiny would further reveal that most fetishists who never *consciously* consider themselves transvestites, or even fantasize about dressing up in women's clothes, nevertheless periodically *wear* their fetish object to subtly identify themselves with the phallic woman, thus behaving in a manner we could fairly describe as transvestic.[11]

This said, however—J. Edgar Hoover, Hemingway was not. To the best of my knowledge, Hemingway, as an adult, never wore women's clothes or high heels—though in 1953 and 1954 he *did* express a strong desire to have his ears pierced and was only dissuaded from doing so by his wife's entreaties. As we

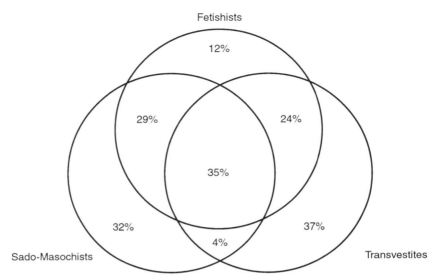

Figure 3.1: The overlap among male fetishist, transvestite, and sado-masochist groups according to a "fantasy questionnaire" studied by non-analytic psychologists Gosselin and Wilson. Psychoanalytic theory and clinical studies would suggest that even the transvestites who now report no fetishistic interest once passed through a phase of fetishism. It is fairly common for fetishistic interest to decline in transvestites as they age.

shall see, what Mary called "the earring crisis" was indeed trans-vestic—not because the wearing of earrings is inherently trans-vestic for men (it isn't), but because Hemingway was interested in piercing his ears specifically as a tool to negotiate an identification with the phallic woman. To say that Hemingway *was* a transvestite would mistakenly give the impression that such fantasies dominated his erotic life; yet within the dominant field of his fetishistic fantasy, the transvestic position was one to which he returned repeatedly. A more thorough consideration of Hemingway's transvestic desires and their influence upon his fiction, however, must wait for a later chapter. For the moment, suffice it to say that these desires are hardly inconsistent with Hemingway's mythic machismo. As Kaplan explains,

> When the impulse to cross-dress is quiescent [which is most of the time], the transvestite dresses in hyper-masculine clothing.

> In contrast to drag queens and transsexuals, transvestites, when they are not cross-dressing, are unmistakably male in appearance and behavior. . . . They enjoy participating in the macho activities that fortify them against the feminine wishes and tendencies that impel them to act out their perverse fantasy. The transvestite's behavior and attitudes are feminine only when he is dressed in female clothes [i.e., wearing the fetish]. However, conscious and unconscious feminine fantasies and illusions are present at all times. (23–24)

The recognition of these desires in Hemingway, moreover, invites a comparison between the sort of behavior Stoller describes as characteristic of the mothers of transvestites and the sort of behavior Grace displayed in raising her son.

The parallels between Grace Hall Hemingway and the mothers described by Stoller are difficult to ignore—as are the parallels between Ernest's father and the weak, or absent, fathers described by Stoller. Grace, who identified with her father and whom Ernest considered "androgynous" (i.e., "phallic"), gave every indication, at least "on occasion," that she wanted Ernest to be a girl. And, as Spilka demonstrates, she clearly identified with her son. If, as I have suggested, Grace thought of her voice as phallic, she may well have *also* unconsciously considered Ernest her own feminized phallus. The baby bonnet episode demonstrates her willingness to humiliate her children; it is no stretch to imagine that she might have felt an *unconscious* need to humiliate young Ernest by dressing him and treating him like a little girl. As for the issue of merger, Lynn records that "with his first breath of life, Grace had drawn baby Ernest into a deliciously intimate dependency. For six months he slept in her bed, where she allowed him to pat her face, squeeze up close to her and feed at her pillowy breasts. 'He is contented to sleep with Mama and lunches all night,' she happily recorded in her scrapbook" (43).

This issue of merger is crucial, since excessive identification and physical intimacy can inhibit the child's attempt to separate and individuate from its early near-symbiosis with the mother, and it is now generally accepted in the psychoanalytic community that a failure of separation and individuation figures prominently in the etiology not only of fetishism, but of all the perversions.[12] For instance, in her essay, "Perversions: General Considerations Regarding Their Genetic and Dynamic Background," Phyllis Greenacre writes:

There generally seems to be a definite disturbance of development in the first two years of life affecting and undermining the
orderly progression of the work of separation and individuation. A failure of satisfactory maternal care, the mother either
depriving or overwhelming the infant, makes a fertile ground
for the later development of perverse tendencies, but this failure by itself does not offer conditions for the specific perverse
content. It means that there is a prolongation of the uncertainty about the "I" and the "other," and that there already
exists a situation conducive to continued oscillation in relationships. (306)

Common to all of the perversions is a prolonged and intense experience of primary identification with a concomitant "fear of
fusion and merging with the mother, a tendency to lose ego
boundaries, and a fear of loss of self or ego dissolution" (Socarides 61). That is, since the process of separation-individuation is the crucible in which the ego comes into being, a failure
to successfully or fully negotiate this process hinders the
formation of a stable ego. And for little boys it is difficult to dis-
associate the process of ego-formation and separation-individuation from the process of gender-identity formation. As Ralph
Greenson has argued, little boys form their gender identities
partly by identifying with their fathers and partly by *dis*-identi-
fying from their mothers and establishing their own egos. If the
process of dis-identification from the mother is disturbed, the
formation of a stable gender identity will likely be disturbed as
well.[13] This, then, creates a vicious circle, for the recognition of
sexual difference is reciprocally a tool for reinforcing the male
ego, symbolizing as it does the boy's separateness from the
mother; if this recognition is intolerable or disavowed, as it is in
the fetishist's imagoes of the phallic woman or castrated man,
the ego remains all the more prone to merger and fragmentation.[14] The problem is only exacerbated if, as in Hemingway's
case, the little boy has little incentive to identify with a weak or
denigrated father. (Hemingway clearly loved his father and identified with him as a hunter and naturalist, yet this identification remained problematic for him and was generally disavowed
since Ernest imagined his father—rightly or wrongly—as weak
and browbeaten, essentially emasculated, by Grace.[15]) In such
cases a bisexual spilt in the ego—which incorporates the mother
and the mother's image of the self as female within a split-off
unconscious section of the emerging masculine ego—offers it-

self as a stabilizing "solution" at the cost of perpetuating the very "problem" it seeks to resolve.

This brings to mind "Mourning and Melancholia," in which Freud claims that normal mourners initially introject the lost object as both present and absent, "simultaneously conceding and denying its loss." But whereas the normal mourner eventually admits the loss of the object, the melancholic "will cling to a mode of 'disavowal' [much like that engaged in by the fetishist] and maintain the article both alive and dead, there and not there, good and bad, within a split-off unconscious region of the ego" (Moorjani 23). Significantly, "Mourning and Melancholia" grew out of Freud's essay on narcissism, for the loss of primary identification with the mother (and in Ernest's case also his sister) inherent in separation-individuation is the prototype of all such loss. By creating a split-off feminine half based upon an introjection of his mother's feminine version of him, his mother herself, and his "twin" sister—and sustained in adulthood by the continued introjection of his wives (particularly Hadley)—Hemingway never *fully* conceded the loss of primary identification.[16] On the other hand, his *partial* acknowledgment of this loss may help to account for the overwhelming sense of loss which permeates his fiction and which is perhaps best summed up in Catherine Bourne's haunting complaint, "I wish I could remember what it was we lost" (*GE* 118). While the biological and genetic origins of Hemingway's depression are irrefutable, the sustained introjection of lost objects may have contributed to the psychodynamic aspects of Hemingway's depression that have recently been analyzed so well by Pamela Boker.

Yet even were we to ignore the issue of Grace's unusually intense merger and identification with her son, her pseudo-twinning of Ernest with his sister, and her insistence on perpetuating the illusion that they were *twins of the same sex* (though just what sex that might be oscillated unpredictably), would have been *more than enough* to prolong Ernest's experience of primary identification, to inhibit his formation of a stable ego, body-image, and gender identity, and to encourage a bisexual splitting of the ego—in short, to create in her son a predisposition to a clinical perversion, if not a predisposition to fetishism in particular. According to Socarides, all of the perversions involve a "conscious and/or unconscious faulty gender-defined self identity . . . . [that] plays an important role in propelling them in the various directions in search of psychic equilibrium:

. . . the transvestite toward accepting his feminine identification contrary to anatomy; the fetishist toward alternately being man and woman (consciously not accepting his feminine identity but unconsciously desiring it)" (61). While a failure to separate and individuate fully from the mother can lead to precisely such a "faulty gender-role identity," one can easily imagine how the twinning of Ernest with Marcelline would produce nearly identical results.

By giving Ernest a "matching" "other" for the first seven years of his life, Grace fostered in her son a prolonged experience of primary identification played out through his sister. Young Ernest's "reflection" in Marcelline and repeated changes of costume—not to mention his internalization of his mother's feminine image of himself—must have raised troubling questions for him. "What do I look like?" "Am I a boy or a girl?" "Where do *I* stop, and where does the *other* begin?" Ernest's relationship with Marcelline seems like a virtual recipe for producing the sort of confusion between the "I" and the "other" that Greenacre considers a hallmark of the perversions and that we see so clearly in Hemingway's fiction when his lovers merge identities, misrecognize themselves in mirrors, or experience themselves as split personalities.[17] Thus, it should come as no great surprise to learn that in her 1953 essay, "Certain Relationships between Fetishism and the Faulty Development of the Body Image," Greenacre calls attention to precisely such twinning and pseudo-twinning of opposite-sex children in the etiology of fetishism:

> In the early history of the prefetishist, there may be an insecure and unstable early body image, developed from any combination of causes. . . . As a natural result of this there is a continuation of the state of primary identification. . . . *In several patients who later developed fetishism—a sufficient number to make me think it might be of some import—the boy child was in very close visual contact with a female, either the mother or more importantly a sister relatively close in age, so that there may have been a state of primary identification which resembles that seen in twins, with a well-forecast bisexual splitting of the body image even antecedent to the phallic phase.* (my emphasis, 25)

Thus, writing about children with the sort of gender-identity confusion which predisposes them to the perversions, in her 1958 essay, "Early Physical Determinants in the Development of the Sense of Identity," Greenacre contends, *"Probably the clear-est instances of the nature of this confusion in sexual identity oc-curs in twins or pseudotwins of opposite sexes, who are brought up together from their earliest years"* (my emphasis, 121). And by 1968, when she wrote "Perversions: General Considerations Re-garding Their Genetic and Dynamic Background," Greenacre was even more confident about the importance of such opposite-sex twinning in the history of many fetishists. Describing the confusion between the "I" and the "other" and the repeated exposure to the female genitals that can inspire preoedipal cas-tration fear in little boys (for if "I" am like my sister, and she doesn't have a penis, castration certainly looms as a prospect), Greenacre writes:

> These conditions exist in families in which the parents fre-quently appear nude before the child, *but even more in situa-tions in which there are two children of opposite sex, either twins or only a year or two apart in age, who are constantly cared for together, daily bathed and dressed together.* If early exposure is thus repeated and almost constant, both an interest in and confusion about the genitals may develop. *These conditions pre-dispose to confusion even in children whose separation and indi-viduation have not been seriously interfered with.* (my emphasis, 307)

Imagine Ernest's confusion when comparing bodies with his otherwise identical "twin" sister during their summertime skinny-dipping sessions in Walloon Lake. Marcelline recalls, "We had no bathtub at the cottage, of course, and we were often in and out of the water three or four times a day. Sometimes, as a special treat, we would be allowed to go into the water without bathing suits in the evening. This we called our 'Secret Society.' We felt so free as the water slid past our naked bodies. Even in our teens, our parents let us swim this way on hot nights" (San-ford 75). Here we probably have an important source for Hem-ingway's castration anxiety, and perhaps this is why nude sunbathing and swimming figures so prominently in the fetishistic rituals that preoccupy David, Catherine, and Marita in *The Garden of Eden.*

While Greenacre has given more attention to opposite-sex sibling relations than any other psychoanalytic theorist of the perversions (largely because within the dynamics of perverse eti-ology sisters are easily, and not entirely wrongly, dismissed as

"mother substitutes"), corroborating evidence of their importance can easily be found elsewhere. In his essay "The Phallic
Woman: The Ubiquitous Fantasy in Perversions," for instance,
three out of the five cases of fetishism and transvestism Bak
presents involve unusually close brother-sister ties. In one case,
a male fetishist actually had a twin sister. In a second case, Bak
writes: "The fetishistic and transvestite phases clearly demonstrate the revival and impersonation of the phallic woman, pre-
dominantly the mother and the *sisters*" (my emphasis, 20). And
in yet another case, that of a male transvestite, Bak notes: "The
compulsion to dress up in female clothing, especially to put on
his sister's garments, appeared after a separation from her" (my
emphasis, 25). Hamilton records the case of a shoe fetishist,
also given to transvestism, who shared a bed with his older sister until he was eleven years old, and Fenichel reports the case
of a transvestite who engaged in "all manner of sexual games"
with his sister. "His sister used to play at 'dressing dolls,' and
she would dress up the living doll—her little brother—putting
clothes of her own on him" ("Transvestitism" 172). In his study
of a shoe fetishist, Gillespie offers an interesting variation on
this theme. In an anaysis "completely dominated" by the patient's powerful castration complex and his "desperate defense
against feminine identification," it turned out that the fetishist's
mother, who was the "prime castrator" in his version of the family romance, "wanted both him and his one-year-younger
brother to be girls." (Gillespie notes that the brother indepen-
dently became a boot fetishist.) "The mother made a religion out
of a dead and angelic sister, whom the patient never saw," and
she had obviously tried to use him and his brother as "replace-
ments" for her dead child ("Notes" 400). Finally, there is Freud's
most famous patient, Sergei Pankeiev, better known as the Wolf
Man, who among many other things was also a fetishist. Though
Freud's study of Pankeiev stresses not the perversions but,
rather, the oedipal dynamics behind his neurosis (significantly a
bisexual, bipolar oedipal, with strong negative oedipal leanings,
not unlike Hemingway's Oedipus complex), Freud mentions
Pankeiev again—if only indirectly—in his essay on fetishism
(Abraham & Torok 31). Thus, Freud's recognition that Pankeiev's sister, who was two years older than her brother, "seduced him into sexual practices" when he was still very young
by rubbing his genitals suggests yet another case of abnormally
close opposite-sex sibling relations in the infantile history of a

fetishist (*SE* XVII, 14). As for the gender confusion so central to Greenacre's argument, Pankeiev's parents used to say when he was quite young that he was such a tractable, good-natured child "that he ought to have been the girl and his elder sister the boy" (*SE* XVII, 9). And in a dazzling argument, Nicolas Abraham and Maria Torok have demonstrated that Pankeiev's extremely close relation with his sister, and his introjection of her into a split-off feminine half of his ego, was fundamental to etiology of his condition.

While Greenacre contends that such close opposite-sex sibling ties can lead to ego instability and gender-identity confusion even in cases where separation-individuation has *not* been seriously interfered with, how much the more so when it *has* been seriously interfered with? We would be mistaken to isolate either Ernest's relationship with his mother or his relationship with his sister as a single source of his childhood gender confusion and later fetishism. Rather, as we shall soon see, Hemingway's dreams, fantasies, and, most importantly, his fiction, all bespeak the powerful influence of both relationships.

Having begun to answer the question "Why Hemingway?" we are now in a position to address my second question, "Why hair?" As we have seen, hair was a ready-made hypercathected symbol in the Hemingway household (as it is to a lesser degree throughout Western society) employed to disavow and affirm gender identity, to negotiate masculine and feminine identifications, and to maintain and deny a symbolic union with the object of primary identification—*to function, that is, precisely like the fetish object.* If, as I have suggested, the twinning symbolized by the matching hairstyles of Ernest's youth was a primary cause of his preoedipal castration anxiety, since it equated Ernest with his "castrated" sister and hindered the formation of a stable ego and body-image, how better to memorialize and ward off castration anxiety than to transform the very symbol of *identity* into a substitute *phallus*? Hair was a symbol easily accessible for satisfaction, intimately associated with the body, available for symbolic cutting yet capable of magically growing back.[18] More importantly, it was a symbol intimately linked to memories of Hemingway's childhood. It evoked memories both of his prolonged primary identification with his sister and of his mother's trasformational powers, specifically her power to feminize or masculinize him.

Thus, throughout Hemingway's fiction—in a combined representation of his own feminization and his father's symbolic
emasculation at his mother's hands—his male characters are
fetishistically feminized by their female partners. The experience
can be exciting, as it is when Catherine Barkley proposes that
Frederic grow his hair out to match her own, and it can be profoundly erotic, as it is when Catherine Bourne transforms David
by cutting and bleaching his hair. But as the association between haircuts and castration helps to explain, and as we see in
David's divided attitude toward the metamorphosis orchestrated
for him by Catherine, such transformational experiences can
also be profoundly unsettling, shameful, or threatening for Hemingway's male characters. Insofar as they promise union they
tend to be desirable (though even this can raise anxiety about
the loss of the ego); insofar as they threaten a castratory feminization, as opposed to a transvestic "phallic feminization," they
tend to be undesirable (though, as I have suggested, an intense
unconscious desire to identify with the phallic woman in her
"castrated" aspect contributes significantly to fetishistic castration anxiety). We see something of this when, after making love,
Maria tells Jordan that she will look out for his every need and
nurse him if he is wounded. Jordan asks what she will do for
him if "I'm neither wounded nor sick and I give up smoking and
have only one pair of socks and hang up my robe myself. What
then, rabbit?" he asks. "Then," she replies, "I will borrow the
scissors of Pilar and cut thy hair" (172). Yet while Jordan fantasizes about playing games with Maria's hair so that she can look
exactly like him—thus reproducing the conditions of his twinship with Marcelline, allowing him to shore up his ego through
the incorporation of an identical "other," and enabling him to see
a feminine version of himself—the prospect of being transformed, "castrated," by Pilar's more maternal scissors strikes
him as less than erotic, and he tells Maria, "I don't like to have
my hair cut" (172). Long hair, like short hair, could be a tool for
feminization, but at least it repressed the implied threat of castration that Hemingway always associated with feminization.

For Hemingway, however, hair was more than a fetish *ob-
ject*, "hair" was a fetish *word*, or better yet, a "word-thing."
Hence, Hemingway's universe is populated by Harrys: *Harry*
Morgan, *Harry* Walden, and *Harold* Kreb's, whose sister calls
him "*Hare*." In *The Sun Also Rises*, Jake and Mike fish with the
Englishman, *Harris*. Then there is the *Harris* in "Homage to

Switzerland" whose father has recently shot himself (as had Hemingway's father a few years before he wrote the story). In his "African Journal" from his 1953 safari, Hemingway adopts the names "Mr. Wilson *Harris*" for the white hunter Philip Percival (elsewhere called "Pop") and "Harry Steele" for the pilot, Roy Marsh; in "The Strange Country," Roger and Helena assume the name "Mr. and Mrs. Robert *Harris*" when they check into a hotel; "Big Harry" contemplates suicide in *Islands in the Stream*; and in *To Have and Have Not*, Frederick *Harrison* reports Harry Morgan for running liquor. In the manuscript to *Islands*, Hudson remembers his stay in Switzerland when he was always addressed formally as *Herr* Hudson (K113). The nickname Hemingway gave to his wife Mary, his African "finacée" Debba, and Marita in *The Garden of Eden*, "Heiress," chimes perhaps significantly with "hair" (Mary Hemingway 218 & 220; *SL* 826).[19] It's certainly no coincidence that Colonel Cantwell drinks at *Harry's* Bar in Venice. Nor is Robert Jordan's horribly inappropriate nickname for Maria, "little rabbit"—with its linguistic slipage to "hare" and "hair"—any mistake, as I will demonstrate in the following brief detour which will emphasize the linguistic mechanism of fetishistic association while, I hope, also resolving an ongoing critical debate about the significance of Maria's nickname.

Rabbit Stew and Blowing Dorothy's Bridges: Slips of the Tongue, Incorporation, and Aggression

"Then you and me are the same," Maria said. She put her hand on his arm and looked in his face. He looked at her brown face and at the eyes that, since he had seen them, had never been as young as the rest of her face but that now were suddenly hungry and young and wanting.

"You could be brother and sister by the look," [Pilar] said. "But I believe it is fortunate that you are not."

"Now I know why I have felt as I have," Maria said. "Now it is clear."

"*Qué va*," Robert Jordan said and reaching over, he ran his hand over the top of her head. He had been wanting to do that all day and now he did it, he could feel his throat swelling. She moved her head under his hand and smiled up at him and he felt the thick but

silky roughness of the cropped head rippling between
his fingers.

—*For Whom the Bell Tolls*

"Everybody has a private language around here, like
Basque or something. You got an objection if I speak
mine?"

—Willie in *Islands in the Stream*

There is something a little perverse about love at first sight.
Powerful and poetically beautiful, such love is nevertheless constituted by a sort of blindness unlike the ordinary blindness of
dull sublunary lovers' love. The lover who truly loves passion-
ately at first sight somehow fails to *see* the immediate object of
his devotion. Instead he *recognizes* some quality that speaks to
him, or "hails" him in an almost Althusserian sense; but this
quality isn't *in* the object so much as it is projected onto the object and then "discovered" there. It is as if the unwitting love object had stumbled by chance onto the stage of an imaginary
drama, long in progress, only to be immediately and unconsciously recognized as a replacement for another object lost in
the opening scene. The quality in the love object that hails the
lover can't really do so from "outside" because in the "other
scene" the subject was formed partly in a dialectical relationship
with precisely the quality that now appears to hail and subject
him from without. Thus, colored by nostalgia from the moment
of its inception, this love so refined that it knows not what it is
takes the immediate object of devotion as a counter-melancholic
replacement for a lost object whose absence cannot be admitted
and for whom mourning has long been forbidden.[20]
    When Maria, lithe and fragile, first steps forth from the
darkness of the cave carrying a big iron cooking platter, in *For
Whom the Bell Tolls*, Robert Jordan falls in love at first sight. As
she sets the platter before him, Jordan admires her features—
her high cheekbones, her bright smile and eyes, her irises and
skin of the same golden tawny brown, her full lips, and her
"small up-tilted breasts" showing through her grey shirt—but
there is something else, something that clearly hails Jordan and
that he immediately recognizes as "the strange thing about her":
"Her hair was the golden brown of a grain field that has been
burned dark in the sun but it was cut all over her head so it was

but little longer than the fur on a beaver pelt. She smiled in Robert Jordan's face and put her brown hand up and ran it over her head, flattening the hair which rose again as the hand passed" (22). "She'd be beautiful if they hadn't cropped her hair," Jordan muses; yet when his throat swells up so that he can't speak (indicating a swelling elsewhere) it seems fairly obvious that Jordan *is* moved, and he is moved precisely by Maria's cropped hair. Running her hand over her head, Maria has to remind Jordan not to stare, and to divert him, or perhaps suspecting with prophetic accuracy that the way to this man's heart is through his stomach, she tells him to eat.

The communal meal that follows bonds Jordan with his new comrades, but the dish also establishes a more subtle bond between the two lovers: "It was rabbit cooked with onions and green peppers and there were chick peas in the red wine sauce. It was well cooked, the rabbit meat flaked off the bones, and the sauce was delicious" (23). As Jordan carefully piles the bones to one side of his plate and uses his bread to sop up every last drop of the sauce, the girl continues to watch him. Jordan dips his cup full of wine and drinks, but the thickness remains in his throat as he asks her, "How art thou called?" "Maria," she replies, but Jordan soon adopts another name for her—"little rabbit"—a name apparently intended to capture her fragile vulnerability and Jordan's infinite tenderness for her.

Yet as Arturo Barea pointed out soon after the publication of *For Whom the Bell Tolls*, Robert Jordan's pet name for Maria is either a vicious nickname for a young woman who has recently been raped, a horrendous slip of the tongue, or an embarrassing testament to Hemingway's limited Spanish. In Spanish, rabbit is *conejo*, also the common Spanish slang term for *coño*, or "cunt," a fact that Robert Jordan, as a college instructor of Spanish, should certainly have known. This apparent gaffe has baffled Hemingway critics for years. James Mellow can't believe that Hemingway, who possessed a working knowledge of Spanish slang derived from his bullfighter friends and hours spent in Cuban bars, could have used this term unknowingly—though he is at a loss to explain why Hemingway would knowingly want to do so. Wolfgang Rudat has suggested, rather unconvincingly, that Jordan's slip is a joke at his own expense, a jab by Hemingway aimed at academics who fail to apply their ivory-tower knowledge to the real world. Allen Josephs, however, sees Jordan's unfortunate choice of a nickname for Maria as simply the

most egregious and ironic of some sixty different errors in Spanish peppered throughout the novel. If Hemingway had been
aware of the term's double-meaning, Josephs argues, he obviously never would have used it.[21] Jordan clearly loves Maria,
treats her gently, and uses "little rabbit" only as a term of en-
dearment. Indeed, Josephs' case appears to be the most convincing, but I would like to suggest another explanation for
Maria's nickname. Jordan's tender feelings for Maria mask an
element of hostility that is somehow bound up with "the strange
thing about her," and thanks to a split in Hemingway's ego, one
part of him knew exactly what it was doing in naming his heroine, while another part of him was entirely innocent.

The object that hails Jordan when he first meets Maria—her
cropped hair—had indeed been a significant object in one of the
novel's opening scenes, where the bald General Golz somehow
associates Jordan's long hair with his "irregular" military service
and irregular sex life. "Look, do you have many girls on the other
side of the lines?" Golz asks. "No," Jordan replies. "There is no
time for girls."

> "I do not agree. The more irregular the service, the more ir-
> regular the life. You have very irregular service. Also you need
> a haircut."
> "I have my hair cut as it needs it," Robert Jordan said. He
> would be damned if he would have his head shaved like Golz. "I
> have enough to think about without girls," he said sullenly. (7)

Yet the power of hair (or its absence) to hail Jordan originates in
another scene entirely: in Hemingway's fetishism.

The trail of Jordan's "rabbit" leads right to Hemingway's
fetish: "rabbit" = "hare" = "hair"—an equation which Hemingway
all but spells out for us. When Jordan chastises the gypsy,
Rafael, for leaving his post and thereby allowing a fascist horse-
man to wander silently into the camp, the gypsy apologizes but
explains that he had been tempted away by the prospect of
shooting that night's dinner: "It was the *hares*. Before daylight I
heard the male thumping in the snow. You cannot imagine what
a debauch they were engaged in" (my emphasis, 274). But it
shouldn't escape the reader's notice that two other little rabbits,
or "hares," were engaged in a similar debauch in the snow at
much the same time: Jordan and Maria. (I say "two" because
there is an element of psychological "truth" to Maria's assertion

that she is identical with her lover: "I am thee and thou art me and all of one is the other" [262]. Thus, Jordan also becomes a "rabbit.") The connection between the gypsy's hares and the "little rabbits" making love in Jordan's sleeping bag is underscored a few pages later when Agustín warns Jordan that if he thought Jordan didn't really love Maria he would have shot him in the night while he lay with her—the very fate suffered by the two hares. Thus, instead of "little rabbit," Maria might more appropriately be nicknamed "little hare," for with her closely cropped head she in fact has only "little hair."

But there is a good deal more to the matter than a dreadful pun. Hemingway *was* also preconsciously aware of the slang meaning of *conejo*, a fact perhaps attested to by Agustín's protestation that Maria isn't a whore (which is yet another slang connotation of *conejo*).[22] Given the fetishist's use of the fetish object, or *word*, as a substitute female phallus, both a monument to and a tool for disavowing the penisless state of women, Hemingway simply couldn't pass up the opportunity provided by *conejo* to conflate the words "hare," "hair," and "cunt." The word "cunt" may stand in as a monument to Maria's penisless state (remember, Jordan thinks of her hair as being as short as a "*beaver pelt*"[23]), but by putting "rabbit"/"hare"/"hair" on her "cunt," Jordan *also* phallicizes her, turning her into the phallic woman. More importantly, by equating "hair" with the female genitals, Hemingway disavows the penisless state of women in general. By merging with his little rabbit, deeply romantic and spiritual as the image may be, Jordan probably satisfies a number of different urges in the characteristically overdetermined manner of the fetishist—having it all ways at once. Jordan's merger with Maria, who according to Pilar looks enough like him to be his own sister, testifies to his fluid ego boundaries and satisfies his narcissistic desire to recapture the world of primary identification and blissful twinship. But this merger, facilitated by Jordan's plans for identical haircuts, also probably satisfies Jordan's and Hemingway's urge to identify with the "castrated" woman (since *conejo* means "cunt"), while simultaneously managing to ward off the castration anxiety implied by such an identification through identifying with the phallic (hare/hair) woman and literally becoming the phallus (hare/hair) himself.

This last interpretation may help us to understand Jordan's consumption of rabbit stew throughout the novel. Jordan first meets Maria when she brings him a plate of rabbit cooked with onions and green peppers, and rabbit again figures as Jordan's last supper. I realize, of course, that rabbit, one of the glories of Spanish cuisine, would be one of the easiest game animals to catch in the mountains of Spain, and its presence needs no excuse in the work of a man who loved good food as Hemingway did—but given the long reach of his fetishism one can't help but wonder whether Jordan eats his words to bolster his and Hemingway's genitality. Greenacre speculates that for the fetishist one function of sex with the fetishized feminine partner may be the incorporation of the phallus through her: "According to my view of the situation, the fetishist not only endows his partner with the removable and adaptable penis, but in doing this he can incorporate the penis himself through vision, touch, and smell, and thereby bolster his uncertain genitality" (182). Greenacre contends that such incorporation is most often visual, but it may also be oral, and I see no reason why it can't also be *verbal*. As Lacan and Granoff observe in their essay on fetishism, language is "subtle matter, but matter nonetheless" (269). Jordan's consumption of the phallus in the guise of rabbit/hare/hair is a striking example of just this sort of incorporation. Moreover, Jordan simultaneously bolsters his *ego* by incorporating his "little rabbit." Stabilizing an uncertain body-image by incorporating the phallus already reinforces the ego, but Greenacre further explains that the search for identical partners ("twins") can involve a "taking in" of "a similar person" to intensify one's sense of identity (119).

Yet there is also an obvious element of aggression in Jordan's cannibalistic consumption of rabbit, piling the bones to one side of his plate, as there is as well in the insulting slang slippage of the word *conejo*. Almost every major theorist of the perversions now acknowledges that the role of aggression in the perversions is powerful, ubiquitous, and undeniable. (See Bach, Bak, Gillespie, Glasser, Greenacre, Kaplan, Kernberg, Khan, Lacan, McDougall, Payne, Romm, Socarides, and Stoller.) The reasons for this are multiple, ranging from the fierce primitive aggressions that accompany preoedipal fixations and anxieties to the aggressions that accompany an unresolved and unresolvable Oedipus complex. In *Perversion: The Erotic Form of Hatred*, Stoller offers one of the most compelling explanations: "In men, perversion may be at bottom a gender disorder (that is, a disorder in the development of masculinity and feminity) constructed out of a triad of hostility: *rage* at giving up one's earliest bliss

and identification with mother, *fear* of not succeeding in escap-
ing out of her orbit, and a need for *revenge* for her putting one in
this predicament" (99). Thus Stoller advances the following thesis: "Perversion is made from a story in which someone is
harmed" (*Observing* 18).[24]

In the case of fetishism, aggression can be sublimated more
successfully than in many other perversions since the violent
impulses, particularly the desire to "castrate" the object (in
Hemingway's case, to cut the hair of his female characters), can
be acted out upon the *fetish* object instead of the *love* object;
nevertheless, Greenacre writes: "The fetish . . . contains con-
gealed anger, born of castration panic" (333), and Stoller agrees:

> Fetishes are benign enough: no one is killed, mutilated, or
> raped. In fact, the action is played out with an object, not a
> whole person, and whatever is done to that object—the fetish—
> it is either inanimate or a body part not apt to feel devastated.
> . . . Fetishes are only symbols, highly compacted stories that
> subliminally signal their fuller meanings; they do not stab, bite,
> poison, smother, crush, or demolish. Nonetheless, hidden in
> these symbols . . . are scripts that portray hostile acts. That
> fetishists really harm no one need not be confused with the fact
> that their behavior hides, among other things, this hostility dy-
> namic. (*Observing* 17)

But to focus exclusively on the aggression directed at the fetish
object would be myopic. The fetishist takes great care to do no
permanent harm to the fetish object, and the object chosen as a
fetish must be able to withstand the fetishist's assaults.[25] More
importantly, by *deflecting* murderous, sadistic, and castratory
rage onto an inanimate object the fetish actually binds aggression and shields the love object from the fetishist's mutilating
rage. In fact, it is precisely when a perverse scenario can no
longer protect a love object, when *illusion* can no longer suffice
and gives way to violent *delusion*, that perversion most clearly
slips into psychosis. "For example, the transvestite who wants to
merge into his mother's identity will play at being in her skin by
dressing up in female clothes. . . . In contrast to this, the man
(whose case made newspaper headlines) who killed his girl
friend in order to wear her skin for erotic purposes was psychotic, not perverse" (McDougall 84).[26]

It is certainly curious that one of Hemingway's first acts
after writing the conclusion of *For Whom the Bell Tolls* was to or-

ganize a monumental slaughter of rabbits. In the early fall of 1940, right after mailing off the final proofs of the novel, Hemingway went on a jackrabbit hunt with his family. According to Carlos Baker, Hemingway's sons, "Patrick and Gregory killed eighty each, and Ernest and [his third wife] Martha swelled the total to almost four hundred" (352). The aggression implied by this slaughter, however, may have been directed at Martha, with whom Ernest had a stormy relationship, as much as it was at her historic ancestors in Ernest's affections. A number of critics have suggested that Martha served as a model for the fictional Maria. Martha shared Maria's golden hair, and according to Jeffrey Meyers, she even cut her hair like Maria's to please Ernest (435). More importantly, in the first chapter of an aborted novel—a sort of cross between *For Whom the Bell Tolls* and Hemingway's other major work about the Spanish Civil War, the 1939 play *The Fifth Column*—Hemingway calls Martha's fictional counterpart "rabbit." The ten typescript pages of the novel begin the story of a couple staying at a hotel in Madrid during the shelling of the city. Ernest and Martha had stayed in the city under precisely these circumstances in 1937, and the story's Don Enrique is an obvious self-portrait: "Ernesto" has been crossed out in the text only to be replaced by "Enrique." Don Enrique and his lover share a meal of rabbit cooked in onions and a red wine sauce and then try to get some sleep. When they are awakened by shelling in the night, Enrique/Ernesto tries to wake his "rabbit," only to be scolded sleepily that they had eaten the rabbit, and that he musn't call her rabbit when they had eaten the rabbit (K522a).[27] (The story also contains a maid—the "only inefficient servant" in the hotel—named *Marta*.) Thus, it is no mistake that Jordan's mission in *For Whom the Bell Tolls* is to blow a *bridge*. Hemingway had named Martha's fictional counterpart in *The Fifth Column*, "Dorothy *Bridges*," and Dorothy is described as being "charming like the snake with *rabbits*" (51). Because this aggression couldn't bear conscious expression in a love story, Hemingway re-channeled it into Maria's brutal rape and symbolic "castration" for which Jordan becomes the savior—though, as we have seen, he is subtly and significantly aligned with her attackers.

Yet, however much Hemingway's aggression may have been directed at Martha, it tended to express itself in terms of a more fundamental aggression directed at more archaic sources. Describing his play in the preface to *The Fifth Column*, Hemingway writes, "There is a girl in it named Dorothy but her name might also have been Nostalgia" (vi)—a curious thing to write about the fictional counterpart of a woman he had only just married. Keeping with the culinary theme of this section, a passage from *The Fifth Column* will testify to Dorothy/Martha's ancestry in Ernest's affections and will lead us into the terrain of the next chapter. Making do with what she can find in war-ravaged Madrid, Dorothy serves up a curiously familiar dish for Philip Rawlings:

> PETRA: What are you cooking, Señorita?
> DOROTHY: I don't know, Petra. There wasn't any label on it.
> PETRA: [*Peering into the pot*] It looks like rabbit.
> DOROTHY: What looks like rabbit is cat. But I don't think they'd bother to put cat in a tin and ship it all the way from Paris, do you? Of course, they may have tinned it in Barcelona and then shipped it to Paris and then flown it down here. Do you think it's cat, Petra? (55)

As we shall soon see, Dorothy's inability to distinguish between rabbit and cat reflects more than her lack of kitchen experience. Canned cat masquerading as rabbit was a genuine problem in war-ravaged Spain, but when this mystery meat is cooked by a woman *named* "rabbit," the symbolic value of such confusion merits our attention. "Rabbits" and "cats" were both fetishistically-invested "word-things" for Hemingway. Hemingway possessed an entire personal lexicon of such fetishistically-invested word-things, or *archeonyms*—word-things like hair, rabbit, cat, lion, ivory, silk, and pilar—that signified in special ways within his field of fetishistic fantasy. An understanding of this lexicon not only clarifies the etiology and function of Hemingway's fetishism, it reveals the overdetermination of the fetish object and opens up new possibilities for reading Hemingway's fiction.

CHAPTER 4

Loss, Fetishism, and the Fate of the Transitional Object

"What Looks Like Rabbit Is Cat"

> He no longer dreamed of storms, nor of women, nor of great occurrences, nor of great fish, nor fights, nor contests of strength, nor of his wife. He only dreamed of places now and of the lions on the beach. They played like young cats in the dusk and he loved them as he loved the boy.
>
> —*The Old Man and the Sea*

> I don't know how many people and animals have been in love before. . . . It is probably a very comic situation. But I don't find it comic at all.
>
> —*Islands in the Stream*

Hemingway occasionally expressed his lifelong scorn for "head doctors" in curiously ironic and revealing ways. In one celebrated incident from the time he spent as a war correspondent during World War II, this scorn sparked a confrontation between Hemingway and Meyer Maskin, the psychiatrist assigned to the Fourth Infantry Division during the Battle of the Bulge. According to Carlos Baker, Hemingway accused Major Maskin, who was in charge of identifying men with battle fatigue to be sent to the back of the lines, of knowing "everything about fuckoffs and nothing about brave men." Legend has it that, after a heated exchange, an angry Maskin shook a trembling finger at Hemingway and predicted forebodingly "You'll be coming to me yet" (642–3).

Hemingway critics are fond of recounting this story, some as an outlet for their own scorn of head doctors, some for the tragic

119

accuracy of Maskin's reply. I am interested, however, in another incident between Maskin and Hemingway, one in which Ernest told an unintentionally revealing analyst-baiting story one night after "the doctor invited himself into Ernest's billet and began to ask his probing, subtle questions."

> Ernest put on a sober face, saying that he needed Maskin's advice. He was troubled about his cats at Finca Vigía. He had twenty or thirty and kept getting more. "The little bastard was fascinated," said Ernest. "His eyes were bugging out." Many people liked cats, said the doctor. That was no problem. "With me it is," said Hemingway. "My problem is that I can't seem to stop having intercourse with them." (Baker 435)[1]

As a psychoanalytic critic, I suppose the joke is on me as much as it was on Maskin. Yet, had the doctor only known how unusual Hemingway's attachment to cats really was, he might have enjoyed the last laugh.

Freud taught us long ago that jokes often play upon unconscious desires; he also taught us that the first words of an analysis are always especially significant. Both generalizations apply all too easily to this mock-analysis. Hemingway truly *was* erotically obsessed with cats, kittens, and lions, and a little analysis reveals that his intentionally absurd claim that he couldn't help sleeping with his cats wasn't too far from the truth. As he said of himself in *Death in the Afternoon*, "I do not love dogs as dogs, horses as horses, or cats as cats"; instead he loved them for their individual attributes or through some pattern of "association" (6). And a look at the names of his innumerable cats at the Finca Vigía reveals a complex pattern of association indeed. Most of the names seem trivial enough—Fatso, Princesa, Uncle Willy, or Uncle Wolfie—but a significant number of his cats sported fetishistically-invested names that alluded to various aspects of his erotic desire. Could a hair fetishist choose a better name for a cat than "Barbershop," later shortened to "Shopsky"? Then there was "Big Goats," whose name was derived from "*bigotes*," Spanish for "mustache" or "whiskers." "Boise," shortened to "Boy," would, like "whiskers," be an entirely innocuous name if it weren't for the fetishistic implications of the word "boy" in the Hemingway lexicon, or at least in *The Garden of Eden*, where Catherine's tonsorial transformations always turn her into a "*boy*" but never a *man*.[2] Hemingway christened one cat "Spendy" (sometimes called Spendthrift) after the bisexual poet Stephen Spender. Finally, Hemingway's cat "Ecstasy" slinks quitely into *The Garden of Eden* manuscript. When Catherine complains that in English we have the worst words for the loveliest things, like erotic "ecstasy," David replies that "ecstasy" sounds like a "name for a cat," and this response becomes a sort of mantra, repeated twice more in the chapter (K422.1 10.5).

I don't mean to suggest that, strictly speaking, Hemingway fetishized cats. A genuine erotic fetish, as should be clear by now, is an object used by the fetishist to, among other things, make intercourse with women tolerable by disavowing their penisless state. (Here I am distinguishing between the fetish proper and other *eroticized objects*—objects which may represent the maternal or paternal phallus, but which may be worn by the self instead of being used to endow the partner with a symbolic female phallus. One might choose to ignore this distinction and call all eroticized objects "fetishes," but one does so at the risk of unnecessarily diluting psychoanalytic terminology and blurring important differences in etiology, psychodynamics, and the use of the object.) Hemingway would never ask a woman to *wear* a cat to make intercourse with her possible—but he might *associate* her with a cat for a very similar purpose. For Hemingway, cats were *fetishistically-invested objects*, totem animals which were always connected symbolically to his fetishism and which could perform some functions of the fetish object. (To call cats personal "totem animals," however, implies a revision of the traditional Freudian interpretation of totemism. Whereas Freud read totemism as a masculine "positive" oedipal drama in which totem animals represent the *father*, we need to recognize the connection between the totem animal and the *mother* for those men, such as Hemingway, with largely *negative*, or "inverted," Oedipus complexes.)[3] Hemingway didn't desire to sleep with actual cats—some truly bizarre evidence to the contrary notwithstanding—but "cats," "kittens," and "lions" were "word-things" *representing* an object intimately linked to his fetish that he genuinely *did* desire. Following the path of this investment invokes the overdetermined path of the fetish object and leads us back to the origins of Hemingway's fetishism.

One can't help noticing the abundance of cats in Hemingway's life and fiction, nor can one miss Hemingway's easy alignment of cats with women—a culturally sanctioned equation to be sure, but one which usually lacks the insistence and complexity of Ernest's feline associations. Hemingway thought of at least two of his wives as "cats." One of his favorite pet names for Hadley was "Feather Kitty" or "Feather Cat"—a name he sometimes shared himself, though more often he played the role of her "little waxen puppy." Hemingway also regularly called his fourth wife, Mary, "Kitten," and he often referred to himself as her "Big Kitten."[4] In *A Farewell to Arms*, Frederic calls Catherine Barkley "Cat" for short, and David Bourne chooses the same nickname for *his* Catherine in *The Garden of Eden* (that is, when he isn't calling her "Devil"). In both novels, Hemingway was apparently attempting to conjure up the ghost of his lost love, the "good" first wife whom he had betrayed and forfeited. In 1929, the year *Farewell* was published and two years after her divorce from Ernest, Hadley signed at least one of her letters to him, "Katherine" (Desnoyers 120). Then there is a letter from Ernest to Hadley, written in 1939, addressed to "Kath. Kat" (*SL* 496). In another letter from 1942, Hemingway calls Hadley "Miss Katherine Kat"—this after describing the cats at the Finca and remembering an old song about his "Feather Kitty" (*SL* 537):

> *A feather kitty's talent lies*
> *In scratching out the other's eyes.*
> *A feather kitty never dies*
> *Oh immortality.*

And in yet another 1943 letter, in which Ernest calls Hadley "dearest Katherine Cat," he tells her wistfully, "When it is really rough on ocean [I] sing old songs like Oh My Gentlemen, If You've Got Any Feather-Cats, and a Feather Kitty's Talent Lies, the Basque crew think these are folk songs of my *Pais*. So they are. So, my *Pais*, get well quickly . . ." (*SL* 556).

This connection between cats and women, a connection most often mediated by hair, pervades Hemingway's fiction. As Mark Spilka has noted, the name of Nick Adams's short-haired sister, Littless, in "The Last Good Country" was derived from the name of one of Hemingway's cats at the Finca. In *Across the River*, during their lovemaking in a gondola, Cantwell discovers feline properties in raven-haired Renata: "She talks like a gentle cat, though the poor cats cannot speak" (155). In *To Have and Have Not*, the lovely blonde-haired daughter of a wealthy, virtuous, and dull family aboard a yacht curls up "like a cat" while she dreams of her fiancé (233). Likewise, in *For Whom the Bell*

Tolls, when Robert Jordan rubs Maria's closely-cropped head, "she stroke[s] under his hand like a kitten" (68). We can only feel a sensation of *déjà vu*, then, when David Bourne, in *The Garden of Eden* manuscript, strokes Catherine's hair after her new haircut and she moves under his hand just "like a cat" (K422.1 5.6.2).[5] In fact, throughout *The Garden of Eden*, which begins in a town on "The Gulf of Lions," Catherine is repeatedly described by David, by Barbara, and by herself as a "lioness." When, for instance, David expresses his surprise that Catherine could become so dark in spite of her blonde hair, she explains with a strange logic, "I can because I'm lion color and they can go dark" (*GE* 30). But Hemingway must have created this association for reasons beyond a simple attempt at characterization, for Marita as well has her catlike dimension. After one of *her* haircuts, David strokes *her* hair, with predictable results. "I'm so proud of you and you look wonderful," he tells her. "Stroke once so I can purr," she demands coyly. "Can you purr?" David asks. Marita replies, "I've been purring ever since we did it" (K422.1 36.3).[6]

Perhaps the most amusing instance of such purring, however, is to be found not in Hemingway's fiction, but in the memoir of his youngest son. There, Gregory offers the following account of his father's use of one of his favorite cats as a prop in demonstrating how to pet a "pussy":

> The key to making a woman happy in bed is so simple, Gig. They have a thing down there about a third the size of your little finger. It's called the clitoris. It's right in the middle. If you want to make a woman happy, really happy, not just satisfy yourself, first stroke it gently, over and over, *like you're petting a cat*, ever so gently. (*He was stroking our cat Boise under the chin and Boise was purring ecstatically.*) It's a woman's sexual trigger, a *sort of miniature penis*. And if you don't know about it you might as well forget about pleasing women in bed. (my emphasis, 98)

But Hemingway's passion for cats burns most brightly in the bizarre second book of *Islands in the Stream*, where his attraction to women with feline qualities gives way to an attraction for *cats* (male or female) with feminine attributes.

Grieving over the loss of an ex-wife and three sons (the ex-wife and two younger sons by a car accident, the eldest son by war), Thomas Hudson takes consolation in his cat Boise, with whom Hudson has an almost spousal relationship. At one point

Hudson thinks, "I don't know how many people and animals
have been in love before. . . . It is probably a very comic situation. But I don't find it comic at all," and for some forty pages of
text, Hudson strokes, sleeps with, and talks to Boise (212). Such
behavior, aside from the length of Hemingway's description of it,
may not seem so odd, but the off-color sexual jokes that pervade
Hudson's relationship with his cats are certainly unusual.
Throughout this chapter there are repeated references to
Boisie's "lovemaking" and status as a "lover" (239). Upon waking
up to find Boise still asleep beside him, for instance, Hudson
thinks, "I never had a girl that waked when I did. . . . And now I
haven't even got a cat that does" (220). And when Hudson runs
into another kind of "cat," the housewown prostitute Honest Lil,
she asks him: "Tell me. Willie said there was a cat in love with
you. That isn't true, is it?" "Yes. It's true," Hudson corrects her,
letting her think that by "cat" he means prostitute. "I think it's
dreadful," Lil scolds. "No. It's not," Hudson replies. "I'm in love
with the cat, too" (275). Or when Hudson's silky-haired first
wife—a cross between Hadley and Ernest's blonde friend Mar-
lene Dietrich—visits him, he implies that his only sex objects are
a pillow and a cat, eliciting the promise from her, "I'll make up
for the cat" (311). And later, after learning that her ex-husband
has kept the news of their son's death from her for three weeks,
she rebukes him, adding, "Just because I'm a non-combatant
and you're in something so secret you have to sleep with a cat so
you won't talk" (324).

Hudson's most interesting feline attraction, however, is not
to his cat "Boy," but to another of his cats, "Princessa."
Thoughts of this dainty Persian, who nevertheless behaves like a
regular hussy when in heat, elicit a strange series of associations:

> *Thomas Hudson knew that he did not want to die without hav-
> ing made love to a princess as lovely as Princessa.*
> She must be as grave and as delicate and as beautiful as
> Princessa before they were in love and made the love and then
> be as shameless and as wanton in their bed as Princessa was.
> *He dreamed about this princess sometimes in the nights and
> nothing that could ever happen could be any better than the
> dreams were* but he wanted it actually and truly and he was
> quite sure he would have it if there were any such princess.
> The trouble was that the only princess that he had ever
> made love to outside of Italian princesses, who did not count,

was a quite plain girl with thickish ankles and not very good legs. *She had lovely northern skin, though, and shining well-brushed hair.* . . . (my emphasis, 221–2)

Hudson then recalls making love with this shiny-haired princess against the rails of a passenger ship while sliding through the Suez Canal. Tellingly, just before they made love, the princess had quipped, "A *mink coat* is good for something finally in the tropics" (224).

The connection between cats and women in fur coats is hardly accidental. Cats, like rabbits, are furry animals, and Hemingway frequently displaced his hair fetish onto furs. When Yogi, in *Torrents of Spring*, remembers the Parisian dream-woman who seduced him only to be revealed later performing for an audience of voyeurs peeping through a slit in a wall, he specifically remembers her doffing her hat and "long fur coat" (139). Early in *Across the River*, Cantwell admires an "extremely desirable . . . sleek girl" in a "long mink coat," and thinks to himself, "She is damned beautiful. I wonder what it would have been like if I had ever had the money to buy me that kind and put them in the mink?" (39). In *A Moveable Feast*, Hemingway admires the appearance, if not the minds, of the two blondes with long mink coats who accompany Ernest Walsh. One of Hemingway's first pieces for the *Toronto Star* chronicled the ins and outs of fox farming ("Canadian Fox-Ranching Pays Since the Wild-Cats Let the Foxes Alone," May 29, 1920). And in a satirical 1922 piece for the *Star*, "Two Russian Girls the Best-Looking at Genoa Parley," Hemingway notes favorably the Russian girls with their "hair bobbed in the fashion started by Irene Castle," but better still are the "wonderful wealth-reeking fur coats" worn by other women at the conference: "*The fur coats are the most beautiful things in the hall*" (my emphasis, *Dateline* 146; 144).

All of Hemingway's wives owned fur coats. In a 1922 article for the *Star*, Ernest mentions christening Hadley's "new fur coat" with an airplane trip, and as we have already seen, Pauline's chipmunk fur coat attracted Ernest well before *she* did (*Dateline* 206). After Hemingway's 1933–34 safari, Pauline even sported a cheetah-fur coat.[7] Likewise, Martha owned a silver fox coat—a gift from the Abraham Lincoln Brigade, but of no less psychological importance to Ernest for all that. The silver fox coat that her fictional counterpart Dorothy Bridges wears in the midst of the Spanish Civil War serves almost as her blazon in *The Fifth Col-*

umn, representing her superficiality and frivolity in the face her own hypocritical rhetoric and the horrors of the war beyond the walls of her hotel. The Hemingwayesque hero, Philip Rawlings— who by contrast wears a leather coat—denounces Dorothy for war profiteering, but her coat, which compliments her silky, blonde hair, exercises a curiously corrupting magnetism upon him. He can't help telling his Venus in furs how "fine and soft" the furs feel and how wonderful it is to feel her in them. Soon he is "shamelessly" telling her, "They feel really marvelously. I'm glad you bought them" (74). And a few years after Ernest and his new wife, Mary, returned to the states from their journalistic duties in the Second World War, Ernest sent his bride on yet another mission: "Operation Mink Coat" (Mary Hemingway 245).

In a September 22, 1949, letter addressed to "My dearest Kitten," Ernest urges Mary, who was then in Chicago, to "please get a lovely coat" (qtd. in Mary Hemingway 244). On September 30, 1949, he wrote giving her directions about the coat *and her hair*: "I don't think we ought to bleach it again until just before we leave [for Europe]. But . . . if they have really good hair-cuts a good hair-cut would be sound. We know how to bleach from the best people that ever did it and *then you can be silver-headed in your natural mink coat.* Will look awfully lovely." (In a postscript, he reconsiders the question of bleaching: "If you think your hair is OK to have it done very light with Clairol Silver-Blonde it would be very exciting to see. . . . I'd love to see it as light as it could be and then we'd get brown as could be on the boat" [my emphasis, ©1998, Ernest Hemingway Foundation].) When he wrote again on the following day Mary's coat and hair were still on his mind: "Am so excited about the coat. Can't wait to see my kitten in it. . . . If you want to have your hair done red instead of silver-gold that is just as wonderful. . . . I love it silver and love it red too. But never seen it a beautiful red yet like the red that copper kettles have. . ." (October 1, 1949, ©1998, Ernest Hemingway Foundation).

Another theme runs through these 1949 letters to "Kitten." While Mary was in Chicago, Ernest met and cultivated a friendship with the lion tamer of a traveling circus which had set up in a lot next to the Finca. Much to Mary's dismay, the old man, who starved himself to feed his lions, allowed Ernest to play with them in their cage. Ernest wrote on September 24 that he had received eight "chickenshit scratches" before he and the two lions became completely friends; nevertheless, he boasted to

Mary that the old man had said that Ernest "knew more about cotsies than anyone he knew." And trying to dispel any anxieties Mary might have about his flirting while she was away, Ernest explained in a letter written a few days later: "I am polite and loving to all these dames but who I love is you. You ought to begin to suspect that by now. It is just that they are fun, probably, like going in the cage with the big cotsies" (qtd. in Mary Hemingway 244–5).

That Ernest associated Mary herself with the "big cotsies" is most evident in one his dreams from his 1953 trip to Africa—an amazing dream not unlike Hudson's dreams of his princess, Princessa, but at least superficially unlike those other lion-dreams in *The Old Man and the Sea* and "The Short Happy Life of Francis Macomber."

> In my nocturnal dreams, I am always between 25 or 30 years old, I am irresistible to women, dogs and, on one recent occasion, to a very beautiful lioness.
>   In the dream, this lioness, who became my fiancée, was one of the most delightful creatures that I have ever dreamt about. *She had some characteristics of Miss Mary* and she could become irascible. *On one occasion, I recall she did an extremely perilous act. Perilous to me, that is.* When I recalled the dream to Miss Mary and Denis Zaphiro at breakfast, they appeared to be appreciative of the dream, but they seemed slightly shocked. Denis invited me to share a bottle of beer with him, a thing that I almost never do at breakfast, and I sat drinking this beer and remembering with great pleasure the night I had spent with the beautiful lioness. (my emphasis, "Christmas Gift" 86)[8]

After his account of the dream in a rambling article for *Look* magazine, Hemingway tells his readers that this is "the type of dream" he has "more or less habitually" and, in a maneuver curiously reminiscent of the Maskin incident, invites Freudian scholars to take their best crack at him ("Christmas Gift" 86).[9]

In *Hemingway's Genders*, Comley and Scholes cite this dream to argue that "miscegenation across species lines is erotic in itself in the Hemingway Text, but it is also a metaphor for racial miscegenation, which had a special eroticism for Hemingway" (96). I couldn't agree more. Yet in the absence of psychoanalytic theory the reasons for this association remain murky, merely metaphorical, governed by an overwhelming *somehow*. And why *lions* and *cats*? Aren't sheep more traditional? It is certainly significant that Ernest compares the lion not only to Miss Mary, but to the "African girl" of his 1953–54 safari, that "dark symbol," Debba. Hemingway calls the lioness his "fiancée," and "Fiancée" was Ernest's nickname for Debba. ("Fiancée" also becomes the name for David Bourne's boyhood "African girl" in *The Garden of Eden* manuscript.) When Catherine Bourne becomes obsessed with suntanning in *The Garden of Eden*, she tells David that she can become so dark because she is "lion color and they can go dark" (30). But the mechanism behind this association reveals itself only when we realize that, as I shall argue in my next chapter, Hemingway fetishized race along with hair, and cats and lions for Hemingway are fetishistically-invested objects.

The association may hinge in part on the word "tawny" which Hemingway frequently and accurately used to describe lions, but which also seems to have been one of his fetishistically-invested "word-things." (See, for instance, the "tawny" hide of the lion in "The Short Happy Life of Francis Macomber" [*SS* 19].) Thus, Hemingway describes Audrey, in *Islands in the Stream*, as having a "beautiful face and clear brown skin and *tawny hair*" (my emphasis, 172). (In the *Islands* manuscript, Hudson's first wife, Jan, also has "tawny hair.") In *The Garden of Eden*, Catherine Bourne's hair is "tawny" before she bleaches it, and Hemingway uses this same word to describe Maria's skin, in *For Whom the Bell Tolls*, and Catherine Barkley's skin in *A Farewell to Arms* (*FWBT* 22; *FTA* 18). Moreover the fact that Hemingway uses this word in his *initial* descriptions of both Maria and Catherine Barkley lends even more importance to it— as does the fact that the "tawniness" of Catherine Barkley's skin seems to be at odds with its "ivory" status, being like "piano keys" (*FTA* 144). (That Catherine's skin is like "ivory" has its own significance, as we shall eventually see.) The word "tawny" may owe its significance to a pun on the French *tanner* ("to tan"), thereby invoking the mechanism by which characters work their racial metamorphoses in *The Garden of Eden*. Yet, as these examples demonstrate, the radical overdetermination of Hemingway's primary fetish object, *hair*, still functions as a nexus for these associations. Thus, trying to explain her compulsive desire to tan so deeply in *The Garden of Eden* manuscript, Catherine can only say, "I don't know why I want it so much. It's like I wanted to have my hair cut" (K422.1, 2.4.2).

Given Hemingway's displacement of his hair fetish onto fur, his interest in small furry animals such as rabbits and cats already makes *some* sense, but the matter is more complicated than this. While he could covertly satisfy his fetishism by carrying a rabbit's foot or stroking his cats at his leisure, this can't explain his interest in lions, which are hardly so gentle or comforting. Yet if the fetish object, among other things, serves to simultaneously disavow and memorialize the anatomical distinction between the sexes, it is surely significant that the most obvious visual signifier of a lion's sex is the presence or absence of a *mane*. Thus, while Catherine Bourne is continually compared to a lioness in *The Garden of Eden*, Nick Sheldon describes his long hair as being heavy like the "mane" of a lion (K422.1 3.13). If this "mane" in a sense marks Nick's masculinity, however, its fetishistic connection to the female phallus simultaneously undermines that very masculinity. While Hemingway at times would wear the fetish object himself to negotiate a transvestic identification with the phallic woman, like many men he confused a feminine identification in *other* men with homosexuality. Thus in his fiction when any man who is not clearly a cognate for himself wears the fetish object (with the notable exceptions of pigtailed bullfighters and George Armstrong Custer, a.k.a. "Long Hair"), he is clearly and disdainfully identified as being homosexual.[10] When the crowd of gay men enters the bar in *The Sun Also Rises*, for instance, Hemingway pointedly draws attention to their "newly washed, wavy hair" (20). Likewise, in *Death in the Afternoon*, Hemingway relates a story of a "dark-haired young man's" painful initiation into homosexuality, and his appearance soon thereafter with hennaed hair (180). There is the young painter in *Across the River and Into the Trees*, with a "wave in his hair," who Renata explains was "a little bit *pédéraste* once," but who now "goes with very many women to hide what he is" (96). And there is a curious fragment in the Hemingway Collection at the Kennedy Library in which a young man ventures into a Parisian coiffeur's to get a permanent wave. Before entering, the young man stares at his deeply tanned face in a mirror in the shop window. The shop has two doors, one for *Dames* and one for *Messieurs*. In the manuscript, Hemingway initally wrote that the man went through "the" door. This, however, is crossed out. Two women walk through the door marked *Dames*, and the young man enters through the "other door." After a shampoo, watching himself in the surrounding mirrors with a sort of uneasy self-alienation, the young man asks if he can get a permanent. Trying to avoid the glance of the young man in the next chair, he thinks, "I thought he was a pimp. Just an upsidaisy. Why should I think he wasn't. Because I'm in here myself. Just like an upsidaisy. He looked at himself humorlessly in the mirror" (K355a, qtd. in Comley and Scholes 90). Thus, in spite of any masculine attributes that accompany the possession of a "mane," Nick Sheldon worries that his haircut makes him look like a "sodomite," and using what he calls an "Indian trick," he hides his hair under his hat.

(What do we make of the fact that *wavy* hair seems to be a common denominator in Hemingway's portrayal of male homosexuality? Two of Hemingway's female characters, Marie Morgan and Catherine Barkley, also get waves, and from the mention of clicking "tongs" in these passages we can infer that they get "*marcel* waves," not permanents. The marcel, a kind of artificial wave produced with heated curling tongs, was at the height of its popularity in the twenties, and the coiffeur who invented it, Marcel Grateau, was the toast of Paris.[11] Given the linguistic nature of Hemingway's fetishistic associations, could it be that these *marcel* waves allude to Ernest's sister *Marcel*line? If so, we can see how the wearing of marcelled hair by men would signify for Hemingway a cross-gender twinship that entails a loss of gender identity—mistakenly projected onto others as "homosexuality." There may be a further allusion to *Marcel* Proust in these homoerotically-invested waves. After all, Proust is an almost serpentine presence in Hemingway's *Garden*. For Hemingway, then, as for many men according to Robert Stoller, homophobia at bottom seems to have been a fear of turning into the opposite sex, a fear of losing his gender identity. To fear and desire the same thing is a deeply human condition, but this dilemma was undoubtedly intensified in Hemingway by the split in his ego. One half craved gender-obliterating merger; one half feared it.)

When we recognize the slang connotations of "pussy," with its ability to represent the female genitals while conflating them with phallic hair or fur, we begin to see that indeed "what looks like rabbit is cat."[12] But this association becomes even clearer when we learn about one of the more exotic items on Hemingway's menu during his 1953 safari in Africa. After one of his lion hunts, apparently feeling a bit peckish, Ernest decided to nibble at the dead beast. Mary relates the story as follows:

> Ernest's lion was a young male in his prime, four or five years old, with immense fore- and hind-leg muscles and thick bones

and muscles in his paws. Watching the skinning, Ernest bent down and with his pocketknife cut out a bit of the tenderloin beside the spine, chewed some and offered me a tidbit. We both thought the clean pink flesh delicious, steak tartare without the capers. Denis [Zaphiro] scoffed that it would make us sick and Philip [Percival] politely declined to taste. In Kenya neither the natives nor the whites ate lion, having some taboo against it which they would never define for me. Thereafter, Ernest and I had the lion marinated in sherry with some herbs and grilled over N'bebia's cookfire. It was firmer than Italian veal, but not tough, and as bland in flavor without a hint of the wilderness. Later we dressed it up with garlic and onion and various tomato and cheese sauces, as we had done with *vitello* in Italy. (347–348)

Hemingway even wrote up a recipe for "filet of lion," which begins with solid advice: "First obtain your lion" (K376). Ernest then describes how to cut the steaks and hang them beyond the reach of hyennas, covered with cheesecloth to keep off the blowflies. He suggests grilling the tenderloins, dipped first in egg and breaded, over an open fire. If eggs aren't handy, one can always baste the steaks with lard made from eland fat. The results, he promises, will be delicious.

Nevertheless, Hemingway wasn't finicky about how he cooked his cat. In his 1953–54 *African Journal* (about a third of which was published by *Sports Illustrated*), Hemingway relates that the same unconscious cat-eating impulse overtook him on a leopard hunt later that year. After shooting a leopard out of a tree, only to have the animal escape into some brush, Hemingway inspected the spot where the cat had fallen. Out of a clot of blood, one of the gunbearers picked a sharp bone fragment and passed it to Hemingway: "*It was a piece of shoulder blade and I put it in my mouth. There is no explanation of that. I did it without thinking. But it linked us closer to the leopard and I bit on it and tasted the new blood, which tasted about like my own . . .*" (my emphasis, 3.8). While this act invokes a primitive hunting magic of the sort one might encounter in *The Golden Bough* (and Hemingway's identification with his Wakamba gunbearers is intense throughout this passage), it also reads like a textbook description of identification through unconscious incorporation. Hemingway writes that the splintered bone in his mouth cut the inside of his cheek so that he could "taste the familiarity of [his] own blood now mixed with the blood of the leopard" (9). This mixture of blood, however, was a mere formality. Hemingway thought he had female cat blood, anyway. As he explains in the *African Journal*: "A *lioness* was a cat, a true cat, and I always thought that I could think inside *her* head. Cats are supposed to be very mysterious but they are not if you have any cat blood. *I had a lot of cat blood; too much for my own good*, but quite useful around cats. . . . A male lion never really seemed like a cat. He had some other kind of blood . . ." (my emphasis, 3.3). In the manuscript, Hemingway explicitly connects the ingestion of lion with cannibalism. After remembering how he had once shot a cheetah, Ernest thinks about how the Wakamba were still cannibals when his friend M'Cola was a boy. Hemingway has nothing against cannibalism in the abstract, he says, but he thinks that because of a taboo he could not eat human flesh, just as some people could not eat lion.

Somehow the aroma of rabbit stew lingers about these totemic meals. Yet when Ernest ate *hare* he was clearly incorporating the fetish object, his lover, and an "identical" ego-supporting "other." What was he trying to ingest by eating *leopard* or *lion*?

Most immediately, he seems to have been trying to incorporate his "Kitten," Miss Mary. Yet the loss of Ernest's "Feather Cat," Hadley, haunted him throughout the 1940s and 50s, and soon after his 1953 dream of marital bliss with a lioness, he dreamed of being together again with Hadley in Switzerland, "her head . . . under my chin . . . sleeping as close and as trusting as *kittens* sleep" (my emphasis, *African Journal*, 3.15). *A Moveable Feast* nostalgically and beautifully chronicles an idealized version of Ernest's life with Hadley before it was ruined by the infiltration of "outsiders." *The Garden of Eden*, both in the excised relationship between the Sheldons, and in the triangle involving David, Catherine, and Marita could with some fairness be read as a meditation on what went wrong with this marriage (though with the blame shifted to the novel's female characters). In *Islands in the Stream*, Hudson's Hadleyesque first wife returns to console him and replace the cat and pillow which serve as objective correlatives for his loss. And though Hudson's grief is absolutely genuine, it is difficult not so see a morbid element of wish-fulfillment in the novel, whereby Hemingway indirectly admits, through Hudson, that he would give up his second and third marriages and all of his children if only he could exist again with Hadley as they did before their own child was born. Was Heming-

way's appetite for lion cutlets, like Hudson's obsessive cat petting, an attempt to conjure up, or incorporate, Hadley's ghost
and thereby ward off an overwhelming sensation of loss? Ernest's
friends in Africa noted that his almost constant drinking veiled
an underlying depression. This depression may have been largely
chemical and hereditary in etiology, yet how could Ernest avoid
connecting it with the major losses in his life, and how could he
overcome it without trying to undo those losses?

But if in the 1940s and 50s Hemingway used cats and lions,
in part, to console himself for the decades-old loss of Hadley,
what do we make of his 1924 short story, "Cat in the Rain," written during those happy years with Hadley so beautifully and
nostalgically rendered in *A Moveable Feast*? Here, too, a cat
seems to function as a replacement for some unnamed lost object, but Hadley was yet to be lost.

Feather Kitty, Mama Kitty, and the Lost Object

"I wish I could remember what it was we lost."

—Catherine in *The Garden of Eden*

In this enigmatic little story, remarkable for the tension between what it does and doesn't say, an American girl looking out
of the window of her Italian hotel room spies a "poor kitty" in the
rain "trying to keep dry under a table" (SS 167). Not knowing
anyone at her hotel and alone in a strange country with a husband who seems less than attentive, she projects her own alienation onto the cat, empathizes with it, and decides to go
downstairs to its rescue. But once outside in the rain, a maid
holding an umbrella for her, she finds that the cat is gone. When
the maid asks, "*Ha perduto qualque cosa, Signora?*" the American girl explains about the cat, saying "Oh, I wanted it so much.
I wanted a kitty" (168). Empty-handed, she returns to her room,
stares at herself in the mirror, and in an apparent non sequitur
asks her husband, "Don't you think it would be a good idea if I
let my hair grow out?" In contrast to his previous indifference,
this finally gets his attention.

> George looked up and saw the back of her neck, clipped
> close like a boy's.
> "I like it the way it is."

Figure 6. Hemingway with his cat Boise at the Finca Vigía. (John F. Kennedy Library, courtesy Hans Malmberg, Stockholm)

    "I get so tired of it," she said. "I get so tired of looking like a boy."
    George shifted his position in the bed. He hadn't looked away from her since she started to speak.

"You look pretty darn nice," he said.

She laid the mirror down on the dresser and went over to the window and looked out. It was getting dark.

"I want to pull my hair back tight and smooth and make a big knot at the back that I can feel," she said. "I want to have a kitty to sit on my lap and purr when I stroke her."

"Yeah?" George said from the bed.

"And I want to eat at a table with my own silver and I want candles. And I want it to be spring and I want to brush my hair out in front of a mirror and I want a kitty and I want some new clothes." (SS 169)

By this point, though, George has had enough and snaps "Oh, shut up and get something to read." The girl looks out the window at the rain falling on the war monument and palms in the square and adds, "Anyway, I want a cat. . . . I want a cat. I want a cat now. If I can't have long hair or any fun, I can have a cat" (169). In the story's final lines the maid appears with a present from the hotel's Padrone, a "big tortoise-shell cat"—apparently not the "kitty" that had been outside in the rain. We might wonder why two of Hemingway's favorite erotic symbols, cats and boyishly cut hair, appear in a story seemingly devoid of erotic interest, but an examination of manuscript revisions to the story reveals that the story is *not* so devoid of erotic investment. Hemingway sketched his earliest notes for "Cat in the Rain," during his and Hadley's February 1923 stay at Rapallo, where they visited Ezra Pound and where Ernest first read Eliot's *The Waste Land*. This false start, with its allusion to Eliot's poem, implies that it was Ernest, not his wife, whose nickname "Kitty" appears in an early draft of the story (K321), who looked out the hotel window and saw not one cat, but two:

> Cats love in the garden. On green tables to be exact. The big cat gets on the small cat. Sweeny gets on Mrs. Porter. Ezra gets nowhere except artistically of course. . . . Hadley and I are happy sometimes. We are happiest in bed. . . . Sleeping is good. I used to lie awake all night. That was before. This is after. . . . (K670.4, qtd. in Smith, *Reader's* 43)

That Ernest connected the sex life of the two cats with his own sex life with his wife, "Feather Kitty," makes at least semantic sense, but why did he associate it with the tawdry sexuality of Eliot's Sweeny, and later with the mood disorder which most likely caused his sleeplessness in the early 1920s?[13]

In a 1925 letter to F. Scott Fitzgerald which, as Paul Smith observes, "confirms more with its denials than it asserts" (*Reader's* 45), Hemingway explained that "Cat in the Rain" "wasn't about Hadley," though he "knew" that Scott and Zelda "always thought it was." Instead, he claimed that the story was about a "Harvard kid and his wife" whom he had met in Genoa. "Hadley," he curiously explained to Fitzgerald, "never made a speech in her life about wanting a baby because she had been told various things by her doctor and I'd—no use going into all that" (*SL* 180). Yet the fact that the American girl in the story never makes any such speech either—at least not *directly*—and that Hadley had, in fact, first told Ernest of her own pregnancy in February 1923, suggests, as John Hagopian argued decades ago, that the cat in the story functions as a replacement for a child that the young woman—clearly based on Hadley—either cannot have, or is under some pressure to abort. (In Hemingway's letter to Fitzgerald, he even admits that Hadley was pregnant in February 1923 when he began "Cat in the Rain," but he claims that she was "4 months pregnant with Bumby"—a curious claim since Bumby was born early in October, implying a highly unusual twelve-month gestation.) Whether Hemingway and Hadley actually discussed aborting their first child, or whether Hemingway simply imagined what such a situation might be like, or what it might have been like if Hadley had not been able to conceive, matters little. The theme of abortion clarifies the story's allusions to *The Waste Land*, invoking the pub monologue on Albert and Lil (Smith, *Reader's* 45), and it also clarifies the near hysteria of the American girl and the symbolic "something" that feels "very small and tight inside the girl" when the hotel's Padrone looks at her (*SS* 169). For our purposes, however, it is most important simply to recognize that the cat serves here, as in *Islands in the Stream*, as a replacement for an unnamable lost object.

Aside from Hadley's perhaps unwelcome pregnancy, and the prospect of a baby drawing Hadley's undivided attention away from himself, loss and depression must have been subjects much on Ernest's mind in the months before he began "Cat in the Rain." In December 1922, Hadley famously tried to surprise Ernest by packing all of his manuscripts into a small valise and taking a train to join him for the Christmas season in Lausanne where he was covering a peace conference for the *Star*. When the valise was stolen, along with almost all of the work Hemingway had done since his arrival in Europe, Ernest and Hadley were both devastated. In the abortive early chapters of *Islands in the Stream* published posthumously as "The Strange Country," Roger tells a heavily fictionalized tale of this loss and, in language eerily resembling that used to describe Hudson's reaction to the loss of his ex-wife and three children, explains what he did after he returned to Paris and verified that indeed *all* of the manuscripts had been lost: "I locked the door of the cupboard and went into . . . the bedroom . . . and lay down on the bed and put a pillow between my legs and my arms around another pillow and lay there very quietly. I had never put a pillow between my legs before and I had never lain with my arms around a pillow but now I needed them very badly" (*CSS* 648). This loss, in addition to the imagined loss of an unborn child, may lie submerged beneath the action of "Cat in the Rain," the first story Hemingway tried to write after losing his manuscripts.[14]

But if Hadley, Ernest's "Feather Cat," was yet to be lost, why are lost objects at this early date still signified or replaced by *cats* of all things? Clearly and importantly, cats can be cradled and stroked and loved as a baby is loved. Yet the same could be said for a lapdog. Of course, if we acknowledge the American wife's name from the manuscript, "Kitty," her identification with the "poor kitty" offers the perfect substitute for her identification with her unborn, aborted, or unconceived child. Thus, she knows whereof she speaks when she complains, "It isn't any fun to be a poor kitty out in the rain" (169). Illuminating as this connection is, however, it fails to explain the logic behind the American girl's claim that "*If [she] can't have long hair or any fun, [she] can have a cat*" (169). Her proposal to grow her hair out reflects a loss of symbiotic identity with her husband and thereby signifies the stress on their relationship, but, given the ubiquitous connection in Hemingway's work between fetishism and cats, I suspect that the matter runs much deeper than this. The story's preoccupation with "*replacement cats*"—the "big tortoise-shell cat" replacing the original "kitty," which in turn replaced an unborn child—can be read as a hint that Ernest's "Feather Cat," Hadley, was *herself* a "replacement cat" for Ernest's *original* fetishistically-invested lost love object: his mother.

According to James Mellow, "Kitty" was Ernest's childhood nickname for Grace (6), and a look at two of Ernest's favorite childhood games casts an entirely new light on the association between Hemingway's eroticized attachment to cats and his interest in women in mink coats. In her well-kept "memory books," Grace describes how her five-year-old son would cuddle around her neck and plead, "*I'm Mama's little mink, ain't I? Will you be my Mama Mink?*" Elsewhere in the memory books, she notes, "*He loves to play kitty and be the baby kitty, and Mama be the mama kitty and stroke him and purr*" (qtd. in Spilka 57). And it would seem from the passage in *For Whom the Bell Tolls* where Maria strokes under Jordan's hand like a kitten, or from the passage in *The Garden of Eden* manuscript where Marita demands to be stroked so she can purr, that Hemingway simply never outgrew a taste for these games—though his adult penchant for playing the role of the caressing "mama kitty" was indeed a new development.

The nostalgic longing for Hadley that so haunts Hemingway's later work, in fact, is merely the most obvious example of a much more general and pervasive pining for lost "original love objects" that permeates almost all of Hemingway's fiction. The actual representative, or real-world cognate, of the "original love object"—whether it be Hadley, Agnes von Kurowsky, Marjorie Bump, Prudy/Trudy Boulton, Catherine Barkley, Robert Jordan's Maria, Nick Adams's little sister, or the "African girl" of David Bourne's youth—often seems to matter less than her *firstness*. When Frederic Henry first meets Catherine Barkley, he tells her that he has never loved anyone before, and Robert Jordan says much the same thing to Maria: "'I have never run with many women,' he said truly. 'Until thee I did not think that I could love one deeply'" (344). Years after his divorce, Thomas Hudson still carries a torch for his first wife. As an adult, Nick Adams nostalgically remembers the Indian girl who "did first what no one has ever done better" (*SS* 497), and Catherine Bourne, in *The Garden of Eden* manuscripts, is intensely jealous of David's boyhood African "fiancée." In "The Snows of Kilimanjaro," Harry's first wife—based clearly on Hadley—functions as a mere replacement for an earlier love based on the wartime nurse Agnes von Kurowsky, "*the first one. The one who left him . . .*" (Hemingway's emphasis, *SS* 64). Unable "to kill his loneliness," Harry, while away on a trip to Constantinople, the circumstances of which correspond closely to those of Hemingway's own 1922 trip there, writes her

a letter telling her how he had never been able to kill it. . . . How when he thought he saw her outside the Regence one time it

made him go all faint and sick inside, and that he would follow
any woman who looked like her in some way, along the Boule-
vard, afraid to see it was not she, afraid to lose the feeling it
gave him. How every one he had slept with had only made him
miss her more. How what she had done could never matter since
he knew he could not cure himself of loving her. (64–65)

Of course, romantic literature has always privileged "first loves,"
but for Hemingway, adult love very often seems like a reaction
to, or imitation of, some original affair in the distant past. Thus,
it is no coincidence that the "first loves" who populate his fiction
frequently turn out to be "nurses."

    That Catherine Barkley is a wartime nurse; that Brett Ash-
ley is an *ex*-World War I nurse; that Maria, named after a nurse
Hemingway met in Mataro in 1938, promises to nurse Robert
Jordan if he should ever be wounded; that Hadley had spent the
year before Ernest met her *nursing* her dying mother; and that
Ernest called his fourth wife, Mary, his "practical nurse" for his
old age and kids—all could be read (perhaps not inaccurately) as
a testament to Hemingway's never having gotten over his first
adult love, Agnes von Kurowsky. Yet Agnes, who was seven
years older than Ernest, who shared Grace Hall Hemingway's
height and chestnut-colored hair, and whom Ernest fictionalized
as "Cat," felt herself to be a replacement for an even earlier
"nurse" in Ernest's life. In her "Dear John" letter to him, Agnes
called attention to the disparity in their ages, writing: "I know I
am still very fond of you, but more as a mother than as a sweetheart" (qtd. in Villard & Nagel 246). This age disparity, however,
hardly bothered Ernest; on the contrary, two years later he married a talented musician with the kind of auburn hair that his
mother so admired, a woman even older than Agnes, his
"Feather Kitty," Hadley Richardson.
    Influenced by negative oedipal hatred and a positive oedipal
need to deny his own unusually intense maternal bonds, Hemingway referred to his mother throughout most of his adult life
as "that all-American bitch" and chafed under the sort of sug-
gestions that I am making here. Writing of his mother to Charles
Scribner in 1949, Hemingway bluntly declared, "I hate her guts
and she hates mine" (*SL* 670). And to Arthur Mizener, Hemingway complained, "Hell this love or hate your mother thing is too
simple. What if you've been in love with two of your sisters, five
dogs, maybe twenty cats, four different airplanes, two cities and

five towns, three continents, one boat, the oceans, and Christ count them, womens. So it was your mother. That's much too simple any way one plays it" (*SL* 697).[15] Were I *reducing* the various loves of Hemingway's life to his love (and hate) for his mother (and his sister, Marcelline), his complaint to Mizener would hit uncomfortably close to home. My point, however, is not that Ernest's love for Grace was his single, *essential*, love; my point, rather, is that Grace was Ernest's *first* love, and this love, and loss, served as a model for his later loves and losses. Insofar as Hemingway's later loves were mediated by his fetishism, they were mediated by his love for Grace (and Marcelline). This first love, intimately tied to the etiology and psychodynamics of his fetishism, provided him with a *language* for expressing his later loves and losses. Its traces can be found not only in Ernest's attraction to mink, his obsessive petting of cats, or his ingestion of lion, but also in his description of the fetish object itself, most notably in his fascination with *silky* hair.

When young Ernest wasn't calling his mother "Kitty" or "Mama Mink," he had another nickname for her: "Silkey Sockey."[16] And whether or not it is the sound of silkworms eating mulberry leaves which sparks Nick Adams's memories of his parents and childhood in "Now I Lay Me," the word "silk" does appear with an unusual frequency in Hemingway's fetishistically-invested descriptions of hair. Thus, in *Islands in the Stream*, Audrey Bruce has lovely "silky" hair that swings when she walks (172). Likewise, Hudson's ex-wife brushes her hair "to please him, and because of what she [knows] it [does] to him," and she sits so it swings "like a heavy *silken* load" when her head moves (my emphasis, 315); later, when Hudson dreams of a sexual reunion with her, her dream-hair hangs down and lies "heavy and *silky* on his eyes and on his cheeks" (my emphasis, 343). In *Across the River and Into the Trees*, the wind blows Renata's hair up around Cantwell's neck, and he kisses her, feeling the hair "beating *silkily* against both his cheeks" (my emphasis, 261); later, when he watches her sleeping without first "having done anything to her hair" he thinks: "She is sleeping with it spread out on the pillow and all it is to her is a glorious, dark, *silky* annoyance, that she can hardly remember to comb. . ." (my emphasis, 179). In *To Have and Have Not*, Marie Morgan remembers her reaction to her hair after first bleaching it: "it shone so in the sun and was so soft and *silky* when I put my hand and touched it, and I couldn't believe it was me and I was so excited I was choked with it" (my emphasis, 259). When, in *For Whom the Bell Tolls*, Robert Jordan rubs his hand over the top of Maria's head, something "he had been wanting to do . . . all day," his throat swells as he feels "the thick but *silky* roughness of the cropped head rippling between his fingers" (my emphasis, 67). Later, in his sleeping bag, Jordan remembers an erotic dream of Greta Garbo, whose "hair swept over his face," and who appeared to him "wearing a soft *silky* wool sweater" (137). When Maria's cropped head rubs up against his chin and cheeks, Jordan notes that her hair feels "soft but as alive and *silky* rolling as when a marten's fur rises under the caress of your hand when you spread the trap jaws open and lift the marten clear and, holding it, stroke the fur smooth"; once again a "hollow aching from his throat" nearly overwhelms him (378).

In *Hemingway: The Paris Years*, Michael Reynolds quotes a 1924 fragment from one of Ernest's stories which never took off: "There is a girl *selling [silk?] stockings* under a canvas shelter in the square. . . . The girl is letting her bobbed hair grow out. It is very hot under the canvas and she tosses her hair back" (my emphasis, 196). In his notes for this story, Hemingway, whose hair was then almost as long as his wife's, "put down two new ideas: a story about a man who always wanted to have his hair long, and another about a woman who always wanted to cut hers short, finally did and how she felt" (196). When, over twenty years later, Hemingway finally did write a version of this story, the word "silk" still figured prominently in his tonsorial associations. Early in *The Garden of Eden*, Hemingway describes Catherine Bourne's pre-cropped hair as feeling "silky" against David's cheek (11), and her hair remains silky even after it is cut: "[David] held her head close against his chest and felt it smooth close clipped and coarsely *silky* and she pushed it hard against him again and again" (my emphasis, 45). In the manuscripts, after Catherine transforms herself into a "new girl" yet again by cutting and bleaching her hair, she asks her husband how he likes his new girl: is she "dark enough," "light enough," and "*silky* enough"? (K422.1 12.18.10).

But if the trail of Hemingway's eroticized cats and minks leads back to childhood memories of his "mama mink" or "mama kitty," and if such memories are encoded within the "silky" symbolism of the fetish object itself, *why* does this link exist? And how does it help us to understand the relationship between fetishism and loss? Answers to both questions are to be found in the relationship between the fetish object and that all-important first pregenital *not-me* object that D. W. Winnicott calls the "transitional object."

If fetishism results largely from a failure of separation-individuation and a "prolongation of the introjective-projective stage in which there is an incomplete separation of the 'I' from the 'other' and an oscillation between the two" (Greenacre 302), we should hardly be surprised to learn that the fetish object often retains traces of the transitional object, which "represents the infant's transition from a state of being merged with the mother to a state of being in relation to the mother as something outside and separate" (Winnicott, *Playing* 14). The child's first *not-me* object, typically a blanket, teddy bear, or piece of soft cloth, the transitional object functions as a bridge, separating and joining the infant to the mother's body. Soft, warm, and endowed with bodily odors, the transitional object allows the child to leave the mother's orbit and explore the world beyond without ever fully leaving the maternal presence. Like the fetish object, which exists outside the fetishist's body but is the subjectively-invested product of illusion, "the transitional object is *not an internal object* (which is a mental concept)—it is a possession. Yet it is not (for the infant) an external object either" (Winnicott's emphasis, *Playing* 9). The transitional object, which generally becomes the child's first symbol, "stands at one and the same time for the baby and for the mother. It is both, though it is neither. . . . The paradox demands acceptance as such, and need not be resolved. This is permitted madness, madness that exists within the framework of sanity" (Winnicott, *Explorations* 285).[17] But, however "mad" it may be, and however much it may resemble the Janus-faced fetish object, the transitional object is by no means "perverse." As Winnicott takes great pains to explain, almost all children, boys and girls alike, use transitional objects in the process of separation-individuation. With separation from the mother and the gradual formation of a stable ego, most children gradually de-cathect their transitional objects by the time they enter the phallic phase, so that Winnicott has compared transitional objects to those old soldiers who never die but who simply fade away.

The fetishist, however, never successfully negotiates separation-individuation and therefore fails to form an entirely stable ego or sense of gender-identity. Thus, as Greenacre explains, "It is exactly the period of the transitional object which is the first disturbed one in the fetishist" (63). For the fetishist, the transitional object, the child's first tool for becoming able to accept difference and similarity, develops into something new: a tool for affirming and denying the anatomical difference between the sexes.[18] As Stoller explains, the transitional object and the fetish object both "stand as a bridge between the infant's wanting to stay merged with mother and to become an independent person" (*Presentations* 128), but from the phallic position where the fetishist is fixated and where separation from the maternal body has become symbolized by sexual difference, merger and individuation can only be imagined through the presence or absence of the signifier of sexual difference: the phallus. Merger thus becomes an Edenic always-already-lost state which promises blissful union at the price of complete ego loss, fragmentation, castration, and gender-identity dissolution. By holding onto a sort of phallic-position substitute for the transitional object, the fetishist remains in a perpetual state of ego-suspension and separation-individuation, tied to but separated from the maternal body.

Thus Greenacre writes, "Whereas the transitional object is derived from the mother-me association and is somewhat focused on the mouth-nose and *breast*, the fetishist's mother-me combination is distinctly concerned with the *genitals*" (my emphasis, 321). And just as the adult fetish object will often contain a trace of the infantile transitional object, it will often as well contain a trace of the original attachment to the mother's breast, thereby invoking the equation "breast = penis."[19] For instance, when Hemingway displaced his hair fetishism onto fur or fuzzy sweaters, both of which are themselves classic fetish objects but which also suggest the soft cloth of the transitional object, he was always keenly aware of the movement of the breasts beneath the fur. While this equates the breasts with the phallic fetish object, it simultaneously reveals the maternal presence beneath Hemingway's construction of the phallic. Robert Jordan fondly remembers the "*silky* wool sweater" that Greta Garbo wears in his dream (*FWBT* 137); Jake Barnes admires Brett Ashley's "curves" beneath her "wool jersey" (*SAR* 22); Richard Gordon, after breaking up with Helen, looks wistfully one last time at her "curly black hair [and] her small firm breasts under the sweater" (*THHN* 192)[20]; Colonel Cantwell stares with fascination at Renata's "silky" hair and "her true breasts under [her black] sweater" (*ART* 179); Thomas Hudson appreciates Audrey Bruce's breasts beneath her sweater (*IITS* 178); and, after one of her haircuts, Catherine Bourne appears triumphantly wearing a cashmere sweater with her hands provocatively held beneath her breasts (*GE* 43). Nor was this merely a literary phenomenon. When Hemingway first met Mary, she noticed that like a number of other men who had stopped by her lunch table that day, Hemingway was attracted to her brassier-less breasts beneath her sweater, and one of his first presents to her was a white imitation angora sweater.

Mary's well-endowed chest aside, though, Hemingway more often than not seemed to favor small, hard, "boyish" breasts, like Trudy Boulton's "*hard little breasts*" (*SS* 497), Helen Gordon's "small *firm* breasts" (*THHN* 192), Catherine Bourne's "*hard erect* freshness" (*GE* 17), Renata's "*upraised* breasts" (*ART* 152), or Maria's "small *up-tilted*" or "*firm-pointed*" breasts (*FWBT* 22; 70).[21] In "The Strange Country," for instance, when Roger kisses Helena, he feels "the *silk of her hair* over his arm and their bodies *hard and taut*" as he drops his hands to her breasts "*to feel them rise, quick-budding under his fingers*" (my emphasis, *CSS* 615). Michael Reynolds has attributed Hemingway's taste in breasts to his youthful reading of Havelock Ellis, who described short women with "small breasts, wide hips, dark hair, [and] brilliant eyes" as being unusually sexually active (*Young Hemingway* 121). But while such reading clearly could have reinforced Hemingway's predilections, it hardly accounts for Hemingway's fascination with *hard, erect* breasts, and it fails to explain why these breasts so often appear in conjunction with the fetishized hair or furry sweaters. The "breast = penis" equation explains both phenomena, and Hemingway invokes this equation explicity when *The Garden of Eden*'s Marita plays with the sleeping David; after giving him an erection, she touches him with her breasts and takes pride in their ability to "do the same thing he does" (K422.1 27.33.34). The "breast = penis" equation further explains the significance of the covertly phallic "*stiff*" "*men's*" shirts that Catherine Bourne wears in *The Garden of Eden*:

> People did not wear fishermen's shirts then and this girl that he was married to was the *first girl* he had ever seen wearing one. She had bought the shirts for them and then had washed them in the basin in their room at the hotel to take the *stiffness* out of them. They were *stiff* and built for hard wear but the

> washings softened them and now they were worn and softened enough so that when he looked at the girl now her *breasts showed beautifully* against the worn cloth. (my emphasis, 6)

Here, in addition to the "breast = penis" equation, we may again find a trace of the soft cloth of the transitional object.

The link between the transitional and fetish objects illuminates not only the maternal presence beneath the fetish, it also clarifies the relation between fetishism and loss. Winnicott describes the ego-reinforcing transitional object as "*a defense against anxiety, especially anxiety of the depressive type*," and he further notes that "patterns set in infancy may persist into childhood, so that the original soft object continues to be absolutely necessary at bedtime or *at a time of loneliness or when a depressed mood threatens*" (my emphasis, *Playing* 4). Even after the child has apparently relinquished the transitional object, he or she will find it again when it is needed. Winnicott describes the passing of the transitional object as follows: "The transitional object tends to be relegated to the limbo of half-forgotten things at the bottom of the chest of drawers, or at the back of the toy cupboard. It is usual, however, for the child to know. For example, *a boy who has forgotten his transitional object has a regression phase following a deprivation. He goes back to his transitional object*" (my emphasis, *Explorations* 56).

In the case of the fetishist, the transitional object develops during the phallic phase into a fetish object that still shores up the body image and ego while establishing a link to the maternal body; hence, this object, much like the transitional object, can ward off depression and anxiety. Thus Greenacre writes, "*Both the fetish and transitional object are security props which serve to bring the current anxiety-provoking situation under the illusory control of the individual infant or man*. But the fetishist becomes addicted to the use of his prop, for his dilemma is clearly due to an extraordinarily stubborn fixation and arrest of development with a special infarct in the reality sense" (my emphasis, 321). (Gosselin and Wilson have, likewise, called attention to the fetish object's magical power to relieve stress and anxiety. In their book, the wife of a fetishist explains, "'John builds up tension from his work a bit, and sometimes the strain shows. But if I go upstairs and slip into one of the special dresses he bought me, the tension just flows out of him like melted butter.' [John confirmed this, adding that to him the material was 'partly arousing, partly relaxing—though I don't suppose you'd understand that.']" [44].) So Thomas Hudson's obsessive cat-petting and erotic tonsorial dreams are more than mere kinky quirks of his character unrelated to the plot of *Islands in the Stream*; rather, they are expressions of, and defenses against, his profound loneliness and depression after the loss of his ex-wife and three sons. Likewise, we can now understand why the American girl in "Cat in the Rain" so desperately wants a cat or long hair; she imagines that either object could be used somehow to alleviate her sense of loss and depression.

The fetish object's status as a "security prop" partially explains why, aside from superstition, Hemingway carried a rabbit's (or "hare's") foot during his Paris years. In *A Moveable Feast*, Hemingway remembers, "For luck you carried a horse chestnut and a rabbit's foot in your right pocket. The fur had been worn off the rabbit's foot long ago and the bones and the sinews were polished by wear. The claws scratched in the lining of your pocket and you knew your luck was still there" (91). A few pages later, he adds: "I felt the rabbit's foot in my pocket guiltily. . . . *In those days you did not really need anything, not even the rabbit's foot, but it was good to feel it in your pocket*" (my emphasis, 96). Together the rabbit's/hare's foot and horse chestnut form a rather suggestive unit—a sort of magical pocket phallus capable of warding off loneliness, anxiety, depression, and danger. Greenacre, in fact, has suggested that it is precisely in such lucky pieces that the fetish and the transitional object merge, and Hemingway was never without a charm in his pocket (Hotchner 61). In *The Garden of Eden*, Catherine plucks an olive out of her drink, chews it, and hands the pit to David: "Semiprecious stone. . . . Put it in your pocket." A few lines later she laments, "I wish I could remember what it was we lost" (118). In *Across the River*, Cantwell carries two "stones" in his pocket (Renata's emeralds) to ward off loneliness and fingers them with a hand that bears the stigmata of castration. And now we can finally understand Robert Jordan's otherwise inexplicable response to wartime anxiety in *For Whom the Bell Tolls*. Waiting before the assault on the bridge, Jordan watches a squirrel clatter down the trunk of a tree. "Robert Jordan looked down through the pines to the sentry box again. *He would like to have had the squirrel with him in his pocket. He would like to have had anything that he could touch*" (my emphasis, 433). But in addition to explaining such literary tidbits, an understanding of the relation between fetishism, depression, and loss may explain why Hemingway's fetishism grew more flagrant as he aged (witness *The Garden of Eden*); as Hemingway's depressive phases grew in intensity (normal behavior for a mood disorder, particularly when it is "self-medicated" with alcohol), his fetishistic defenses grew in intensity to compensate.

An appreciation for the relation between fetishism, depression, and loss also invites a rereading of one of Hemingway's most famous stories: "Soldier's Home."

A Fetishist's Home

> There were so many good-looking young girls. Most of them had their hair cut short. . . . They all wore sweaters and shirt waists with round Dutch collars. It was a pattern. . . . He liked the round Dutch collars above their sweaters. He liked their silk stockings and flat shoes. He liked their bobbed hair and the way they walked. . . . He did not want them themselves really. They were too complicated. There was something else. . . . He liked the pattern. It was exciting.
>
> —*"Soldier's Home"*

Traditionally understood as a story about post-traumatic stress disorder—or at least post-war malaise—and superficially intended to be exactly that, "Soldier's Home" in fact offers a fictionalized account of the onset of Hemingway's fetishism.

Virtually indistinguishable from the Nick Adams of so many of Hemingway's short stories, Harold Krebs, whose name is perhaps intended to distance him from the author who is often so difficult to distinguish from Nick, hails from Oklahoma, Hemingway's oft-used substitute for his native Oak Park (*Oak*-la-*home*-a).[22] An enlisted Marine returned from the First World War long after "the greeting of [mostly drafted] heroes was over," Harold, "who had been at Belleau Wood, Soissons, the Champagne, St. Mihiel and in the Argonne," at first finds it difficult to talk about the war—only to find that by the time he finally *is* ready to talk no one cares to hear about it anymore (*SS* 145).

> Krebs found that to be listened to at all he had to lie, and after he had done this twice he, too, had a reaction against the war and against talking about it. A distaste for everything that had happened to him in the war set in because of the lies he had

told. All of the times that had been able to make him feel cool
and clear inside himself when he thought of them . . . now lost
their cool, valuable quality and *then were lost themselves*. . . .
    Krebs acquired the nausea in regard to experience that is
the result of untruth or exaggeration, and when he occasionally
met another man who had really been a soldier and they talked
a few minutes in the dressing room at a dance he fell into the
easy pose of the old soldier among other old soldiers: that he
had been badly, sickeningly frightened all the time. *In this way
he lost everything*." (my emphasis, 145–146)

Suffering from this loss and a general ennui, Harold sleeps in
late, wanders about town, reads until he is bored, and then
dozes some more. Meanwhile, his parents grow worried.
    From the importance given to the theme of post-war psychic
trauma in Hemingway's work—particularly in such Nick Adams
stories as "Now I Lay Me" and "A Way You'll Never Be"—one
might suspect along with Philip Young, Denis Brian, and Malcolm Cowley that Hemingway, himself, suffered from post-traumatic stress disorder. Yet Michael Reynolds and James Nagel
convincingly contend that Hemingway demonstrated none of the
traditional signs of "shell shock" after his wounding at Fossalta:
"Agnes von Kurowsky, who treated Hemingway virtually every
day, and Henry Villard, who was in the room next to him in August of 1918, and who talked with him at length, saw no sign of
shell shock whatever. Indeed, they remember him as being almost incessantly cheerful" (Villard & Nagel 214). Thus Nagel argues that instead of writing from personal experience
Hemingway probably read about cases of shell shock and "found
them an intriguing metaphor for the cultural destruction Western civilization had just experienced" (214). Nagel's case is persuasive, and to be sure, Harold Krebs, an enlisted Marine who
fought in France and whose father works in the real estate business, is hardly a simple portrait of the artist as a young man.
Nevertheless, while Hemingway probably never suffered from
shell shock, he may very well have *thought* that he did.
    If, as I have suggested, Hemingway's fetishism manifested
itself after the ego-threatening and symbolically castratory explosion at Fossalta, and if his clinical depression first manifested itself soon after his loss of Agnes and return to America,
Hemingway may very well have felt that the war left him a bit
"crazy." Crazy or not, after his break with Agnes, he was cer-

tainly depressed, and he responded to this depression in a manner which Winnicott would have easily understood. According to Marcelline's memoir, Ernest, who moped about the house much like Krebs, "usually . . . had his Red Cross knitted cover spread over him on top of his other bedclothes. . . . He didn't like to be without his cover somewhere around. When we asked him why, he said it kept him from being so homesick for Italy" (Sanford 178).[23] It may also have kept him from missing so desperately the Red Cross nurse, Agnes.

While Krebs doesn't reach for a transitional object, he *does* reach for the fetish. Somehow the war has impaired his ability to deal with women. He likes various aspects of feminine garb, but like all "perverts" according to Masud Khan, he must place an *impersonal object* between himself and the object of his desire. Krebs can no longer deal with the local girls as *people*:

> Nothing was changed in the town except that the young girls had grown up. But they lived in such a complicated world of already defined alliances and shifting feuds that Krebs did not feel the energy or the courage to break into it. He liked to look at them, though. There were so many good-looking young girls. Most of them had their *hair cut short.* When he went away only little girls wore their hair like that or girls that were fast. They all wore *sweaters* and shirt waists with round *Dutch collars. It was a pattern.* He liked to look at them from the front porch as they walked on the other side of the street. He liked to watch them walking under the shade of the trees. *He liked the round Dutch collars above their sweaters.* He liked their *silk stockings* and flat shoes. *He liked their bobbed hair* and the way they walked. . . . *He did not want them themselves really. They were too complicated. There was something else.* (my emphasis SS 147)

Though he vaguely wants a girl, Krebs feels that he couldn't stomach the lies necessary to court one. "Besides," he tells himself, "he did not really need a girl. The army had taught him that. It was all right to pose as though you had to have a girl. Nearly everybody did that. But it wasn't true. You did not need a girl. That was the funny thing" (147). Men posed as if they could get along without women, or posed as if they had to have a woman all the time: "That was all a lie. It was all a lie both ways. You did not need a girl unless you thought about them" (148). Krebs remembers the French and German girls fondly, since conversation with them had never been a concern. "But here at home it was all too complicated. . . . He liked the girls that were walking along the other side of the street. He liked them much better than the French girls or the German girls. . . . *They were such a nice pattern. He liked the pattern. It was exciting.* But he would not go through all the talking" (my emphasis, 148).

One look at the "pattern" that Krebs finds so "exciting"— bobbed hair, silk stockings, sweaters, and round Dutch collars (Ernest and his sister shared "Dutch boy" haircuts for much of their youth, and Ernest's mother had been fond of calling him her "little Dutch dolly")—reveals that Krebs's alienation from the local girls rests on something more than his experience as a soldier which he could never explain and which they presumably would never want to hear about or would never be able to understand. While Krebs's fetishism defends against his depression, it places an impersonal object between himself and the object of his desire, thereby alienating him from the local girls. Like all fetishists, Krebs can't risk an unmediated intimacy that might render him vulnerable to further loss. As Joyce McDougall explains, perversion is the "very essence of independence from others and self-sufficiency," but it thereby "creates loneliness and the need to make sexuality into a desperate game" (187).

There is, however, at least one local girl with whom Krebs can talk: his tomboyish little sister. When Harold goes down to breakfast, his sister greets him, "Well, *Hare*, . . . You old sleepyhead. What did you ever get up for?" (my emphasis, 149). Explaining that there will be a softball game that day, she tells her brother, "I can pitch better than lots of the boys. I tell them all you taught me. The other girls aren't much good." "Yeah?" Harold responds.

> "I tell them you're my beau. Aren't you my beau, Hare?"
> "You bet."
> "Couldn't your brother really be your beau just because he's your brother?"
> "I don't know."
> "Sure you know. Couldn't you be my beau, Hare, if I was old enough and if you wanted to?"
> "Sure. You're my girl now. . . ."
> "Will you love me always?"
> "Sure." (150)

But a little later when Krebs' mother asks much the same question, she gets a very different answer. After encouraging her son to do something with his life, she pleads, "Don't you love your mother, dear boy?"

> "No," Krebs said.
> His mother looked at him across the table. Her eyes were shiny. She started crying.
> "I don't love anybody," Krebs said.
> It wasn't any good. He couldn't tell her, he couldn't make her see it. It was silly to have said it. He had only hurt her. He went over and took hold of her arm. She was crying with her head in her hands.
> "I didn't mean it, he said. "I was just angry at something. I didn't mean I didn't love you."
> His mother went on crying. Krebs put his arm on her shoulder.
> "Can't you believe me, mother?"
> His mother shook her head.
> "Please, please, mother. Please believe me."
> "All right," his mother said chokily. She looked up at him. "I believe you, Harold."
> *Krebs kissed her hair.* (my emphasis, 152)

"I'm your mother," Mrs. Krebs explains. "I held you next to my heart when you were a tiny baby." Feeling "sick and vaguely nauseated," Krebs consoles her, "I know, Mummy. . . . I'll try to be a good boy for you" (152).

Krebs's "nausea" here, which clearly echoes the "nausea in regard to experience that is the result of untruth or exaggeration" mentioned earlier in the story (146), and his realization that his mother "had made him lie" place this final scene squarely within the broader context of the story's thematic interest in lies (153). In fact, "Soldier's Home" could fairly be described as a story about lies, depression, and alienation. Like so many other war-scarred Hemingway heroes, Krebs craves simplicity and order, a "life without consequences," and mistakenly comes to believe that both will follow from a strict adherence to the truth. But a look at Krebs's reasons for initially telling his two war-related lies complicates this quest for simplicity and reveals much about his motives for supposedly refusing to lie at the end of the story.

Krebs returns from the war depressed and alienated, unwilling or unable to talk about his experiences. Yet when he finally *is* ready to talk, presumably to ease his depression and break down the walls of his isolation, no one, not even his mother, is prepared to listen. Krebs then tells his lies not so much to deck himself with borrowed glories as simply to be listened to. When he finds, however, that this only causes him to "lose everything," thereby deepening his depression, he stops telling lies. Thus, though he vaguely wants a girl, he refuses to lie to get one and instead combats his depression, at the cost of confirming his isolation, by taking whatever fetishistic and voyeuristic pleasure he can find in watching girls from a distance. In the story's final scene, it is partly Krebs's ironic desire to be *understood*, to be integrated instead of alienated, that drives him to tell his mother the alienating "truth" that he no longer loves anybody; only when he realizes that his mother can't understand him and that he cannot bridge the chasm between them does he give in and "lie" to her, telling her that he didn't mean it when he said he didn't love her. However, as the quotation marks around "truth" and "lie" imply, I find the relationship between truth and falsehood in the final scene more complex than the story would superficially suggest.

If the "truth" is that Krebs "[doesn't] love anybody," why did he tell his little sister only a few minutes before that he would love her forever? And why didn't he complain that his sister had forced him to lie? Either Krebs lied to his sister, or his initial response to his mother's question—not his retraction—was a lie. The story clearly asks us to consider Krebs's retraction the lie forced upon him by his mother, but what if Krebs's real lie is his *denial* of his love for his mother? What if this denial symbolizes the very depression and alienation that plagues him and remains unresolved at the story's conclusion? Such an either/or logic is probably misplaced; one can easily imagine Hemingway's response: "Hell, this love or hate your mother thing is too simple"—not because the focus on the mother is misplaced in this instance, but because a better response has been offered by Krebs in another context: "It was all a lie both ways." Love and hate, revenge and reparation, in this instance are too inextricably mixed for simple "truth." Whatever the case, Krebs's nickname, "Hare," and his fascination with *silk* stockings, short hair, sweaters, and Dutch collars—not to mention the final benedictory kiss that he bestows upon his mother's hair—all bespeak a deep and abiding attachment to his mother of which Krebs is no longer aware.

The theme of incest, implied by the playful banter between Krebs and his sister, might be taken as further evidence—however displaced—of Krebs's attachment to his mother, but it more clearly alludes to the fetishistically-invested presence of the sister who replaced Grace as the early object of Ernest's narcissistic identification. As has long been recognized, brother-sister romance is one of the dominant themes of Hemingway's fiction. We find it in Littless's desire to marry her brother and have his child in "The Last Good Country." We find it again in the lovers of *For Whom the Bell Tolls* and *The Garden of Eden* who look enough alike to be brother and sister. And we find it in "The Battler," where the blond-haired ex-fighter, Ad, has gone crazy after marrying a woman who may or may not have been his sister, but who looked enough like him "to be his own twin" (SS 137). In relating this story to Nick, Bugs at first calls her Ad's sister, but he later "corrects" himself: "Of course they wasn't brother and sister no more than a *rabbit* . . ." (my emphasis, 137). As we now know, however, "what looks like rabbit is cat," and both are inseparable from hare/hair. Thus, it should come as no surprise to learn that Ernest's memories of his sister Marcelline, like his memories of Grace, are inextricably tied to the language of his fetishism—a fact which will figure prominently in my next chapter.

Ebony and Ivory:
Hemingway's Fetishization of Race

Ebony

Isn't it nice our dark things are so simple and so complicated too?

—*The Garden of Eden* Manuscript

In 1950, reminiscing about his youth in Paris, then a quarter of a century behind him, Ernest Hemingway, using the clipped "pseudo-primitive" language he was so fond of in his later years,[1] told his friend and crony A. E. Hotchner a curious yarn about one of his adventures at the club, *Le Jockey*:

> Was in there one night with Don Ogden Stewart and Waldo Pierce when the place was set on fire by the most sensational woman anybody ever saw. Or ever will. Tall, coffee skin, ebony eyes, legs of paradise, a smile to end all smiles. Very hot night but she was wearing a coat of black fur, her breasts handling the fur like it was silk. She turned her eyes on me—she was dancing with the big British gunner subaltern who had brought her—but I responded to the eyes like a hypnotic and cut in on them. The subaltern tried to shoulder me out but the girl slid off him and onto me. Everything under that fur instantly communicated with me. I introduced myself and asked her name. "Josephine Baker," she said. We danced nonstop for the rest of the night. She never took off her fur coat. Wasn't until the joint closed she told me she had nothing on underneath. (Hotchner 52–53)

Hemingway of course, like so many writers, was a notorious liar. Famous both for mythologizing his genuinely remarkable life and for trying to live up to that myth, Hemingway, in spite of his reputation as a hard-boiled realist, was frequently less than diligent when it came to distinguishing between fantasy and reality in his own life. His evening with Josephine Baker, reeking as it does of the men's locker room and stale detective novels, is surely one of his lies. Baker's 1925 debut in *La Revue Nègre* had made the exotic African-American dancer literally an overnight sensation in Paris; Hemingway could not have failed to recognize her. Hemingway's major biographers apparently agree, for none of them even allude to the story, much less credit it.[2]

The Baker story *does*, however, bear a more than suspicious resemblance to a passage in Hemingway's heavily autobiographical story, "The Snows of Kilimanjaro." Gangrenous and dying in remote Africa, Harry recalls his trip to Constantinople years before, and how, angry with his wife and lonely for an earlier love, he had slept with "a hot Armenian slut" whom he "took away from" a "British gunner subaltern" at a dance hall (*SS* 65). Hemingway, like Harry, quarreled with his wife before his 1922 trip to Constantinople to cover the Greco-Turkish war, but whether the story about the Armenian woman has its origin in fact or fantasy is unclear.[3] If the passage is pure fiction, we are left wondering why Hemingway felt inclined first to invent it and then to pass it off as the truth in another guise. If, on the other hand, the passage is grounded in autobiographical truth, its connection to the Baker story does more than demonstrate how Hemingway used the raw material of his life to forge fiction only to use that fiction to reinterpret and fictionalize his life (a process that bedeviled him and continues to bedevil all but the most careful of his critics). By now we should be able to explain a good deal of the symbolism in the two passages—for instance, the special status of Constantinople for Hemingway, or the significance of Baker's breasts "handling the fur like it was silk"—but troubling questions remain. Why does Hemingway substitute Josephine Baker for the "Armenian slut," and why the attention to her dark skin, "ebony eyes," and her nakedness beneath the fur? Why the gunner subaltern, and why does Hemingway compare himself to a "hypnotic"? If, as Byron in a Freudian mood once quipped, a lie "'tis but / The truth in masquerade," what do we ultimately make of these details of the Baker fantasy?

There is surely nothing so extraordinary in a man's comically cliché-ridden fantasy about a beautiful woman, but Hemingway's fabricated evening with the beautiful, dark-skinned, short-haired, fur-clad Baker seems to be something more than this; it reads like a Freudian "screen memory," a distillation of the raw stuff of Hemingway's daydreams. Perhaps we should not be surprised to discover, then, that the concerns of Hemingway's fantasy bear a remarkable resemblance to those of one of his major projects of the forties and fifties, the posthumously published, fantasy-laden novel, *The Garden of Eden*. The Baker story in fact reads like a crystallization of those concerns—concerns which, if understood psychoanalytically, clarify, without resolving, indeterminacies central to the dynamics of *The Garden of Eden*—concerns which, moreover, both invoke and clarify an eroticization of race by white male authors which has inspired studies of American literature from Leslie Fiedler's seminal 1948 essay, "'Come Back to the Raft Ag'in, Huck Honey!'" to Toni Morrison's recent and equally important *Playing in the Dark* (1992).

In an essay devoted to *The Garden of Eden* in *Playing in the Dark*, Morrison herself explores some of these concerns brilliantly—as do Comley and Scholes in *Hemingway's Genders*. But with a psychoanalytic understanding of fetishism and with archival evidence unavailable to Morrison, I hope to extend her analysis into new territory and to clarify how the socio-psychology she explores, a psychology by which American authors have traditionally defined themselves as "white" and "male" in relation to an insistent and ever-present racial and sexual otherness, relates to the individual psychology of Hemingway. Moved by a distaste for reductivism, Comley and Scholes explicitly avoid a psychoanalytic interpretation of Hemingway's work, opting instead to study Hemingway's unique deployment of *cultural* codes. Yet by employing some of Hemingway's *personal* codes, I hope to show precisely how a psychoanalytic reading can be useful *without* being reductive. Thus I use psychoanalysis not to reveal a "*deeper*," *more real*, or *essential* truth about my subject (for I realize that no such thing exists), but rather to reveal a different, more theorizable, pattern uniting what Comley and Scholes call the "threads" of the Hemingway Text.

The "sea changes" undergone by the various lovers in *The Garden of Eden* manuscript—changes which have understandably received a good deal of attention from Hemingway scholars in the past few years—involve something more than gender swapping and unisex hairstyles. Sun-tanning, an obsession which seems innocuous enough, is in fact integral to each character's sexual metamorphosis. David acknowledges as much when (in some lines which incidentally read like a gloss of Hemingway's 1931 short story "The Sea Change") he lies awake one evening pondering Catherine's transformation:

> She changes from a girl into a boy and back to a girl carelessly and happily and she enjoys corrupting me and I enjoy being corrupted. But she's not corrupt and who says it is corruption? . . . . Now we are going to be a special dark race of our own with our own pigmentation, [and we have our own tribal customs— *crossed out in the manuscript*] growing that way each day as some people would garden or plant and raise a crop. The trouble with that is that it will not grow at night too. It can only be made in the sun, in strong sun against the reflection of the sand and the sea. So we must have the sun to make this sea change. The sea change was made in the night and it grows in the night and the darkness that she wants and needs now grows in the sun. (K422.1 2.4.4)[4]

The fact that all of the major characters in *The Garden of Eden* are well-tanned, that brown skin is one of the most pervasive images in the manuscripts, that Catherine, David, and Marita spend endless hours tanning at the beach, and that Nick and Barbara even tan on the ski slopes during the winter, may seem like nothing more than a quirk of personal taste, coming from an author who spoke of his wives "when things were going well . . . in a standard phrase: they were happy, healthy, hard as a rock, and well-tanned" (Baker x). Yet in this novel, and for Catherine in particular, a tan is clearly *more* than a tan. As Morrison and Comley and Scholes have argued, the "sea change" is racial as well as sexual.

The skillfully but radically edited version of the novel published by Scribner's in 1986 mutes Hemingway's concern with race considerably, but the concern is hardly subtle in the original. Throughout the manuscripts, Catherine seems desperately concerned with being "dark enough not to be white" (K422.1 4.3.1). Tanning on the beach at le Grau du Roi, Catherine claims she wants to be as "brown as a Kanaka" (K422.1 2.1.1). In Madrid, she delights when a bootblack mistakes her for a Gypsy and when the Colonel tells her she looks like "the young chief of a warrior tribe" and calls her "the darkest white girl I've

ever seen" (K422.1 6.9.2 & *GE* 62). After waking up late one
morning, she calls herself David's "lazy naked octoroon half-
caste wife" and "wild girl" (K422.1 5.5.2).[5] She provides an ex-
ceedingly odd excuse for her jealousy about David's success as
a writer: "I can't help it any more than if I were a negro" (K422.1
2.3.3). Later she tells David, "I'm your Kanaka and when we go
to Africa I'll be your African girl too" (K422.1 2.4.1). Even David
wonders why his "wife want[s] to seem to be of a different race
and have completely different pigmentation" (K422.1 2.2.3).
When, lying in bed one night, he finally asks her why she wants
to be so dark, she gives an interesting but vague reply and
sparks an equally interesting conversation:

> "Right now it's the thing that I want most. . . . and we're so far
> along now. I don't know why I want it so much. It's like I
> wanted to have my hair cut. But this takes so long. Maybe
> that's part of it. It's like growing something. But it makes me
> excited too. Just good excited all the time. The fact that it's
> happening. Doesn't it make you excited to have me getting so
> dark?"
> "Uh-huh. I love it. . . . But we have to be careful with you."
> "You *are* so careful and good. Look how nice it is against
> the sheets with only this much light."
> "It's lovely."
> It was too and strange in the small light.
> "I don't want to be a white girl anymore and I'm half-caste
> already and I think I can be darker and it still be good. Did you
> think I could ever be this dark?"
> "No because you're blonde."
> "I can because I'm lion color and they can go dark. . . . But
> I want every part of me dark and it's getting that way and you'll
> be darker than an Indian and that takes us further away from
> other people. You see why it's important. . . . I wish I had some
> Kanaka blood or some Indian blood but then it probably would-
> n't mean anything. It's the changing that is as important as the
> dark. But I'm going to be so dark you won't be able to stand it
> and you'll be helpless. White women will always bore you."

David can only reply, "They bore me already" (K422.1 2.4.3–4).
    For the others as well, a tan isn't simply a tan. Nick is de-
scribed repeatedly—by himself, by Barbara, by Andy, and by
David—as looking like a "reservation Indian." David jokes about
being a "half-assed Tahitian," and Catherine, who calls him a
"renegade Kanaka," plans to make him "darker than an Indian"

(*GE* 154 & K422.1 4.3.4). When Hemingway introduces us to the Italian heiress, Marita, she isn't only the "dark girl"; she is so dark that her skin seems almost "Javanese" (*GE* 236). And while Marita initially imagines that David might like one of his "girls lighter than the other" (*GE* 101), after constant gender-flipping drives Catherine mad, Marita decides to fill Catherine's old shoes (not to mention the bare feet of David's boyhood African "fiancée") by cutting her hair to become David's "M'Bulu girl" (K422.1 36.25). In David's opinion, she ends up looking more like "a Bizerte street urchin" or "waterfront Arab," but he assures her, "You do look like Africa. . . . But the very far north and you mix up the genders" (K422.1 36.1).

This racial transformation, like all aspects of the "sea change" the characters undergo after seeing Rodin's statue, *The Metamorphoses of Ovid*, is radically overdetermined, partaking of manifold cultural, literary, and psychological associations and numerous—almost always troubling—racial stereotypes. On the surface, both Catherine and Marita want to fill in for David's boyhood African sweetheart. But Hemingway also clearly associates racial otherness with a primitivism that must have struck him as only appropriate for his theme: the Garden of Eden. When Andy tries to relate the story of Nick and Barbara, he insists that the "things they did were primitive. . . . It was all very primitive" (K422.2 40.inserts.10). Lurking behind Andy's assertion are all of the stereotypes by which the West has traditionally constructed the "primitive" as something "original," "simple," "spontaneous," and "pure," yet simultaneously "mysterious," "lustful," "irrational," and "defiled" (Torgovnick 19; 80). This interest in the "primitive," however, is as characteristically modernist as it is Edenic. In a sense, the wealthy white woman Catherine, who expresses an interest in the "primitive" art of Picasso, plays at being a Kanaka much like whites played at being black in their visits to the nightclubs of Harlem in the twenties and thirties.

Yet Catherine isn't *simply* playing, nor is she searching for some sort of Laurentian or Andersonian mythical authenticity lying just beyond the color-line; she sees her dark skin as an integral part of her identity. When the Colonel asks her what she plans to do with her tan, she replies: "Wear it. . . . It's very becoming in bed. . . . I don't really wear it. It's me. I really am this dark. The sun just develops it. I wish I was darker" (*GE* 64). Catherine's dark skin, like that of all the other characters, signifies her alienation from "proper" (read *white*) society and her transgression of social taboos. It also clearly signifies—what Hemingway regarded as—her moral "darkness," a moral darkness in us all just waiting to be "developed." If Catherine's insistence on being "Kanaka" clearly connects her to the supposedly innocent, Edenic, sexually-liberated, tropical islands of Margaret Mead's Pacific, it also carries an implicit threat so long as we remember Captain Cook's reputed fate at the hands of cannibal Kanakas. And while Catherine's honorary status as a Kanaka links her to Richard Henry Dana's Kanaka companion, Hope, likewise a sick friend who must be cared for, her darkness may as well link her to the Babo of Melville's "Benito Cereno," the supposedly subservient partner who, like Bugs in Hemingway's story "The Battler," in fact commands the ship. Yet the obvious titillation she derives from tanning, her repeated insistence that her tan looks wonderful in *bed*, and her tendency to link her obsession for tanning to that obvious signifier of gender status in *The Garden of Eden*, her obsession for haircutting, all suggest (as do Morrison and Comley and Scholes) that Catherine's racial transformation also has to be read as part and parcel of her psychosexual transformation.

Ivory

I am happy because I have [a] little African fetish from Angola. It is very beautiful and gives me pleasure.

—*Hemingway, random notes, 1923*

"Do you remember when all I wanted was to be so dark and now I'm the darkest white girl in the world?"
"And the blondest. You're just like ivory. That's how I always think. You're smooth as ivory too."

—Catherine and David, *The Garden of Eden*

According to Leslie Fiedler, "When . . . the [white male] American writer does not make impotence itself his subject, he is left to choose between the two archetypes of innocent [racially charged] homosexuality and unconsummated incest: the love of comrades and that of brother and sister" (348). Whatever we may think about the breadth of this claim, in *The Garden of*

Eden Hemingway seems to take up both of these archetypes which Fiedler aptly enough describes as "Edenic affair[s] . . . lived out in a Garden in the process of being destroyed" (351). More importantly, Hemingway takes up the two archetypes in a manner that ultimately clarifies how they form—at least in his case—part of a unified psychology.

In *The Garden of Eden*, the friendship between the native hunter, Juma, and the boy, David, in the story of the elephant hunt fits nicely (at least initially) into Fiedler's litany of innocent homoerotic (or "homosocial," to employ Eve Kosofsky Sedgwick's term) lovers, one white and the other dark: Dana and Hope; Leatherstocking and Chingachgook; Ishmael and Queequeg; Huck and Jim; Ike McCaslin and Sam Fathers. We might easily add to Fiedler's list such colonial British duos as T. E. Lawrence and Ali or Kipling's Kim and the old lama—duos which Fiedler with his American emphasis ignores but to which Hemingway plainly alludes in the *Eden* manuscript. (At one point, David and Marita imagine getting married as Mohammedans and imagine the sort of daughter they might have, a little girl who would be like both of them and like Kim in the bazaars [K422.1 36.19]). In this archetype, Fiedler explains, dark skin signifies for the white male imagination, among other things, an escape from feminine civilization and the super-ego into the mythical masculine wilderness and forbidden sexuality of the uncivilized id.

Kipling's *Kim* both exemplifies this archetype and offers a key to Hemingway's treatment of the elephant story. Kim repeatedly flees the constraints of British decorum and feminine society for the freedom of the Indian road with the beloved old Tibetan lama, changing races like a chameleon—*or like Catherine*—all the while. And in one scene, which must have appealed to Hemingway immensely, the Irish boy, Kim, has his hair cropped and his face painted by a prostitute so he can pass as a "low-caste Hindu boy" on the road, though he tells the prostitute that he does this to visit his twelve-year-old Hindu lover. (This scene, in fact, may have inspired Hemingway and Pauline to paint their own faces during their honeymoon at Le Grau du Roi in 1927, a vacation which provided much of the background for *The Garden of Eden*. According to Lynn, "While walking naked on deserted stretches of beach, the newlyweds . . . developed deep tans, which they further augmented one day by staining their faces with berry juice, for they had decided to bicycle to a local festival disguised as gypsies" [362].)[6] But even more impor-

Figure 7. Hemingway and Pauline at San Sebastian, 1927. (John F. Kennedy Library)

tantly for understanding *The Garden of Eden*, the power of male homosocial bonding in Kipling's novel is conveyed most poignantly in the old lama's comparison of himself and the boy to the two elephants who save one another in Buddhist legend, Shakyamuni and his disciple Ananda in earlier lives. Hemingway, moreover, evidently recognized the homoerotic undertow of this bonding: "Andy do you believe it about women for breeding, boys for pleasure, and melons for delight?" Catherine asks. "I always thought of it as everything that Kipling left out. . . . Imagine how he would have been with all that in. Sometimes it's almost there but then it moves away. He knew it for a while and then he was ashamed of it" (K422.1 6.9.14).

In *The Garden of Eden*, the old lama's parable lurks behind the story the adult David writes of the old elephant's return to the bones of his long-deceased friend and partly explains the boy David's break with his father and Juma, the "god damned friend killers" (*GE* 198). The elephant's final charge, which almost kills Juma, who "had always been David's best friend and had taught him to hunt," seems a sort of wish fulfillment aimed both at Juma and, indirectly, at David's father, signifying a failure, or rejection, of the homosocial bonding of Fiedler's archetype (*GE* 171). David more or less admits as much when he says he wishes the elephant had killed Juma. His anger might even display a touch of homoerotic jealousy; he thinks to himself, "Juma will drink his share of the ivory or just buy himself another god damn wife" (*GE* 181). Through his identification with the elephant, homoeroticism becomes for David inextricably linked with death—either his father's or his own at the hands of his father. It is linked as well with a sort of primal repression: "I'm going to keep everything a secret always," he tells himself. "Never tell anyone anything again" (*GE* 181).

Gender affiliation, however, is never stable in this novel, and the old bull elephant who becomes David's "hero" and "brother" in the place of his father and Juma is symbolically as feminine as it is masculine. Thus, the killing of the elephant with his oversized tusks, which the adult David clearly associates with the "ivory"-haired Catherine, and David's subsequent boyhood rejection of his father and Juma, force the adult David into Fiedler's second archetype, a pseudo-incestuous love for a woman whom he calls "brother," and who thinks she's a "boy" (or a "girl and a boy both"), but who looks enough like him to be his "*sister*"—a love which recovers the lost object represented by the elephant while blending innocence with an overwhelming sense of sin (*GE* 192; 6).[7] David may jokingly assure Marita (whose brother "was in love with her") that he "never minded incest if it was in the same family," but he can never entirely shake the feelings of "corruption" and "remorse" which follow his sexual experiments with Catherine (K422.1 33.22). Yet if Hemingway manages to link both of Fiedler's archetypes, one nevertheless suspects, given what we have learned about his psychosexuality, that the connection he establishes has little, if anything, to do with any sort of Jungian collective unconscious and quite a lot to do with the vicissitudes of his own boyhood.

A work of as much importance to the background of *The Garden of Eden* as *Kim* is Proust's *Remembrance of Things Past*, which Catherine is reading in the Madrid section of the novel. True to form, she skips immediately to book four, *Sodome et Gomorrhe*. The biblical allusion to the cities of the plain is rich enough in itself, suggesting a homoerotic and "perverse" parallel for the more epistemophilic/narcissistic/oedipal loss of Eden.[8] (In *The Garden of Eden* manuscript, we might recall, Nick is afraid that his haircut makes him look like a "sodomite," so, using what he calls an "Indian trick," he hides his hair under his hat.)[9] The connection to Proust is important, however, not only for the allusion to sodomy, not only because Proust shares Hemingway's interest in male and female homosexuality, not only for the weight Proust gives to loss and the impermanence of love, but also for what it suggests about the importance of involuntary unconscious memories (both David's and Hemingway's) in the genesis of *The Garden of Eden*—a suggestion further underscored by still another book on David's and Catherine's reading lists: W. H. Hudson's memoir of his boyhood, *Far Away and Long Ago*. Moreover, it may be no coincidence that Hemingway uses *Marcel* Proust to allude to these unconscious memories, since, as we shall see, they are deeply concerned with his sister, *Marcel*line.

As Toni Morrison and Marianna Torgovnick have so convincingly demonstrated, white male authors have traditionally constituted and shored up their own egos in dialectical relation to racial and sexual "otherness," but Hemingway seems to have been particularly driven to do so due to an intensely fragile ego troubled by his own remembrance of things past. David's attachment to the "African girl" of his boyhood (excised from the published novel)—like the hero's attachment to "first loves" elsewhere in Hemingway's work—suggests a fascination with "original love objects" more complex than simple nostalgia. (In the manuscript, David returns to his African "fiancée" after the elephant hunt. Marita and Catherine both try to emulate this African girl, and Catherine is jealous of her firstness in David's heart.) And if Hemingway's concerns strike us as "archetypal," I would like to suggest that, aside from his sheer verbal artistry, some element of Hemingway's vast cultural appeal may reside

precisely in how the psychosocial dilemmas of his age—an age
in which many of his white male compatriots felt challenged by
the rising power of racial and sexual "others"—found a magni-
fied mirror-image in Hemingway's personal psychology.

In spite of the Conradian cultural associations revolving
about its status as the white core within the heart of darkness,
the "ivory" which symbolically links Catherine to the elephant of
David's African story was also a profoundly personal and eroti-
cally-charged symbol for Hemingway. In *Islands in the Stream*,
Hemingway gives ivory a place within his fetishistically-invested
description of the aging prostitute Honest Lil:

> She had a beautiful smile and wonderful dark eyes and lovely
> black hair. When it would begin to show white at the roots
> along the line of her forehead and along the line of the part, she
> would ask Thomas Hudson for money to have it fixed and when
> she came back from having it dyed it was as glossy and nat-
> ural-looking and lovely as a young girl's hair. She had a skin
> that was as smooth as olive-colored *ivory*, if there were olive-
> colored *ivory*. . . . (my emphasis, 273)

In a work of juvenilia entitled "The Mercenaries" (1919), the
story's protagonist spends an amorous night with an Italian
beauty with "blue-black hair and a face colored like old *ivory*"
(my emphasis, qtd. in Griffin 109). As Nick makes love to Kate in
"The Summer People," he thinks that her skin feels "like piano
keys" (*CSS* 502), and in a passage from *A Farewell to Arms*, we
find this same phrase in a description of Catherine Barkley:

> She had wonderfully beautiful hair and I would lie sometimes
> and watch her twisting it up in the light that came in the open
> door and it shone even in the night as water shines sometimes
> just before it is really daylight. She had a lovely face and body
> and lovely smooth skin too. We would be lying together and I
> would touch her cheeks and her forehead and under her eyes
> and her chin and throat with the tips of my fingers and say,
> "Smooth as piano keys," and she would stroke my chin with
> her finger and say, "Smooth as emery paper and very hard on
> piano keys." (114)

"Ivory," however, just happens to have been Ernest's boyhood
nickname for his sister Marcelline.[10] In fact, as late as 1921,
Hemingway still used the salutation "Dearest Carved Ivory" in
his letters to her (*SL* 5; 9; 49). And here, in memories of his iden-

tically-coifed sister, we have located a significant chunk of the
ivory core within Ernest's very personal, fetishistically-invested,
heart of darkness. When Catherine Bourne tells her coiffeur,
Jean, that she wants David's hair cut and dyed exactly like her
own so that the two of them will look like "brothers," or at least
"brother and sister," her instructions are explicit: Jean has to
create the "same ivory colour" (K422.1 25.2). And the magical
project is a success, for when Marita sees David's newly cut and
dyed hair, she tells him that he looks like Catherine's "twin
brother" (K422.1 26.12).

    As I have already argued, Grace Hall Hemingway's "twin-
ning" of Ernest and "Ivory," with its concomitant gender-flipping
and hair-matching, played an important role in profoundly disturbing the early formation of Hemingway's ego, gender identity,
and body-image. Having a "matching" sister must have, among
other things, prolonged and intensified Ernest's stage of primary
identification while simultaneously leading to an intense and irreconcilable need to individuate, casting doubt upon such fundamental questions as "Am I a *boy* or a *girl*?" and "What is *me*
and what is *not me*?" This upbringing seems to have given Hemingway both his tremendous ability to identify with others and
his powerful need to fend off exactly this sort of identification
through the process of objectification.

    These abilities, desires, and anxieties surface in *The Garden
of Eden* when Catherine flip-flops between genders and (like her
namesake in *A Farewell to Arms*, like Maria in *For Whom the Bell
Tolls*, and like her replacement, Marita, in *The Garden of Eden*)
tries to merge identities with her lover. She dresses like David,
talks him into having his hair cut and dyed to match her own,
and insists that she wants to be exactly like him. Such unity between lovers clearly had a symbolic and spiritual significance for
Hemingway, who apparently strove for a similar unity in his relationships with Hadley and Pauline (Diliberto 79), but it just as
clearly invokes psychosexual concerns (such as castration anxiety) which partly explain the feelings of "remorse" and "corruption" that David associates with this unity. Like infants
narcissistically trapped in the Lacanian mirror stage, David and
Catherine stare endlessly into mirrors to confirm and constitute
their body-images and egos. Their love itself is such a mirror.
Thus, when David refuses to look into a mirror after cutting and
bleaching his hair to match his wife's, he nevertheless finds that
he is talking to a mirror-image of himself. "I wish you'd look in

the glass," Catherine cajoles. "I couldn't," replies David. "Just look at me," Catherine answers. "That's how you are and I did it and there's nothing you can do now. That's how you look."

> "We couldn't really have done that," David said. "I couldn't look the way you do."
> "Well, we did," Catherine said. "And you do. So you better start to like it. . . . We're damned now. I was and now you are. Look at me and see how much you like it."
> David looked at her eyes that he loved and at her *dark face* and the incredibly *flat ivory color of her hair* and at how happy she looked and he began to realize what a completely stupid thing he had permitted. (my emphasis, *GE* 177-178)

This experiment which so disturbs David (though it also clearly excites him when first undertaken earlier in the novel), allows Hemingway to repeat, and perhaps temporarily master, the traumatic aspects of his childhood twinship with his sister, "Ivory," likewise forced upon him by a woman. Robert Stoller, for instance, hypothesizes that "a perversion is the reliving of actual historical sexual trauma aimed precisely at one's sex (an anatomical state) or gender identity (masculinity or feminity), and that in the perverse act the past is rubbed out. This time, trauma is turned into pleasure, orgasm, victory" (*Perversion* 6). More than a mere return of the repressed, David's adult twinship with his wife phallicizes Catherine (who repeatedly claims to be a "boy," or "a boy and a girl both") by equating her with a man while allowing Hemingway, through David, to experience himself as a phallic/fetishized woman, thereby shoring up the split-off feminine half of his ego with a minimum risk of castration anxiety. The attempt to incorporate an "identical" "other" represents an attempt to shore up a fragile ego, yet in this fun house of mirrors and perverse *méconnaissance* with no boundaries between the self and the other, Catherine and David seem to intensify the very gender-related and ego-related anxieties which they, or Hemingway, are trying to escape.[11]

Hemingway apparently tried to confront these anxieties like a colonial magistrate, by making color the signifier of "otherness." Yet this doesn't solve David's, or Hemingway's, problem: David himself tans like Catherine and becomes, after Catherine takes him to the coiffeur, a "white headed Indian" (K422.4 4.inserts.18). Racial differences are disavowed, and David, in a sense, becomes other than himself. Insofar as Marita allows

David to play the "sahib" or "effendi" to her "Arab street urchin,"
insofar as she promises to leave David unchanged in her attempts to look and be just like him (K422.1 35.31), she seems
less threatening than Catherine. Yet she resembles Catherine
more closely than she would have David believe. Thus when
Marita looks at David's "whitish" hair against his "dark face" she
thinks, "I wish I'd done that to him" (K422.1 36.14).

    By turning Catherine into David's "African girl," Hemingway
may allow David (who imaginatively "becomes his father" in the
process of writing the African story) to identify with his father,
the seducer of African girls, when David with his gender status
challenged needs such an identification most (GE 147). Yet as he
grows darker himself, and as Catherine tempts him to play
games with his own gender, he perhaps also becomes his father's African girl. Such narcissistic indeterminacy is all the
more frightening for Hemingway's characters since the otherness against which the ego defines itself is absolutely yoked to
sexual otherness—invoking the most terrifying aspects of masculine anxiety about body image. Thus, while Mark Spilka wonders whether the narcissism which has long been recognized in
Hemingway's fictional romances "altogether explain[s] these relations," claiming that "feminization, or better still androgyny,
might further explain them" (217), I want to suggest that what
Spilka calls "androgyny" in Hemingway's texts is largely the result of precisely such narcissistic desires and anxieties.

    In "Toward a Functional Definition of Narcissism," Robert
Stolorow describes narcissism in terms that can't help but remind us of the Bourne's fun house of love: "Narcissism refers
not to the love of oneself but to the love of one's mirror image. . . .
Narcissistic object relationships are understood as regressive ef-
forts at identity maintenance through mirroring in the object"
(199). This is precisely what Catherine explains to David (without the help or hindrance of psychoanalytic jargon) in a marvelously eerie sentence: "But now you're me, you're you so much
better" (my emphasis, K422.1 25.35). And while disturbances in
the separation-individuation stage of development, like those
suffered by Hemingway, are generally considered the source of
pathological narcissism in adults, opposite-sex twinning and
pseudo-twinning that similarly disturb the early formation of the
ego can produce similar narcissistic results.[12] Thus, in a paper
on the "Early Physical Determinants in the Development of the
Sense of Identity," Greenacre cites a version of the myth of Nar-

cissus that while quite unlike Ovid's would nevertheless have sounded remarkably familiar to Hemingway.

In his account of his second-century AD Greek travels, Pausanias describes the spring of Narcissus as follows:

> They say that Narcissus looked into this water, and not understanding that he saw his own reflection, unconsciously fell in love with himself, and died of love at the spring. But it is utter stupidity to imagine that a man old enough to fall in love was incapable of distinguishing a man from a man's reflection. There is another story about Narcissus, less popular indeed than the other, but not without some support. It is said that Narcissus had a twin sister; they were exactly alike in appearance, their hair was the same; they wore similar clothes, and went hunting together. The story goes on that Narcissus fell in love with his sister, and when the girl died, would go to the spring, knowing that it was his reflection that he saw, but in spite of this knowledge finding some relief for his love in imagining that he saw, not his own reflection, but the likeness of his sister. (Pausanias 311)

Far from being opposed to what Spilka describes as "androgyny," the sort of narcissistic opposite–sex–pseudo-twinning described by Pausanias, Greenacre argues, leads not only to a disturbance of *identity* but to a disturbance of *gender-identity* that predisposes little boys to the perversions. Socarides, in fact, claims that "the relationship to the object in all forms of perversion may be described as 'narcissistic' . . . since the object is a narcissistic one, that is, it represents the self. . . . The fetish, for example, represents the self free from disintegration and fragmentation," and like the transitional object to which it is related, "it embodies a feminine identification with the mother . . ." (84)— and sister (insofar as she, too, is an object of primary identification).

If boys frequently cope with the fragile body-images, bisexual identifications, and intensified castration anxiety that result from prolonged opposite-sex pseudo-twinning by adopting a fetish—an object which can paradoxically both stand in for and confirm the absence of the maternal or female phallus—we can begin to understand how and why Hemingway relates the themes of "androgyny," narcissistic brother-sister love, and latent homosexuality. For the fetishist, fixated at the phallic position, women must be androgynous: simultaneously "castrated" and "phallic," "other" and *not* entirely "other." *That is, the fetishist disavows not only the penisless state of women, he disavows sexual difference itself, as well as the difference between the "I" and the "other."* The fetishist's divided attitude toward his object, which corresponds to the split in his ego, results in an uneasy slippage between imagoes of "woman" that can be symbolized by the four corners of a semiotic square:

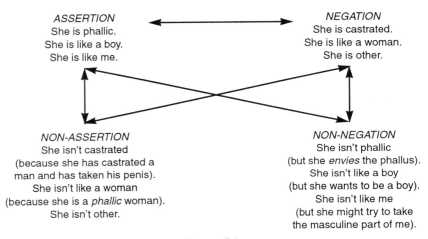

ASSERTION
She is phallic.
She is like a boy.
She is like me.

NEGATION
She is castrated.
She is like a woman.
She is other.

NON-ASSERTION
She isn't castrated
(because she has castrated a
man and has taken his penis).
She isn't like a woman
(because she is a *phallic* woman).
She isn't other.

NON-NEGATION
She isn't phallic
(but she *envies* the phallus).
She isn't like a boy
(but she wants to be a boy).
She isn't like me
(but she might try to take
the masculine part of me).

Figure 5.1

By disavowing the difference between the sexes, moreover, the fetishist disavows the distinction between hetero- and homosexuality. That is, just as one part of the fetishist's ego is hyper-aware of sexual difference while a submerged part of the ego denies this difference, so the fetishist will often be overtly homophobic while covertly suspecting himself of harboring homosexual impulses. Freud claimed that the fetish "saves the fetishist from becoming a homosexual, by endowing women with the characteristic which makes them tolerable as sexual objects" (*SE* XXI 154), but Greenacre corrects him by noting that the fetish doesn't "save" the fetishist from homosexuality so much as it prevents him from "*recognizing* his own homosexuality, since every intercourse with a woman [becomes] for him a relationship with a *phallic* woman" (my emphasis, 13). It might be even fairer to say that by endowing women with a *substitute phallus* that wards off the apparent threat of homosexuality while covertly preserving an outlet for homoerotic desire in a *female but phallic* object, the fetishist calls into question any simplistic or stable dichotomy between homo- or heterosexuality. Yet, however we settle (or unsettle) this issue, by endowing the old elephant with the enormous, overstated tusks that David associates with the "ivory"-haired Catherine, which Hemingway associated with his troublingly identical "twin" sister, Ivory, and which David's father and Juma will hack off the dead animal in an act confirming their presence/absence, David denies and displaces his own attachment to a homoerotic male bonding. The roots of the fetishism that allow him to do this, moreover, lie precisely in the narcissistic anxieties inherent in the innocent brother-sister love of "Soldier's Home," "The Last Good Country," and Fiedler's second archetype.

In *The Garden of Eden*, racial otherness and dark skin become a symbolic nexus for these issues precisely because Hemingway treats them as *fetish objects*. After all, Marita's racial transformation "mixes up the genders" (i.e., phallicizes her), and Catherine can only compare her obsession for tanning, which she links to her "lion color" and insists is like "growing something" (a female phallus we might presume?), to her obsession for haircutting.[13] Moreover, an understanding of this fetishization clarifies Hemingway's treatment of race considerably. The fetish, as a marker of both absence and presence, is an inherently paradoxical, unstable object. As Catherine, that daughter of a "dark" father and "fair" mother (*GE* 63), explains herself, her darkness would signify nothing if she were *really* Kanaka: "It's the *changing* that is as important as the dark."[14] Catherine isn't simply "the darkest white girl in the world," she is also "the blondest," with hair "just like ivory." Her dark skin always has to be counterpointed against the whiteness of sheets, her pearls, her clothes, or her hair.[15] The fetish, as imaginary female phallus, is a marker of gender difference that paradoxically somehow fails to mark exactly this difference.[16] Catherine Bourne, oscillating between boyhood and girlhood, in possession of the fetishized but *closely cut* ("phallic" yet "castrated") hair, both has and does not have the female phallus, she is both *other* than David and yet paradoxically identical to him. Her racial transformation, which is not *really* racial transformation (she both "wears" her tan and yet *really is* this dark), is the marker of precisely this difference/non-difference.

Yet Hemingway's female characters aren't the only ones to wear the fetish, and they aren't the only ones to be simultaneously phallic and castrated. In the *Eden* manuscript David stares at his own deeply tanned face in the mirror. With ivory hair nearly as light as his wife's, he almost doesn't recognize himself. On his face, he sees what seem to be "tribal scars," the remembrance of a long-ago plane crash. As he stares at his image, he tries to come to terms with his role in his sexual games with Catherine, and he realizes that he needs a haircut before going to Spain; he can't go looking like a "white headed Cherokee" (K422.1 23.insert.18). With his suntan, tribal scars, and ivory hair, David wears the fetish objects himself in what is essentially a transvestic act; that is, he identifies *himself* with the phallic woman. Thus when the "wild girl," Catherine, becomes the phallic "Peter" in bed, David *becomes* Catherine:

"Now you can't tell who is who can you?"
"No."
"You are changing," she said. "Oh you are. You are. Yes you are and you're my girl Catherine. . . ."
"You're Catherine."
"No. I'm Peter. You're my wonderful Catherine. You're my beautiful lovely Catherine. You were so good to change." (*GE* 17)[17]

Such transformations, moreover, were hardly confined to Hemingway's fiction. Like Marita, who speaks of sharing the same "tribal rules" with David, Hemingway, in the manuscripts to *A Moveable Feast*, describes his sexual and tonsorial experiments with Hadley in now familiar terms: "We lived like *savages* and kept our own *tribal* rules and had our own customs and our own standards, secrets, *taboos*, and delights" (my emphasis, qtd. in Kennedy 135). Hemingway always enjoyed pretending to be part Ojibway, and on his last trip to Africa he developed a complusion to "go native" so overwhelming that it unsettled his wife.[18] Hemingway not only appears to have had a dalliance with a Wakamba girl, Debba—whom he called his "fiancée" and compared to Nick Adam's boyhood love, Prudy—he shaved his head "to the scalp, *like a Masai girl's*," dyed his clothes various shades of Masai rusty pink ochre, developed a desire for pierced ears and tribal marks, and took up spear hunting by the light of the moon (my emphasis, Mary Hemingway 367).[19] In a letter to Slim Hayward written in late September 1953, he described himself and Mary as "*burned black by the sun*" and raved, "Wonderful African womenies. . . . Hope you won't mind me with *head shaved.* Maybe it will grow out by April. Maybe not. Let me know how you feel about *piercing of ears* and *tribal marks.* Can do to please our mob The Honest Ernies [Ernest's Wakamba spear-hunting pals], or can skip pleading The White Man's Burden" (my emphasis, ©1998, Ernest Hemingway Foundation). And in a January 1954 letter to Harvey Breit, he wrote: "*Have my head shaved because that is how my fiancée likes it.* . . . My girl is completely impudent, her face is impudent in repose, but absolutely loving and delicate rough. I better quit writing about it because I want to write it really and I mustn't spoil it. *Anyway it gives me too bad a hardon*" (my emphasis, *SL* 827). Macho spear-shaking aside, Hemingway's attempt to go native, insofar as it involved a sort of fetishistic cross-dressing, was, like David Bourne's transformation, inherently transvestic. The spear-throwing itself seems to be on some level but a playful game of *fort!/da!* through which Hemingway could attempt to master the anxiety inherent in playing the role of the phallic/castrated "Masai girl."

If such an interpretation seems far-fetched, the entries in Mary's diary from December 1953 (some of which appear in her memoir, *How It Was*) should make it much less so. On December 19, after a night of "long gay love" with Ernest, Mary recorded the following mock-interview between Papa and the reporter of "Recondite" magazine:

> "Reporter: 'Mr. Hemingway, is it true that your wife is a lesbian?'
> "Papa: 'Of course not. Mrs. Hemingway is a boy.'
> "Reporter: 'What are your favorite sports, sir?'
> "Papa: 'Shooting, fishing, reading and sodomy.'
> "Reporter: 'Does Mrs. Hemingway participate in these sports?'
> "Papa: 'She participates in all of them.'
> "Reporter: 'Sir, can you compare fishing, shooting and cricket, perhaps, with the other sports you practice?'
> "Papa: 'Young man, you must distinguish between the diurnal and the nocturnal sports. In this later category sodomy is definitely superior to fishing.'" (*How It Was* 369)

Of course, this is a joke—"to laugh at," as *The Sun Also Rises*' Georgette would remind us—but it was also something more

Figures 8 and 9: Hemingway's shaved head, Africa, 1953. (John F. Kennedy Library)

than a joke. Mary had closed a letter to Ernest written a few weeks before in Shimoni with a picture of a kitten and the following words: "Dearest—much love from half a woman—or half a boy." And the day after his mock-interview, *Ernest* made the following entry in Mary's diary:

> We decided last night to lay off all huntings and shootings today . . . and *devote the day to rest and Miss Mary's Christmas haircut.* . . . Her hair is naturally blonde to reddish golden blonde to sandy blonde. Papa loved the way it looked naturally, but Miss Mary had made him a present of saying to make her hair really blonde . . . and this made him want to have her as a *platinum blonde*, as she was at Torcello where we lived one fall and part of a winter, burnt the Beech logs in the fireplace and *made love at least every morning, noon and night* . . . and had the loveliest time Papa ever knew of. . . .[20] Loving Mary has been such a complicated and wonderful thing for over nine years. . . . Mary is . . . a prince of devils and has wonderful breasts that rise like the Chuly-Chuly hills. . . . She has the loveliest place I have ever known and almost any place you touch her it can kill both you and her. *She always wanted to be a boy and thinks as a boy without ever losing any femininity.* If you should become confused on this you should retire. *She loves me to be her girl, which I love to be, not being absolutely stupid, and also loving to be her girl since I have other jobs in the daytime. In return she makes me awards and at night we do every sort of thing which pleases her and which pleases me.* She has a skin smoother than any Chinese girl and before Miss Mary they were the loveliest girls I knew and if I had no responsibilities I would have remained with them always. Mary has never had one Lesbian impulse but has always wanted to be a boy. *Since I have never cared for any man and dislike any tactile contact with men* except the normal Spanish abrazo or embrace which precedes a departure or welcomes a return from a voyage. . . , *I loved feeling the embrace of Mary* which came to me as something quite new and *outside all tribal law.* On the night of December 19th we worked out these things and I have never been happier. EH 20/12/53.[21]

When Mary's diary resumes again in her own voice, she adds, "We had a day of *Hapana Kuwinda* [no hunting]. . . . We cut and bleached and washed my head, gay and happy."

Here we can glimpse some of the complexity behind Hemingway's desire. We can trace how he used his fetishistic relationship with Mary, a relationship mediated by earrings, ivory

Figure 10. Ernest and Mary Hemingway in Torecello, Italy, 1948. (John F. Kennedy Library, courtesy Interfoto, Venice)

hair, and tribal law, a relationship which under the pull of narcissism turns *both* partners into masculinized feminine objects,
as a defense against and substitute for the embrace of a homoerotic desire which itself stemmed in part from the dangerous
power of a feminine whose touch can "kill both you and her." It
is in this Edenic, polymorphously perverse, yet anxiety-laden,
desire that we should look for Hemingway's quarrel with what
Spilka defines more vaguely as "androgyny."[22]

If the act of writing in *Mary's* diary doesn't in itself strike us
as vaguely transvestic, it is hard to overlook Ernest's desire to be
Mary's "girl." Nor should we overlook the ensuing "earring crisis." Describing Ernest's unusual behavior some three months
after he wrote this note in her diary, Mary recalled, "For days he
had been talking about becoming 'blood brothers' with his
Wakamba friends among our servants. That night I noted cryp-
tically: 'We got home before six. Papa had started ceremonies for
face-cutting and ear-piercing'" (391).[23] Playful as this might
sound, Mary didn't find it playful then, nor did she find it playful
over a year after their return from Africa when Ernest again insisted on piercing his ears: "Writing every morning about Africa
and his native friends there, Ernest had developed a fever for
some outward sign of kinship with the Wakamba. He wanted to
have his ears pierced and wear gold earrings in them *as I did*.
Wouldn't I do the piercing for him, with a sterilized needle and
cork?" (my emphasis, 426).[24] With the aid of a note explaining to
Ernest how such behavior might affect his literary reputation,
Mary managed to put him off. The note, dated October 4, 1955,
is in the Hemingway Collection at the John F. Kennedy Library:

> Honey Papa—
>   For the well-being of both of us, I ask you please to recon-
> sider having your ears pierced. The only good that can come
> from it would be the momentary sensation you get at the time
> of the pricking, a sensation you've already had from the taking
> of blood for tests. But it could cause a variety of trouble, pri-
> marily because it would be flouting the mores of western civi-
> lization. I do not defend the modern idea that men, except for a
> few sailors, rakish fellows, do not wear earrings—but I think we
> should recognize that it exists.
>   Everything you do sooner or later gets into print, and I feel
> truly that your wearing earrings or having your ears pierced
> will have a deleterious effect on your reputation both as a
> writer and as a man. If you were a chorus boy, it wouldn't

make any difference. But you are an important man with a reputation for seeing reality and the truth more clearly than any other writer of your time. The fiction that having your ears pierced will make you a Kamba is an evasion of the reality, which is that you are not and never can be anything but an honorary Kamba, and it is out of harmony with your best character which is that of a wise, thoughtful, realistic adult white American male.

I know that you are impassioned about Africa and the Africans, writing about them, and allured by the mystery and excitement of becoming one of them. And you know that I love the fun of make-believe as much as you do. But the attempt to convert fantasy into actuality can only result, I think, in distortion and failure. There are other ways of proving brotherhood between you and the Kamba. I do hope you will find them, my Big Sweetheart—

Mary

Yet the most amazing evidence of Ernest's transvestic behavior in Africa links his cross-racial and cross-gender identifications directly to the games of Catherine and David Bourne in *The Garden of Eden*. What's more, it does so in a manner that suggests how inseparable David's African stories really are from the surrounding honeymoon narrative. On December 19, 1953, right after the mock-interview with "Recondite" magazine in Mary's diary, there is another entry in Ernest's hand that Mary didn't include in her memoir:

New Names Department.
    Mary Peter Hemingway
    Peter Mary Welsh-Hemingway
    Pedro Maria Hemingway y Welsh (for social columns of the
Diario de la Marina)
    HRH Mary Peter Welsh-Hemingway
    Lady Mary Welsh-Hemingway
    Ernest Welsh-Hemingway
    E. Kathrin Welsh
    Kathrin Ernest Hemingway
    E. K. Hemingway-Welsh
    Ernest Cathrin Inez Hemingway y Welsh (for *Diario de la
Marina*)

Just as the fetish magically transforms Catherine Bourne into "Peter," Mary has become "Peter"; just as David Bourne becomes

"Catherine," Ernest is "Kathrin." If we were looking for a smoking gun, this is it.

Only now can we adequately understand Hemingway's daydream of Josephine Baker and its relationship to "The Snows of Kilimanjaro." Baker (pronounced as "Bak*hair*" by the French) was the quintessential *garçonne* (French for "flapper"), and she was virtually an ambassador for the sexual adventurousness of bohemian Paris in the twenties. As Marjorie Garber notes, cross-dressing was a staple of Baker's shows, and Baker's associations with transvestism were "ubiquitous":

> When she danced the Charleston onstage Baker "sang in a man's voice." She described herself as having "pointed knees and the breasts of a seventeen-year-old boy." Her famous banana skirt, worn at the Folies-Bergère, is unforgettably described by Phyllis Rose as looking, when she danced, "like perky, good-natured phalluses" in "jiggling motion"; later, when she appeared with the Ziegfield Follies, the bananas had transmuted into tusks. (279)

The (ivory?) tusks (which in pictures I must admit look more like spikes to me) may be little more than a happy coincidence, but I am less inclined to find coincidence in Baker's famous pet cheetah, in her well-known eponymous product for plastering down hair (*Bakerfix*), or in the scandal surrounding her appearance in a blonde marcelled wig to sing "*Si j'étais blanche!*" a satirical song about the then new (1932) French fad for sunbathing.

In Hemingway's fantasy, Baker, the banana-skirted phallic/castrated boy/girl, is clearly more than a glamorous substitute for an anonymous racial other, the "Armenian slut," who in turn functioned as a substitute or "cure" for an original love, a fictional counterpart of the nurse Agnes von Kurowsky. Instead of meeting his dream girl in *Harry* Walden's Constantinople, which Hemingway associated with his own transvestic memories of post-head-lice baldness and skirted Greek soldiers, Ernest meets Baker at *Le Jockey*, a club that Robert McAlmon equated with transgressive sexuality. He replaces the "Armenian slut" with a short-haired beauty whose breasts "handle" her fur coat as if it were "*silk*," and whose "coffee skin" and "*ebony*" eyes throw her *ivory* smile into bright relief. (If my interpolation of the word "ivory" seems like an interpretive stretch, we might recall that, in *A Farewell to Arms*, Catherine Barkley's skin "like piano

Figure 11. The phallic woman personified. Josephine Baker in her celebrated banana skirt
(courtesy of Bryan Hammond's private collection).

keys" is chafed by Frederic's "emery" beard. "Emery" here seems
to encode the linguistic slippage "ebony," establishing a contrast
of color as well as a contrast of texture.) When Hemingway, driven by a "hypnotic" unconscious attraction, "*cuts in*" on Baker,
separating her from the big phallic gunner subaltern, he confirms her psychosexual "castration"; yet Baker, perhaps like
Hemingway's "*hard-as-rock*" wives, functions as a walking—or,
rather, dancing—fetish. Hemingway's daydream of her "coffee
skin," short hair, boyish breasts, and "coat of black fur," not
only collapses his favorite fetishes into a single icon, it exposes
the very nature of the fetish—it is that which like Baker's fur
coat both stands in for and conceals a *lack*, the "nothing under-

Figure 12. The fantasy of the phallic woman meets the object of racial and tonsorial fetishism. An advertisement for Baker's eponymous hair-dressing product, designed to plaster hair down as if it were painted on with black shellac. This product was well-known in France and remained on the market for over thirty years. (Photograph courtesy of Bryan Hammond's private collection.)

neath." Beneath Hemingway's tie to this phallic presence and absence, beneath the narcissistic tension between his insepara-bility from Baker with whom he dances all night and his contra-dictory need to objectify her entirely, beneath the noun-clipping pseudo-primitive language which allows him to transvestically "go native" in the very act of telling his story, lurk memories of a lost "nurse," memories of the maternal breast and transitional object (Baker's breasts beneath the fur), memories of Heming-way's mother ("Silky Sockey"), memories of his sister ("Ivory"), memories of cross-dressing (the Greek Evzones), and memories of a castration threat and the threat of bodily disintegration (Hemingway's shaved head and Harry Walden's gangrene). In short, this dazzlingly economical screen memory single-hand-edly illustrates Sylvia Payne's maxim: "A study of what the fetish means to the fetishist" indeed reveals that "every component of the infantile sexual instinct has some connection with the fetish object."[25]

Bisexuality, Splitting, and the Mirror of Manhood

Reading *The Rift*

"Anybody may crack."

—Catherine Barkley in *A Farewell to Arms*

They held each other and he could feel himself start to be whole again. He had not known just how greatly he had been divided and separated because once he started to work he wrote from an inner core which could not be split nor even marked nor scratched. He knew about this and it was his strength since all the rest of him could be riven.

—*The Garden of Eden*

"There's two of me and there are the two of you. You and Nicky. Nicky makes three because I made him two. . . . At first I thought it would be nicer if you could be two. . . . But now I know better."

—Barbara Sheldon to Andrew Murray
The Garden of Eden Manuscript

Of the three memoirs overtly alluded to in *The Garden of Eden* manuscripts, Marcel Proust's *A Remembrance of Things Past*, W. H. Hudson's *Far Away and Long Ago*, and David Bourne's *The Rift*, the significance of the latter is surely the most difficult to assess. The barely mentioned product of an entirely fictional author, David's first novel is a remembrance of things past, recalling his boyhood long ago and far away in East Africa. Other than the fact that David's father figures in the sad novel, and the implication that his "African girl" does as well, we have little more than the title to work with. Yet this is suggestive enough. Most obviously, the title fuses East Africa's Great Rift Valley with the rift between David and his father (likewise the subject of the elephant story), but it may as well allude to the rift separating David from his "African girl," the narcissistically-invested "first love" whom Catherine and Marita strive to replicate by transforming themselves into David's "M'Bulu girls" or "Somali wives." Yet more importantly, I would argue that it invokes an even more profound rift—a rift at David's point of origin—a primary rift in his sense of gender identity and in the basic structure of his ego—a rift shared by each of the novel's characters and by Hemingway himself, and one of fundamental importance to any interpretation of *The Garden of Eden* and to any understanding of the figure beginning to emerge from the recent reconsiderations of Hemingway's sexuality.

On some level David Bourne clearly functions as a proxy for his creator, and, thus, it is no coincidence that the discussion of *The Rift* is prompted by confusion about David's place of birth, a site symbolically riven between Oklahoma and East Africa. Catherine, Marita, and David are all lunching one afternoon in the south of France when Catherine jokingly complains that Marita "spends money like a drunken oil-lease Indian." "Are they nice?" Marita asks in her childlike manner. "David will tell you about them," Catherine explains. "He comes from Oklahoma." But this information surprises Marita:

> "I thought he came from East Africa."
> "No. Some of his ancestors escaped from Oklahoma and took him to East Africa when he was very young."
> "It must have been very exciting."
> "He wrote a novel about being in East Africa when he was a boy."
> "I know."
> "You read it?" David asked her.
> "I did," she said. ["It's called *The Rift*."][1] "Do you want to ask me about it?"
> "No," he said. "I'm familiar with it."
> "It made me cry," the girl said. "Was that your father in it?"
> "Some ways."
> "You must have loved him very much."
> "I did." (*GE* 111)

Figure 13. In Oak Park, Ernest and Marcelline, in matching dresses and hats, take their baby sister Ursula for a stroll, September 1902. (John F. Kennedy Library)

This division between Africa and Oklahoma reflects a real gender-inflected split in Hemingway's childhood between winters spent in his native domestic, suburban, Oak Park—where his pseudo-twinship with Marcelline was characterized by matching dresses—and summers spent in the "manly," Indian-inhabited, wilds of Michigan—where matching dresses more often gave way to matching overalls and Huck Finn-style straw hats. Writing of Hemingway and Nick Adams, for instance, Jackson Benson has argued that

> the gentility of the Hemingways, like the gentility of the Oak Parks of America, was based largely on female-inspired standards of conduct. Typically, in the youth of Ernest Hemingway, all those aspects of masculinity associated with aggressive male behavior were either held in abeyance or transferred to more "appropriate" locations. All the basic aspects of living—birth, sex, and death—are discovered in the Michigan woods by Nick . . . , and Nick's initiation to the masculine role and male activities—hunting, fishing, drinking, and the problems of courtship—takes place in the woods also. (5)

Of course, as Mark Spilka has observed, the gender-inflected division between Oak Park and Michigan was probably not so clearly defined in reality, but that certainly didn't prevent Hemingway from imagining it largely in these terms.

Yet *The Garden of Eden*'s transformation of Oak Park into Oklahoma, a transformation familiar to us from such stories as "Soldier's Home" and "The Last Good Country," complicates any simple gender-inflected dichotomy of place. (In "The Last Good Country" Nick is from Michigan, but he has "family" in Oklahoma.) Much as David's ancestors had "escaped" from Oklahoma, Hemingway spent most of his career trying to escape the feminizing influence of Oak Park. The mutation of genteel suburbia into a rugged site of cowboys and Indians, or into the Indian Territory itself, seems to disavow the feminine component of David's (and Hemingway's) past, but if Hemingway fetishized racial otherness along with his more obvious fetishization of hair, David's status as an "honorary Indian" involves an appropriation of the fetish object by the subject, a sort of fetishistic cross-dressing (i.e., transvestism) that makes Oklahoma into anything but an entirely stable "masculine" signifier. Beneath its macho veneer, Oklahoma remains linked to Oak Park and memories of cross-dressing and, thus, serves as a monument to the divided nature of David's and Hemingway's ego, simultaneously Rotarian and Indian, domestic and wild, male and female.

Nor is David's Africa monolithically masculine, though it is clearly tied to the Michigan of Hemingway's youth. David's

Figure 14. Marcelline and Ernest in matching overalls at Walloon Lake in 1901. (John F. Kennedy Library)

African hunting trips with his father recall Hemingway's boyhood hunting trips with his father in Michigan, and, as we
have seen, there is an easy slippage throughout *The Garden of
Eden* between references to Africans and references to Native
Americans. Prudy Boulton, the "Indian girl" of Hemingway's, or
at least Nick Adams's, Michigan youth becomes in *The Garden
of Eden* the "African girl" of David's youth. In fact, on his 1953
trip to Africa, Hemingway explicitly compared his Wakamba "fiancée," Debba, to the mythical Prudy, and Debba's tie to the
"African girl" of *The Garden of Eden* manuscript is made abun-
dantly clear when Catherine grows jealous of David's boyhood
African "fiancée." But far from merely memorializing a masculine or colonialist conquest, the link between the Africa of
David's youth and the Africa of Hemingway's middle age also
links the sexual acrobatics of *The Garden of Eden* to Hemingway's own sexual acrobatics during his 1953 stay in Africa.
For it was on this same trip that Hemingway "went native," developed a compulsion to wear earrings, shaved his head "like a
Masai girl," and fantasized about his wife being a "boy" and
himself being her "girl." For Hemingway, Africa, like Oklahoma, is the outwardly "masculine" site of fetishistic cross-
dressing. The "rift" that concerns us, then, is not simply
between Oak Park and Michigan, nor between Africa and Oklahoma; it is inescapable, omnipresent, built into the very structure of David's and Hemingway's ego and sense of gender
identity.

Harold Bloom has astutely described Hemingway as "an ele-
giac poet, who mourns the self, who celebrates the self (rather
less effectively), and who suffers divisions in the self" (3). And
Peter Messent devotes an excellent Lacanian-inspired essay in
his recent book on Hemingway to the divided subjects who populate the pages of Hemingway's stories and novels. According to
Messent, in Hemingway's work, "A recognition that the notion of
coherent subjectivity is a myth vies with the urge to represent
the self as autonomous and independent. A presentation of the
self as unstable, caught between subject positions, confined and
partly defined by the social formation in which it is positioned,
conflicts with an urge to celebrate the self, to endorse individual
freedom and authority" (44). Yet while, for Messent, Hemingway's attention to divided subjects turns him into a sort of
proto-postmodernist, I would like to suggest that Hemingway's

interest in divided subjects, postmodernist or not, was not so
much a matter of abstract philosophizing as it was a matter of
the heart, a matter of personal experience. As Freud and Lacan
have taught us, the notion of coherent subjectivity is indeed a
myth, but Hemingway recognized this and dwelled on it precisely because an unusually profound rift at his point of origin
forced the issue.

According to Freud's fragmentary late essay "The Splitting of
the Ego in the Defensive Process," the sort of riven relation to
reality characterized by the fetishist's irreconcilable but tenaciously held phallic-position attitudes toward feminine "castration"—his recognition that women don't have the phallus and
his simultaneous disavowal of this same intolerable fact which
seems to threaten the possibility of his own castration—creates
nothing less than a "rift in the ego which never heals but which
increases as time goes on" (*SE* XXIII 276). More recent theory
and clinical evidence, however, suggest that fetishism not only
perpetuates and reinforces a split in the ego, it is itself largely a
response to a profound confusion about gender identity and an
unstable ego already deeply riven and prone to merger and fragmentation. In words that make it sound almost as if she had
Hemingway specifically in mind, Greenacre, who pioneered this
revision of classical Freudian theory, explains:

> My own work and . . . clinical reports by others indicated that
> the splitting of the ego was along lines of fission already pre-
> sent though not readily apparent. . . . The early disturbance
> had occurred in the preoedipal time, usually during the sec-
> ond year as well as in the anal-phallic period when suscepti-
> bility to castration fear is very great. *But this was often placed
> on a background of chronic milder disturbance dating from the
> first months, especially involving an overly close dependence
> on the mother or a sister with an intensification and prolonga-
> tion of confusion of sexual identity.* . . . [T]his identification . . .
> occurred the more readily when the influence of the father was
> weakened by his being absent or devalued.* (my emphasis,
> 168–169)

That is, the rift in the fetishist's ego is a "bisexual" one dating
back to the time when the ego was in the very process of formation.[2]

The rift in Hemingway's ego and sense of gender identity is
woven into the very fabric of *The Garden of Eden*. Desire in the

manuscript seems to spring from a single source—Hemingway—
but this desire is always divided, tempered by anxiety, and dis-
tributed amongst a set of characters who (as the epigraphs to
this section suggest) are each internally riven, masculine and
feminine, and yet incredibly prone to merger with those around
them. A sort of perverse *roman à clef*, the novel is torn across
time not only by the tension between the "present" and David's
or Hemingway's "past," for although Hemingway began to write
the novel in 1946 or early 1947, the "past" is constructed with
props left over from Hemingway's 1953 trip to Africa, and the
"present" is an amazing amalgam infused with its own nostalgia
and based on two different decades and three entirely different
sets of people.[3] Catherine, for instance, who insists she is "two
people," in fact seems to be a crazy cocktail blending three of
Hemingway's wives with a shot of Zelda Fitzgerald for spice,
and—as one would only expect from Catherine's semi-identity
with David—more than a jigger of Hemingway himself. *The Garden of Eden* manuscript's three male protagonists, David, Nick,
and Andy, are all in some way or another transparent cognates
for Hemingway, but the author's identity with his female characters is only slightly less apparent—a sort of projective identification reflecting both a need to split off his feminine, "crazy," half
and a contrary desire to merge with the feminine in others, a
fetishistic need to phallicize his women and a transvestic urge to
identify himself with the phallic woman.

A number of critics have noted Catherine Bourne's resemblance to that other "crazy" Catherine in Hemingway's work,
the nurse of *A Farewell to Arms* who wants to merge identities
and hairstyles with her lover, and who wants to cut her hair to
become a "new girl" for her man even if that means "ruining"
him (*FTA* 305). But why does Hemingway "resurrect" this earlier "Catherine" in *The Garden of Eden*, and why is she, returned from the grave, so much more threatening than before?
In a gesture with profound consequences for our understanding
of each novel (and which, by extension, should transform our
understanding of Hemingway's entire *oeuvre*), I want to argue
that both "Catherines" (even more than his other heroines) represent on some level the split-off, "crazy," feminine half of Hemingway's ego. What's more, I will support this assertion with
evidence from a remarkable series of previously unpublished
letters written by Hemingway in 1947 during a time of such intense stress that he was forced to put aside his work on *The*

Garden of Eden. But before we can fully appreciate these letters, we must first understand what Hemingway meant by "things of the night."

Day and Night

> "Young man, you must distinguish between the diurnal and the nocturnal sports."
>
> —Hemingway's mock interview with himself in Africa 1953, from Mary Hemingway, *How It Was*

Hemingway is famous for distinguishing between daytime and nighttime "reality," and the split in his ego could aptly be described as a matter of night and day. For instance, in *The Sun Also Rises*, when Jake Barnes muses, "There is no reason why because it is dark you should look at things differently from when it is light," he immediately recants: "The hell there isn't!" (148). Just exactly what this difference between night and day is, however, is seldom entirely clear. Nevertheless, a brief survey of Hemingway's deployment of this distinction suggests that he structured it around two basic themes: depression and psychosexual transgression. Building on the argument of chapter 4, I would like to suggest how these themes are related and how they relate to the split in Hemingway's ego.

Consider, for instance, the following passages from throughout the course of Hemingway's career (and one could easily point to a dozen others):

> Luz wrote him many letters. . . . They were all about the hospital, and how she loved him and how it was impossible to get along without him and how terrible it was missing him at night. ("A Very Short Story" [1923], SS 141)

> It is awfully easy to be hard-boiled about everything in the daytime, but at night it is another thing. (*The Sun Also Rises* [1926], 34)

> I know that the night is not the same as the day: that all things are different, that the things of the night cannot be explained in the day, because they do not then exist, and the night can be a dreadful time for lonely people once their loneliness has started. But with Catherine there was almost no difference in

the night except that it was an even better time. (*A Farewell to Arms* [1929], 249)

"I am of those who like to stay late at the café," the older waiter said. "With all those who do not want to go to bed. With all those who need a light for the night. . . . Each night I am reluctant to close up because there may be some one who needs the café." ("A Clean Well-Lighted Place" [1932], *SS* 382)

DOROTHY: But aren't we going to go and live together and have a lovely time and be happy? The way you say always in the night?
PHILIP: No. Not in a hundred thousand bloody years. Never believe what I say in the night. I lie like hell at night. (*The Fifth Column* [1939], 73)

"The earth moved," Maria said, not looking at the woman. "Truly it was a thing I cannot tell thee." . . . .
"*Cómo que no, hija?*" Pilar said. "Why not daughter? When I was young the earth moved so that you could feel it all shift in space and were afraid it would go out from under you. It happened every night."
"You lie," Maria said.
"Yes," Pilar said. "I lie. It never moves more than three times in a lifetime. . . . It is common and proven knowledge with *Gitanos.*" . . . .
All right, Robert Jordan said to himself. . . . I've known a lot of gypsies and they are strange enough. But so are we. . . . Nobody knows what tribes we came from nor what our tribal inheritance is nor what the mysteries were in the woods where the people lived that we came from. All we know is that we do not know. We know nothing about what happens to us in the nights. When it happens in the day though, it *is* something. (*For Whom the Bell Tolls* [1940], 174–175)

"Are you glad I brought back the boys and that I come and be a devil in the night?"
"Yes. I'm glad of everything and will you swing your hair across my face and give me your mouth please and hold me so tight it kills me?" (*Islands in the Stream* [1946–1951], 344)

"Let's . . . lie very quiet in the dark," David said and lowered the latticed shade and they lay side by side on the bed in the big room in The Palace in Madrid where Catherine had walked in the Museo del Prado in the light of day as a boy and now she would show the dark things in the light and there would, it seemed to him, be no end to the change. (*The Garden of Eden* [1947–1959], 67)

Hemingway associated night, then, with loneliness, depression, and a mysterious transgressive psychosexuality, "nocturnal sports" that had to be denied by the light of day. Moreover, throughout his work—particularly in such stories as "Now I Lay Me" and "A Way You'll Never Be"—Hemingway associates insomnia and night-terrors with that nexus for his depressive and fetishistic associations, his World War I wounding at Fossalta. Yet if, as I have suggested, Hemingway didn't suffer from shell shock after his wounding but instead mistook the combined onset of his fetishism and depression for the symptoms of shell shock, how can we explain the undeniable link between insomnia and the wounding at Fossalta? Seventy to eighty percent of patients suffering from clinical depression experience some form of insomnia (Klerman 312). Thus, if Hemingway confused the symptoms of clinical depression with the symptoms of shell shock, it should hardly come as a surprise that he associated his post-war insomnia with his experience at the front.

Hemingway's tendency to associate night with depression, however, rests on more than symptomatic insomnia. Both his fiction and personal correspondence suggest that his depressive phases—which he called "black-ass" or "the horrors"—were habitually manifested with particularly frightening ferocity *at night*.[4] In an incomplete 1926 letter written to Pauline Pfeiffer, during the famous "100 days" separation forced upon them by Hadley as a condition for granting Ernest a divorce, Ernest complains of "horrors at night and a black depression." "You see Pfife," he explains,

> I think that when two people love each other terribly much and need each other in every way and then go away from each other it works almost as bad as an abortion. . . . The deliberate keeping apart when all you have is each other does something bad to you and lately it has shot me all to hell inside. . . . *You lie all night half funny in the head and pray and pray and pray you won't go crazy.* (my emphasis, SL 234-5)

And in another terrifying and suicidal letter from the same period, Hemingway complains to Pauline of a "despair" that comes every night "about five o'clock like a fog coming up from a river bottom" (December 2, 1926, ©1998, Ernest Hemingway Foundation).[5]

In *The Fifth Column*, Philip Rawlings complains about getting "the horrors" at night and adds a little later, "It's getting almost daylight, and I'm getting sensible again" (68). Likewise, in
For Whom the Bell Tolls, Pilar confides to Jordan, "'All my life I
have had this sadness at intervals. . . . It may be it is like the
times of a woman" (90). She assures him, however, that her
"sadness will dissipate as the sun rises. It is like a mist" (89).
This same nighttime depression is the essential clinical backdrop behind the more philosophically-endowed suicidal impulses of the old man in Hemingway's masterpiece, "A Clean
Well-Lighted Place." And in "The Sea Change" this same association between depression and the night may color Phil's reply to
his wife's admonition to be "understanding" of her need to have
a lesbian affair: "Sure . . . I'll understand all the time. All day
and all night. Especially all night" (SS 398).

   But why would Hemingway's depression manifest itself
more intensely *at night*? One might speculate about the influence of light, which can have a profound effect on mood. A more
fruitful line of inquiry might question the influence of his drinking habits on his mood disorder. If Hemingway covered his daylight depression with a veil of alcohol, and if, as he always
claimed, he never drank at night (in order to have a clear head
to work in the morning), the veil covering his depression may
have been torn asunder after sunset. Whatever the case, habitual nighttime depression is unusual but hardly unheard of. In
his memoir of his own struggle with major depression, William
Styron describes an experience much like Hemingway's:

> Most people who begin to suffer from the illness are laid low in
> the morning, with such malefic effect that they are unable to
> get out of bed. They feel better only as the day wears on. But
> my situation was just the reverse. While I was able to rise and
> function almost normally during the earlier part of the day, I
> began to sense the onset of the symptoms at midafternoon or a
> little later—gloom crowding in on me, a sense of dread and
> alienation and, above all, stifling anxiety. (11–12)

To describe his nightly depressions, Styron even uses language remarkably like Hemingway's: "Beginning at about three
o'clock, . . . I'd feel the horror, like some poisonous fogbank, roll
in upon my mind, forcing me to bed" (58).
   Styron, further, suggests a link between depression and a
sort of ego-splitting: "A phenomenon that a number of people

have noted while in deep depression is the sense of being accompanied by a second self—a wraithlike observer who, not
sharing the dementia of his double, is able to watch with dispassionate curiosity as his companion struggles against the oncom-
ing disaster, or decides to embrace it" (64). Thus, Hemingway's
depression could have deepened the rift in his ego. Such an association between depression and splitting would have been
stronger still if Hemingway was indeed *manic*-depressive. Speculating about the connection between manic-depression and
creativity, Kay Jamison—who suffers from the disease herself—
claims that "extreme changes in mood exaggerate the normal
tendency to have conflicting, or polar, selves" (*Touched* 127). And
if extreme mood swings "exaggerate the *normal* tendency to have
conflicting, or polar, selves," we might only wonder at what
might be true for an artist with an *abnormal* predisposition to
such a rift in his identity. But while the splitting associated with
Hemingway's affective disorder suggests a symbiosis between
depression and perversion, we have yet to explain the erotic
component to the "things of the night." An explanation, however,
is at hand.

    If, as I argue in chapter 4, perverse acts function to reduce
suffering due to both anxiety and depression, we can easily see
how Hemingway's nighttime depression (regardless of its hereditary or chemical etiology) might have provoked those erotic defenses which Hemingway likewise associated with the "things of
the night." The ebb and flow of Catherine Bourne's psychosexual
madness suggests nothing so much as the cycles of manic-
depression: "It lasted a month, [David] thought, or almost. And
the other time from le Grau du Roi to Hendaye was two months.
No, less, because she started thinking of it in Nimes" (*GE* 57).
Likewise, she complains of mild hallucinations characteristic of
mania but entirely unrelated to the perversions that structure
her more obvious concerns. One afternoon when she is afraid
that her madness is coming back, she reports that colors have
become disconcertingly all "too bright." Trees shimmer unnatu-
rally, and even the greys are "brighter than El Greco yellows"
(*GE* 162; K422.1 21.16). Thus, suffering from depression,
Thomas Hudson dreams of his silken-haired ex-wife returning
like a ghost "in the night," and Catherine Barkley, recovering
from the loss of her childhood love, becomes "the same person"
with her new love, Frederic, in the night. To be sure, Catherine
and Frederic fuse during the act of sex, which they just happen

to do at night, but the thoroughness of their fusion is remarkable and entirely characteristic of the "overwhelming merging tendencies" that are a hallmark of the perversions (Rosen 50). Even if nighttime depression was not the source of Hemingway's erotic "nocturnal sports," there can be little doubt that Hemingway's erotic imagination was nonetheless especially fertile at night, and similar twilight phenomena can be found in the literature on fetishism and transvestism. For instance, one of Havelock Ellis's transvestite correspondents ("C.T.") noted: "I tend to be much more affected by 'Eonist' [i.e., transvestite] impulses in the evening than in the daytime" (2.2.70). Hemingway's fetishistic and transvestic impulses apparently ran on the same clock.

The erotic component to Hemingway's "night things" is at its clearest in the dizzying gender-acrobatics of Catherine and David Bourne in *The Garden of Eden*. Early in the novel, soon after her first haircut and transformation into the phallic/castrated boy/woman "Peter," Catherine assures her husband, "Truly you don't have to worry darling until night. We won't let the night things come into the day" (22). But while she promises, "I'll only be a boy *at night* and won't embarrass you," she finds it literally impossible to keep her word, and it is this release of the private "night things" into the bright public light of the sun which so disturbs her husband (my emphasis, 56).[6] This transgression, moreover, is particularly threatening for David because the "things of the night" in this novel involve his own nighttime transformation into a "lovely girl" named "Catherine."

At times David's transformation seems like a figment of Catherine's nocturnal imagination, such as when she pleads with her husband: "Now you change. Please. Don't make me change you. Must I? All right I will. You're changed now. You are. You did it too. . . . I did it but you did it. Yes you did. You're my sweet dearest darling Catherine. You're my sweet my lovely Catherine. You're my girl my dearest only girl. Oh thank you thank you my girl—" (56). But elsewhere it is clear that David feels this transformation deeply:

> During the night he had felt her hands touching him. And when he woke it was in the moonlight and she had made the dark magic of the change again and he did not say no when she spoke to him and asked questions and *he felt the change so that it hurt him all through* and when it was finished after they were both exhausted she was shaking and she whispered to

him, "Now we have done it. Now we really have done it." (my emphasis, 20)

And since the transvestite mediates his identification with the phallic woman by *wearing* the fetish object, we should hardly be surprised to learn that David's transformation into the "girl," "Catherine," is intimately bound up with his own series of tonsorial metamorphoses. During one of David's transformations, Catherine coos to him,

> "Let me feel your hair girl. Who cut it? Was it Jean? It's cut so full and has so much body and it's the same as mine. Let me kiss you girl. Oh you have lovely lips. Shut your eyes girl."
> He did not shut his eyes but it was dark in the room and outside the wind was high in the trees.
> "You know it isn't so easy to be a girl if you're really one. If you really feel things."
> "I know."
> "Nobody knows. I tell you so when you're my girl. . . . Just be my girl and love me the way I love you." (86)

But if Hemingway, like David, genuinely felt such transvestic desires, why does David put up such resistance, and why do we so often get the feeling that Catherine is trying to hijack David's body?[7] A partial answer to these questions lies in Catherine's link to the split-off feminine half of Hemingway's ego—a ghost from the past which could rise from the grave whenever the fetish object beckoned.

Letters from Catherine

> Catherine was not his enemy except as she was himself in the unfinding unrealizable quest that is love and so was her own enemy.
>
> —*The Garden of Eden*

> "Anyway I am you and her. . . . I'm everybody. You know that don't you?"
>
> —Catherine to David in *The Garden of Eden*

> "Say 'I've come back to Catherine in the night.'"
>
> —Catherine to Frederic in *A Farewell to Arms*

Sometime in the wee hours of the fourteenth of May 1947—longing to return to Catherine in the night—Hemingway decided to dye his hair bright red, or in his own words, "as bright red as a French polished copper pot or a newly minted penny."

It wasn't the first time. He had dyed his hair red once before, in 1933, and had written to his second wife, Pauline, asking how to get it from red to blond. Now, in 1947, Hemingway had been absolutely obsessed with hair for weeks. He was also suffering from an extraordinary combination of worry, sleep-deprivation, separation anxiety, castration anxiety, and alcohol-exacerbated depression. His son Patrick had been confined, and occasionally strapped, to his bed for the better part of a month, ranting incoherently from a post-head trauma psychosis—the result of an auto wreck. Worried sick, Hemingway had been keeping vigil by his son's bed almost around the clock. Meanwhile, his fourth wife, Mary, was in Chicago tending to her father, who was suffering from prostate cancer. The prognosis was not good, and the recommended treatment—castration—inspired Ernest at least once during these weeks to recount an anecdote about a boy whose penis had been sliced off mistakenly by an irresponsible quack.

Hemingway's letters to Mary from these weeks reveal what may seem like a surprising response to the crisis. A few weeks earlier, he had been busy at work on *The Garden of Eden*, and he had apparently been playing the coiffeur for Mary, dyeing her hair blonder and blonder àla Catherine Bourne. Now his interest in hair grew still more intense. While he continued to report on Patrick and inquire about Mr. Welsh, his letters to Mary are dominated for pages at a time by his exhortations for her to get hot oil treatments or dye her hair ash blonde or smoky silver. In between complaints about his sleeplessness, loneliness, and gloominess, he worries for pages about the various combinations of gold and drab necessary to lighten Mary's hair as much as possible without damaging it, and he even assures her that if she can't find the time to get her hair done in Chicago, he will gladly dye it for her himself when she returns to Cuba. Ernest rationalized his need to write at such length about hair with what must seem like a curious logic: "You can tell I've been a long time without my Kitten, but with so much *awful* lately is OK to talk about our jollities and secrecies" (May 2, 1947, ©1998, Ernest Hemingway Foundation). His logic seems less strange, however, if we remember that a fetishist uses his fetish, among other things, as a tool to ward off anxiety and depression.

But the "jollities and secrecies" that Ernest shared with Mary were something more than fetishistic. They were transvestic. Ernest's games with Mary's, and eventually his own, hair resembled the nocturnal sports of David and Catherine Bourne more closely than anyone has imagined. These games even involved the tonsorial transformation of Mary into "Peter" and of Ernest into "Catherine." The only significant difference was that Ernest, not Mary, was the director of this private erotic theater. On the evening of May 2, Ernest wrote to his wife:

> Get [a] good hot oil[,] see about ash blonde if you want to— Don't see how [it] could hurt us—but if you don't want to, I can always look after dear head with great pleasure and what skill have acquired—But there is a sort of drab silver colour that is not negative—not just our lovely de-coloring that goes so beautifully with the sun and tan—But is a positive coloring that might be wonderful and we could always cut off as grew out if you unlike it or unavailable here or a nuisance to keep up. . . .
>
> Still think could be a lot of fun to go . . . to NY and come back redheaded. . . . Maybe you could do [that] for my birthday—you could pick out a couple of shows to see and . . . see Willie and Connie . . . and could tell them you were making surprise present of red-headed kitten for Papa—(*also for Pete and for Catherine*) correct the spelling to Katherine from your letter and which is much nicer.

He closed his letter affectionately, "*Your girl Katherine sends her love*, also your cat Boise" (my emphasis, ©1998, Ernest Hemingway Foundation).

In another letter, on May 5, Ernest noted that it had been twenty-two days since he had last dyed Mary's hair, and he was happy to hear she had found a place in Chicago to get it lightened. Then after another page about the intricacies of dyeing hair, he finished his letter with some lines that should remind us of *The Garden of Eden*: "My God it will be wonderful to have my blessed dearest wife and partner and friend and *Pete* home. *Your girl hasn't been around at all except before daylight times[,] but know very well will turn up when you ask for her*" (my emphasis, ©1998, Ernest Hemingway Foundation).[8]

The shades of *The Garden of Eden* are impossible to deny. True, one of Ernest's closest friends, General Buck Lanham, did have a wife nicknamed "Pete," but Lanham is mentioned nowhere in these letters, and he did not go to Cuba to visit Hemingway in the spring of 1947. By "blessed dearest wife and partner and friend and *Pete*," Hemingway was plainly referring to Mary, and Mary alone, endowing her with the same phallic moniker assumed by Catherine Bourne in her nighttime metamorphoses. And who could "Katherine" and Mary's nighttime "girl" be if not Ernest? After all, we know about "Peter Mary Welsh-Hemingway" and "Kathrin Ernest Hemingway" from the "New Names Department." This was the same man who on safari shaved his head like a "Masai girl," developed an overwhelming compulsion to wear earrings, and wrote of his wife: "Mary . . . has always wanted to be a boy and thinks like a boy without losing any femininity. . . . *She loves me to be her girl, which I love to be, not being absolutely stupid.*" And if the nighttime "girlhood" of America's erstwhile icon of literary machismo still seems at all unlikely, Ernest's letter of May 14 should dispel any doubts.

Ernest begins the letter by promising Mary that if he could do anything for her father, it would be as much a privilege as it would have been to have helped his own dead father whom he was unable to help when he had needed it most. That Hemingway associated Mary's soon-to-be-castrated father with his own dead father suggests an important source of anxiety behind Ernest's decision to dye his hair. Hemingway (entirely unjustly) blamed his father's suicide on his mother, and he interpreted this suicide both a result of and as a confirmation of his father's emasculation at his mother's hands. Ernest needed to disavow his identification with his father and the significance of castration. He also needed to undo his loneliness and depression. Since desperate times call for desperate measures, Hemingway decided to dye his hair bright red. According to Carlos Baker and Kenneth Lynn, Hemingway explained his red hair to everyone at the Finca by telling them that he had mistakenly picked up a bottle of shampoo left over from Martha's time, but the letter he wrote to Mary tells a very different story:

> Last night I . . . had to make the all night standby [Patrick's bed] and thought you would be coming back soon and what [I]

could do to amuse me and please you and *remembered how you used to talk about Catherine in the night and how her hair was and so decided would make red*—So started on test piece with just the drab—and only tiny bit of mixture and it made fine red in about 35 minutes—(I was checking on Mousie [Patrick] all the time.) Hair as dark as mine has to go through red before can be blond—So I thought, what the hell, I'll make really red for my kitten and did it carefully and good, *same as yours*, and left on 45 minutes and it came out as red as a French polished copper pot or a newly minted penny—not brassy—true bright coppery—*and naturally in the morning I was spooked shitless*—and then thought what the hell—with everything the way it is and we free people able to do anything we want that doesn't hurt other people, whose business is it but yours and mine—

So I just *had* red hair—and I loved it for you and was proud of it—and nobody said anything about it any more than they said to Gen. Custer when he wore his down to his shoulders. Because right now have quite a little credit with my troops. . . .

So now I am just as red headed as you would like your girl Catherine to be and don't give a damn about it at all—(like very much).[9] It's not deep red—but light, bright, coppery, like shiny copper pans—and I'll do it again before you come home—or do it again when you get here. . . . *If a girl has a right to make her hair red I have*—I've fought enough fights so no one can say anything to me . . . except really wonderful fighting people and maybe they didn't fight as many times over such a long space of years and months and days—

So I will be red-headed kitten when I see you and very proud to be and hope will please my kitten—

Actually me and Catherine both would be better dark red than this jolly new copper tinker's colour. But you can't do that at home—(my emphasis, ©1998, Ernest Hemingway Foundation)[10]

The mysterious Catherine of this letter sounds suspiciously like Hadley, Ernest's "Katherine Kat." As we've seen, in a 1921 work of juvenilia entitled "The Current," Ernest described Hadley's hair as being the color of "*old country burnished copper kettles.*" But if the Catherine of this letter invokes Hadley's memory, *this* Catherine is *Mary's* girl, and Ernest's identification with her is obvious. She is the split-off feminine half of himself, a sort of female alter-ego typical of transvestic fantasy. She is the internalized precipitate of Ernest's first maternal "Cat" (who con-

sidered auburn the ideal color for hair), sustained through the
introjection of his lovers and identified with by transvestically
wearing the fetish object himself. (Taylor, in his work with transvestism, has called attention to precisely such "contradictory
personality organizations" or "dual identities, based on a split in
the ego" [511], and Money notes that transvestites typically
adopt "two names, two wardrobes, and two personalities."[11]) Like
Frederic Henry's nighttime union with Catherine Barkley, or like
David Bourne's nocturnal transformation into "Catherine"
which inspires "remorse" only after Catherine's games spill over
into the day, Hemingway's split-off feminine half was apparently
confined to the night, and in spite of his declaration that if a girl
has a right to color her hair then he does as well, this half of his
ego only surfaced in the day at the risk of "spooking him shitless."

What can this split-off feminine half teach us about Hemingway's heroines, particularly the Catherines of *A Farewell to
Arms* and *The Garden of Eden*? First, it suggests an explanation,
aside from Ernest's friendships with a great many lesbians, for
Hemingway's lifelong fascination with lesbian eroticism—a fascination reflected most obviously in "The Sea Change," "The Last
Good Country," *For Whom the Bell Tolls*, and *The Garden of
Eden*. As Catherine Barkley explains to Frederic, she wants to
sleep with all of his ex-lovers so she can be *exactly like him* (*FTA*
299). And in doing so, she would simply be playing the part of
the split-off feminine half of the male ego during the act of heterosexual intercourse. In a sense, this part of Hemingway felt
like it *was* a lesbian. This is why Phil can experience his wife's
lesbian affair by proxy in "The Sea Change." This is why, as
Mark Spilka has argued, Jake Barnes at times seems as much
like a lesbian as he does like a castrated man. This, more than
his liberalism, is why David Bourne finds it comparatively easy
to tolerate Catherine's brief affair with Marita (not to mention
her plans in the manuscript for an affair with Barbara Sheldon).[12]

In his work with a case remarkably like Hemingway's, Winnicott observed that his patient recognized a split-off feminine
half in himself but considered this a "crazy" idea—an attitude
which only makes sense, as this "internal woman" represents
that psychotic half of a divided ego which repudiates the reality
of sexual difference.[13] That is, whereas the pervert *disavows* reality, balancing two contrary attitudes about sexual difference in

a riven ego, this single split-off feminine half of the perverse ego
holds an attitude that *in isolation* is psychotic. Instead of arriving at an illusory compromise to the contrary demands of delusion and reality, it merely *repudiates* reality in deference to the
delusion.[14] (Whereas Freud saw "disavowal" [*verleugnung*] as the
characteristic defense of the perversions, he saw "repudiation"
or "rejection" [*verwerfen*] as the characteristic defense of the
psychoses.) The madness of Catherine Barkley and Catherine
Bourne clearly owes much to the instability of Hadley, Pauline,
Zelda Fitzgerald, and Jane Mason (all of whom were to a greater
or lesser degree introjected by Ernest), but it owes even more to
Ernest's own manic-depression and psychosexual disorder, and
we can now understand why instead of projecting his "madness"
onto his more immediate cognates, Frederic Henry and David
Bourne, Hemingway projected it onto those female characters
who represented the split-off psychotic feminine half of his own
ego.[15] Yet Hemingway had another reason for projecting this
madness onto his female characters: by doing so he protests
that it was his *mother* (not himself) who was mad when she saw
a little girl where there was in fact only a little boy.

Winnicott further reports that the split-off other-sex half of
his patient was intensely jealous of the masculine half. "*She [did]
not want the man released. . . . What she want[ed] [was] full acknowledgment of herself and of her own rights over [his] body.
[And] her penis envy especially include[d] envy of [him] as a male*"
(combination of Winnicott's emphasis and my own, *Playing*
75).[16] Hemingway's work abounds with phallic women who enjoy
this status only by dint of their partner's emasculation. Brett
Ashley with her fetishized short hair possesses the phallus by
virtue of Jake's lacking his. Marie Morgan with her bleached-
blonde hair and man's hat takes a strange erotic pleasure in
Harry's missing arm, much as raven-haired Renata does in
Cantwell's misshapen hand which bears the stigmata of castration. Margot Macomber wields her Mannlicher and phallic authority by virtue of Francis's emasculating cowardice and crew
cut, and Pilar assumes the phallic scepter of her authority at the
expense of Pablo, who becomes a "castrated boar" or a "sick kitten." While critics like Leslie Fiedler have traditionally dismissed
such heroines as "castrating bitches," Hemingway could never
dismiss them precisely because they gave expression to his *desires* as well as his *fears*. No *mere* expression of misogyny, these
women spoke for the split-off part of Hemingway that felt that *it*

was a woman. This should hardly turn Hemingway into a feminist hero, nor can it mask the genuine elements of misogyny that often taint his images of women, but we need to recognize that Hemingway was fighting an imaginary battle of the sexes within himself. In short, he can no longer be seen as the simple male chauvinist pig of much early feminist criticism.

The target of much of that criticism, Catherine Barkley, generally considered (along with *The Garden of Eden*'s Marita) to be one of the most pliant of Hemingway's heroines, nevertheless swings her leather-bound swagger stick only because the boy who originally owned it has been blown to bits—as Frederic almost is himself. And the evidence traditionally cited for Catherine's "pliancy"—namely, her plea to Frederic, "There isn't any me. I'm you. Don't make up a separate me" (115)—must now be seen in an entirely new light. More than an expression of Frederic's or Hemingway's narcissism and wish-fulfilling chauvinistic demand for a woman to surrender her identity in the matrix of heterosexual love, Catherine's plea is a demand for *recognition* and an attempt, however lovingly expressed, to commandeer her lover's body. More than a mere sex toy, Catherine *uses* her sexuality as a tool to hijack Frederic's body. Thus, when Catherine asks Frederic to grow his hair out to match her own haircut, she is asking him to transvestically identify with the phallic woman, *herself*; meanwhile she assumes phallic/masculine properties by fetishistically cutting her own hair.

Such an interpretation adds a sinister new dimension to Frederic and Catherine's playful banter.

> "You know, darling, I'm not going to cut my hair now until after young Catherine's born. . . . But after she's born and I'm thin again I'm going to cut it and then I'll be a fine new and different girl for you. We'll go together to get it cut, or I'll go alone and come and surprise you."
>
> I did not say anything.
>
> "You won't say I can't, will you?"
>
> "No. I think it would be exciting."
>
> "Oh, you're so sweet. And maybe I'd look lovely, darling, and be so thin and exciting to you and you'll fall in love with me all over again."
>
> "Hell," I said, "I love you enough now. What do you want to do? Ruin me?"
>
> "*Yes. I want to ruin you.*"
>
> "*Good,*" I said, "*that's what I want too.*" (my emphasis, 304)

However playfully intended, Catherine's desire to "ruin" Frederic can no longer be laughed off so easily, and this desire, along with more obvious and important artistic motives, may have unconsciously contributed to Hemingway's decision to kill off his heroine at the novel's end.

Catherine Bourne's need to "ruin" David—though clearly based on Hadley's loss of Ernest's manuscripts and Zelda Fitzgerald's purported need to ruin Scott—is far more virulent than Catherine Barkley's desire to ruin Frederic.[17] In Catherine Bourne, it seems almost as if Catherine Barkley has returned from the grave, mad as hell and out for revenge. As Catherine's transvestic experiments spill over into the day, and as she transforms David through tonsorial experiments into another version of herself, David's need to shore up his masculinity builds. Naturally, he returns to the rift, to the Africa of his boyhood, there to find his masculine self through an identification with his father. Indeed, the Scribner's version of the novel implies that David's mission is a success; in spite of Catherine's torching of his African stories, Marita insists on David's having male friends, and she is emphatic about her own girlhood. As the story ends, David is once again, through the magic of his art, at one with his father in Africa and secure in his own masculinity. The manuscript, however, tells a very different story. Here, Catherine and Marita both play transvestic and fetishistic games, and both become obsessed with co-opting David's Africa by becoming his "M'Bulu girls" or "Somali wives." David's identification with his father may still promise to shore up his masculinity, but what he finds in Africa is precisely the rift itself: on one side stands his father (for whom he has profoundly ambivalent feelings); on the other side stand his fetishistically and narcissistically-invested African girls. What he finds, in short, is the bisexual rift in his own ego. Hemingway can no longer simply kill off the Catherine of *this* novel, for now, perhaps through his own nighttime experience of *being* "Catherine," he realizes that "Catherine was not his enemy except as she was himself in the unfinding unrealizable quest that is love and so was her own enemy" (*GE* 193). To kill her is to kill an essential part of himself. Thus, short of an impossible psychotic integration that would deny the rift itself, there is only one "solution" to David's and Hemingway's dilemma: the contemplated double-suicide of the manuscript's "provisional ending."

Transvestism, Homeovestism, and the
Mirror of Manhood

"I wish you'd look in the glass."
"I couldn't."
"Just look at me. That's how you are and I did it
and there's nothing you can do now. That's how you
look."

—Catherine and David, *The Garden of Eden*

I looked in the glass and saw myself looking like a fake
doctor with a beard.

—Frederic in *A Farewell to Arms*

In his recent book, *The Face in the Mirror*, Robert Fleming argues that Hemingway used the motif of the mirror throughout his career as a tool for his fictional writers to explore their identities "and the sins that necessarily accompany the artist's obsession with his art" (138). Fleming notes that in *The Garden of Eden*, for instance,

> David frequently looks at his own image in the mirror, as if to
> seek external evidence of the depths of his own depravity;
> Catherine looks at herself in the mirror in imitation of David,
> the true artist; David and Catherine look at each other and at
> themselves together as a couple in the mirror they have bought
> for the bar at their hotel; finally, they use each other as mir-
> rors: if husband and wife are one, each may see his or her own
> present state reflected in the other. (138)

But David finds aspects of his "present state" in Catherine that Fleming doesn't seem to anticipate, and if Hemingway habitually used mirrors as a tool to examine his own identity, we need to realize that, for him, even more than for most men, questions of *identity* and questions of *gender-identity* were always inseparable. Thus it is only appropriate that when Hemingway stared into the mirror he occasionally saw a man and occasionally saw a woman, and the gender-signifier of choice was almost always the fetish.

Thanks largely to the bisexual split in Hemingway's ego—and to the magic of symbolic barbering—his characters don't so much recognize themselves in the mirror as *mis*recognize themselves in it. We might remember how Catherine and David Bourne react to

their specular images after visiting the coiffeur: "She looked in
the mirror as though she had never seen the girl she was looking
at" (*GE* 80), and "He looked in the mirror and it was someone else
he saw. . ." (84). In "The Sea Change," after Phil reluctantly ac-
cedes to the entreaties of his tanned, blonde, and short-hair
lover, telling her to go ahead and have a lesbian affair, with the
proviso to come back and tell him "all about it," Hemingway
writes: "He was not the same-looking man as he had been before
he had told her to go." And when his lover is gone, Phil, who
shares her deep and fetishistically-invested tan, walks over to the
barman and declares, "I'm a different man, James. . . . You see in
me quite a different man. . . .' As he looked in the glass, he saw
he was really quite a different-looking man" (*SS* 401). The same
motif pops up yet again in *To Have and Have Not*. After bleaching
her hair, Marie Morgan responds to her image in the mirror with
the same perverse *méconnaissance*: "I looked strange to myself. .
. . I couldn't believe it was me" (259). Then we should remember
the rape of Maria in *For Whom the Bell Tolls*: "I saw my face in the
mirror of the barbershop and the faces of those who were holding
me and the faces of three others who were leaning over me and I
knew none of their faces but in the glass I saw myself and them,
but they saw only me. . . . My own face I could hardly recognize
. . . but I looked at it and knew that it was me . . ." (351).

For most of us, Maria's brutalization should seem far from
erotic (though we have seen that the rape of her body and her
locks epitomizes the aggression inherent in perversion), but
such misrecognition in the mirror, like the fluid ego boundaries
it signifies, becomes a tool for erotic—ultimately transvestic—
merger when Jordan proposes that after cutting Maria's hair to
match his own, "We will sit in the famous bed together and look
into the mirror of the *armoire* and there will be thee and there
will be me in the glass . . ." (346). The transvestic impulse is
there when Jake Barnes inspects his mutilated body before the
mirror, or when Cantwell sees Renata's portrait in the mirror instead of his own image or is reminded by a mirror that he needs
a haircut if he is to avoid "looking like Joan of Arc" (*ART* 169).
When David Bourne gazes into a mirror at his bleached hair in
the *Eden* manuscript, thinking about Catherine and a Danish
girl he had seen in Biarritz, he gets an "erection" and thinks to
himself that he looks like "that girl in Biarritz" *and he likes it*
(K422.1 12.18.12 & 17). And if the transvestic implications of
this scene aren't clear enough, they should be a few pages later

when in bed that night David somehow "becomes" the Danish girl.[18] In still another scene, Catherine and David stand naked before a mirror admiring each other's almost identically dark skin. Catherine calls attention to the matching color of their bleached hair and, after noticing David's erection, asks him to touch her "firm erect breasts" (K422.1 24.12).[19] Here, the very confusion between the "I" and the "other" which played such an important role in the etiology of Hemingway's fetishism becomes a mechanism whereby he can transvestically *identify* with the phallic woman instead of constructing her solely as an *object*.

The face in the mirror, where subject becomes object and object is revealed as subject, is precisely the site where fetishism most clearly slips into transvestism, and this is why masturbation in front of the mirror while cross-dressed (i.e., wearing the fetish) is *the* defining act of the transvestite. Take, for instance, the case of "A.T.," a thirty-year-old artist and transvestite, who wrote a brief autobiographical sketch for Havelock Ellis. A.T., who wore petticoats until age seven or eight, became in late adolescence a confirmed underwear fetishist. He would follow short-skirted women for miles hoping only to catch a glimpse of some underthings peeping out beneath their skirts, and he remembers going every day one summer to "some cliff steps behind a girl's school in order to enjoy looking up their clothes," eyeing every detail of "their pretty drawers and petticoats" (2.2.46). Then one day, his fetishism gave way to a transvestic revelation:

> While one day enjoying being naked in my sister's bedroom, where there was a large mirror in which I delighted to see my naked body and limbs reflected, I came across a lot of her prettily trimmed underclothing, and was seized with the desire to put it on. I did so—and from that moment I date what I term my change of sex. I cannot describe to you the pleasure I felt when dressing myself for the first time in female garments. It was exquisite, delicious, intoxicating, far and away transcending anything I had before experienced, and when, after some trouble, I was completely attired as a girl, and placed myself in front of the glass, it was a positive revelation. I felt that here at last was what I had been longing for. . . . Here before me was a pretty girl, whom I could see in any stage of dress or undress, whom I could pose in any position I liked that would show off her body or limbs or underclothing. . . . I was both boy and girl at once, and since that time I have never been a male pure and simple again. . . . (2.2.46)

Just so, Greenacre records the case of a fetishist/trans-
vestite who bound himself with ropes and masturbated in front
of a mirror "nude except for his carefully polished shoes" (20).
Lihn, likewise, reports the case of a fetishist with strong transvestic leanings whose favorite masturbatory ritual consisted of
"put[ting] on a pair of his mother's panties, conceal[ing] his
penis between his thighs, and with them apply[ing] pressure to
his penis while looking at himself in the bathroom mirror, imagining himself to be a woman with a penis" (352). Bak relates the
case of a transvestite who would dress up in his sister's clothes
and pose in front of the mirror with his "penis . . . bandaged and
very forcefully tied backward."[20] And Murray Lewis tells an almost identical tale of a transvestite patient who "would put on
some of his sister's clothes before a mirror, then add a tight belt
around his waist and push his penis between his thighs so that
his body contours even more resembled a girl's" (345). Langevin
records the monologue of a transvestite whose twin personalities
and nightly anxiety-soothing mirror-masturbation should remind us of Hemingway's experience with "Catherine": "I feel like
there are two persons in me, a man and a woman. At work during the day, I am the man and at night when I come home, I will
dress up for 'us'. . . . As the 'she' in me unfolds in front of the
mirror, I can feel the tension drain from me" (213). Finally,
Glasser records the case of a transvestite whose mirror-masturbation fantasy illuminates Hemingway's interest in lesbian love.
The patient would dress as a woman,

> paying careful attention to the minutest details: the exact size
> and shape of the padding put into his brassiere and the precise
> degree of tightness in its straps; the smoothness of the texture
> of the panties and the feel of their tightness round his waist;
> the matching blouse and skirt, tights and shoes; the hairstyle
> of the wig; and so on—all to ensure that what he saw in the
> mirror was a neatly and attractively dressed woman. . . . He
> would then masturbate looking at himself in the mirror, ar-
> ranging himself in such a way that his penis was not visible in
> the reflection. *A frequent fantasy was to imagine himself as a
> woman being made love to by a woman.* (my emphasis, 163)

Again and again and again, in case studies by Fenichel, Feigelson,
Jucovy, McDougall, Ostow, Segal, Stoller, Taylor, Zavitzianos, and
others we find the identical ritual. Bradlow and Coen have even
devoted an entire article to the topic of mirror masturbation.

Of course, Hemingway's characters don't masturbate in front of the mirror. But David Bourne's erection signals *something* and Jake Barnes's missing penis is conspicuous by its absence, much like the concealed penises in so many of the cases above.[21] I can't imagine—nor do I *want* to imagine—Hemingway posing in front of the mirror wearing lipstick, high heels, and an evening gown; yet the deeply tanned, earringed, bleach-blond or redhead that I suspect Hemingway occasionally imagined when he gazed into the mirror *was* a transvestic self-image. Nor is this image really at odds with the macho public persona that Papa so lovingly cultivated. Rather, as I suggested in chapter 3, Hemingway's transvestic impulses go a long way toward explaining his machismo, since transvestites, when they are not cross-dressing, often tend to overcompensate for their feminine impulses by adopting hyper-masculine garb. As Stoller explains in a passage which indirectly suggests a good deal about Hemingway's character, transvestites, unlike transsexuals,

> distinguish themselves (at least those who are articulate about the matter) by emphasizing a *split in their identities*. They wish to live alternating roles in *both* genders, each successfully maintained in the eyes of the public, their wives, and themselves. In their role as men, they are masculine enough in dress and mannerisms, are often married and have children, maintain potency with their wives so long as this potency can be protected by the fetishistic act (clothes = fetish . . .) and more often than not have a dread of and abhorrence of homosexuality in themselves. The absence of any homosexual genital activities whether dressed as men or women is a rule most of these men assiduously try to obey in order to maintain themselves as heterosexuals. *While dressing as women starts with these men* [sometimes well into middle age] *as a primarily fetishistic act, in which a single piece of female wear is sufficient, over the years the condition* [often] *progresses to an equally compelling need to pass undetected in public as a woman. . . . Their feeling when 'dressed' that they are women with a phallus is another aspect of their need to be both masculine and feminine. Even when being feminine, the transvestite is keenly charged with the awareness of having a penis.* (my emphasis, "Mother's Contribution" 390)

Elsewhere, Stoller is a little more precise about the transition from fetishism to transvestism, and we can see that one need not adopt a completely feminine costume to behave like a transvestite. For many transvestites,

> *a single garment or class of garments remains the preferred*
> *fetish*; for another group, the original preference sooner or later
> spreads to a desire to be completely clothed in women's gar-
> ments and to pretend for a period of time—minutes to hours—
> to be a woman; men of the third group (far fewer than the first
> two), with some transsexual tendencies (the extreme being sec-
> ondary transsexuals), learn to pass as women and spend peri-
> ods living as women. (my emphasis, "Gender Disorders" 124)

Insofar as he behaved like a transvestite, Hemingway clearly belonged to the first group of men—dyed, shaved, or long hair, earrings, "tribal marks," and deeply tanned skin being the preferred
fetish objects.

Yet the misrecognition in the mirror that bewilders so many
of Hemingway's characters was by no means exclusively transvestic. Frederic Henry's misrecognition of himself in the mirror
continually points to a *failure to identify* successfully with his, or
Hemingway's, *father*—an identification which may have been all
the more necessary and all the more impossible since Hemingway revised the novel in the months after his father's suicide.[22]
With his gender status challenged by Catherine's long-haired
plans for him—plans which recall Hemingway's own alpine idyll
in the early 1920s, "In the winter in Schruns I wore a beard
against the sun that burned my face . . . and did not bother having a haircut" (*MF* 205)—Frederic tries to shore up his masculinity by growing a beard to identify with his or Hemingway's
father, but he instead ends up feeling like a participant in a
masquerade.[23] At first the sensation of inauthenticity seems to
center around his desertion from the military—"In civilian
clothes I felt a masquerader" (*FTA* 243); "I . . . looked at myself
in civilian clothes in the mirror behind the bar" (245); "Knotting
my tie and looking in the glass I looked strange to myself in the
civilian clothes" (258)—but the matter runs deeper than this.
Perhaps Frederic's civilian clothes trouble him so much because
they were given to him by an *opera singer*—a male singer, to be
sure, but one who may nevertheless represent the opera-singing
mother who cross-dressed Hemingway in his youth. (This male
opera singer may, in fact, represent the *phallic* mother or a
"combined parent figure.") Frederic's failed specular connection
to Hemingway's bearded doctor father only becomes clear toward the end of the novel when Frederic uses the fetish object—
hair—in what George Zavitzianos would call a *homeovestic*
manner—that is, as a tool to negotiate a latently homosexual

bond with the father, a bond inherently undermined by an aura of masquerade: "I could not shadow-box in front of the narrow long mirror at first because it looked so strange to see a man with a beard boxing" (311). Then when Catherine enters labor, Frederic dresses in a medical gown to see her, but this "costume" again leaves him feeling like an impostor: "I looked in the glass and saw myself looking like a fake doctor with a beard" (319).[24]

Whereas the fetishist takes the phallic woman as an *object* by fetishizing part of his female lover's body or attire, and the transvestite *identifies* with the phallic woman by wearing fetishized female clothing, the homeovestite's perverse behavior involves—perversely enough—"wearing clothes of the same sex." His inanimate hypercathected object (beards or uniforms in Hemingway's case) represents not the maternal phallus but rather the

> *penis of the parent of the same sex with whom the [homeovestite] wishes to identify.* Consequently, in the case of a male homeovestite it would represent the incorporated penis of the father. The object is worn by the homeovestite during sexual activity and is considered in his fantasies a part of himself. [One might say, rather, that the wearing of the object *is* a sexual activity.] It is significant that in the man it is often an athletic article or a military uniform. The homeovestite act of the male does not symbolize a sexual relation with the phallic mother, as is the case in fetishism, but a homosexual relation with the father which has as a goal the incorporation of the paternal penis. ("Object" 489)[25]

Significantly, Zavitzianos writes that one of his homeovestic patients became excited gazing into *mirrors*: "By projecting his image of the father on to the mirror and looking at it, he created a sexual relation with the father which resulted in an erection. The image of the father was then introjected through vision and led to an identification with the omnipotent father. By the same token he warded off his identification with the mother" ("Object" 489–490). This patient had to ward off this latter identification, moreover, because "he had been a transvestite before resorting to homeovestism" ("Homeovestism" 474). According to Zavitzianos, this patient "had a pre-phallic bisexual splitting of the body image and [identified] . . . especially with his sister, whom he often felt inside himself" ("Homeovestism" 474).[26]

The persistence of this patient's identification with his sister and mother suggests that Zavitzianos's contention that his patient had *formerly* been a transvestite *before* becoming a homeovestite should not be taken to mean that the two conditions are in any way mutually exclusive. As almost every major theorist of the perversions acknowledges, the perversions tend to manifest themselves as clusters rather than in isolation. "Characteristically one perversion assumes dominance. Nevertheless, the scenario that is built up around the dominant perversion will bring in elements from nearly all the other perversions" (Kaplan 21). There is no reason to consider homeovestism an exception to this rule. Rather than existing as fixed and isolated conditions, transvestism and homeovestism in this case could more usefully be seen as two "logical moments" within a single psychodynamic, one or the other of which may dominate for any given period of time. In fact, the tension between homeovestism and transvestism within individuals suggests why so many transvestites adopt hyper-masculine clothing when they take a vacation from evening gowns and high heels. One of the great tragedies in the later life of the Chevalier d'Eon, that most famous of transvestites, was Louis XVI's refusal to let him wear the uniform of his beloved dragoons (Buhrich and McConaghy 4).[27] And Brierley, for instance, records the case of "Ida," a transvestite who kept two remarkably detailed diaries: one of his transvestism, the other celebrating "his exploits as a soldier" (95). Phyllis Greenacre seemed to recognize this coexistence of transvestism and homeovestism when she wrote that "some transvestites represent both parents in themselves and play out different parental roles with different parts of their own bodies" (312). In Hemingway's case, since hair symbolized the illusory, present/absent *female* phallus, it should hardly surprise us that *beard*-hair, as a synecdoche of his father and specifically masculine manifestation of the fetish object, functioned as a symbol for the *paternal* phallus.

Catherine Barkley, thus, describes Frederic's beard in reassuringly "masculine" phallic terms: "It looks so *stiff* and fierce and it's very soft and a great pleasure" (303). But whereas the fetish object, as maternal phallus, establishes an *identity* between lovers by disavowing the anatomical distinction between the sexes, the homeovestic object, as paternal phallus, wards off cross-gender identification and reinforces the anatomical *difference* between the sexes. Before Frederic grows his beard,

Catherine complains that his beard stubble chafes her skin which is as "*smooth as piano keys*" (114). And given Hemingway's association of the word "ivory," with his eponymous pseudo-twin sister, it would seem that by using a beard to establish the sexual difference between Frederic and Catherine, Hemingway was trying to ward off the more threatening aspects of merger with the split-off feminine part of himself that was so intimately tied to his memories of Marcelline. Yet in trying to disavow the feminine half of his ego, Hemingway can't help but call attention to the bisexual nature of the rift in it. By disavowing his femininity, he establishes a masculinity, but it is unstable, parodic, openly performative, found not in the self but in the specular, alienated image in the mirror.

Dad, Granddad, and Long Hair: The Castrated Father and the Idealized Paternal Phallus

> So now I just *had* red hair—and I loved it for you and was proud of it—and nobody said anything about it any more than they said to Gen. Custer when he wore his down to his shoulders.
>
> —Hemingway, Letter to Mary Hemingway,
> May 14, 1947

The embodiment of specular masculinity in Hemingway's work is none other than that *beau sabreur* General George Armstrong Custer, who appears in no fewer than six of Hemingway's novels. Custer's autographed portrait comically hangs alongside those of Mary Austin, D. H. Lawrence, Henry Wadsworth Longfellow, and Jim Thorpe in the committee room of the pseudo-British "town-Indian" club in *Torrents of Spring*. The famous F. Otto Becker lithograph of the Last Stand hangs in Freddy's bar in *To Have and Have Not*, just as it did in Hemingway's real Key West hangout, Sloppy Joe's. In fact, thanks to an Anheuser-Busch promotion, over 200,000 copies of this lithograph made their way into American saloons and homes between 1896 and the Second World War, so it is little wonder that Robert Jordan should remember this same picture of Custer hanging in a Montana bar in *For Whom the Bell Tolls*, nor should we be surprised that the mention of Custer's name prompts Willie to wish for a cold Anheuser-Busch in *Islands in the Stream*. Yet in Hemingway's work Custer is more than a picture on the wall. He functions as a pivotal symbolic figure in both *For Whom the Bell Tolls* and *Across the River into the Trees*.

Custer is a more ghostly, but no less important, presence in *The Garden of Eden*. He never actually appears in the manuscript, but he is replaced by an equally long-haired substitute whose identity was inextricably bound up with the Custer myth: Buffalo Bill.[28] It was after a meeting with Cody that Custer adopted the "scout" image in dress and manner that characterized his style between 1874 and his death. Cody returned the compliment after the Last Stand by "modifying his own appearance and dramatizing his adventures" to emphasize "his Custer likeness and his close relation to the Custer story" (Slotkin 408). With Custer safely buried, Cody became Custer's sidekick on stage and in dozens of dime novels, and after 1886 Cody regularly "reenacted" Custer's Last Stand for cheering fans in his Wild West Show. His name appears in the *Eden* manuscript, significantly enough, when Nick Sheldon is worried about the length of his hair. Although Nick likes having his hair the same length as his wife's, it makes him uncomfortable and he tells Andy that he's afraid he looks like a "sodomite." This, Nick explains, is why he uses "an Indian trick" to hide his hair under a hat. Nick also has another name for this disguise: "*Systeme* Colonel William F. Cody." Nick explains that when Cody would go out at night he, too, would hide his hair under his hat, using a "single big silver pin" to hold it up (K422.2 40.insert.15). Andy protests that Cody was a "showman" and that Nick isn't. This apparently doesn't matter to Nick, but to us it should. Cody was an *impersonator* of a man Hemingway used as a symbol of a sort of male male impersonation.

Dubbed by the admiring New York press "The Boy General with the Golden Locks," "the Gold-Haired Cavalryman," and "a Viking in long yellow locks," known to his soldiers as "Old Curly" and to the Lakota as "Pahuska" ("Long Hair"), celebrated by Whitman as "Thou of the tawny flowing hair," and memorialized by Whittier and Longfellow as "the White Chief with the yellow hair," General Custer was for obvious reasons a key figure in Hemingway's fetishistic imagination. But while Custer's flowing yellow hair is the crucial element in his iconography—so much so that pictures of the Last Stand almost invariably portray him with long hair in spite of the fact that he had shorn his locks shortly before his final campaign—he was almost as famous for his flamboyant uniforms, and these, too, are essential both to his public iconography and to his position within Hemingway's field of fetishistic fantasy.[29]

Although our national perception of Custer has become fixed by images of the Last Stand (supposedly the most repre- sented scene in American history), the genesis of the Custer myth and the key elements of its iconography date back to Custer's meteoric rise through the ranks during the Civil War to become at twenty-five the youngest major general in the history of the United States Army. It was during this war that Custer's hair became so famous, and it was soon after his promotion to the rank of brigadier general in 1863 that Custer designed a special and spectacularly gaudy uniform for himself:

> Known as his "fighting trim," it consisted of a tight hussar jacket and trousers of black velveteen garnished with yards of gold lace, a blue sailor shirt bearing a white star on each side of the collar, a long cravat of flaming scarlet, a black broad- brimmed hat adorned with a gold cord and a silver star, and a pair of high-topped boots sporting gilt spurs. With his blond mustache, imperial, and shoulder-length hair, he looked like the reincarnation of some seventeenth century cavalier. (Urwin 17)

It was an impressive uniform, unlike any other in the Union Army, and it caught the public's imagination. "Reporters loved him: he was good for a story every time he put on, or took off," his "plumed piratical sombrero" (Slotkin 386). But if Custer's Civil War uniform captured the national imagination, the equally flamboyant light buckskin "scout" suit of his Indian-fighting days (and of so many Hollywood westerns) has become even more firmly ingrained in our national consciousness. Only two years after his death, Custer's dual costumes were already so in- timately tied to his mythic identity that when Henry Steinegger came to create his well-known print, *General Custer's Death Struggle: The Battle of the Little Big Horn* (1878), he felt com- pelled to draw in TWO long-haired Custers fighting heroically side by side, one in buckskin and the other in dress blues. "The viewer is left to choose for himself between them!" (Dippie 36).[30]

Steinegger's double image is suggestive, for Custer has al- ways been a profoundly complex, divided, and ambivalent figure in the national consciousness. In his brilliant reading of the

Custer myth in *Fatal Environment*, Richard Slotkin has demonstrated that, as early as the Civil War, Custer was represented
by the press as an androgynous "liminal hero," a "boy-man" of
questionable judgment but unquestionable bravery "whose sexual character is on the border between masculine adulthood and
the passionate nature of womanhood" (454). This liminal status
was then solidified by the Eastern papers during the Indian
wars, when Custer was portrayed (often by himself) as a
Leatherstocking-like figure whose "kinship with his dearest foes
. . . paradoxically enable[d] him to sympathize with them and to
be a more effective agent of their destruction" (Slotkin 351). Simultaneously "Sioux chieftain" and representative of the "White
Race," symbol of the fading frontier and agent of "prosperity"
(i.e., industrialism), savior of captive white women and murderer
of innocent Indian men, women, and children, the Custer portrayed by the Eastern press was a true mythic hero: the embodiment of the ideological conflicts of his age, representing in
himself the polar opposites of a network of national struggles:

> Custer is presented as the meeting point of the positive and
> negative forces in American culture—masculinity and feminin-
> ity, adulthood and childhood, civilization and savagery, sanity
> and madness, order and disorder. As one who balances on a
> turning point between these orders and qualities, he is able to
> draw knowledge and power from both; but that very position
> makes him the embodiment of trouble and conflict, unstable
> and dangerous as a moral reference point. (Slotkin 454-5)

When Frederick Van De Water began his 1934 biography of
Custer, *Glory Hunter* (from which Hemingway excerpted the
chapter on the Last Stand for his 1942 anthology of war stories
Men At War), he did so by describing Custer at length as a man
so riven by contradictions that one thing alone held him
together: his insatiable thirst for glory. Van De Water thereby
added yet another contradiction to the Custer myth, offering
to balance the heroic youth enshrined in national mythology
with the image of a reckless glory-hunting fool. But if Custer
was, and is, a complex and ambivalent figure in the national
mythology, he was even more so in Hemingway's *personal*
mythology, and the "trouble" he embodied was, above all, *gender* trouble.

History and mythology both lend themselves to a reading of
Custer as curiously androgynous. At West Point, "his eyes were

bright blue, his hair golden yellow and his complexion so innocent a pink and white that the cadets, to his horror, nicknamed
him 'Fanny'" (Van De Water 27). His famous dead-last class-
standing at graduation was largely due to demerits "earned for
eccentric behavior, hair-styles, and dress," and his Civil War
image was

> distinctly dependent on the parallel symbolism of his youthful
> or adolescent qualities, his ambiguous sexuality, and his re-
> semblance to warriors from a primitive or savage stage of social
> development. Many correspondents and memoirists empha-
> sized the 'almost feminine' qualities of the Boy General—his
> long fair curls and smooth skin, his high voice that 'fairly
> screeches' calling his troops to charge, his 'Merry eye and rosy
> lip,' his vanity and self-display. (Slotkin 376; 386)

Custer's first and idolizing biographer, Frederick Whittaker, describes the boy general as "girlish in appearance" (33), writes of
him blushing "like a girl" (91), and describes Custer's appearance in his self-designed Civil War uniform as follows: "The boy
general looked so pretty and effeminate, so unlike the stern re-
alities of war, that he was certain to be quizzed and ridiculed un-
mercifully, unless he could compel the whole army to respect
him"—something he never achieved, in spite of Whittaker's
protests to the contrary (169). Soon after the Little Big Horn, one
of General Sheridan's aides remembered Long Hair with fondness but not respect. "[He] used to go about dressed like one of
Byron's pirates in the Archipelago," the aide recalled, conde-
scendingly tempering his critique of the vain and reckless boy
general with a telling analogy: "You see we all liked Custer and
did not mind his freaks . . . any more than we would have
minded temper in a woman" (qtd. in Slotkin 454).

  Yet whatever history and mythology imply about Custer's
ambiguous sexuality, Hemingway, with his special attention to
the symbolism of hair and uniforms, must have had his own
highly individual, and uniquely sharp, understanding of the
matter. He was certainly well read on the subject. He probably
first read about Custer as a boy, perhaps in Whittaker, and he
would have learned a good deal about Custer from his extensive
reading on the Civil War. His 1940 Key West book inventory lists
copies of Van De Water's *Glory Hunter* and Elizabeth Bacon
Custer's *Tenting on the Plains* (1887); at the Finca Vigía, he
owned copies of David Humphreys Miller's *Custer's Fall* (1957),

Jay Monaghan's *Life of George Armstrong Custer* (1959), and Charles Windolph's *I Fought with Custer* (1959). These latter volumes, published when they were, could hardly have influenced Hemingway's fiction, but their presence in his library suggests that Long Hair remained an abiding interest for Hemingway even during the final years of his life. In a humorously hyperbolic 1950 letter to Arthur Mizener, Hemingway boasted that he alone knew "the exact details of how [God] killed George Armstrong Custer" (*SL* 694). And when Hemingway on his second safari regaled his Wakamba hosts with tales of life in America, he told them of hunting for brontosauruses, mammoths, and American soldiers: "At night I tell them how we killed George Armstrong Custer and the 7th Cavalry and they think we are wasting our time here and should get the hell to America" (*SL* 827).

That Hemingway should tell such tales in the very same letter to Harvey Breit in which he explains that he has just shaved his head to please his African fiancée, and that he can't write any more about her because to do so gives him "too bad a hardon," is, I submit, no mere coincidence. "Gone native" and with his head shaved, Hemingway was using the ghost of Long Hair to negotiate the transvestic aspects of his own identity— just as he did in the May 1947 letter to Mary that I quote in my epigraph. An identification with Custer, however ambivalent and indirect, is somehow built into Hemingway's identification with "Catherine" and with his need to dye his hair red. With his flowing mane that Hemingway—a good deal of historical evidence to the contrary notwithstanding—simultaneously imagined as *scalped*, Custer embodied for Hemingway the phallic/castrated transvestic position.[31] Yet with his theatrical uniforms that staged a symbolic relation to masculinity that exposed that relation precisely *as staged*, Custer also functioned for Hemingway as an icon of homeovestism and as a defense against the more threatening aspects of transvestic identity. Custer, thus, represented for Hemingway not only a rift in the national consciousness but also the bisexual rift in his own ego. Hemingway could identify with the courageous Custer to negotiate a transvestic or homeovestic position, but he could as easily dismiss him disdainfully as a fool, thereby disavowing the sensation of masquerade that undermined his gender negotiations. Custer's long hair assured Hemingway that other brave fighting men ("real men") shared his secret desires, but Custer's bravery (like Paco's in "The Capital of the World") was the sort of foolish, suicidal bravery that Hemingway could never respect. Hemingway's disparagement of Long Hair, fed by Van De Water's Custerphobic biography, not only allowed him to maintain an optimal distance from those aspects of himself that he found threatening, it seems to contain and project outside of himself an element of self-loathing. But Hemingway's attempts to *disidentify from* Custer are structured by the logic of disavowal and always betray the depth of the identification that must be denied. Thus if Hemingway, head shaved and spear in hand, often identified with Custer's killers, he almost as often identified himself with Long Hair—and with good reason.

Hemingway, who spent many of his adult summers in the "Custer Country" (now much more appropriately known as "Crow Country") of Wyoming and Montana, had a good deal in common with the Boy General. Though born in Ohio, Custer was raised in Michigan by an older half-sister with whom he identified strongly; yet he identified just as strongly with his militaristic father. This dual identification seems to have produced in Custer's childhood, as in Hemingway's, a tension between genteel, "feminine," values and those militaristic values more often associated with masculinity. (In Hemingway's case, however, militaristic values were represented by his grandfathers, both of whom were Civil War veterans.) According to Slotkin, Custer's sister and father represented "the moral and symbolic poles of his character," and Custer negotiated between these two powerful influences primarily through the symbolism of his hair and his uniforms:

> Lydia spoke from the bourgeois values of respectability and self-discipline which Custer's society had traditionally vested in "Woman"; and Father Custer represented masculine combativeness, defiance of respectability, and love of display. . . . These elements first found symbolic expression in the young boy's search for a personal style. Frequent changes of costume and hairstyle throughout his life marked his ambivalent play with different roles. His hairstyle was especially symbolic: he alternately grew his hair long and clipped it short, got his head 'peeled like an onion' or let his curls swing below his shoulders perfumed with cinnamon oil. The 'long-haired' phases suggested his father's flamboyance; yet the style itself made him appear "feminine," and he enjoyed the implication of sensual attractiveness that the adjective implied—and enjoyed also the

ambivalent linkage with his half-sister Lydia. Yet "respectable"
virtues often required him to shear his locks, Samson-like—it
was characteristic of him to clip his mustache and mail it to his
wife. (375-6)

Hemingway not only played similar gender-inflected games with
his own hair—growing it out, shaving it, dyeing it, or combing it
over the top as he began to bald—he also, at least in his youth,
shared Custer's fondness for flamboyant uniforms.

Returning to Oak Park after serving as an ambulance driver
for the Red Cross in the First World War, Ernest wore a dashing
"British-type khaki-colored uniform, partly covered by a long
black broadcloth cape flung over his shoulders . . . [and] fastened
at the neck with a double silver buckle" (Sanford 177). Hardly
standard issue for an American Red Cross ambulance driver,
Hemingway's uniform had been custom-tailored by Spangno-
lini's, the most fashionable men's tailoring establishment in
Milan. It featured a Sam Browne belt which Ernest was unautho-
rized to wear and a "U.S." insignia on the shoulder which he did
not rate. Neither did Ernest rate his Italian officer's cape. Though
he was fond of implying otherwise, Ernest never served with the
Italian Army, much less with its Arditi shock troops. Ambulance
drivers for the American Red Cross attached to the Italian Army
were considered "honorary" second lieutenants, a status which
gave them priority on roads and which allowed them to mess
with the Italian officers when they were near the front, but they
were not entitled to wear Italian uniform.

Yet, to be fair, Ernest was hardly the only Red Cross ambulance driver to sail home in a custom-tailored uniform. As
Michael Reynolds explains, many drivers returning from overseas went to some lengths to disguise their Red Cross affiliation
in response to changing public attitudes toward the Red Cross
at the close of the war:

> The Y.M.C.A. and the Red Cross, linked in the public mind by
> their drives for donations and their war work, had begun to
> smell a little tainted by 1919. Embarrassed by riches, the
> Y.M.C.A. coffers were filled with one hundred million undistrib-
> uted dollars when the war ended in November, 1918. Soldiers
> from the front could not understand why they had been
> charged money for cigarettes and coffee. Had not the home font
> donated the money? Was the Y.M.C.A. profiteering from the
> war? (*Young Hemingway* 22)

As the Red Cross became ever more associated with nursing, society matrons, and "benevolent, if somewhat misinformed,
home-fronters," those who had served in the line of fire overseas
became ever more uncomfortable with uniforms that failed to
distinguish their service. Thus Reynolds observes:

> It is little wonder that Hemingway, along with other Red Cross
> men, began to invent a different war for himself. He had gone
> to the war in search of heroics. If what befell him was an "in-
> dustrial accident," it would serve. The Red Cross, however, be-
> came an embarrassment that he simply eradicated. In Milan he
> and other Red Cross drivers spent good money on fitted uni-
> forms made to order, which resembled the ones worn by the
> American Expeditionary Force. Change the uniform, change
> the story. (23)

Nevertheless, as Reynolds realizes, Hemingway's uniform
was laden with psychological import. Could it be that it helped
to shore up a masculinity threatened by a wounding that Hemingway always interpreted as a threat of castration? Home from
the front, Ernest continued to wear his uniform for as long as he
possibly could, even though it made him feel like a masquerader
amongst civilians. Convalescing, he would sleep in late, appear
downstairs for lunch in his uniform and polished high cordovan
leather boots, and then sally forth in full military regalia for a
walk about town. The newspapers reminded soldiers "that they
had only three months after demobilization to get into mufti, to
store old uniforms for Memorial Day parades and such," but
Ernest was still wearing his uniform daily some four months
after his return (*Young Hemingway* 40). Reynolds speculates,
quite reasonably, that Hemingway was simply reluctant to take
off a uniform that he associated with his new, largely fictional,
identity as a man of the world. He may have also had a more
practical reason for wearing the uniform. In *At the Hemingways*,
Marcelline remembers attending a matinee in Chicago one Saturday in the spring of 1919 when she overheard two women in
the row behind her talking about her brother: "'Why does that
boy have to flaunt that fancy uniform around town all these
months?' said a voice in my ear. 'He's been home from war since
last winter. Why doesn't he stop trying to be a hero and put on
civilian clothes? I've got no patience with these kids that keep
trying to show off'" (190–191). When Marcelline angrily turned
around she discovered two teachers from Oak Park High; out-

Figure 15. Hemingway in Oak Park, January 1919. (John F. Kennedy Library)

raged, she dressed them down, explaining that Ernest needed to wear his high boots to support his wounded legs. And she was probably right. Pictures of Hemingway in swimwear from the summer of 1920 still show him with a large bandage around one knee. Nevertheless, as Reynolds notes, Ernest could have worn the boots without the uniform.

Whatever Ernest's practical reasons were for ordering a custom-made uniform and for wearing it for months around Oak Park, he must have recognized the flamboyance of it, for he soon gave it a safely distanced position in his field of fetishistic fantasy. In one of his earliest stories, "The Mercenaries," the protagonist, down-to-earth Percy Graves, cuckolds the "Italian ace of aces," "Il Lupo," a caricature of the bald Italian soldier-poet Gabriele D'Annunzio, another of Hemingway's homeovestic icons. When Il Lupo, "a good-looking fellow with a scar across his cheek and a beautiful blue theatrical-looking cape and shining black boots and a sword," walks through the door of his mistress's house in Sicily to find Percy having breakfast with the beauty, a woman with "blue-black hair and a face colored like old ivory," he immediately challenges him to a sword duel. Bold but prosaic (and perhaps inspired by Mark Twain's battling axes or Gatling guns at fifteen paces from *A Tramp Abroad*), Percy proposes different terms: pistols at four feet on the count of three. He then proceeds to shoot Il Lupo's gun out of his hand when the coward draws on the count of two. "Wolf, hell no," Percy recalls. "He was a coyote" (qtd. in Griffin 110).

Hemingway could clearly recognize the homeovestic use of a uniform in others when he saw it. In "Gaudy Uniform Is Tchitcherin's Weakness," that dispatch from the 1923 Lausanne Conference mentioned briefly in chapter 3, Hemingway wrote at length about the Russian diplomat, opining that Tchitcherin's weakness for military posturing and uniforms, in spite of his having never served in the army, was his single weakness and the result of his having been "kept in dresses until he was twelve years old" (*Dateline* 259). And given the homeovestic significance of beards for Hemingway and his intimations of Tchitcherin's effeminacy, it is surely significant that Hemingway repeatedly calls attention to Tchitcherin's "indefinite beard," "thin beard," or "wispy red beard" (*Dateline* 146; 153; 257). In *Across the River*, Cantwell offers Renata a fair definition for a type of homeovestite: "We call a pistol-slapper a non-fighting man, disguised in uniform, or you might even call it costume, who gets an erection every time the weapon slaps against his thigh" (238). Cantwell, however, is careful to distance himself from such types. When Renata gives him the two emeralds that he keeps in his pocket to ward off loneliness and castration, she explains her own disinclination to wear them by comparing them to a fancy dress from Paris, asking Cantwell, "You don't like to wear your dress uniform, do you?" "No," replies Cantwell. "You don't like to carry a sword, do you?" Renata presses, to which Cantwell responds emphatically: "No, repeat, no." Renata concludes, "You are not that kind of a soldier and I am not that kind

of girl" (103). Nevertheless, this fails to dull Cantwell's interest in
the topic. He criticizes General Montgomery for changing "from
his proper uniform into a crowd-catching kit" for his evening
strolls (125), and in a bar he snaps at a staring couple of Vene-
tians, "I am sorry that I am in uniform. But it is a uniform. Not a
costume" (38). Yet would Cantwell need to protest so much if
this were entirely the case? It sounds more like a classic example of negation betraying its opposite: there *is* an element of
masquerade to Cantwell's military demeanor. The face that he
sees in the mirror certainly suggests as much.

Cantwell negotiates his identity partly through a series of
disavowed identifications with three famous theatrical soldier-
lovers: Othello, Gabriele D'Annunzio, and George Armstrong
Custer. As dozens of critics have noted, Cantwell's protest that
he and Renata are not Othello and Desdamona invites the comparison more effectively than it denies it. With greedy ears, the
Venetian Renata devours her foreign soldier's discourse of war,
and Cantwell's present to Renata—the ebony head of a moor
with a bejeweled turban—is as much a symbolic self-portrait as
the painting that Renata offers in return.

Cantwell, likewise, both identifies with and distances himself from D'Annunzio, "writer, poet, national hero, phraser of the
dialectic of Fascism, macabre egotist, aviator, commander, or
rider, in the first of the fast torpedo attack boats, Lieutenant
Colonel of Infantry without ever knowing how to command a
company, nor a platoon properly, the great, lovely writer of *Notturno* whom we respect, and jerk" (*ART* 52). Cantwell admires
D'Annunzio's writing and bravery, but he doesn't think much of
the man as a soldier. "D'Annunzio . . . had moved through the
different arms of the service as he had moved into and out of the
arms of different women," Cantwell thinks, and he calls attention to the poet-soldier's flair for the theatrical.

> All the arms were pleasant that d'Annunzio served with . . . ex-
> cept the Infantry [Cantwell's own branch of the service]. He re-
> membered how d'Annunzio had lost an eye in a crash, flying as
> an observer, over Trieste or Pola, and how, afterwards, he had
> always worn a patch over it and people who did not know . . .
> thought it had been shot out at the Veliki or San Michele or
> some other bad place beyond the Carso where everyone died, or
> was incapacitated. . . . But d'Annunzio, truly, was only making
> heroic gestures with the other things. . . . He . . . flew, but he
> was not a flier. He was in the Infantry but he was not an In-

fantryman and it was always the same appearances. (*ART* 49-50)

Yet Hemingway, whose fascination with D'Annunzio began soon after the First World War when he gave D'Annunzio's novel *Il fuoco* to a number of young women, had a good deal in common with the man he described in 1923 as "that old, *bald-headed*, perhaps a little insane but thoroughly sincere, divinely brave swashbuckler, Gabriele D'Annunzio" (my emphasis, *Dateline* 256). John Paul Russo has argued that in *Across the River* D'Annunzio functions as "a scapegoat for certain qualities that Hemingway secretly admired and wished to reject in himself" (172).

> Like D'Annunzio, Hemingway [was] . . . a famous writer, a paramilitary figure, and lover—married four times. Hemingway, likewise, "flew but he was not a flier." He flew as a journalist during the Second World War. As the leader of a rolling canteen in World War One, and as a journalist in World War Two, Hemingway "was in the Infantry but he was not an Infantryman". . . . Cantwell may be partially justified in his criticism, and yet Hemingway could be accused of "the same appearances" as D'Annunzio, and with much less credit to them. D'Annunzio was a genuine and much-decorated war hero, he did the military part better—he also did it first. (172–3)

Cantwell's (and Hemingway's) disavowed identification with D'Annunzio becomes even clearer when we recognize Hemingway's debt in *Across the River* to D'Annunzio's novel *Il fuoco* and memoir *Notturno*. Cantwell thinks he passes "the house where the poor beat-up old boy had lived with his great, sad, and never properly loved actress" (51). But according to Adeline Tintner, Cantwell (another "beat-up old boy") is wrong about the villa. Cantwell passes not the house where D'Annunzio had the affair with Eleonora Duse that inspired *Il fuoco*, but rather the house described in *Notturno* where D'Annunzio stayed in 1916 with his lovely raven-haired daughter, Renata, while he was recovering from the eye wound that he suffered in a plane crash.

During his last stand in Venice, Cantwell is at similar pains to disidentify with Custer, but the more he struggles against the identification the more he reveals the strength of the identification that must be struggled against. Cantwell often calls himself "boy," but when we are first introduced to him Hemingway makes a point of noting that "he was *not* a boy. He was fifty and

a Colonel of Infantry in the Army of the United States. . . . reduced from being a general officer . . ." (my emphasis, 8).
Cantwell's age and fondness for disparaging the cavalry distance
him from the Boy General, but his rank betrays the underlying
identification. Cantwell owes much of his character to Hemingway's friend Buck Lanham, who was *promoted* from colonel to
general after losing many men following orders in the Hürtgen
Forest. Yet in *Across the River* Hemingway reverses the situation,
demoting Cantwell from brigadier general to colonel. No doubt,
as James Meredith contends, Hemingway did this to "emphasize
the tragic condition of his fictional hero" (64), but I would suggest that he also did it to establish an identification (however
ambivalent and disavowed) with Custer, who was demoted from
general to colonel after the Civil War. Like Custer, whose brigade
by the end of the Civil War could claim the unenviable honor of
having "the highest number of casualties sustained by any
mounted organization of equivalent size in the Union Army"
(Urwin 7), Cantwell had been a fighting general with a well-
deserved reputation for losing men; but whereas Custer lost his
men at the Little Big Horn by *disobeying* orders, Cantwell lost
his men by trying to *follow* impossible orders.

Cantwell's battles are, nonetheless, aligned with the Little
Big Horn. Cantwell received his symbolically castratory wound in
the hand "on a rocky, bare-assed hill" (135). The too-obvious allusion, of course, is to *Calvary* and to Christ's stigmata, but the
pun on *cavalry* reveals a further association with Custer's castratory scalping on another bare-assed hill. Thinking about how he
had lost three battalions and three wives, a phrase pops into
Cantwell's mind: "GENERAL WHERE IS YOUR CAVALRY?" (95). Having
served with the Montana National Guard, Cantwell is from
"Custer Country," and he apparently has an intimate understanding of the Last Stand. When, over drinks at Harry's Bar,
Cantwell and Renata plan an imaginary trip across the U.S.,
Cantwell tells Renata that they will go to Sheridan, Wyoming,
and "drive up on the way to Billings, to where they killed that fool
George Armstrong Custer, and you can see the markers where
everybody died and I'll explain the fight to you" (265). Renata
thinks this will be lovely and naively asks, "Which is Sheridan
more like, Mantova or Verona or Vicenza?" Cantwell's reply
clearly connects the Last Stand with his and Hemingway's youthful castratory wounding at Fossalta: "It isn't like any of those. It
is right up against the [Big Horn] mountains, almost like Schio"

(265). Schio had been where Hemingway worked as a Red Cross ambulance driver shortly before he was wounded in 1918.

Cantwell's (and Hemingway's) disavowed identification with Custer, then, points to a disavowed symbolic castration—a castration equated with the loss of infantile omnipotence that accompanies separation and individuation from the maternal body. Cantwell thinks that what he really lost at Fossalta was his illusion of personal "immortality," something Custer, who fought in the thick of battle through the entire Civil War without ever being seriously wounded, is accused of never having lost until it was too late. Cantwell's defenses against castration are multiple. Renata's fetishized hair wards off the threat of castration, as do the emeralds that she gives "Dick" to keep in his pocket. Most importantly, Renata's love makes Cantwell feel as if he were "out on some bare-assed hill where it is too rocky to dig . . . and all of a sudden instead of being there naked, [he is] armoured" (129).

Like Zavitzianos's patient, who used his homeovestic identification with his father to ward off troubling aspects of his transvestic identification with his mother, Cantwell uses his ambivalent identification with Custer to negotiate between the masculine (homeovestic) and feminine (transvestic) aspects of his identity. Regarding his face in the mirror before a homeovestic shave, Cantwell thinks to himself, "Boy, . . . you certainly are a beat-up, old looking bastard."

> Now you have to shave and look at that face while you do it. Then you must get a hair-cut. . . . You're a Colonel of Infantry, boy. You can't go around looking like Joan of Arc or General (Brevetted) George Armstrong Custer. That beautiful horse-cavalryman. I guess it is fun to be that way and have a loving wife and use sawdust for brains. But it must have seemed like the wrong career to him when they finished up on that hill above the Little Big Horn . . . and nothing left to him for the rest of his life but that old lovely black powder smell and his own people shooting each other, and themselves, because they were afraid of what the squaws would do to them.
> The body was unspeakably mutilated. . . . Poor horse-cavalryman, he thought. The end of all his dreams. (169)

Cantwell confronts in the mirror nothing less than the bisexual rift in his (and Hemingway's) ego. "Beat up" and scarred like the mutilated Custer, Cantwell balances his homeovestic beard-stubble and disavowed identification with the Boy General against his transvestic long hair and identification with Joan of Arc. (When Marita cuts her hair like an "African girl" in *The Garden of Eden* manuscript, she, too, worries about looking like "Jeanne D'Arc" [K422.1 36.1].) The young French heroine is but a substitute for the more immediate object of his transvestic identification: Renata. Inspired by what he has seen in the mirror, Cantwell spends the night thinking of Renata, and as soon as it is light enough to see, he begins pages of "conversation" with her portrait, addressing the image as "*Boy or daughter* or my one true love" (173). His use of the word "boy" suggests both the androgynous nature of his love object and his identification with the image—as if it were in a mirror. And when the portrait fails to reply to his questions, he reflects, "She probably would speak to a horse-cavalryman. . ." (173).

It is a little jarring to think that Cantwell might see the image of a nineteen-year-old girl when he looks in the mirror, yet he and Renata attempt to "become" each other through their love-making rituals, and Hemingway engaged in similar attempts to merge identities with Renata's closest real world counterpart, Adriana Ivancich. In his letters to Adriana, Hemingway addresses her as "Adriana Hemingway" or "Hemingstein" and signs himself "Ernest Ivancich" or even "A. Ivancich."[32] Earlier in the novel, after Renata tells Cantwell, "Now I will comb my hair and make my mouth new and you can watch me," the Colonel steps into the bathroom momentarily to look at his own scarred face in the mirror to check for "any traces of lipstick" (111). He's none-too-pleased with what he sees, but he thinks that at least his (fetishized) tan takes some of "the curse" off his face. He tells the mirror to go to hell and asks his image, "Should we rejoin the ladies?" As the Colonel steps out of the bathroom, he feels "as young as at his first attack" (112). And what does he find in the hotel room? Renata, the girl whose name means "reborn" and who *is* exactly as young as Cantwell was at his first attack (and symbolic castration), standing in front of the mirrored armoire combing her hair. "She was not combing it for vanity, nor to do to the Colonel what she knew it could and would do. She was combing it with difficulty and without respect, and, since it was very heavy hair and as alive as the hair of peasants, or the hair of the beauties of the great nobility, it was resistant to the comb" (112). Cantwell offers to help, but Renata needs none, though they talk about how to arrange her hair for the entire next page. Alienated from her image in the mirror, Renata complains: "The mirror bores me. . . . Putting on lipstick . . . and combing your too heavy hair is not a life for a woman . . . who loves someone. When you want to be the moon and various stars and live with your man and have five sons, looking at yourself in the mirror and doing the artifices of a woman is not very exciting" (118). Cantwell, however, finds it quite exciting—just as he can appreciate the beautiful hair that she merely takes for granted.

Cantwell, likewise, has a special appreciation for Renata's portrait. He assures Renata that he isn't abnormal enough to prefer the portrait to "the real thing," but at night it does help him to negotiate the transvestic and homeovestic aspects of his identity. After a nighttime identity-merging ride in a gondola with Renata, the Colonel returns to his room and looks in the mirror. Staring back at him is the image of a woman: "The inner doors of the armoire, the mirrored ones, were opened in such a way, that he could see the portrait from the side" (164). To relieve his loneliness, he talks to the portrait—at great length— just as he talks to his own alienated image in the mirror:

> "Portrait," he said. "You better look the other way so that you will not be unmaidenly. I am going to take a shower now and *shave*, something you will never have to do, and *put on my soldier-suit* and go and walk around this town even though it is too early."
>
> So, he got out of bed, favoring his bad leg, which hurt him always. He pulled the reading light with his bad hand. . . . He walked past the portrait, only looking casually, and looked at himself in the mirror. He had dropped both parts of his pajamas and he looked at himself critically and truly.
>
> "You beat-up old bastard," he said to the mirror. Portrait was a thing of the past. Mirror was actuality and of this day.
>
> The gut is flat, he said without uttering it. The chest is all right except where it contains the defective muscle. *We are hung as we are hung, for better or worse, or something, or something awful.* (my emphasis, 180)

Turning away in disgust, Cantwell decides to take his shower and don his "soldier suit." The homeovestic shave and military disguise may be a bit of a masquerade, but at least they cloak his feminine identifications and compensate for any deficiencies in the way he is "hung."

Scalped, mutilated, and symbolically castrated, Custer doesn't function very well as a paternal ideal to shore up Hemingway's fragile masculinity. But, then, neither did Hemingway's real father. It is a biographical commonplace that despite some genuine identification with and admiration for his father's prowess as a naturalist and woodsman, Hemingway regarded him largely as an object for *dis*identification, a disappointing coward emasculated by a domineering wife. This, in fact, is a classic portrait of the perverse family. According to Joyce McDougall, by disavowing sexual difference and separation from the maternal body, the pervert also disavows the significance of the *primal scene*, the fantasy of parental intercourse. That is, for the male child to disavow sexual difference, retain his narcissistic union with the mother, and function as her substitute phallus, the role of the father's penis as the object that completes the mother's genital must be disavowed.[33] *Ergo*, father must be "castrated"; and the mother is almost invariably presented as the agent of castration. Moreover, as Pamela Boker has recently argued in her study of repressed grief in Hemingway's work, the reverse is equally true and reciprocally reinforcing: if the male child refuses to identify with a disappointing real father, adopting an abstract idealized paternal imago in his stead, he will find it difficult to separate from the mother, negotiate the Oedipus complex, and establish a mature masculinity.[34]

McDougall could easily be describing Grace Hall Hemingway when she writes, "One is tempted to surmise that the mother of the future pervert herself denies sexual reality and denigrates the father's phallic function. It is possible that she also gives the child the feeling that he or she is a phallic substitute. In the histories of these patients we frequently find that another model of virility was held up to the child, sometimes the mother's own father or brother, sometimes a religious figure or God is the one phallic object of value" (79). It may well be, as Max Westbrook has suggested, that Grace was guilty only "of having the strength that Clarence lacked" and that Clarence "was unmanned not by Grace but by himself" (31); yet in Ernest's *imagination*—and, unjust as it may be, this is what counts—Grace clearly denigrated his father's phallic function. One need only think of Mrs. Adams's Christian Science and patronizing tone in "The Doctor and the Doctor's Wife" or her destruction of the doctor's preserved snakes and Indian artifacts in "Now I Lay Me."[35] We've already speculated that Grace used young Ernest, the "little man" that she sometimes dressed as a little girl, as a "phallic substitute." And instead of holding up Clarence as a model of virility for her son, she celebrated the idealized virility of her own father. Ernest grew up "with the reminder ringing in his ears that she had named him for 'the finest purest noblest man I have ever known, Ernest Hall.'"[36] It is tempting to put into Ernest's mouth the complaint of one of McDougall's patients, Professor K (a fetishist, transvestite, and sado-masochist): "Always talking about her wonderful father . . . the man I was supposed to emulate. Actually it was *she* who wanted to be exactly like him. She told me she had always wanted to be a boy. Well I was supposed to be that boy—not for myself but for her" (45). After all, "Grace Ernestine Hall was always her father's child" (Reynolds, *Young Hemingway* 106).

As a result of these family dynamics, the pervert's identification with the father is deeply ambivalent and disavowed. Yet beneath this disavowal of the father and his role in the primal scene lurks a vital recognition of both. According to McDougall, "We discover in the course of analysis that *the father, invariably presented as a castrate, a figure unworthy of identification, conceals his idealized counterpart, that of an uncastratable phallus, the only one capable of completing the mother*" (my emphasis, 44). The pervert splits the paternal imago, then, into a denigrated, castrated imaginary father and an idealized unassailable phallus or symbolic father often based upon the ideal of virility held up by the mother. The mother, whose imago is likewise split into an idealized love object and a dangerous castrator, thus remains on some level the arbiter of masculinity and the conduit for the idealized paternal phallus. This idealized phallus, however, "is only defensively attributed to the mother, hidden so to speak behind her own primordial phallic role" (McDougall 60).

Despite its split-off quality, the idealized paternal phallus "plays an important structuring role in the personality" (McDougall 60). Although the pervert disavows his identification with the father to maintain the illusion of union with the mother, the representation of the father as an absence profoundly threatens his sense of individual identity. To ward off the threat of an absolute merger with the mother that would annihilate his ego, the pervert needs to maintain some tie, however tenuous, to the father. "Only the perverse . . . sexual act permits some illusory recovery of the paternal phallus, albeit in idealized and disguised forms; it thus fulfills an essential function in affirming separate identity and affords some protection against the overwhelming dependence on the maternal imago, and the equally dangerous desire to merge with her" (McDougall 73). The fetishist attempts incorporate the idealized paternal phallus (along with the maternal phallus) during intercourse; the transvestite disguises himself as his (phallic) mother to incorporate it through her; and the homeovestite hopes to borrow and incorporate it by impersonating the father and having a sexual relation with his specular image in the mirror. Through yet another trick, the fetishist/homeovestite can impersonate the heroic idealized paternal imago and then identify with his female partner during intercourse to incorporate the idealized paternal phallus through her. "This eternal quest for the father, for something which stands between the child and the omnipotent mother, contributes to the compulsive character of perverse sexuality" (McDougall 60).

This relation between the mother, the denigrated father, and the idealized paternal phallus is unmistakable in *For Whom the Bell Tolls*. As dozens of critics have noted, the "family" of guerrillas in Pablo's cave is on some level an imaginary portrait of the Hemingways. There is the strong, castrating, phallic mother, Pilar; the denigrated and "castrated," but dangerous, father, Pablo; the twin-like love object, who looks enough like Jordan to be his sister, and who wants to wear her hair exactly like his, Maria; and the idealized, dignified, grandfatherly Anselmo. The role of the idealized, grandfatherly paternal phallus is clearest, however, in Jordan's memories of his youth in the "Custer Country" of Montana.

These memories of his family surface after Jordan is shaken by the distant sound of El Sordo's last stand and the news that El Sordo and his men have all been decapitated. As Dean Rehberger observes in an excellent ideological reading of Hemingway's use of the Custer myth, El Sordo's battle on a hilltop shaped like "the breast of a young girl with no nipple" both invokes and inverts the traditional iconography of the Last Stand (309). The outnumbered and encircled leader on the hilltop, El Sordo, has a "thin-bridged, hooked nose like an Indian's" and has more in common with Sitting Bull than with Custer (141). El Sordo speaks in the clipped pidgin-English of a Hollywood Indian: "When blow bridge?" and "Heard last night comes English dynamiter. Good. Very happy. Get Whisky. For you. You like?" (156). Likewise, the Fascist cavalry captain, who foolishly re-

fuses to listen to his subordinates and who is tricked by El
Sordo's false suicide, looks with his blue eyes, blond hair, and
"blond, British-looking mustache" suspiciously like Custer
(316). As Rehberger notes, "In Hemingway's retelling of the
Custer myth . . . savagery is displaced to the side of military
order and technological superiority," for it is the Fascists who
mutilate their dead enemies (177). Yet the inversion of the
Custer myth has a further effect; it allows Jordan and Hemingway to disavow their identifications with Long Hair, just as both
disavow their identifications with their emasculated fathers.
After all, Robert Jordan, who hails from a town not far from the
Little Big Horn, has a distaste for haircuts and wears his hair
long enough to provoke some teasing from General Goltz. Likewise, while he was writing El Sordo's last stand, Hemingway was
engaged in growing his own hair out, having taken a vow to
leave his hair uncut until he finished the novel.[37]

For both Jordan and Hemingway, the decapitation of El
Sordo and his men represents the terrors of castration. During
the standoff on the hill, El Sordo feels "as naked . . . as though
all of his clothing and even his skin had been removed. . . . A
flayed rabbit [hare/hair] is as well covered as a bear in comparison" (310). And when Jordan learns of the decapitations, he
struggles to contain a horror which he equates with a loss of
hair: "What is a little brush between a guerrilla band and a
squadron of cavalry? That isn't anything. What if they took the
heads? Does that make any difference? None at all. The Indians
always took the scalps when Grandfather was at Fort Kearny
after the war" (336). Jordan combats the castration anxiety that
he so urgently tries to deny by calling upon his identifications
both with Maria and with his grandfather: "Your grandfather
fought four years in our Civil War and you are just finishing
your first year in this war. You have a long time to go yet and
you are very well fitted for the work. And now you have Maria,
too. Why, you've got everything. You shouldn't worry" (336).
From Maria, he can acquire the female phallus that denies castration by denying sexual difference. From his grandfather, he
hopes to acquire the idealized, uncastratable paternal phallus.

Jordan's grandfather is no mere mortal but, rather, an exalted heroic paternal ideal. Both of Hemingway's grandfathers
were Civil War veterans; but while Ernest's maternal grandfather had served with the cavalry, Jordan's grandfather was
nothing less than the finest cavalryman who ever lived. True,

Jordan's grandfather modestly calls John Mosby "the finest cavalry leader that ever lived," but Jordan has a letter from General Phil Sheridan calling his grandfather "a finer leader of irregular cavalry than John Mosby" (339). Jordan had even been told that Custer never would have been sucked into the trap at the Little Big Horn if his grandfather had only been along with him that day. Thinking about scalping and his grandfather's role in the Indian wars, Jordan remembers his grandfather's "quivers of hunting and war arrows, and how the bundle of shafts felt when [he] closed [his] hand around them." This phallic memory magically steadies his nerves, so he tells himself,

> Remember something like that. Remember something concrete and practical. Remember Grandfather's saber, bright and well oiled in its dented scabbard and Grandfather showed you how the blade had been thinned from the many times it had been to the grinder's. Remember Grandfather's Smith and Wesson. It was a single action, officer's model .32 caliber and there was no trigger guard. It had the softest, sweetest trigger pull you had ever felt and it was always well oiled and the bore was clean although the finish was all worn off and the brown metal of the barrel and the cylinder was worn smooth from the leather of the holster. . . .
> You could take the pistol out of the drawer and hold it. "Handle it freely," was Grandfather's expression. But you could not play with it because it was "a serious weapon." (336)

Yet Jordan ultimately can't separate the idealized paternal phallus from the imago of the denigrated and castrated father. Memories of his grandfather's well-oiled Smith and Wesson remind Jordan of his father's inadequacies. For Jordan's father, like Hemingway's, had used his father's Smith and Wesson to commit suicide, and Jordan interprets this suicide as an expression of cowardice and as a sort of emasculation.

Within a page of remembering how sick it made him feel the first time he knew his father was a coward, Jordan remembers another deflating experience—its symbolic equivalent:

> "George Custer was not an intelligent leader of cavalry, Robert," his grandfather had said. "He was not even an intelligent man."
> He remembered that when his grandfather said that he felt resentment that anyone should speak against that figure in the buckskin shirt, the yellow curls blowing, that stood on that hill holding a service revolver as the Sioux closed in around him in

the old Anheuser-Busch lithograph that hung on the poolroom
wall in Red Lodge. (339)

Jordan comes to realize that his grandfather was the better
man—better than Custer, better than his father. Yet while he desperately craves his grandfather's courage (idealized paternal
phallus), Jordan can never shake his fear that he might instead
turn out like his father (castrated). He tries to identify with his
grandfather, thinking, "It's a shame there is such a jump in time
between ones like us. . . . Maybe he sent me what little I have
through that other one that misused the gun. . . . Maybe the
good juice only came through straight again after passing
through that one?" (338). But Jordan has a hard time believing
that the idealized paternal phallus could pass through the loins
of a man who was emasculated by his wife, a man who was a
coward. "Because if he wasn't a coward he would have stood up
to that woman and not let her bully him." The image of his father
as the victim of a castrating phallic woman, however, gives Jordan a new theory. "Maybe the bully in her helped to supply what
was missing in the other. And you" (339). In other words, maybe
she is the conduit for the idealized paternal phallus. Or maybe he
simply doesn't have it. He realizes that he is getting ahead of
himself. He won't really know what kind of "juice" he has until he
is tested at the bridge. As Jordan makes his last stand in the
novel's final pages, wounded, lying on his stomach, awaiting the
Fascists, he still worries aloud—as much to his grandfather as to
himself—"Oh let them come. . . . I don't want to do that business
my father did" (469). The problem is, though, that without an
identification with a realistic paternal imago, Jordan is left with a
choice between suicidal castration and a fraudulent and impossible identification with his heroic idealized paternal imago. A
stable, realistic, mature masculinity is out of the question.[38]

Although his more astute critics have always found an element of gender masquerade, a sort of hypermasculine posturing, in his art, Ernest Hemingway has remained for decades a
cultural icon of unadulterated masculinity. Countless American
men—and women—have looked to him for a model of manhood.
But if, as should now be evident, Hemingway was *not* monovocally masculine, where can we look for such a model?

Perhaps the more interesting question would be *why* are we
ever tempted to look for models of ideal masculinity? Is the

quest to find such a model in Papa, or anyone else, really so un-like Frederic Henry's staring into the mirror to shore up his masculinity by incorporating that of his father? Is such a quest an attempt to understand masculinity, or simply an attempt to incorporate and identify with it to shore up our own masculinity? Hemingway's art should remind us that there *is no such* thing as an entirely monovocal masculinity. Rather, precisely where masculinity (or femininity) is most insistent, most *at issue*, it is likely to be concealing an equally insistent (though perhaps split-off) dialectical partner.

What is interesting about Hemingway, then, isn't that he had bisexual identifications and impulses. One of Freud's earliest and most profound insights into the human condition was that we are all on some level profoundly bisexual. We all harbor traces of infantile polymorphous perversity, access to which allows us some freedom of erotic response. In this sense, one can behave fetishistically without *being* a fetishist. In an organized adult "perversion, however, there is no freedom, but only a driven compulsion" (Kaplan 384). What makes Hemingway's bisexuality interesting is that instead of integrating the elements of bisexuality in his ego, he organized these elements into relatively "pure" and dissociated masculine and feminine halves structured around the split in his ego.

It would be pretty to think that an extraordinarily talented, sensitive, and insightful writer like Hemingway was a gender hero who "transgressed the oppressive norms of patriarchal culture"; but unfortunately he was no such thing. His masculine and feminine selves were founded upon rigid, infantile gender stereotypes. As Louise Kaplan explains, transvestic and homeovestic fantasies always employ "an infantile ideal of masculinity to disguise what is felt to be a shameful and frightening femininity." In fact, all perverse strategies deploy "one gender stereotype as a way of keeping hidden other gender stereotypes that are felt to be shameful and frightening" (249). However "transgressive" the gender-blurring of transvestism and fetishism may appear, "the feminine and masculine roles that are enacted in a perversion, male or female, epitomize in dramatic form the very social gender stereotypes and social role conventions that a perversion pretends to be subverting and undermining" (509).

My point, however, isn't to reduce Hemingway's representations of gender to these stereotypes. I would never want to deny the very real complexity and sensitivity with which Hemingway could consciously address gender identity and gender relations. My point is only that *insofar as his work was driven and shaped by the perverse aspects of his psyche*, these stereotypes were his stock in trade. Hemingway's more sensitive and complex considerations of gender were rooted in other—more creative—aspects of his psyche. But to understand this distinction we need to explore the relation between perversion and creativity.

CHAPTER 7

Perversion, Pornography, and Creativity

The Garden of Eden and the Structure of Transvestite Pornography

"Don't you ever talk on any other subjects? Perversion is dull and old fashioned. I didn't know people like us kept up on it."

—David to Catherine in *The Garden of Eden*

In his monumental work *Studies in the Psychology of Sex*, Havelock Ellis prints a brief autobiographical statement by one of his transvestite correspondents, "T.S.," an established novelist who blamed his mother for his transvestism. According to T.S., his mother "cordially disliked him." When he was a boy, she beat him and humiliated him at every opportunity. More importantly, she taunted him almost "daily" with the threat that she would dress him in his sister's clothes. Although she supposedly never made good on these threats, T.S. complains, "I was made to part my hair in the middle 'like a baby girl' and my resemblance to a girl was consistently pressed upon me" (2.2.57). He suspects that he really did look rather feminine, but he claims that he never cross-dressed until he was fifteen or sixteen and home from school for the holidays. He remembers that his sister had first cross-dressed him and that she had been disappointed that his hair was not long enough to be curled, since this alone betrayed an otherwise flawless feminine illusion. As an adult, strangely enough, T.S. developed a Hemingwayesque taste for big game hunting. After a long day in his safari suit trekking wild beasts, he would return to camp and lie beneath the stars—mentally dressing himself "garment by garment, as a woman" (2.2.59). When he finished this mental dressing—not so unlike Nick Adams's mental trout fishing in "Now I Lay Me"—he would mentally undress and begin the process all over again.

But T.S. had more in common with Hemingway than an unusual childhood and a taste for big game hunting. "A successful author and man of high-minded character," T.S. had a long-term book project that should sound vaguely familiar (2.2.56):[1]

> For many years now I have found satisfaction in writing an account of imaginary circumstances under which I adopt woman's dress altogether. The scheme of the thing is always much the same. In the capacity of private secretary I take up residence with a woman my own height and figure whose taste is the counterpart of my own. She thirsts to dress as a man, and I must take her place to adjust matters. She forces change of clothes on me, first in jest, then by persuasion, until I am committed. For some obscure reason an element of compulsion enhances the delights of the situation for me. I am allowed a week-end once a month to come home, but always on the understanding that I resume skirts without protest as soon as I return, that my employer may resume male dress. Refusal on my part would entail public exposure . . ., and I submit. I have worked out this idea a score of times in minute detail, introducing variations which seem to bring it within the ambit of the possible. . . . (2.2.62–3)

This transvestite fantasy should sound so familiar to us because in many ways it is almost a plot summary of *The Garden of Eden*. The props have been changed, but the script is in many respects essentially the same. Replace the fetishized female clothing with fetishized bleached hair or identical haircuts, and one has a fair outline of the novel that occupied Hemingway for well over a decade. There is the Bourne-like twinning implied in the woman whose physical features and tastes mirror those of the transvestite protagonist; this woman, like Catherine Bourne, longs to be transformed into a man, and when she dresses as a man, the transvestite must "take her place," just as David Bourne must *become* "Catherine" when Catherine *becomes* "Peter"; most importantly, the male protagonist of T.S.'s novel, like David Bourne, is cross-dressed against his will, but to his secret delight.

Whatever its similarities to *The Garden of Eden*, though, T.S.'s novel would sound familiar to plenty of men who have never read a word of Hemingway. According to Robert Stoller, the plot behind T.S.'s novel—and behind *The Garden of Eden*—is the classic script of transvestite pornography. "In all samples . . . of transvestite pornography the fundamentals are the same: the heterosexual young man, unquestionably totally male, innocent, is captured by females who do so not by physical power but by the mysterious power inherent in femaleness and femininity. Humiliated, he is forced by them into women's clothes"— that is, to wear a fetish object to negotiate a feminine identity. "That," writes Stoller, "is the essential story." For the transvestite it is a winner. "For the rest of us it is uninteresting. If we wondered about it, we would only be puzzled about how this could be erotic" (*Observing* 24).

As an example, Stoller cites a story from a transvestite magazine brought to him by one of his patients. The protagonist of "Panty Raid," Bruce King, is a young fraternity pledge who undertakes a solo panty raid against a sorority as part of an initiation rite. In the story, Bruce desperately craves acceptance from his fraternity brothers, "and if he had to steal feminine underclothes and lingerie, not to mention some silly bloomers, to gain their respect, he would do it!" Under a "cloak of velvet" darkness, Bruce creeps up to the sorority and begins rifling through the panties and lingerie on the clothesline. While lost in the act of savoring the fabrics, he is suddenly captured by a half dozen sorority girls who promptly tie him up with silken robe belts and gag him with "a silky-soft sheer stocking." Promising to teach him a lesson he'll never forget, they carry him inside to a bedroom as he twists and wiggles and tries to squirm free. "This brought much raucous laughter from the victorious vixens who thrilled at the helpless struggles of their male captive." At the direction of Lori, a sort of phallic sorority dominatrix who commands "obedience and respect," the girls strip Bruce of his masculine clothes. (The breast = penis equation is obvious in the cover illustration of the sorority "Amazons," both of whom hold riding crops. Bruce, in high heels and a corset, is pinned in a chair, humiliated and crying, with one arm twisted gently behind his back.) Standing "proudly erect," Lori teases, "'Good boys shouldn't wear such sloppy things. We'll teach our Brucie how to dress." "See, Bruce," she taunts, dangling a brassiere before him "as if threatening his manhood." After ridiculing his athletic supporter ("Look—he wears a G-string!"), the girls dress Bruce in a "vampire red" evening gown, described in mind-numbing detail. (An absorption with fabrics and the smallest details of feminine costume is a hallmark of transvestite fiction. In Hemingway's case, a similar sort of attention is paid to hair.) "As the dress was lowered upon Bruce, he found his heart was pounding, his emotions were stepped up and he was breathless with eager anticipation. He dared not admit his true feelings to anyone; even to himself! After all, he had been FORCED into this whole thing . . . by his frat brothers and then he was CAPTURED and BOUND BY FEMALES and compelled to follow their orders." The story ends with an illustration showing Bruce pinned beneath "four beauties, kicking and bawling as they apply makeup to him and dress him in their shoes and undergarments" (qtd. in *Observing* 25–27; *Perversion* 63–70).

Stoller overstates his case when he claims to have isolated the fundamental story in *all* samples of transvestite pornography, but he is close enough. Severe humiliation isn't quite as prevalent as "Panty Raid" would have us believe, but in these stories the male protagonist seldom freely chooses to cross-dress. In all but thirteen of the seventy-three published novels and twenty unpublished manuscripts in Beigel and Feldman's 1963 study of transvestite fiction, the protagonist was compelled by circumstances to cross-dress; and in all of the stories, the protagonist was at least initially reluctant. In Buhrich and McConaghy's 1976 study of twenty transvestite stories (from the Australian journal *Feminique*, the British *Beaumont Bulletin*, and the American *Transvestia*), all but one told tales of "innocent" males who were forced to cross-dress by circumstances beyond their control. And in Bullough and Bullough's 1993 study of ninety-six transvestite stories, "seventy-six percent of the stories tell of a situation in which the hero is forced to cross-dress by a mother, sister, other woman, or circumstances beyond his control" (291). As T.S. explains, "an element of compulsion"—even though it implies an element of reluctance, humiliation, and what Hemingway calls "remorse"—"enhances the delights of the situation" for the transvestite novelist and reader. Seen in this light, David Bourne's resistance to his wife's plans for gender-swapping and barbering must seem more than a little suspect. As both Catherine and the Marita of the *Eden* manuscript know, David "corrupts" easily and his hoarse "no" is but a variation of "yes."

But is a story like "Panty Raid" really *pornographic*? It lacks the obsession with copulation and exposed genitalia that we generally consider the hallmarks of pornography. And am I trying to reduce *The Garden of Eden* to a work of transvestite pornography?

I should address the second question first. By no means am I trying to *reduce* Hemingway's novel to the status of pornography. I never mean to reduce *any* of Hemingway's works to their underlying psychosexuality, which is but one of their components and one which I have only begun to explain. (My very point about this single aspect of Hemingway's work is that it is so overwhelmingly overdetermined and complex and rich that one couldn't hope to ever explain it in its entirety. If I neglect other aspects of Hemingway's work—and I do—it is only because this single aspect alone demands my full attention if I am to do it any semblance of justice.) I do, however, want to argue that *The Garden of Eden* is a work of erotica with an *element* of pornographic intent and function, and this element needs to be understood *as pornography.* (I define erotica as art that *contains* but also *transcends* a component of pornographic intent and function. To the degree that a work functions as more than a pretext for masturbation it becomes something more than mere pornography.) An understanding of this fetishistic/transvestic pornographic kernel in *The Garden of Eden* will help us to understand what this story "did" for Hemingway psychosexually; it will help us to understand why he constructed the story as he did and why his characters behave as they do; and it will ultimately help us to understand the part played by perversion in Hemingway's creativity.

But what does it mean to understand a narrative "as pornography"? In its most obvious sense, pornographic literature is literature *intended to produce* erotic excitement, and a 1948 letter to Mary Hemingway reveals that this was precisely Ernest's intent in *The Garden of Eden.* (Hardly his *only* intent, but an important and interesting one.) In the letter, Ernest gives Mary detailed instructions to give to her hair stylist, Gustavo Dorio, because he wants Mary's hair to be exactly like Barbara Sheldon's in *The Garden of Eden* manuscript:

> Tell him you have decided . . . to wear your hair sleek and long instead of short and curly. But you are keeping the same style of hair-cut. You don't want to lose any of the length and you want the very front, that was so short, to grow into the sweep of the back. You would like the bottom of the hair neatened; trimmed in the same style as it is. . . .

> Ask Gustavo if there is anything he can recommend . . . to
> be absolutely harmless to the hair . . . to keep it straight and
> sleek. . . . *[T]he girl in my book* [*The Garden of Eden*] *will have
> her hair the way you are fixing yours . . . and some 500-000 up
> people will have d'erections about it.* (my emphasis, qtd. in Bur-
> well 212)

Surely the promise to produce a half million erections—quite a
feat of levitation—establishes Hemingway's pornographic intent.
Writing about hair lit Hemingway's fire. For instance, in one of
the hair-obsessed letters that I cite in chapter 6, Ernest tells
Mary that "Mr. Scrooby" (Ernest's pet name for his penis) made
a "tent" out of the bed as he was writing, and he was afraid it
would "do an Old Faithful" before she got home. After a slight
detour he lapses back into a reverie about Mary's hair and "up
comes Mr. S. again" (May 3, 1947). It worked for him. It's only
reasonable to think that Hemingway expected it would work for
at least some of his readers.[2]

So was it good for you? Or does Hemingway's project to produce a legion of hard-ons leave you feeling a little left out?
Women need not feel particularly excluded. If Catherine's haircuts failed to arouse you sexually, if T.S.'s novel or "Panty Raid"
failed to move more than your curiosity, you're hardly alone. As
pornography (and therefore as erotica), *The Garden of Eden*
would probably fail for about 99 percent of the population. But
then how could Hemingway be so "wrong" about what excites
people? And how can a work be pornographic if it manifestly
fails to excite? The answer to both questions is pornography rule
number one: not all pornography is pornographic for all people.[3]

A glance at the back of any porn magazine makes this abun-
dantly clear. In *Observing the Erotic Imagination* Stoller offers a
brief but graphic sampling of porn ads to make precisely this
point:

> "Scissor Stories!" "Cigar-Smoking Females," "Barefoot Girls
> Who Never Wear Shoes," "White Male Slave," "Saddle Shoe
> Fetish," "Oral Service Given Free!" "Pussy Galore!" "Wrestling
> Goddess 6'3"," "Horse Mating," "Pregnant or Lactating?" "Rape,"
> "Bizarre Fashions," "Forbidden Beastiality" [sic], "High Heels
> and Other Sensuous Delights," "Roots Toilette!" "Twenty-Two
> Inch Negro Penis Worn by 200lb. Negress while disciplining
> young white boys," "The Most Beautiful Transsexuals in the
> World!" "Dominant Goddess Trains Generous Slaves in Private

Dungeon," "Seeks French Slaves," "Lean and Mean Skilled Mistress!," "Forced Enemas," "Fun Loving & Dominant," "Couple offers total discretion to generous people. Threesomes, bisexuality, cross-dressing, S&M," "Enchanting Chestnut Dominatrix," "Foot Loving Male in Delaware," "Fighting Mad About Gals With Sexy Looking Feet," "Need Tickling Victims," "Female Wrestler/Writer," "Dominant Black Stud," "Big Strong Ladies," "Bizarre Photos-Dirty Panties. Will Exchange Shit-Piss Photos. Also sell dirty panties," "Fighting Female Wanted," "Spit and Saliva," "Tattooed-Pierced Women," "Golden Showers & Cunnilingus," "Discrete [sic] Submissive Females," "[Finger] Nail Fans," . . . "Unbelievably Submissive Male," "Male Shit Photos Wanted," "High Heel Shoe Lover," "Submissive Male Lesbian," "Dress Me Up and Put Me Down," "Might is Right," "Honky Slave," "Crippled Female," "Amputee Lovers." (13)

Clearly, most of us aren't "fighting mad about gals with sexy looking feet," nor are "amputee lovers" everyone's cup of tea. Yet just as clearly they are *someone's* cup of tea. Consider, for instance, one of Aarons's patients, a foot and shoe fetishist (also a creative writer) with a taste for female amputees. He was "addicted" to pictures of such women and would insist, "I need to see a one-legged girl, it's like looking at her genital, *it's pornographic*" (my emphasis, 207). And, as much as we might like to think otherwise, Aarons's patient is hardly unique. Why else would an ad for "amputee lovers" run in the back of a magazine? As Chasseguet-Smirgel notes, "in times past, any thriving brothel featured a 'wooden-legged woman'" (81). Men who share this inclination have even begun to organize, calling themselves *amelotatists* (Greek for "one inclined toward those lacking limbs"). They divide themselves into SAKs (the vast majority, nearly 80 percent, who prefer women with a single amputation above the knee), DAKs (those who prefer double amputees), and such exotica as COLBAs (combination, one leg, both arms).[4] Thus Stoller arrives at a simple but powerful conclusion: "Pornography is the communicated sexual fantasy of a dynamically related group of people" (*Perversion* 115).

Thanks to this exclusivity—one is either a member of the "club" or one isn't—pornography is characterized by a radical split between two forms of invisibility, *obviousness* and *incomprehensibility*. As Stoller notes, "There are probably few people who do not recognize their favorite erotic script when they meet it," yet when we bump right into someone else's favorite erotic script we often fail to even recognize it *as erotic* (*Observing* 9). At most it obtains the status of a curiosity ("Whatever turns you on—") or an outrage ("How dare you be turned on by *that!*"). Pornography hails individuals, much like someone in the street shouting, "Hey, you there!" And pornography never misses its mark. The one hailed always turns in acknowledgment: "Someone is calling me!" Meanwhile, those not hailed will in all likelihood stroll calmly along as if they were entirely deaf.[5] Thus the senator who demurs at defining pornography but who declares that he "knows it when he sees it" is, in a sense, correct. What he "knows" as pornography *is* pornography—for him. We can learn to recognize other people's pornography, but it will never *function* as pornography for us; it will never turn us on. (One must, of course, grant substantial leeway for reading against the grain—interpreting an alien erotic script in a way that converts it into our own favorite script, something that *can* turn us on.) The pornography that excites the perverse individual "is psychodynamically about the same as his perversion." It is nothing less than "the highly condensed story of his perversion." This is why Stoller has only half-facetiously suggested "that a test to establish the diagnosis of transvestism or any perversion in men would be to show its pornography to several subjects: only those with increased penile blood flow would fit the diagnosis" (*Perversion* 66; 83). And while Stoller may have been joking when he suggested this diagnostic tool, I suggest we try it in earnest.

The subject of pornography does "pop up" in *The Garden of Eden* manuscript when David and Marita discuss the kind of literature that gives them "erections." At this point in the manuscript, David is recovering from the destruction of his stories, and Marita is well on her way to becoming Catherine's replacement. Marita has cut her hair short in an attempt to be "exactly" like David's boyhood "African girl," but the haircut somehow transforms her into a boy-girl. David protests that she shouldn't have to do "Catherine things," but Marita assures him that with her these things will be different. Catherine, she explains, wanted to change him and was torn apart by her oscillations between boyhood and girlhood; she, however, doesn't need to change David because she is already exactly like him: a boy and a girl at once. With her, their games won't be "perversion," they'll just be "variety," and he won't suffer from any "remorse." (Marita's promise to leave David unchanged shouldn't fool us. She understands that a "no" from David really means "yes," and she is intensely jealous of Catherine for having bleached David's hair.) It is against this backdrop of haircutting, race-changing, and gender-swapping that Marita playfully offers to be David's girl disguised as a young Cossack officer.

David asks if she has ever read Gogol's tale of the Cossacks, *Taras Bulba*. He suspects that a girl couldn't maintain a disguise for long amongst a rough crowd of Cossacks like old Taras Bulba's band. Following the theme of cross-dressing, Marita asks what about Gautier's *Mademoiselle de Maupin*? The heroine of that novel, Madelaine de Maupin, successfully passes herself off as a man amongst men. She outrides her male companions, drinks with them, and regularly defeats them in duels. David explains that Gautier's novel is just "pleasant fancy writing to make excitements," not "dirty like pornography," just "what we do made into musical comedy." Yet when he asks Marita if Gautier's novel gave her "an erection," she replies, "Of course. Didn't it you?" "Sure," says David. "That's why he wrote it. For himself and his friends. That's how all books that are just fun are written" (K422.1, 36.22).

David's claim that *Mademoiselle de Maupin* isn't pornographic should be taken with a grain of salt. He recognizes that the novel was written for a select group of people "to make excitements." It gave him an erection, and he suspects that it will give other people (even women) "erections." That sounds an awful lot like pornography. To be sure, Gautier's novel *isn't* pornographic in the same sense that *The Garden of Eden* isn't pornographic. It is a work of *erotica* with an *element* of pornographic intent and function. Insofar as it was written expressly to produce erections, the novel *is* pornographic; insofar as it was written for purposes beyond this, it transcends mere pornography. But this isn't David's point. He equates pornography with "dirtiness," and he wants to assert that Gautier's novel isn't dirty. Hemingway nevertheless suspected that there *was* something "dirty" about *Mademoiselle de Maupin*. In *Islands in the Stream*, Thomas Hudson's eldest son, young Tom, is reading *Mademoiselle de Maupin*. He finds Gautier wonderful, but he's afraid that his school's headmaster will think he is "dirty-minded" if he reads the book to his classmates (68). David Bourne's claim that the book isn't pornographic or "dirty" is simply a classic example of negation, revealing a truth by denying that very truth.

So what kind of story turned Hemingway on? As Gautier's novel opens, the male hero, d'Albert, is searching for a mistress, a prize which for him will be "like the robe of manhood for a young Roman" (62). Criticized for his theatrical manner, "effeminate" clothes, and too-carefully-curled hair, d'Albert is a poet of lofty ideals and a great connoisseur of feet, shoes, fabric, and hair. Seeking a mistress of surpassing beauty and wit, he unfortunately finds no woman entirely to his satisfaction. The problem is that he already loves an imaginary ideal. As he confides to a friend, he loves someone he's never seen, "someone who must exist," someone he hopes to find. He promises, "I know quite well what she is like, and, when I meet her, I shall recognize her" (66). D'Albert, however, has another problem: his notion of ideal beauty. He finds it embodied in the image of Hermaphrodite: "It is indeed among the most subtle creations of the pagan genius, this son of Hermes and Aphrodite. You can't imagine anything more ravishing in the world than these two bodies, both of them perfect, harmoniously fused together" (196).

D'Albert eventually settles for Rosette, a remarkably beautiful woman and his intellectual equal—but not his ideal. He and Rosette have a passionate affair full of variety (at one point d'Albert dons a bear suit to take his mistress as a savage representative of the wild), but neither loves the other and both are losing interest in the affair when one day a beautiful cavalier and page ride up to the château where d'Albert is staying with Rosette. The master is "as beautiful as a woman" and the page "as beautiful as a young girl" (148). D'Albert thinks what a pity it is that the master isn't a woman, or that he himself isn't a woman so he can possess him. But later as the page sleeps off his travels, the reader catches a glimpse of what looks like a woman's breast beneath "his" unbuttoned shirt. After some deliberate blurring of the matter ("The reader may think what he likes. . .; we know no more than he does. . . . The curtains are drawn, and the light in the room is subdued" [149]), the reader's suspicions are confirmed: the master and page are women disguised as men. D'Albert and Rosette, however, are none the wiser. Even the page doesn't know that "his" master, Théodore de Sérannes, is really a woman. (This in spite of the fact that the page was first cross-dressed by Théodore and that he/she regularly sleeps with him/her.) Rosette, the reader discovers, has long suffered from an unrequited, or at least unconsummated, love for Théodore. And soon d'Albert, too, is in love with the young cavalier. He is horrified to find himself in love with another "man," but he simply can't help himself. Théodore is what he's always been waiting for: the perfect embodiment of his androgynous ideal. As the days pass, d'Albert half suspects and fully hopes that Théodore might just be a woman, but he can't figure out why a woman would want to wander about dressed as a man. He can understand why a man would want to dress as a beautiful woman, but the reverse baffles him.

The reader eventually learns that Théodore de Sérannes is really Madelaine de Maupin, a young woman who has adopted a masculine disguise to discover what men are "really" like when unaccompanied by women. Yet Madelaine's cross-dressing becomes something more than a masquerade. After changing her clothes, she feels she is no longer herself, but "someone else": "I remembered my old deeds like the deeds of an unknown person which I had witnessed, or like the beginning of a novel which I hadn't finished reading" (207). She describes herself as neither man nor woman, but a member of a third and as yet unnamed sex, and she dreams of having "each sex in turn" to satisfy her "dual nature" (330). Attracted both by Rosette's beauty and by d'Albert's more feminine qualities, Théodore/Madelaine indeed "has" each sex in turn in the novel's climactic conclusion. She reveals herself to and sleeps with both d'Albert and Rosette in the same night. With daybreak she rides off leaving only memories behind.

Because d'Albert is never cross-dressed and humiliated by any of the women in the novel, *Mademoiselle de Maupin* doesn't entirely fit Stoller's scenario for transvestite pornography. Nonetheless, d'Albert dresses effeminately, he occasionally desires to be a woman, and he has little difficulty understanding why a man might *want* to cross-dress. He even stages a performance of *As You Like It*, for which he lovingly designs costumes, so he can see "Théodore" dressed as a woman (Rosalind).[6] A sort of narcissistic mirror-image, Théodore/Madelaine is the ideal love object for a transvestite. A woman who cross-dresses or who secretly desires to be a man (as in T.S.'s novel or *The Garden of Eden*) is a classic accomplice and love object in transvestic male fantasy.[7] Gautier's foot fetishism, moreover, is obvious. Consider, for instance, a scene in which Madelaine/Théodore's page has fallen asleep after a long ride:

> When the servant had withdrawn and the door was shut, [Théodore] knelt before [the page], and tried to take off his half-boots; but his little swollen, painful feet made the operation

rather difficult, and from time to time the pretty sleeper uttered a few vague and inarticulate sighs, as if he were about to wake up; then the young cavalier would stop, and wait for him to go to sleep again. The half-boots finally gave in, which was the important thing; the stockings offered little resistance. When this operation had been performed, the master took the child's two feet, and laid them side by side on the sofa; they were indeed the two most adorable feet in the world . . . as white as new ivory and slightly pink from the pressure of the boots in which they had been imprisoned for seventeen hours. They were feet too small for a woman, feet which never seemed to have walked. What you could see of the leg was round, smooth, transparent and veined, and most exquisitely delicate; it was a leg which was worthy of the foot.

The young man . . . contemplated these two little feet with loving and admiring attention; he bent down, took the left one and kissed it, then the right one and kissed that, too; and then, kiss by kiss, he went up the leg to the place where the material began. (147–8)

Thus, as we might expect, Madelaine's memories of cross-dressing are particularly concerned with her footwear. In a dialogue of self and soul, she asks herself, "Why are you wearing boots, Madelaine? It seemed to me that you had very pretty feet. Boots and breeches, and a big hat with a feather, like a cavalier who is going to war! Why this long sword which is beating and bruising your thigh?" Her soul replies: "My boots stop people from seeing if I have pretty feet; this sword is to defend me, and this feather trembling on my hat is to scare off the nightingales which might . . . sing me false love songs" (208). The problem, then, isn't that *Mademoiselle de Maupin* is not transvestite erotica; the problem is that Stoller's scenario is a bit too narrow to encompass *all* transvestite pornography.

If anyone doubts that Hemingway read Gautier's novel through this perverse lens, we need only look at the context in which it appears in *The Garden of Eden* manuscript. How, after all, did we get from tough old Cossacks to cross-dressing cavaliers? Although no one has ever suggested that *Taras Bulba*, Gogol's macho, anti-Semitic, nationalistic celebration of Cossack warriors, is a work of transvestite erotica, it fits perfectly into Stoller's scenario for transvestite pornography. Given what is known about Gogol's sexuality, this should come as no surprise. His work abounds with phallic and castrating women (see, for in-

stance, "Ivan Fiodorovich Shponka and His Aunt"), and his castration anxiety is palpable in his nonsensical masterpiece "The
Nose."[8] Like Gautier's d'Albert, Gogol had a lifelong passion for
fabrics and always felt that "the closer a man resembles a woman
the more authentically beautiful he is" (Karlinsky 28). His most
sympathetic female characters are much given to self-admiration
in the mirror, and in "Christmas Eve" Oksana initially rejects her
suitor, the blacksmith, because "he cannot match her in beauty
and would look ludicrous if he tried to wear her ribbons and
other adornments" (Karlinsky 38). The fear of looking comic in
women's clothes didn't keep Gogol from cross-dressing. In student plays, he was celebrated for his portrayals of female characters, and later in life, "in complete privacy, he apparently took to
wearing what in a latter age might have qualified as high drag"
(Karlinsky 205).[9] In fact, the magically transformative power of
clothing, perhaps most obvious in "The Overcoat," is one of the
most pervasive themes in Gogol's work.[10] The erotic component of
Taras Bulba, however, is far from self-evident. Whereas *Mademoiselle de Maupin* is about little else but cross-dressing and sexuality, *Taras Bulba* is outwardly almost entirely concerned with
violent battle and masculine military striving. That Hemingway
understood something erotic about this story that Gogol scholars
have yet to recognize both demonstrates the invisibility of transvestite erotica to the non-transvestite and testifies to the power of
transvestite erotica to hail the like-minded. In the absence of theory, it takes one to know one.

Gogol's novel opens with the return home of Taras Bulba's
two sons, Ostap and Andrei, fresh from their studies at the seminary in Kiev. Old Bulba immediately begins to mock the boys'
feminine appearance and long robes. He challenges them to fight
and feels compelled to purge them of any taint of femininity. As
their mother stands by weeping, Bulba vows to send his sons
the next morning to the camp of the Dnieper Cossacks, a land of
men without women. Bulba admonishes his wife, who has not
seen her boys for over a year, "A Cossack's not for hanging about
with women. You'd hide them both under your petticoat and sit
on them as though they were hen's eggs" (24). To bring his sons
into the "world of men," Bulba feels he must sever any association they might have with femininity. His sons can't have
"dainty" food; instead they eat a whole goat and drink vodka,
"not vodka with all sorts of fancies, not with raisins and flavor-
ings, but pure foaming vodka, that hisses and bubbles like mad"

(24). (The oral dynamic is clear: they must incorporate the symbolic father and spit out anything that tastes like mother.) At dawn the next morning the boys ride off with their father to join the "wifeless warriors." A profound sense of loss accompanies this drama of masculine identity formation through separation from the mother: "Farewell to childhood, to play, and to everything, everything!" (32).

As the boys ride by their father's side, Gogol begins to flesh out their characters. The eldest son, Ostap, is a promising young Cossack who "suppressed any interests other than fighting and carousing" (34). Andrei, however, is more sensitive and more interesting.[11] "A yearning for love flamed hotly in him" and "woman was more often the subject of his ardent dreams" (34). During philosophy lessons at the seminary, Andrei's mind had wandered off into minutely detailed daydreams about ethereal women (a form of mourning for his detachment from his mother). "He carefully concealed from his comrades these emotions of his passionate youthful soul, for in those days it was a shame and dishonor for a Cossack to think of a woman and love before he had seen any fighting" (35). Yet long before he had seen any fighting, Andrei fell deeply in love.

One day while he was still in seminary, Andrei had been thrown into the mud by the passing coach of a Polish nobleman. As he lay in the street, "a most musical and melodious laugh rang out above him. He raised his eyes and saw standing at a window the loveliest creature he had seen in his life, with black eyes and skin white as snow. . ." (35). Smitten, Andrei eventually discovers that the girl is the daughter of a visiting Polish military governor. The very next night, Andrei climbs over the fence of her house, up a tree onto the roof, and down through a chimney into the girl's bedroom where she sits before a candle removing her earrings. After recovering her composure, the Polish beauty recognizes him as the youth who had fallen in the mud the day before. Once again she laughs at him. She finds him handsome, though, and decides to amuse herself at his expense.

> The seminary student could not stir a limb, but stood stiffly as though tied in a sack, while the military governor's daughter went boldly up to him, put her glittering diadem on his head, hung earrings on him, and threw over him a transparent muslin chemisette with ruffles embroidered in gold. She dressed him up, and, with the naughty childlike ease characteristic of frivo-

lous Polish girls, played a thousand silly pranks with him, and this put the poor student into even greater confusion. He was a ridiculous sight standing with his mouth open, staring into her dazzling eyes. (36)

A knock at the door forces Andrei to hide, and when he tries to escape over the garden wall he is caught and soundly beaten. He manages to see the Polish beauty only once more in church before she leaves town with her father, but she remains in his daydreams.

Later in the novel, Andrei discovers the Polish beauty starving in a town besieged by the Cossacks. Finding her twice as lovely in her emaciated condition, he forsakes his faith, his family, and the Cossacks for her love. Gogol now becomes oddly insistent about Andrei's manhood, and the result is a homeovestic counterbalance to Andrei's earlier transvestic encounter with his dream girl. Now Andrei berates himself because his manly nature prevents him from finding words of love, and the starving Polish girl is "impressed at the sight of the ruggedly handsome and manly Cossack" (72). More importantly, Andrei's transformation into a Polish warrior is signified by a resplendent homeovestic uniform. As his enraged father soon hears: "Now he is such a great knight. . . . His shoulderpieces are of gold and his armguards of gold and his breastplate is of gold and his cap is of gold and there is gold on his belt and everywhere gold and all gold. So that he is all shining in gold, like the sun. . . (80). Bulba can only ask dumbfounded, "Why has he put on other dress? . . . . Who has forced him to do it?" Yet he knows the answer: woman. "He remembered how great is the power of weak woman, how many strong men she has ruined, how susceptible Andrei's nature was on that side; and for some time he stood without moving from the spot as though struck dumb" (82). When Bulba meets his son in battle a few pages later, he orders Andrei to dismount, and the boy meekly obeys. Then, as Andrei mutters the name of the Polish beauty, Bulba shoots and kills his own son. "Like a stalk of wheat cut by the sickle, like a young lamb the deadly steel at its heart, Andrei hung his head and sank upon the grass. . ." (108). One could hardly find a clearer instance of oedipal castration; yet on another level, Andrei's death represents a penetration by (and internalization of) the idealized paternal phallus (the steel at the heart). This is the aim of the homeovestic act. In a sense, Andrei has duped his father: cross-dressed by the Polish beauty, and therefore disguised as his mother, Andrei has obtained the idealized paternal phallus that guarantees his masculinity. As Bulba stands admiring his dead son's manly beauty, the castrating penetration almost seems like a bizarre token of love.[12]

Gogol's homeovestic assertion of Andrei's masculinity is hardly out of place in a work of transvestite erotica. Strange as it may seem, most transvestite pornography is largely *about* shoring up the transvestite's precarious masculinity. Homeovestic trappings just heap more icing on the cake. Remember, Bruce King undertakes his panty raid as part of a ritual to join an all male club. D'Albert needs a mistress—even if *she* seems to be a *he*—because she will be for him "like the robe of manhood for a young Roman." According to Stoller, all of the male perversions, along with their attendant pornographies, are at bottom essentially about preserving masculinity. The perversion enables the pervert to retain his sense of maleness by retaining the potency of his penis: "that core of masculinity" (*Perversion* 152). Whereas a more traditional Freudian would say that the perversions are fundamentally a defense against castration anxiety, Stoller realizes that concern about the phallus is just the most obvious manifestation of a more sweeping anxiety about gender identity. The transvestite asks,

> "When I am like a female, dressed in her clothes and appearing to be like her, have I nonetheless escaped the danger? Am I still a male, or did the women succeed in ruining me?" And the perversion . . . answers, "No. You are still intact. You are a male. No matter how many feminine clothes you put on, you did not lose that ultimate insignia of your maleness, your penis." And the transvestite gets excited. What can be more reassuringly penile than a full and hearty erection? (Stoller, *Observing* 30)[13]

If transvestite pornography doesn't *look* like pornography to most outsiders, it is partly because the all-important erection usually doesn't appear in the story itself. (In this respect *The Garden of Eden* manuscript is an exception.) Its presence would compromise the transvestite's illusion of *temporary* feminine transformation. We might remember how so many transvestites hide or bind their penises when cross-dressing before the mirror. The penis must temporarily disappear (without ever really being forgotten) only to be recovered in a masturbatory version of *fort!/da!* Masculinity is temporarily set aside so the transvestite can savor it all the more in its jubilant recovery. Thus the crucial hard-on in transvestite pornography belongs not to the story's protagonist but to transvestite writer and reader.[14]

The Garden of Eden—particularly the version published by Scribner's—can easily be read as a novel about the preservation of David's masculinity in the face of Catherine's attempt to "ruin" him by forcing him to wear the fetish and assume a feminine identity. In the final pages of the Scribner's edition, after Catherine's departure, Marita tells David, "You've been over-run with girls. I'm always going to see you have your men friends" (244). Blaming Catherine for depriving David of male companionship, Marita promises, "I want you to have men friends and friends from the war and to shoot with and to play cards at the club" (245). She also assures him that her own gender identity is stable: "I'm your girl. . . . Your girl. No matter what I'm always your girl. Your good girl who loves you" (245). Two pages later, on the final page of the Scribner's edition, David's ability to write returns along with a new understanding of his father: "He found he knew much more about his father than when he had first written this story. . . . He was fortunate, just now, that his father was not a simple man" (247). David's masculinity, shaken by his transvestic games with Catherine (*fort!*), is magically restored and fully intact (*da!*). All is well with the world. The perversion has "worked." Happy ending.

Thus, so long as we are willing to substitute fetishized tans and haircuts for fetishized female clothing, the Scribner's version makes an exemplary piece of transvestite pornography. One could almost call it a transvestite fairy tale. Yet as Robert Fleming has demonstrated, this happy ending is not what Hemingway had in mind. Whatever the importance of the pornographic impulse in this novel, Hemingway's vision was ultimately far more tragic than pornographic. His stories all end with loss. As he explained in *Death in the Afternoon*: "All stories, if continued far enough, end in death, and he is no true-story teller who would keep that from you. . . . If two people love each other there can be no happy end to it" (122). One could interpret (I think unjustly) the loss and death at the conclusion of a novel like *A Farewell to Arms* as just another means of distancing the self from the object, preserving masculinity by fending off the gender-annihilating threat of merger, but one simply can't read the "provisional ending" of the *Eden* manuscript that way. The tentative double-suicide pact between Catherine and David holds out the possibility of merger in mutual obliteration, but it also signifies a recognition on Hemingway's part that he couldn't establish a stable masculinity by killing off the feminine elements in himself. Hemingway recognized, however unconsciously, that those elements were simply too central to his identity. The suicide pact acknowledges the fundamental loss masked by the fetish. It implies that Hemingway recognized that he was trapped in his perversion, since the perversions by their very nature are insatiable. Masculinity is never adequately defended. He must go through it all again or quit the game entirely. There is no victory, no happy ending.

But if the desire to preserve masculinity is central to transvestite pornography, why is an element of compulsion so central to the plot? After all, there is nothing manifestly "masculine" about being cross-dressed and feminized by a more powerful phallic woman. One possible answer may be that this compulsion shifts the responsibility for transvestic behavior from the transvestite himself to the outside world. In a society that proscribes cross-dressing, an element of compulsion may help to establish the "innocence" of the transvestite writer and reader. The story's protagonist doesn't *want* to cross-dress; no, he is "CAPTURED and BOUND BY FEMALES and compelled to follow their orders." Although the transvestite writer and reader want to cross-dress very much, they can through the act of reading identify with an "innocent victim." This, however, is a partial answer at best. Bruce King isn't merely compelled to cross-dress, he is *humiliated* by the sorority girls. Andrei, likewise, discovers the love of his life immediately after being thrown into the mud; the Polish beauty dresses him in her chemisette and earrings to humiliate him; and he is beaten by guards while making his escape. The role of humiliation in transvestite fiction is often more subtle, but it is seldom entirely absent. The very fact that the male protagonist needs to be coerced into wearing the fetish implies a reluctance on his part that is inseparable from an element of humiliation. Nick Sheldon enjoys his long hair, but he hides it under a hat because he fears it makes him look like a "sodomite"; David Bourne is deeply moved by his transformation but is reluctant to travel to macho Spain with his impossibly white hair. Both men are just a little bit humiliated. But how, then, is humiliation related to the preservation of masculinity, and how can humiliation excite?

Once again, Stoller has the answer: *Perversion transforms trauma into triumph.* Consider the case of Mr. M., a fetishist/transvestite analyzed by Kohon. The patient's mother had forced him as child to wear an apron upon returning home from school each day so that he wouldn't get dirty. This, he remembers, had humiliated him terribly. Yet as an adult he always kept an apron in his bedroom, and he had talked his wife into playing along with a strange but mandatory foreplay ritual. "The wife starts by reprimanding him for not having his apron on. Mr. M. resists. His wife gets angry with him, she starts ordering him about, commands him to put it on. He still resists. Wife gets angrier still and . . . forces him to wear it" (Kohon 216). Finally, he puts on the apron and, like magic, up pops an erection. The object and action that had once threatened his masculinity now serve as its best guarantee.

We needn't look far for further examples. It should be obvious that the book project that excites Havelock Ellis's adult transvestite correspondent, T.S., bears a remarkable resemblance to the trauma he suffered as a child. When he was a little boy, his mother had humiliated him and taunted him daily with the threat of petticoat punishment; as an adult he finds his greatest erotic thrill in the fantasy of being cross-dressed by a more powerful woman. Likewise, the story of Bruce King, "Panty Raid," was brought to Stoller by a transvestite patient also named Bruce.

> Suffice it to say . . . that the pornography tells the same story as his traumatic experience of being cross-dressed at age four by women: a defenseless male, who knows the value of being male (it is his core gender identity) but who, at this early age, is not so sure his sense of maleness can withstand assault, is put in girls' clothes; his gender identity is threatened. Then, years later, the perversion surfaces, and now Bruce repeatedly gets excited in women's clothes. But, rather than being traumatized, today he is triumphant when cross-dressing—excited, potent, on his way to maximal pleasure. (*Observing* 27)

Just so with Hemingway. The little boy who had been twinned with his sister and forced to wear his hair exactly like hers grew into an adult who could imagine nothing more erotic than twin-like lovers with identical haircuts. But whereas this prolonged trauma had once threatened his gender identity so profoundly that he feared Santa Claus wouldn't be able to tell if he were a boy or a girl, he could now count on it to produce the ultimate insignia of masculinity: a robust erection.

The perversions, then, not only preserve trauma in their structure, they convert it into the very prerequisite for sexual gratification. In this sense, the perversions, as Stoller observes, seem almost audacious. The pervert becomes most excited when an adult situation most resembles the childhood trauma at the root of his perversion. "This implies that more anxiety is felt during the perverse sexual act than is present in less perverse sexuality. This anxiety—the anticipation of danger— . . . is experienced as excitement, a word used not to describe voluptuous sensations so much as a rapid vibration between fear of trauma and hope of triumph" (*Perversion* 105). The danger so anticipated in *The Garden of Eden* is clear. As soon as the novel opens, Catherine promises to "destroy" David sexually, teasing, "I'm going to wake up in the night and do something to you that you've never even heard of or imagined." David calls Catherine "too sleepy to be dangerous," but she warns him not to "lull [him]self into any false security" (5). Catherine's games with hair are "dangerous" (15); she knows it, and David knows it. It's precisely the *danger* of her "wonderful dangerous surprise" that makes it so exciting (12). All this danger and anxiety may seem at odds with the role of the perversions in *combating* anxiety, but it isn't. *The perversions combat anxiety by mastering it.* This is why the perversions really aren't as audacious as they seem. "One seems to take a risk in approaching the old danger. That is the central part of exciting experiences: uncertainty, a tense hum between the possibility of triumph and the possibility/memory of trauma, failure" (*Observing* 29). But the risk is no longer real. The outcome is assured. Trauma *will* be converted into triumph. The pervert is a playwright who has written his script in advance.

Thus Stoller writes: "Perversion is theater, the production of a scenario, for which characters—in the form of people, parts of people, and nonhuman (including inanimate) objects—are cast. The performance is played before an audience, the crucial member of which is the perverse person viewing (in reality, with mirrors, with photographs, or in fantasy) himself or herself performing" (*Observing* 31).[15] More than an audience and performer, the perverse subject is also the scriptwriter and producer in this theater of illusory erotic self-sufficiency. In the transvestite scenario, he identifies consciously with his story's helpless male protagonist, but he also unconsciously identifies with his story's female aggressor, the phallic woman who coerces the male into wearing the fetish. In *The Garden of Eden*, for instance, Hemingway identified both with David Bourne and with

Catherine. The transvestite not only identifies with the female aggressor, he imagines in fantasy that he is a "better woman" than she is. In his fantasy he is

> a better woman than any woman, for he possesses the best of both sexes. He is always aware of his masculinity (an essential part of transvestism), and he is aware of his femininity. . . . And now identified with the powerful women, he is no longer the humiliated little boy; he no longer consciously experiences that part of him during the act of perversion. It exists overtly only in the script. . . . *In splitting his identification into victim and victor, he is able to satisfy, as it were, two different people inside himself.* (my emphasis, *Perversion* 81)

The obvious victim in transvestite fantasy is the helpless male cross-dressed by the cruel phallic woman. But in another more important sense, the victim is the phallic woman. Through his fantasy the transvestite experiences the ultimate revenge. In spite of everything that had been done to "ruin" him in childhood, he proves with a triumphant erection that his masculinity is intact. Not only that; he gets his erection precisely when he was supposed to fail, when his manhood was most at risk.

The idea of the pervert as impresario, playwright, and performance artist involves something more than a metaphor. It is extremely common for perverse subjects to chronicle their erotic fantasies and performances compulsively through some form of artistic activity that may involve scriptwriting, drawings, or photographs. McDougall notes that for many perverse subjects this artistic activity forms a vital part of their sexual ritual. Three of her "analysands spent many hours each week writing stories, letters, and paragraphs dealing with a fetishistic scene that was to be played out in the near future" (169). One exhibitionist patient would scout and photograph the locations where he planned to exhibit himself "a week or so before the event was to take place" (170). Another "constantly rewrote an erotic stage play in which a couple found themselves forced to have intercourse"; she "then would actually seek out people to play this scene in bars and clubs that lent themselves to her quest" (170). Yet another patient had "written many versions of a story (a classic fetishist script) in which an older woman publicly whips her daughter" (68). This patient had been polishing his script for nearly twenty years.

Bak reports the case of a transvestite who invented elaborate scenarios to photograph himself in his sister's clothes and

who would occasionally venture to professional photographers
to get himself photographed as a woman. Gillespie reports another case, a medical student and fetishist who would make
drawings of his fantasies to facilitate masturbation. Taylor analyzed a 63-year old transvestite and professional writer who
would construct intricate animal masks out of fur that he wore
(often on top of the rubber mask of a woman) while masturbating in front of the mirror.[16] Then there is T.S., the professional
man of letters, with his secret transvestite novel, or Aarons's patient, the creative writer with the taste for female amputees. In
chapter 6 we met "Ida," the transvestite diarist, and A.T., the
artist and transvestite who was magically transformed by wearing his sister's panties in front of the mirror. Stoller and
Greenacre both call attention to the remarkable creative abilities
of many of their perverse analysands. In Sperling's work with
transvestites, she was impressed by the "richness of fantasy life
and creative imagination in the children as well as in the
adults." In her work with one little boy with precocious transvestite tendencies, she noted that "he was a fantastic storyteller
even at the age of three or four," and as he grew older he took to
writing stories and poems (490). Struck by the abundance of
transvestite fiction and autobiography, Brierley speculates that
the act of transferring fantasies to paper may give the illusion of
reality to the fantasies of the transvestite. "The act of making a
statement which has a separate existence which others can read
is rather like the need to appear in public for a confirmation of
the fantasy of femininity" (120).

But while perversion and authentic artistic creativity clearly
can co-exist symbiotically, both within a work and within an individual—witness the examples of Charles Baudelaire, Gustave
Flaubert, Jean Genet, T. E. Lawrence, and Yukio Mishima—the
pseudo-artistic masturbatory creations produced for perverse
rituals are fundamentally different from authentic artistic creations. Moreover, I wouldn't want to bolster the myth of the
stereotypically mad or perverse artist. Artists are as diverse a set
of people psychologically as one is likely to encounter in any pro-
fession; and the overwhelming majority of perverts are not
artists. Nevertheless, many perverse individuals do end up in
professions that are related somehow to their perversion. A man
might become a gynecologist as part of a quest to find the "missing" female phallus, or he might join the military to shore up his
masculinity with a shiny uniform. Lihn records the case of an

electrical engineer who graduated at the top of his class but who became a "lot boy" in a used car lot because he hoped to find discarded panties while cleaning out the back seats of cars. The role of artist offers similar possibilities for transforming sexual fantasy into a full-time paying (pre)occupation. Yet while a writer's perversion may play a crucial role in his or her creativity, the perverse scenario inasmuch as it appears in his or her work will be the *least* creative thing to be found there. To see how this works, let us consider three remarkable chapters that Hemingway sliced out of the manuscript to *Islands in the Stream*.

Islands in the Stream, Perversion, and Creativity

> If you live by the senses you will die by them and if you live by your invention and your head you die by that too. All that is left entire in you is your ability to write and that gets better. You would think it would be destroyed. By everything you have been taught it should. But so far as you corrupt or change, that grows and strengthens. . . .
>
> —*The Garden of Eden* Manuscript

In chapter 11 of the "At Sea" section of *Islands in the Stream*, with everything squared away on his boat for the night, Thomas Hudson retreats to the solitude of the flying bridge. Having just bathed in a rain squall with the rest of his naked, brown-skinned crew, Hudson reclines on an air mattress with a light blanket and tries to "think about nothing," trying to keep his mind off the submarine hunt that will once again occupy him at sunrise. "He felt clean from his scalp to his feet from the soaping in the rain that had beaten down on the stern and he thought, I will just lie here and feel clean. He knew there was no use thinking of the girl who had been Tom's mother nor all the things they had done and the places they had been nor how they had broken up." No, she was gone, just like his sons. Sure, he had seen her only two months ago, but he had lost her. Instead of summoning up her ghost, he dedicates himself to doing "a good job at nonthinking" and quickly falls asleep (383–4).

Here is an excellent, if uncharacteristically obvious, instance of Hemingwayesque omission. The reader is expected to feel with

an immediacy strengthened by its economy, in Hudson's very
need to repress these feelings, his love for his first wife and un-
ease at impending battle. But as Hemingway explained in his
theory of omission, a writer must *know* what he omits. "A writer
who omits things because he does not know them only makes
hollow places in his writing" (*DIA* 192). Thus in an earlier version
of the *Islands* manuscript, in three chapters recently brought to
light by Rose Marie Burwell (items 112 and 113 at the John F.
Kennedy Library), Hudson does remember his first wife, and his
memories echo with the familiar déjà vu of perverse fantasy.

The memories begin in an earlier version of chapter 11
(K112), and they begin with Thomas Hudson's thoughts about
"perversion." Hudson no longer cares about what is and isn't
perversion. As long as everyone does his duty in the daytime, the
pleasures and things of the night are a personal matter. Tom's
mother, he remembers, had taught him this by teaching him to
respect those things which were "old" in people or in their
"blood." When they had first met in Paris years before, Jan had
complained that Hudson was too "wholesome." Sitting with her
at a cafe, Hudson wondered aloud why she would want anyone
"corrupt," but she corrects him. Unlike *The Garden of Eden's*
Catherine Bourne, Jan claims that she doesn't want to corrupt
Hudson. She just wants him to be a bit more adventurous. Because she is blonde and extremely beautiful, Hudson happily
agrees to become her erotic pupil. But before she agrees to take
on a student Jan decides she must first give him an examination. How good of a painter is he? Very good, he ventures with
confidence and modesty. How good is he in bed? she demands.
Again, he answers with confidence and offers to demonstrate.
Wary of male bravado, she wants to know whose pleasure he
thinks about while making love, the girl's or his own. Hudson
replies that he has no self in bed. This apparently pushes a but-
ton for Jan, for it clinches the deal. She is ready to run off with
him; he need only name the place and time.

That night they go to Hudson's studio and make love. It is
wonderful in the dark and without the awful "hunger" that Hudson had feared Jan might display. Afterwards, as they lie in bed,
Hudson admires Jan's lovely "silky" hair, and she lets him know
that he has passed the initial test. But as nice as it was, Hudson's traditional lovemaking is in for a change. Jan promises
new "secrets and surprises." He asks what she has in mind, but
she won't say. She only promises that it will be what she has al-

ways desired but has never done. Tom wonders how Jan can be so sure that he'll play along, but she says she knows that he'll do whatever she asks—and he'll never be the same. In fact, he's transformed already. As a sort of celebratory farewell, they make love as a "wholesome" couple again for the last time.

As soon as they hit the road for Switzerland, the hair games begin. After a late lunch in Auxerre, Jan runs out to a shop while Hudson waits in the restaurant reading the paper. When she returns, her beautiful hair is windblown, and she's very eager to leave. Hudson asks why she's so excited, but she only reminds him that he has promised to do "anything." His "devil" has plans. Nothing too difficult, she says. Just an important first step. But she won't tell him what she has in mind. It's a secret.

At the inn that night, when Hudson goes upstairs to his room, there is something different about Jan, and she's almost quivering with excitement. With her shiny hair brushed "flat and long," she's wearing a white sweater and looking very beautiful. As Hudson stares at her, she makes a drink for him, sits him in a chair, and tries to get him to relax. He does his best, but he's uneasy—especially when Jan wraps a towel around his neck and breaks out her "surprise": a pair of scissors and a barber's comb that she had bought when she ran out to the shop earlier in the day. (*Are we surprised?*) Hudson remembers that his hair was already bleached by the sun and it was long and a little unkempt. He hadn't cared about such things back then—no one in the *Quartier* cared about the length of anyone's hair—but suddenly it was important. As Jan snips away, her excitement is contagious. Hudson gets impatient. He wants a mirror, or at least he wants to feel the length of his hair, but Jan makes him wait. Finally she finishes. As she looks down at Hudson, Jan exultantly pronounces him her "new slain knight."[17]

But Hudson doesn't want to be a "new slain knight," and he's suddenly a bit sullen. Now he refuses to look in the mirror and wants to comb his hair back before they go downstairs to dinner. Jan, however, manages to coax him downstairs without hiding his hair. Over a wonderful meal, she explains that now they'll be exactly the same. Hudson is confused, but Jan seems to know what she's doing. Growing less sullen, Hudson even thanks her for making him "brave." Reconciled to his hair, he now thinks it will be fun in bed.

That night in bed he feels a "strange hollowness" and a "desperation." He is worried, and when Jan asks him if he feels the change—the unnamed mysterious change—he lies. He pretends that he doesn't know what she means—but he does, and he eventually admits it. They both feel transformed, but neither can explain it, and Jan promises that this is only the beginning. Hudson wonders where it is leading, but Jan can only offer vague answers: "Hell" or "Heaven." But how can a few games with hair accomplish this? Hudson can feel the change, he knows it's happened, but he's entirely confused. It makes no sense. Jan can't explain, but running her fingers through his hair she tells him that she has cut it just like her own. Hudson can't believe his hair could ever be as long and as beautiful as Jan's, but she says he has a start. He just needs to let it grow. In two months, it will be the same length and shape. She demands a kiss; then she demands that Hudson be her "girl."

He pleads ignorance. He'd had no idea where this was going. He doesn't know how to be a girl. Nonetheless, Jan tells him that he *will* be her girl, and her declaration works like magic. Hudson is *physically* transformed. As Jan swings her silky hair over him, he can feel a faintness spread from the base of his spine up through his torso. Something inside him feels weak and "destroyed." Yet when it is all over, Hudson admits that he liked being a "girl." With this revelation, Jan admits that she's in love with him. Tom is deeply moved but deeply spooked. He wants a "masculine" haircut again, but Jan talks him out of it. They drift off to sleep, and so ends the chapter.

Item K113 is yet another, entirely different, version of chapter 11 along with a chapter 12 quite unlike the one Hemingway ultimately chose to use. Back on the deck of his boat, Hudson's smooth wet hair conjures up memories of his old "devil," the one who had taught him about "night things" and the one he always daydreamed about when he had the chance. He hopes that thinking about her will encourage her to pay him a visit in his dreams that night. Years before she had been so full of games. She used him as a "plaything," ordering him about as he commands his men now, and he had loved it. She could do little things, seemingly meaningless, silly, innocuous things, like cutting his hair, that nonetheless created almost unbearable pleasure. Feeling his hair, Hudson remembers back to a winter in Switzerland when she wouldn't let him cut his hair at all. During the day he would paint Alpine glaciers, and at night Jan would keep them warm with her erotic games. Both were snow-burned to a deep mahogany, and Jan's shoulder-length hair, streaked and bleached by the sun, was "blonder than blonde." But while Jan supposedly had a grab bag full of erotic games, the rabbit she pulled out of her hat that winter looks all too familiar.

One night, admiring Hudson's long hair, Jan devises a plan to get it cut exactly like her own. Reluctant, Hudson suggests that she cut it herself, but Jan wants it done by the same coiffeur in the village who does her own hair, and (as always) she prevails. Jan has already been busy. She has someone knitting "twin sweaters" for them, and when she walks into the inn the next morning, her breasts show beautifully beneath her sweater. The bar maid at the inn is visibly moved by Frau and Herr/(Hair) Hudson's almost identical hair, and she pleads with Jan not to let anyone cut Tom's long hair. Jan teases her a bit, letting her touch and feel the identical weight of her own and her husband's hair. She wonders what the bar maid would like them to do, and it seems the bar maid has a mind like her own. The bar maid suggests that Frau and Herr Hudson trim their hair exactly alike at the local barbershop. It will look wonderful, she promises. All the men in the village used to wear their hair that way when she was a little girl, and she will be so happy to see that style again. Now even Tom is eager for the new cut, since he loves the games that he plays with Jan in the night. He admits that he wants to look just like her—they're even the same height—but he's not sure that he can. Jan's hair is just too impossibly beautiful. And one thing spooks him: He's not sure that becoming "one person" with Jan will be good for his work.

The significance of hair in "damnation" and in the negotiation of gender identity is prominently displayed on the sign above the door at the coiffeur's: "Herren und Damen." The barber carefully inspects Jan's and her husband's hair. He fears that Frau Hudson's will grow out more quickly than her husband's, but at Jan's directions he cuts both identically. Tom sits anxiously through the barbering, and when it is over, he and his wife have the hair of "twin brothers." Tom loves looking like his devil, but he is a little embarrassed, and he tries once again to hide his hair under his hat. Jan won't let him, though, and back at the inn the bar maid is ecstatic. To her they look just like "brother and sister," or like children from days gone by.

Back in Paris a few weeks later, Tom is absorbed in his work, and Jan knows he will produce something magnificent if she doesn't "ruin" him. Hudson wonders how she could possibly do that, but she replies that she might just do it to amuse herself some night. She calls Tom her "brother" and her "girl," and she's still preoccupied with her hair and her fading tan. She has new plans for making her hair blonder than ever because she wants to drive Tom "crazy." She has to have a deep tan to be so blonde, though, so she decides that they should go to the south of France. A day later, when she meets Tom at a cafe, she strolls in with impossibly blonde hair—hair so light it is almost silver. She begs Tom to feel how "silky" it is and tells him how excited everyone had been at the coiffeur's as her hair became lighter and lighter with each successive rinse. She is entirely transformed, and she's certain that everyone who sees her feels changed. Now she wants Tom to dye his hair as well. He can't bring himself to have it done professionally, but he promises that she can do it by pouring buckets of sea water over his head when they get to the Mediterranean. Like a transvestite driven by the urge to pass in public, Jan needs to be seen, and as item K113 closes she and Tom wander off to a public place to eat dinner.

Needless to say, this all sounds very familiar. In *The Garden of Eden* manuscript, when the reader first meets Nick and Barbara Sheldon, they are in Paris, but their faces are still brown from the snow of Switzerland where Nick had been painting high in the Alps. Barbara has long wanted Nick to wear his hair just like her own and has fantasized about this while making love to him. The miraculous transformation, however, happens not in Switzerland but in Paris. On a cold Parisian morning, Barbara (who with her "red gold hair" and light freckles is clearly a portrait of Hadley) cuts Nick's long hair to match her own, although he is extremely reluctant to comb it as she does. Even after a whisky, he can't muster the courage to look at himself in a mirror. Strangely excited and transformed, though, he makes love with Barbara, and afterward the two sit in bed wearing only their sweaters. Later, they celebrate with a lunch at Lipp's, where they stare at their identical images in the mirror across the room. Emboldened, they venture to a professional coiffeur to have their hair neatened identically, and the barber is so excited that his hand shakes.

It could well be, as Burwell speculates, that items 112 and 113 from the *Islands* manuscript simply evolved into *The Garden of Eden*, but I don't think we can be sure of this. Their omission from the *Islands* manuscript seems as much like an act of self-censorship as of saving material for use elsewhere. Hemingway, indeed, was working on both novels in the late 1940s when he was playing games with his own and his wife's hair, calling her "Peter" and calling himself "Catherine," but he didn't recycle the passages from *Islands* in the *Eden* manuscript. And, in a letter to Adriana Ivancich, Hemingway claimed to be *beginning* the "fighting part" of the "Sea book" (presumably the "At Sea" section of *Islands*) in March 1951—years after he began *The Garden of Eden*.

More importantly, the hair games of the late 1940s were nothing new. Hemingway had been playing them for decades. As early as January 1923 he wrote to Ezra Pound from Switzerland: "I have laid off the barber in order that I won't be able to take a newspaper job. . . . The follicles functioning at a high rate of speed I am on the point of being thrown out from all except the society of outliers like yourself" (*SL* 77). A few days later, he told Pound, "The high altitutde has made me practically sexless" (*SL* 79). Remembering his early days in Paris in the manuscript to *A Moveable Feast*, Hemingway recalls that the easiest way to limit his expenses was to wear his hair so long that he couldn't visit the more respectable establishments on the right bank. But his motives were hardly financial. As his hair grew out, Hadley encouraged him:

> "It's growing wonderfully. You'll just have to be patient."
> "All right. I'll forget about it."
> "If you don't think about it maybe it will grow faster. I'm so glad you remembered to start it so early."
> We looked at each other and laughed and then she said one of the secret things. . . .
> "Tatie I thought of something exciting."
> "Tell me."
> "I don't know whether to say it."
> "Say it. Go on. Please say it."
> "I thought maybe it could be the same as mine."
> "But yours keeps growing too."
> "No. I'll get it just evened tomorrow and then I'll wait for you. Wouldn't that be fun for us?"
> "Yes."
> "I'll wait and then it will be the same for both."
> "How long will it take?"
> "Maybe four months to be just the same. . . ."
> We sat back and she said something secret and I said something secret back.
> "Other people would think we are crazy."
> "Poor unfortunate other people," she said. . . . Do you think other people have such simple things?"
> "Maybe it's not so simple." (qtd. in Kennedy 135)

But Ernest doesn't care if it's simple or not. He just knows that he likes it. Later, when Hadley returns from the hairdresser's with an exciting new haircut, Ernest says something "secret" to her as he strokes her hair and hefts "its silky weight."

So while Frau and Herr Hudson's tonsorial twinning looks uncannily like that practiced by Nick and Barbara Sheldon in the *Eden* manuscript—both, after all, were based on Hemingway's memories of life with Hadley in Paris and Switzerland—it resembles almost as closely Hadley's plans for identical haircuts with Ernest in the *Moveable Feast* manuscript, or Catherine Barkley's plans for identical haircuts with Frederic in *A Farewell to Arms*, or Robert Jordan's plans for identical haircuts with Maria in *For Whom the Bell Tolls*, or Littless's plans for matching haircuts with her big brother in "The Last Good Country." Likewise, brother-sister romances can be found throughout Hemingway's work from the early twenties to the late fifties, and Jan's report of her excitement at the coiffeur's resembles nothing so much as the excitement of Marie Morgan in *To Have and Have Not*. In other words, the problem isn't to explain a remarkable similarity between two texts, or even between the posthumous novels, but rather to explain a remarkable continuity of erotic thematic content throughout Hemingway's entire career.

Those erotic characters, props, and acts that appear in the same combinations again and again in Hemingway's fiction—haircutting, hair-dyeing, sweaters, furs, suntans, cats, silk, ivory, castration, mothers, fathers, brother-sister love, gender-swapping, identity-merging, and mirror-gazing—remain constant because they are the characters, props, and acts of Hemingway's perverse scenario. They are the ambassadors of his core complex to the realm of fantasy. This is why the perverse scenario is the *least* creative thing to be found in Hemingway's work. It is compulsive, fixated, static. Small changes might creep in over the years—a new prop might be found, a new subplot added—but major modifications were out of the question. The script was too fundamental to the regulation of Hemingway's identity to suffer any significant change. The scenario's characters can wear different costumes, but insofar as their roles in any work of fiction are dictated by their roles in the perverse scenario they remain the same beneath the skin. So far as the perverse scenario is concerned, there are no real differences between Catherine Barkley or Maria or Jan Hudson or Barbara Sheldon or Marita

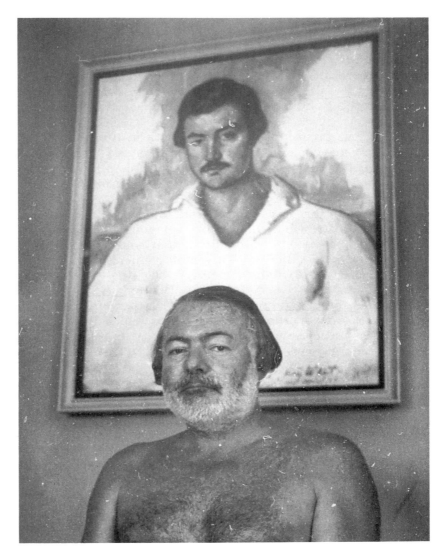

Figure 16. An older Hemingway poses beneath the "Page-Boy" portrait of himself painted in the 1920s by his friend Waldo Peirce. (John F. Kennedy Library)

or Catherine Bourne. It isn't that crucial differences between these characters don't exist; it is only that these differences are insignificant within the context of the perverse scenario; they have their origins elsewhere, in other aspects of Hemingway's psyche. For as McDougall notes, different parts of the personality can be organized differently. In the realm of the perverse scenario, however, Hemingway's male characters all represent either himself, his emasculated father, or his idealized paternal imago; his female characters are the stereotypes classified by Comley and Scholes: mothers, nurses, bitches, sisters, and devils.

What has preoccupied me, then, both in this chapter and throughout this book is a perverse, pornographic kernel embedded in Hemingway's art. I would never want to be misunderstood as equating this kernel with the work itself. It is a mere static, organizing element at the core of the work. It is this organizing function that gives an understanding of it such explanatory power. And while this kernel remained static over the decades—as if Hemingway were prohibited from imagining erotic encounters in any other way—it was nevertheless fundamental to his creativity. Although the perverse scenario itself was anything but creative, the perverse core of Hemingway's psyche regulated itself by generating narratives. His perversion was the crazy old relative at the party who keeps telling the same old story, over and over again. One wonders, "How can he do it? Doesn't he know everyone has heard it a hundred times? Isn't he sick of it himself?" (One thinks of the almost Sisyphean tedium of Sade's novels.) But the rest of Hemingway's psyche, the creative parts of his psyche, could always put a new spin on the old story. Thus, the further one travels from sexuality, the more various and creative his symbols become.

Perhaps Hemingway felt compelled to write his favorite erotic script in part because it wasn't the sort of thing he could buy at any newstand or adult bookstore for a few dollars. Works like *Mademoiselle de Maupin* and *Taras Bulba* might come close in their own ways, but never really close enough. Deeply coded with subtle references to the unique circumstances of his childhood, Hemingway's perverse scenario was a story that he alone could write, and fiction gave him a mechanism for putting the drama of his psyche on paper. There it could have a sort of material reality. There the split-off parts of his personailty could take on flesh and work out some form of integration. There his split-off feminine half could find expression and "pass" in public. There he could work out his relationship with his parents, with his sisters, or with his idealized paternal imago. Even when the perverse scenario didn't provide the seed for Hemingway's narratives, it was bound to surface to the degree that he rooted into his unconscious; and unconscious energies were bound to bubble up to the surface so long as the split-off unconscious portion of Hemingway's ego remained in unbroken contact with forces of the id. Moreover, Hemingway grew to consciously consider the perverse scenario an essential part of his artistic vision—something not to be denied by a man who would confront the world and himself as honestly as possible. In *The Garden of Eden*, David Bourne repeatedly berates himself for trying to deny the nature of his own desire. This is ironic, of course, since a perversion is constructed precisely out of the lies that one tells to oneself. It is an organized system of illusion used to compensate for a reality too traumatic to be faced unaided. Nevertheless, Hemingway showed great courage in probing aspects of himself that in his own words "spooked him shitless."

The positive relation between perversion and creativity, however, is to be found not so much in perversion's thematic content as in its aesthetic. (Here I rely on Christopher Bollas' recognition that creativity consists of both a thematic and an aesthetic.) That is, if the aethetic moment, those all too rare moments when we are captured by a poem or a work of art, consists in a moment of "deep rapport between subject and object"—between reader and text, between author and text, or in our imagination between reader and author—it places us squarely in the realm of what Winnicott calls transitional space, or "potential space" (Bollas 40). This, according to Winnicott, is the location of cultural experience. Such moments of deep subjective rapport rely on a mode of object relating—an ability to use illusion to mediate between inner psychic reality and external reality—that is the legacy of our infantile transitional objects. Insofar as almost all of us once had transitional objects, almost all of us have access to this mode of object relating. Yet for the perverse individual this has remained the *standard* mode of object relating. "In the perversions the object occupies an intermediary position: it is not-self and yet subjective; registered and accepted as separate and yet treated as subjectively created" (Khan 21). For the perverse subject, the relation to the object resembles the aesthetic moment in the reader's relation to a text.

Such a mode of object relating has tragic consequences, alienating the subject from an object whose essential otherness is denied, but could it be that this gives the perverse individual a

somewhat privileged relation to the aesthetic moment? Winnicott suggests that whereas many of us live creatively and experience ourselves most profoundly by drawing freely upon
transitional energies, the creative artist is often driven to create
by a search to find a true sense of self by recapturing the feeling
of being merged with the mother. Blanket assertions about the
psychology of creative artists always merit our skepticism, but
there is something persuasive in Kohut's claim that "the creative
individual, whether in art of science, is less psychologically separated from his [or her] surroundings than the noncreative one;
the "I-you" barrier is not as clearly defined" ("Forms" 75). Kohut
even echoes Kurt Eissler's contention that,

> in certain respects, the artist's attitude to his [or her] work is
> similar to that of the fetishist toward the fetish[.] [This] lends
> support to the idea that, for the creator, the work is a transi-
> tional object and that it is invested with transitional narcissis-
> tic libido. The fetishist's attachment to the fetish has the
> intensity of an addiction, a fact which is a manifestation not of
> object love but of a fixation on an early object that is experi-
> enced as part of the self. Creative artists . . . may be attached
> to their work with the intensity of an addiction, and they try to
> control and shape it with forces and for purposes which belong
> to a narcissistically experienced world. They are attempting to
> recreate a perfection which formerly was directly an attribute of
> their own; during the act of creation, however, they do not re-
> late to their work in the give-and-take mutuality which charac-
> terizes object love. ("Forms" 77)

Thus, while the thematic content of Hemingway's perverse scenario was essentially uncreative, one can't help feeling that, for
Hemingway, it must often have produced in his fiction the
purest experience of the aesthetic moment. And this experience
is perhaps inseparable from our own experience of the aesthetic
moment when reading his work.

   I don't mean to suggest that we respond as fetishists to
Hemingway's fetishistic fantasies, but I would suggest that the
same quest for merger that drove Hemingway's erotic life also
drove him to develop a style that privileges the aesthetic moment. The secrets that Hemingway's lovers share in fetishistic
play and the secrets that Hemingway shares with his readers—
whether they be about wine or fishing or bullfighting or
courage—are tools for creating moments of deep rapport, and I

would suggest that the two forms of secret sharing are ultimately inseparable. We find it so easy to identify with the author
precisely because he was a master at eliciting this response
which was so crucial to the regulation of his identity. To the degree that we are pulled in by such moments, we are pulled in by
Hemingway's fetishistic desire.

Notes

Introduction

1. Carlos Baker recounts the story as follows: one August morning, four years after the publication of "Bull in the Afternoon," Hemingway

> strode into Max Perkins's office and found Max Eastman sitting there.
> . . . Although Perkins was apprehensive over what might happen, he affected a matter-of-fact tone in saying to Eastman what he hoped was true: "Here's a friend of yours, Max." The two men shook hands and exchanged minor pleasantries. Perkins, relieved, had just settled back in his chair when Ernest, grinning broadly, ripped open his own shirt to expose a chest which, as Perkins said, was "hairy enough for anybody." Eastman laughed and Ernest, still grinning, opened Eastman's shirt to reveal a chest "as bare as a bald man's head." The contrast led to further laughter, and Perkins was just preparing for a possible unveiling of his own when Ernest suddenly flushed with anger.
>
> "What do you mean," he roared at Eastman, "accusing me of impotence?"
>
> Eastman denied it. He was just going on to further explanations when he caught sight of his own volume, *Art and the Life of Action*, which happened to be lying on Perkins's desk. It contained a reprint of "Bull in the Afternoon" and he thrust it at Ernest, saying, "Here. Read what I *really* said." Ernest seized the book and began leafing through the pages, muttering and swearing. "Let Max read it," said Eastman.
>
> But Ernest, his face contorted with rising anger, smacked Eastman in the face with the open book. Eastman instantly rushed at him, and Perkins, fearing that Eastman might be badly hurt, ran over to grab Ernest's arm. Just as he came around the corner of the desk, the adversaries grappled and fell. Perkins grasped the shoulders of the man on top, certain that it must be Hemingway. Instead he found himself looking down into Ernest's upturned face. He was flat on the floor and grinning broadly, having regained his temper almost at once.
>
> The newspapers broke the story three days later as Ernest was leaving for France. . . . Eastman believed, and had publicly stated, that he had beaten Ernest fairly in a wrestling match. Ernest assured the

277

> man from the *Times* that this was all poppycock. "He didn't throw any-
> body anywhere," said Ernest. "He jumped at me like a woman, clawing
> . . . with his open hands. I just held him off. I didn't want to hurt him.
> He's ten years older than I am." (317)

This story should interest us for reasons beyond its sheer absurdity. It not only demonstrates Ernest's sensitivity to any questioning of his masculinity; it does so in interesting terms. Eastman's accusation that Hemingway's prose wore "false hair on the chest" clearly hit a raw nerve. After four years it was this phrase—hardly central to Eastman's article—which stuck in Ernest's mind. And this is hardly surprising. Hair—in any form or location, false or otherwise—was no joking matter for Hemingway. His misreading of Eastman, who rightly claimed that he had by no means accused Ernest of "impotence," establishes a symbolic connection between hair and potency which is fundamentally important to my analysis of fetishism in Hemingway's psyche and work.

2. According to Heinz Kohut, this is always the case in fetishism (*Analysis* 177).

3. The conflation of these various forms of fetishism has led to some deeply confused cultural criticism in the past few years. All three forms of fetishism have two things in common: (1) the overvaluation of an object, and (2) a form of disavowal. Yet the link between these disparate phenomena is primarily *semantic*, hinging upon the *word* "fetish." This isn't to say that the same item—say, a rubber jumpsuit—couldn't simultaneously be a sexual fetish *and* a commodity fetish; it is only to say that this confluence is largely a coincidence, a chance meeting of two different phenomena with the same name in the same object. Lorraine Gamman and Merja Makinen sort out this mess admirably in their recent book, *Female Fetishism.*

4. See Louise Kaplan's *Female Perversions.* Some of the most exciting theoretical work on the perversions in the last two decades has been done on the hitherto neglected female perversions. If I ignore much of this research in my analysis of Hemingway, it is not out of any lack of respect for this work but is, rather, due to the fact that my subject is a male author.

5. This remains, however, a point of contention in the psychoanalytic community. In siding with Stoller, my views on homosexuality differ from those of many other psychoanalysts, most notably those of Charles W. Socarides.

6. Joyce McDougall, an expert on the perversions, makes this point well: "A perverse organization cannot necessarily be deduced from, or defined simply in terms of, the incidence of deviant sexual behavior. Sexual aberrations occur in people with differing psychic struc-

ture and the same sexual act may have a significantly different meaning and function according to the personality" (53).

7. For *The Garden of Eden* manuscripts, I cite item number, folder, and page. Thus "(K422.1 3.1)" means Kennedy Library item 422.1, folder 3, page 1. When a folder contains more than one chapter, I cite the chapter number after the folder number and before the page number. Whenever possible I cite the published version of the novel (indicated simply by "*GE*"). All passages cited from the *Eden* manuscript have previously appeared in print, either in Comley and Scholes, in Spilka, in Burwell, or in my own essay "Come Back to the Beach Ag'in, David Honey!" I would like to thank the Hemingway family and the Hemingway Foundation and Society for permission to reprint these passages.

8. Paul Gebhard distinguishes between four levels of fetishistic intensity:

> Level 1: A slight preference for certain kinds of sex partners, sexual stimuli or sexual activity. The term "fetish" should not be used at this level.
> Level 2: A strong preference for certain kinds of sex partners, sexual stimuli or sexual activity. (Lowest intensity of fetishism)
> Level 3: Specific stimuli are necessary for sexual arousal and sexual performance. (Moderate intensity of fetishism)
> Level 4: Specific stimuli *take the place* of a sex partner. (High level fetishism) (qtd. in Gamman and Makinen 38)

My study is concerned primarily with what Gebhard would call moderate and high intensity fetishism. I should also point out that at "level four" fetishism begins to slide seamlessly into transvestism.

9. *Overdetermination* is the product of condensation. A single symbol or symptom may unite "a multiplicity of unconscious elements which may be organized in different meaningful sequences, each having its own specific coherence at a particular level of interpretation" (Laplanche and Pontalis 292).

Chapter One

1. These sentences also appear in the published version of *The Garden of Eden* (37), but the context is entirely different. For these lines in their proper context, see Spilka (295).

2. Note that I imply that we *are* moved by this complexity in some measure whether we fully understand it or not. Most of us are extremely astute psychological observers in our day-to-day lives, even if we could never verbalize the psychological insights implicit in our inter-

actions with others. The same holds true for our experience as readers. Furthermore, one pitfall of a limited or dogmatic verbalization of our psychological understanding is that it can place blinders around our naturally complex psychological perception, focusing our attention too narrowly, closing off aspects of insight which otherwise might have been, at least unconsciously, acknowledged. Still, if we approach any attempt to verbalize the psychological complexity of another with sufficient humility, with an understanding of the ultimate inadequacy of our verbalization, we can avoid this pitfall and use the psychological explanation to open up texts and heighten our awareness of complexity instead of closing off avenues of insight.

3. "[The Maitre d'Hotel] advanced smiling, lovingly, and yet conspiratorially, since they both shared many secrets, and he extended his hand, which was a big, long, strong, spatular fingered hand. . . , and the Colonel extended his own hand, which had been shot through twice, and was slightly misshapen" (*ART* 55). We will eventually see that Cantwell's hand has a significant place in Hemingway's field of fetishistic fantasy.

4. This passage actually combines the secret shared between author and reader with the secret shared between lovers. Marita asks David if his select community of readers knows what *she and David* know about the "*mystère*." David replies that his ideal readers know of its existence and feel it, but he acknowledges that—like myself—they spend more time trying to "explain it" (K422.1 37.20.4th insert).

5. In the aggression-laden relationship between Philip Rawlings and Dorothy Bridges in *The Fifth Column*, Dorothy is excluded from Philip's secret life of counter-espionage which she compares to the "Skull and Bones Society" (73), but she does have fetishized beautiful hair and a silver fox wrap, and she does seem to share erotic "secrets" with Philip at night—"things of the night" which Philip repudiates in the day.

6. From a 1922 letter to Sherwood Anderson: "Bones [Hadley] is called Binney now. We both call each other Binney. I'm the male Binney and she is the female Binney" (*SL* 62). Ernest often shared the nickname "Feather Kitty" with Hadley, just as he shared the name "Kitten" with his fourth wife, Mary. Diliberto notes that Ernest referred to Hadley as the "same guy," and he used the same sort of language in letters to Pauline: Hadley "won't admit it but she knows we're [Ernest and Pauline] the same person—sometimes she has admitted it" (*SL* 221). Pauline reciprocated in her letters to Ernest: "We are one, we are the same guy, I am you" (qtd. in Kert 186).

7. For the "secrets, taboos, and delights," see Kennedy 135. For the "secrets" (which are clearly fetishistic and transvestic) see *GE* 68; for the "tribal rules" see K422.1 36.35. The "jollies and secrecies" are

mentioned in a letter to Mary dated 2 May 1947. In this letter the "secrecies" clearly refer to fetishistic experiments.

8. Traditionally, secret-keeping is linked to anality, but while
there is probably something to be said about anality in Hemingway's
work, his treatment of the secret stresses the *sharing* over the *keeping*,
and this I would argue privileges the fetishistic and narcissistic-
bonding aspect of the secret over its anal-retentive aspect (i.e. keeping
the feces from the mother). Nevertheless, I should note that the French
psychoanalyst Janine Chasseguet-Smirgel has argued that a regressive
anality is central to the perversions. However, while this anality can be
seen fairly clearly in some cases of shoe fetishism (for instance, in a
fondness for smelly, muddy shoes), there is little evidence of it in Hemingway's case, and I think Chasseguet-Smirgel overstates her claims.
Nevertheless, one scene in Hemingway's work does come to mind in
this connection: Colonel Cantwell in *Across the River* defecates on the
site where he suffered his first wound. This is also the site where Hemingway was wounded in the First World War, and it does hold a key
place in Hemingway's field of fetishistic fantasy.

9. Freud noted this fact in his essay on fetishism, and it has been
reaffirmed by many subsequent analysts. While the perversions point
to profound disturbances in ego-formation, the perverse behavior itself
is generally ego-syntonic.

10. Cantwell had been an observer in the Spanish Civil War, not a
combatant.

11. As his hair thinned, Hemingway took to combing long hair
from the back of his head over the top. One tends to overlook this in
pictures from the late 1950s, but with a little attention it is obvious,
and Hemingway was extremely touchy about the subject. According to
Carlos Baker, Hemingway's sensitivity about his balding pate precipi-
tated his only serious argument with his good friend Buck Lanham:

> [Lanham] put his hand fleetingly on Ernest's shoulder in a gesture of
> friendship and remarked that it was only a mere twenty minutes until
> July 21st and [Ernest's] birthday. As he turned away, part of his left arm
> grazed the back of Ernest's head. Ernest winced as if he had been burned,
> and said in a loud clear voice that nobody was permitted to touch his
> head. White with anger, Lanham departed. A while later, Ernest caught
> up with him, apologetic and weeping. He explained that he was bald and
> that he had combed his white, curly back hair forward in a bang in order
> to hide the baldness. If Lanham would forgive him, he said he would go to
> the barber the next day and have his 'goddamned hair' cut short like Lan-
> ham's. Lanham told him to stop talking like a jackass. . . . (548)

12. The pistol/penis is, of course, the most time-worn of phallic
symbols. We find it used in *For Whom Bell Tolls* when Jordan wears his

gun in his sleeping bag at night, and we find it again in a more intriguing way in *Fifth Column*: "I was against the wall and my rifle was between my legs when I leaned back, and I remember [He chokes] in the
dream I—I thought it was my girl and she was doing something—kind
of funny—to me. I don't know what it was. It was just a dream" (40).

13. In a strange passage, Littless playfully fantasizes about getting
knockout drops for Nick from the "Queen of the Whores." Stranger yet
is the lesbian element of this fantasy: "I'm delicately brought up," she
explains. "This makes me intensely desirable to the main whore and to
all of her circle" (97).

14. Margot Macomber would seem to be an exception, but even
Margot has "dark hair drawn back off her head and gathered in a knot
low on her neck" (*SS* 10). The "Macomber" manuscript (K690), moreover, characterizes Margot by her hair. She was the sort who wouldn't
even wear her hair short when that was the style, and you could never
imagine her excited or with her hair mussed. Yet Hemingway is more
insistent about Francis Macomber's crew cut. In fact, Margot shoots
Francis in the back of his "crew-cropped head" (36). Hair signified for
Hemingway regardless of whether it was on men or women, but it signified differently depending on the sex of the wearer.

15. Pauline wrote Ernest a number of letters at this time describing her attempts to dye her hair blonde, but his replies are not extant.

16. A note from Mary's diary (1949) offers a glimpse into the subtlety
of Ernest's fetishistic associations: "Papa also says, 'You're the rich man's
Mary Martin'" (244). With her short blonde hair, Mary Hemingway *did* actually look somewhat like Mary Martin, who as the star of the new hit
South Pacific was much in the news that year. But for Ernest the resemblance ran deeper. Martin's most famous number, sung each evening
from beneath a shower as she washed her hair on stage, had a title which
could hardly be overlooked by a hair fetishist: "I'm Gonna Wash that Man
Right Outa My Hair." (Hemingway, who subscribed to the American edition of *Life* magazine, would have seen a picture of Martin shampooing
her hair featured prominently in a spring 1949 article about the musical.)
Hemingway wanted to meet Mary Martin in 1953 (*SL* 818).

Chapter Two

1. Renata's description of this portrait, painted by a homosexual
"boy" with false teeth and a "wave in his hair," reveals how perceptive
she is concerning Cantwell's fetishism: "It is very romantic. My hair is
twice as long as it has ever been and I look as though I were rising from
the sea without the wet head. Actually, you rise from the sea with the

hair very flat and coming to points at the end. It is almost the look of a very nearly dead rat. But . . . *while it is not truly me, it is the way you like to think of me*" (my emphasis, 97). Of course, Renata's perceptiveness is Hemingway's perceptiveness, just as Cantwell's fetishism is Hemingway's fetishism.

2. In the published version of "The Summer People," a story about Hemingway's close friends in Michigan written during the summer of 1924, the throat thickening is not experienced by the male protagonist, Nick (who is also called "Wemedge," one of Hemingway's many nicknames), but is instead projected onto Odgar when in proximity to Kate. In the manuscript (K725), however, Nick responds "chokily" to Kate's question, "Do you like me with my clothes off, Wemedge?" Hemingway's indifference to the threat of censorship in this story should be clear from the following passage:

> He touched one of her small breasts with his lips gently. It came alive between his lips, his tongue pressing against it. He felt the whole feeling coming back again and, sliding his hand down, moved Kate over. He slid down and she fit close against him. She pressed tight against the curve of his abdomen. She felt wonderful there. He searched, a little awkwardly, then found it. He put both hands over her breasts and held her to him. Nick kissed hard against her back. Kate's head dropped forward.
> "Is it good that way?" he said.
> "I love it. I love it. I love it. Oh, come, Wemedge. Please come. Come, come. Please, Wemedge. Please, please, Wemedge." (CSS 502)

If Gertrude Stein thought "Up in Michigan" *inaccrochable*, what would she have made of this?

3. A proliferation of phallic symbols serves, like the fetish object itself, to ward off castration anxiety while simultaneously serving as a monument to it. See Freud's fragmentary essay on Medusa's head (*SE* XVIII). We should also note that fetishism forces us to distinguish between the real *penis* and the symbolic *phallus*; in fact, the fetish is a symbol not of a real penis but of an *imaginary* penis (i.e., the *mother's* "penis"). For this reason, in his fourth seminor, Lacan introduces the concept of the *phallus* as a means of distinguishing between this imaginary penis and the real biological organ. The fetish is a symbolic phallus, then, that stands in for the absence of the desired imaginary phallus.

4. Some will surely object that Margot's Mannlicher is merely the same gun that Pauline used while hunting with Ernest in Africa. True as this is, however, it hardly prevents the gun from taking on phallic significance. Like all of us, the fetishist finds his symbols most easily in what is at hand. Of course, it is hardly odd for a woman to have a gun in a hunting story, especially if the plot requires her to shoot her hus-

band in a dubious "accident"; yet Hemingway's use of guns as patently obvious phallic symbols in *Islands in the Stream*, *The Fifth Column*, *For Whom the Bell Tolls*, and *Across the River and Into the Trees* leads me to suspect that Hemingway's guns were seldom *just* guns.

5. See Otto Fenichel's famous essay, "The Symbolic Equation: Girl = Phallus." Havelock Ellis refers to the condition of falling in love with statues, or women posing as statues ("a rare form of erotomania") as "Pygmalionism" (1.3.188).

6. When Catherine asks David to make the "sea change" with her, she explicitly invokes this statue of two lesbians kissing:

> "Will you change and be my girl and let me take you? Will you be like you were in the statue? Will you change?"
> He knew now and it was like the statue. The one there are no photographs of and of which no reproductions are sold. (qtd. in Spilka 286)

7. As Freud argued in "The Taboo of Virginity," the phallic properties of the virgin imply a threat to the man's penis at the time of defloration, implying a "castrate" or "be castrated" mentality—an attitude which gives birth to phantasmagoria such as the vagina dentata. The themes of the phallic virgin and the virgin threat to the male phallus can be found quite clearly, for instance, in the biblical story of Judith and Holofernes or in the fourteenth century *Voiage of Sir John Maundeville*, which includes a "tale of virgins who had serpents in their vaginas which 'stongen men upon hire Zerdes, that thei dyeden anon,' i.e., stung men's penises and caused them to die" (qtd. in Rancour-Laferriere, *Signs* 185). This is clearly related to the way Pilar assumes her phallic properties at the expense of Pablo and Finito, or the way Catherine Bourne becomes "Peter" only at the "cost" (which is something *more* than a "cost") of making David "Catherine."

8. Admittedly, the construction of the human voice as *phallic* is bizarre, but Greenacre offers some insight into why such things are possible: "Not only is the whole body of the fetishist more than ordinarily equated with the phallus, but every part of it may become genitalized" (64). Rancour-Laferriere, in his essay "Some Semiotic Aspects of the Human Penis," also notes that both the male and female voice can assume phallic significance in various contexts. "This may occur because the voice is a secondary sexual characteristic which distinguishes males from females" (60). As an example, he offers a sentence from Joseph Heller's *Something Happened* that should remind us of Hemingway: ". . .that's what I'd be left with, a lump in my throat instead of my pants. . ." (60).

9. The very fact that Freud's child-informant *speaks* suggests that he is probably at least three years-old—at the height of the phallic

phase, when such thinking predominates in little boys. Rancour-Lafer-riere cites a number of such examples in *Signs of the Flesh*. There is a report, for instance, of what a two-year-old boy said to his *mother*: "You just have to wait till you grow up, and you'll have a penis too!" (310). Freud's Little Hans provides another classic example of such thought:

> I [Hans's father] explained to him that his sister has not got a widdler [*Wiwimacher*] like him. Little girls and women, I said, have no widdlers: Mummy has none, Anna has none, and so on.
> Hans: "Have you got a widdler?"
> I: "Of course. Why, what do you suppose?"
> Hans (after a pause): "But how do little girls widdle, if they have no widdlers?" (*SE* X, 31)

10. By "primacy of the phallus," I mean specifically Freud's no-tions that the libido is "of a masculine nature whether it occurs in men or in women" (*SE* VII, 219), and that the phallic stage dominates in little girls as well as in little boys before latency sets in and the full genital stage is reached in puberty. Accordingly, "Freud does not recognize any knowledge of the vagina on the part of the girl," and he argues that the little girl thinks of her clitoris simply as a little penis (Laplanche & Pon-talis 311). Yet even a fairly conservative theorist of fetishism like Bak contends that the phallic woman is a "dominantly male fantasy" ("Dis-tortions" 194), and post-Freudian studies by Horney, Klein, and Jones have demonstrated that little girls do typically have an awareness of the vagina that does not square with Freud's model of phallic primacy. (Chasseguet-Smirgel has even argued that "the theory of phallic monism is devised *defensively*—by little boys and psychoanalytic theo-rists alike—to deny the existence" of a frightening vagina that the little boy cannot fill [Whitebook 49].) Nevertheless, the existence of women with other common feminine phallic position fixations, such as penis-envy, suggests that at least some girls do think of the clitoris in phallic terms during the "phallic phase" and fixate on the fantasies provoked by such thought.

11. I focus on the little boy advisedly, for fetishism is overwhelm-ingly a male perversion. Of course I am aware of the recent, and often brilliant, work on "female fetishism" by Naomi Schor ("Female Fetishism: The Case of George Sand"), Elizabeth Grosz ("Lesbian Fetishism?"), Emily Apter (*Feminizing the Fetish*), Teresa de Lauretis (*The Practice of Love*), and Lorraine Gamman and Merja Makinen (*Female Fetishism*). Yet even Schor acknowledges that "female fetishism is a rare, if not nonexis-tent perversion" ("Fetishism" 98); she constructs her arguments around the mechanism of "disavowal," central to fetishism (and many other con-ditions, such as melancholia), rather than around the actual use of a genuine fetish object. Likewise, Grosz "agree[s] with the psychoanalytic orthodoxy that female fetishism is physically inconceivable," with the

proviso that "both 'normal' (i.e., heterosexual) femininity and female homosexuality can be seen—in sociopolitical terms—to be in excess of their
psychoanalytic descriptions as a form of fetishism. . ." (102). Grosz argues for an analogy between masculine lesbianism and male fetishism,
but she recognizes the limitations of her analogy: "It is unimaginable
that women would get sexual gratification from the use of inanimate objects or mere partial objects *alone*" (101). The masculine lesbian's feminine partner, Grosz argues, represents the masculine lesbian's "missing"
female phallus (instead of the *mother's* female phallus). Likewise, in *Female Perversions*, Louise J. Kaplan refers to "fetishism, transvestism, ex-
hibitionism, voyeurism, sexual masochism, sexual sadism, pedophilia,
zoophilia, and necrophilia" as "male perversions," reserving the term "female perversions" for less obviously sexual strategies which nevertheless, like the male perversions, use a parody of traditional gender role
stereotypes to master preoedipal childhood traumas (12). Gamman and
Makinen, on the other hand, explore a genuine non-phallic eroticization
of objects by women which, like male fetishism, has its roots in the infantile transitional object. The object they describe, however, represents
something related to, but quite different from, the masculine/phallic
fetish object; if we are to preserve important psychodynamic distinctions
and distinctions about how the fetishist *uses* his or her object, we
should reserve a separate term for the phenomena they describe.

Nevertheless, Greenacre and Stoller have argued convincingly for the
existence of fetishism in rare cases of women with masculine identifications of delusional or psychotic intensity. Zavitzianos's case of a woman
with a vibrator "fetish," however, is not a case of genuine fetishism.

12. Two examples, both cited in Rancour-Laferriere (*Signs*), offer
helpful illustrations of such thought. In a locker-room conversation between a father and his six-year-old son, the father asked,

> "Johnny, what's the difference between boys and girls?" The little boy
> replied with a long list of differences in clothing, hair style, etc. But the
> father (a university professor) pressed him, saying: "That's not what I
> mean. You know the real difference is that boys have a penis and girls
> don't." To which the little boy emphatically replied: "Oh, I know that,
> but girls *used* to have a penis!" (310)

Thus, this little boy defines girls as "castrated." Yet even the *professor's*
distinction between girls and boys should be classed as a phallic position construction of anatomical difference; the female genitalia are not
acknowledged, and sexual difference is defined instead solely on the
basis of the presence or absence of the penis. Another example demonstrates how such thinking can be symbolized and retained unconsciously even after it has been consciously rejected: "Henry . . . who had
first noticed the difference at 6 years used to think that girls' genitals
were cut off. Even after correction of this notion, he still spoke of the

girl's genital as having "a cut in it" (310). Freud himself was too often guilty of such thought.

13. To Freud's discourse of "castration," Stoller adds that the perversions respond to a "trauma or frustration of childhood [that] was aimed precisely at the anatomical sexual apparatus and its functioning or at one's masculinity and femininity" (*Perversions* 105). That is, Stoller stresses that a childhood threat to one's *gender identity* can be as important to the etiology of the perversions as the threat of "castration"—though on some level for little boys the two threats are inseparable.

14. For another such case, a man in his middle twenties with a *conscious* conviction that women possess penises, see Bak, "The Phallic Woman." (After protesting to his analyst that he *did* see a woman's penis, the man actually took a flashlight to bed so he could finally examine the female organs!) Hamilton's case study of a shoe fetishist might also be helpful here.

> At five, he and a girl playmate urinated behind a bush together, at which time he was sure she had a penis. From that time on, he thought all girls had penises and that the only means of differentiating between the sexes was by the length of hair, which stirred considerable anxiety whenever he was forced to visit a barber. . . . At seven to eight, he began surreptitiously to study an anatomy book belonging to his parents, thought that several of the female drawings looked like his mother, and wondered if she might not have a penis after concluding that the sigmoid colon of one specimen looked like an inverted penis. (326)

15. Technically, "awareness and disavowal" is redundant. Freud contends that disavowals are always "half-measures, incomplete attempts at detachment from reality. The disavowal is always supplemented by an acknowledgment; two contrary and independent attitudes always arise and result in the situation of there being a splitting of the ego" (*SE* XXIII, 204).

16. To the end of his life, Freud remained convinced that boys and girls become aware of their sexual identity only at the phallic/oedipal stage (3 to 5 years of age). "Although [Ernest] Jones and others had objected to this position . . . Freud would not budge. Since then much empirical work has been published, and analysts have generally recognized that Freud's position was mistaken." In their exhaustive psychoanalytic observations of infants, Mahler and her associates "found that girls discovered the anatomical sex differences sometime during the 16–17-month period or even earlier, but more often at 20–21 months. However, the boy's discovery of his own penis usually took place much earlier" (Fine 184).

17. It would really be safer to say that Freud would have arrived at the *origins* of fetish function and formation, not *necessarily* at the *determinants.*

18. "Let me feel your hand," Renata asks at one point. "It's all right," she assures him. "You can put it on the table" (84). Cantwell is reluctant, but Renata persists:

> "I want to feel it because all last week, every night, or I think nearly every night, I dreamed about it, and it was a strange mixed-up dream and I dreamed it was the hand of Our Lord. . . ."
> "What did the hand do?"
> "Nothing. Or maybe that is not true. Mostly it was just a hand."
> "Like this one?" The Colonel asked, looking at the mishapen hand with distaste, and remembering the two times that had made it that way."
> "Not like. It *was* that one. May I touch it carefully with my fingers if it does not hurt?"
> "It does not hurt. Where it hurts is in the head, the legs and the feet. I don't believe there's any sensation in that hand."
> "You're wrong," she said. "Richard. There is very much sensation in that hand." (84–85)

Cantwell's stigmata is a bit much for the reader to stomach, but I think there's more to his wound than the Christ-symbolism. It is interesting that Cantwell mentions the soreness in his legs and feet, the places in which Hemingway was wounded most seriously in World War I. Whereas Cantwell has been shot twice through the hand, Hemingway was also shot twice—once in the foot and once in the knee. Like Jake Barnes and Frederic Henry, Cantwell was wounded in the Great War— at Fossalta di Piave, precisely where his creator was wounded. In fact, in one of the best-remembered scenes from this novel Cantwell defecates on that spot and muses that his right kneecap must still lie in the ground. Given the tie between castration and Hemingway's wounding that informs *The Sun Also Rises* and *A Farewell to Arms*, Cantwell's misshapen hand takes on even more castratory significance. The specific injury to Cantwell's hand—having "been shot through twice" (*ART* 55)—should also remind us of Hemingway's later tall tales about having "been shot twice through the scrotum" when he was wounded in Italy (*SL* 694).

19. As Fenichel notes, this may be because the woman wants to *possess* the man's phallus or because she wants to *be* the man's symbolic phallus.

The reader may well wonder how Hemingway is supposed to have intuited what a *woman* with a phallic position fixation would feel. Winnicott, however, provides an answer for this question. As we shall eventually see, like all fetishists, Hemingway had strong bisexual identifications and an ego split along lines structured largely by gender identity. In short, Hemingway's ego contained a split-off feminine half. This splitting played no small part in helping him to maintain his fragile masculine gender identity in the face of his intense identifications with his mother, sisters, and wives; it also accounts for much of his mythical hypermasculinity. His public face was quite literally "all man"; his face at night, however, was quite different. According to Winnicott, this sort of split-off feminine half in men can "think" remarkably like a real woman. In his work with men with this sort of ego-splitting, Winnicott noted that "the split-off other-sex part of the personality . . . may have girl characteristics, may be breast-proud, experience penis envy, become pregnant, be equipped with no male external genitalia and even possess female sexual equipment and enjoy female sexual experience" (*Playing* 78).

20. Hemingway, of course, claimed that he invoked Stein's epithet for his generation ironically. Soon after publishing *The Sun Also Rises*, he wrote to Max Perkins: "It was refreshing to see someone have some doubts that I took the Gertrude Stein thing very seriously—I meant to play off against that splendid bombast (Gertrude's assumption of prophetic roles). Nobody knows about the generation that follows them and certainly has no right to judge" (*SL* 229). He goes on to explain that in relation to the quote from Ecclesiastes, he wanted to suggest that the earth which "abideth forever" is the true hero of the book.

Yet when Hemingway was writing the novel, he considered using "The Lost Generation" as a title, and he wrote an abandoned preface which lacks the ironic distance that he was soon claiming for the Stein epigraph. After recounting the famous story of how Stein first heard the phrase from the owner of a garage in the Department of Aix, his only complaint about the garage owner's verdict—"*C'est un generation perdu*"—is that "'*perdu*' loses a little something in being translated into 'lost.' There is something much more final about *perdu*." He continues:

> There is only this to say[,] that this generation that is lost has nothing to do with any younger generation about whose outcome much speculation occurred in times past. This is not a question of what kind of mothers will flappers make or where bobbed hair is leading us. This is about something that is already finished. For whatever is going to happen to the generation of which I am a part has already happened. (*SAR* mss 627)

So when did Hemingway change his mind about "the lost generation"? It's significant that he took his title from Ecclesiastes instead of Stein. Nevertheless, he kept Stein as an epigraph. Perhaps when he published the book he already intended the epigraph ironically, but I don't think we can be certain about this, and if we dismiss the Stein quote as mere ironic bombast, I suspect we will miss much of what attracted Hemingway to it in the first place. It can certainly be read ironically, but it has other dimensions as well, and it speaks to that profound sense of loss that permeates so much of Hemingway's fiction.

21. According to Frazer, on the twenty-fourth of March, the Day of Blood, novice priests of Attis (devotees of Cybele) would work themselves into a religious frenzy and sever their own genitals in sacrifice to the goddess. Initiates were then baptized in the blood of a sacrificial bull. As Peter Hays has suggested, Hemingway may have known of these rituals through his reading of Catullus.

If the fetishist creates the imago of the phallic woman to ward off castration anxiety, one might wonder why this same phallic woman can be conceived of as a "castrating woman." The fetishist, however, never really triumphs over castration anxiety. His "phallic women" are really always "phallic/castrated women," and one possibility that suggests itself to the fetishist for the woman's possession of the phallus is that she has taken it from a man. Obviously, the phallic woman so conceived is more threatening than pacifying, but this aspect of the phallic woman, by castrating men, also plays upon the fetishist's genuine desire to identify with the woman who on some level he still sees as "castrated." This should become clearer when we consider the relation between fetishism and transvestism.

22. Brett Ashley's history as a nurse (or Volunteer Aid Detachment member, to be precise) in the war also connects her to Agnes von Kurowsky, the most immediate model for Catherine Barkley in *A Farewell to Arms* and Hemingway's first adult love.

23. Hemingway was particularly concerned with stories about his scrotum during the early 1950s, while he was working on *Across the River and Into the Trees*. Perhaps Cantwell's trip to Fossalta reopened some old wounds for Hemingway, or perhaps it simply confronted these wounds after they had been reopened by other means. Nevertheless, according to Jeffrey Meyers, Hemingway was telling a version of this story in which he had been "shot twice through the scrotum" as early as the 1930s.

24. Bak stresses that regression to the phallic mother can happen quite late in life: "There are cases in which a perversion . . . becomes overt in middle age; such cases again confirm that the fantasy had lain dormant in the id and became reinvested under the impact of fresh traumata, which invariably constituted a severe castration threat" ("Phallic Woman" 23). The notion that Hemingway's wounding at Fossalta might have traumatically reawakened psychological forces with roots in Hemingway's childhood will remind many readers of Philip Young's theory that Hemingway suffered from a post-Fossalta traumatic neurosis with its attendant repetition compulsion and death drive. Yet, while my theory is compatible with Young's and likewise gives importance to adult trauma, fetishism and traumatic

neurosis, while not mutually exclusive, are entirely different; they stem from different forces and lead to entirely different sorts of repetition, with different goals and results. Moreover, Nagel and Reynolds both make convincing cases that Hemingway did not share Nick Adams's shell shock. He may, however, have mistaken his post-Fossalta fetishism and 1919 bout with depression for the effects of shell shock.

25. I *have* found one clear reference to a fetishistic reaction in Ernest before his wounding, but it was remembered long after the event, and it does not involve overt fetishistic behavior on his part. In *Death in the Afternoon*, Hemingway recalls cleaning up the dead after the explosion of a munitions factory in the countryside near Milan, soon after his arrival in Italy:

> I must admit, frankly, the shock it was to find that these dead were women rather than men. In those days women had not yet commenced to wear their hair cut short, as they did later for several years in Europe and America, and the most disturbing thing, perhaps because it was the most unaccustomed, was the presence and, even more disturbing, the occasional absence of this long hair. (136)

Hemingway's friend Milford Baker, who was present with Ernest after the disaster, remembers a site strewn with headless and limbless female corpses, and one can easily imagine how the duty of gathering numberless human fragments might have been as traumatic for Hemingway as his own wounding a month later. Perhaps the two events were linked in his unconscious.

26. Hemingway's father, who suffered from wild mood swings, committed suicide in December 1928. In 1963 Ernest's sister Marcelline died, supposedly from natural causes, but Ernest's brother, Leicester, suspected suicide. Ernest's sister Ursula committed suicide in 1966. In 1982, Leicester committed suicide. Hemingway's "sons Patrick and Gregory . . . have received psychiatric care and electro-convulsive therapy, and his granddaughter Lorian, Gregory's daughter, to the extent that her novel *Walking into the River* is autobiographical, has been hospitalized and given ECT" (Hays, "Depression," 60). Most recently, Ernest's granddaughter Margeaux added her name to this tragic list.

27. In his biography of Hemingway, Jeffrey Meyers dismisses Mary Hemingway's contention that her husband was manic-depressive, stating quite confidently that there is no evidence that Hemingway ever had a manic episode (544). Citing *DSM-III-R* criteria, however, Peter Hays offers convincing evidence for hypomania in his essay, "Hemingway's Clinical Depression." A careful reading of Carlos Baker's biography of Hemingway reveals alternating periods of depression and

abnormal, but not debilitating, elation; Michael Reynolds writes of
"Ernest's cycle of black moods and ecstatic highs" (*American* 210); and
Kay Jamison, one of the country's foremost researchers on mood disorders, diagnoses Hemingway with a bipolar disorder. True, Hemingway never suffered from the sort of wild debilitating manias that
plagued Robert Lowell, but the line between cyclothemia and manic-
depression is often arbitrary, and modern psychiatry recognizes "a
continuum of heightened mood from normal states of happiness, joy,
and pleasure to the extremes of delirious mania in which the patient
may be 'maniacal,' markedly hostile and assaultive, or paranoid and
delusional" (Klerman 314). These last symptoms sound a little like
Hemingway in his final years. In his youth, however, his "highs" were
more characteristic of hypomania and his depressions were frightening
but not debilitating. As Jamison notes, "such milder mood and energy
swings often precede overt clinical illness by years (about one-third of
patients with definite manic-depressive illness, for example, report
bipolar mood swings or hypomania predating the actual onset of their
illness)" (*Touched* 15). Jamison further cautions against any easy distinction between the highs and lows in manic-depression. She stresses
the prevalence and importance of "mixed manic-and-depressive states"
(*Unquiet* 182).

   28. In June 1921, for instance, two years after breaking up with
Agnes, Ernest again displayed symptoms of clinical depression; Hadley
feared that Ernest was suicidal. By November 1922, however, Carlos
Baker tells us that Ernest's "spirits were running high." By the next October, however, Ernest was again deeply depressed. Recovering from
childbirth, Hadley wrote to a friend: "I think we are going to leave
[Canada] as soon as I am safely strong again. It is too horrible to describe . . . and it will kill or scar my Tiny [Ernest] if we stay too long. He
is almost crazy and our hearts are heavy, heavy just when we ought to
be so happy" (qtd. in Baker 117). The gap between Hemingway's 1919
and 1921 bouts with depression should hardly surprise us; according
to Jamison, periods of remission are "common in the early years of
manic-depressive illness" (*Unquiet* 56).

   29. "Castration anxiety and the anxiety of object-loss not only exist
in the relation of part to whole, or of contained to container; they
are mutually reflected in Eros, which holds them together" (Green
222).

   30. Like Frederic, Hemingway came down with jaundice during his
stay in Italy, so here, again, we have a symbolic connection between
Hemingway's war experience and a threat to his genitals.

   31. Given the fetishist's phallic position construction of the female
genitalia as either "phallic" or "castrated," we can hardly be surprised

that the cave—the quintessential symbol of the womb—is "*la cueva de los huevos perdidos*."

32. In "Father's and Sons," when Trudy tells Nick that her half-brother will come some night and sleep with Nick's sister Dorothy, Nick threatens not only to kill Eddie if he even speaks to Dorothy, he threatens to "*scalp* him." "I'd scalp him and send it to his mother," he repeats (SS 494). The threat is clearly ironic, since Trudy and Eddie are Native Americans, but its fetishistic dimension should not be ignored—particularly since mothers and sisters figure more prominently than fathers and sons in the etiology of Hemingway's fetishism.

33. This recalls Hamilton's patient, a shoe fetishist with an anxiety about barbershops who would pull on one of his thumbs when anxious. Once in the midst of doing so, he declared: "I don't want to lose it" and felt faint (330). We find a similar association between barbershops and castration in *Torrents of Spring*. Soon after Scripps O'Neil muses that "in France they geld cats and do not geld the horses," he wanders up to a barbershop (39). He decides, however, that somehow a shave and a haircut "wasn't what he wanted" (42).

34. Tellingly, right before George begins his lecture on razor-fighting, he engages in the following dialogue with the train's chef:

> "Run along," said the chef. "Lackawannius is calling you."
> "I love that girl," said George. "*Who touches a hair—*"
> "Run along," said the chef. "Or those yellow boys will get you." (my emphasis, CSS 574)

The forbidden woman, followed by a castration threat from a man associated by alcohol with Jimmy's father, suggests a traditional oedipal drama—an interpretation reinforced by Jimmy's sexual initiation at the hands of a much older woman. In another scene from the abandoned novel, published in Peter Griffin's *Along with Youth*, a blonde secretary repeatedly and lovingly strokes Jimmy's hair, and he responds in kind: "I was very excited and put my hand on her hair." She then directs his hands elsewhere: "Don't touch my hair. . . . Hold me here" (135). It is after this encounter that Jimmy's father warns his son against "thinking and masturbation," though the fourteen year-old boy strangely doesn't know what masturbation is. (Perhaps, as Michael Reynolds suggests, it is his son's ignorance which inspires Mr. Crane elsewhere in the novel to give his son so much dubious advice about how to recognize homosexuals, "a subject about which he seem[s] to worry a good deal" [*American* 154].) Yet the signifier of desire and the signifier of castration is the fetish—hair—and the importance of the fetish implies a more complex oedipal dynamic than this story superficially suggests. According to McDougall, in the construction of the oedipal primal scene, fetishists fantasize that they really can possess the mother (as Jimmy possesses the older blonde woman) and escape the paternal prohibition by regressing to pregenital behavior, displacing the genitals onto a non-genital object. Hence Jimmy's desire to touch the older woman's hair instead of her genitals. The paternal prohibition in this story might follow, then, from the southward migration of Jimmy's hands.

35. Carlos Baker explains that this story and "One Reader Writes" (essentially a woman's distraught letter about her husband's "sifilus," and thus another story with castratory overtones) grew out of Ernest's friendship with Dr. Logan Clendening, a Kansas City physician who wrote a syndicated medical column. Both stories were inspired by letters in the doctor's mailbag. Some might object that Hemingway's historical source for this story rules out any psychoanalytic interpretation of it. Yet Hemingway's need to retell this story even if he gleaned it from his friend's mailbag suggests just the opposite.

36. As Bak explains, fetishism always involves a "simultaneous and alternating identification with the phallic and penisless mother, corresponding to [a] 'split [in] the [fetishist's] ego.' The identification with the penisless mother leads to the wish for giving the penis up, creating a marked intrastructural conflict" ("Fetishism" 286). That is, if a boy in the phallic position (which defines women as either castrated or phallic) identifies strongly with women (as the fetishist does, since for him the fear of separation from the maternal body is equal to the threat of castration) this identification becomes troubling since it threatens his own castration. He can endow women with a substitute phallus (fetishism), and he can then identify himself with the phallic woman (transvestism) to disavow the threat of castration. Yet on some level, the fetishist always "recognizes" the "lack" which he disavows by endowing the woman with a phallus. This "recognition" persists as an identification with the "castrated" woman.

37. In 1922, Hemingway reported that the Greeks had been betrayed by "bungling politicians and by criminally negligent officers, some of whom had worn face powder and rouge. . ." (Mellow 196).

38. This desire is, of course, the desire for a feminine identification. Each of the patients described in Blacker and Wong's paper "Four Cases of Autocastration," for instance, struggled with "strong pathological feminine identifications" (176). Havelock Ellis reproduces the following passage from the monologue of a transvestite ("C.T.," age 25): "In my tendency to femininity, I have often thought seriously of castration. Only the possible danger has several times prevented me from castrating myself. . . . If I knew anyone who would perform the operation I should immediately have recourse to him. This desire, also, seems to grow stronger,

especially of late" (2.2.66). Given this desire for castration, however, my classification of C.T. as a "transvestite" demands some qualification.

The desire for a sex-change operation is *much* more common among *transsexuals* than among *transvestites*. Transvestism (or what Stoller calls "Fetishistic Cross-Dressing") "is almost always found in men who are overtly heterosexual, of masculine demeanor, in occupations dominated by males; and it occurs only intermittently, most of the subject's life being spent in unremarkably masculine behavior and appearance" (*Presentations* 21). In fact, transvestites typically (if paradoxically) use cross-dressing, in part, to feel *more* masculine. Yet C.T. is certainly not what Stoller would call a "male *primary* transsexual": a biological male who has always regarded himself as female and who feels that the anatomy he was born with is simply a horrible mistake. Male primary transsexuals do not consider themselves homosexual (though they are attracted exclusively to "masculine" men), and "they get no erotic pleasure from putting on females' clothes" (*Presentations* 20). C.T. almost does, however, fit into Stoller's "wastebasket category" of "male *secondary* transsexualism": transsexualism that does not date from childhood (from age thirteen in C.T.'s case) and that may be arrived at via a number of paths—in C.T.'s case, via transvestism with a pronounced erotic attraction to female clothing. But at the time of C.T.'s monologue his transvestism, with only occasional transsexual desires, seems to hold dominant sway. For example, his fetishistic desires are still remarkably strong and he records masturbating "every two to three days, if possible with a woman's garment, preferably something of a silky or velvety texture, or a boot or shoe" (2.2.69).

While this desire for castration among transvestites is uncommon, Ellis nevertheless offers another remarkably similar case, that of a 66-year-old widower and "man of science" ("R.M.") whose mother had wished for a daughter instead of a son. Happily married for years, with one son, R.M. openly envied his wife's femininity, occasionally tried on her clothes, and felt his own feminine urges growing throughout the course of his life. In his correspondence with Ellis, he wrote:

> At this period the desire to be a girl was not very intense; but it was still present, accompanied as it generally had been, by the wish to go through the experience of having a baby. Again, my reflections on sexual subjects were not limited to marriage, but to speculations on abnormalities, such as hermaphroditism and castration. The latter never appeared to me as unnatural or revolting, but only as a curious and perhaps interesting experience, and I should have subjected myself to it after the death of my wife, if I could have carried it out without detection. (2.2.94)

39. This formula is really a bit too neat—psychotics, for instance, also experience a splitting of the ego, and insofar as the fetishist denies the ab-

sence of the penis in females, he denies reality much like a psychotic (though he is curiously denying the *absence* of an object of his own *fantasy*). Gillespie clarifies matters a bit by explaining that in psychotic splitting both or all split parts of the ego remain at a primitive level of object-relationship, whereas in a perverse type of splitting part of the ego "retains a good relation to reality, whilst the other part, using the denial mechanism, clings to what is virtually a psychotic delusion" ("Notes" 402). My aim, however, is to make two essential points: first, that all of the perversions are characterized by a split in the ego structured at least in part around the figure of the phallic woman and a denial of sexual difference; second, that in the perversions (as opposed to the neuroses—though perversions can be and frequently are accompanied by neuroses) the mechanism of repression is comparatively absent—hence Freud's dictum, "Neuroses are the negative of the perversions" (*SE* VIII, 165). As Laplanche and Pontalis warn, however, Freud's dictum cannot simply be reversed, as it too often is, to imply that the perversions are mere expressions of a raw unrepressed infantile sexuality. Rather in the perversions the mechanism of repression is largely replaced by different, more primitive, defenses— namely, disavowal and a splitting of the ego. In trying to differentiate between the psychoses, neuroses, and perversions, then, it would perhaps be most accurate to say that a denial of reality *dominates* in the psychoses, a denial of infantile sexual forces *dominates* in the neuroses, and a more evenly divided attitude *dominates* in the perversions. However, it would be misguided to take the notion of a clearly demarcated division too literally or rigidly.

Masud Khan offers another useful method of distinguishing between the neuroses, psychoses, and perversions:

> The distinction between perversions from neuroses on the one hand and psychoses on the other is the specific modality of the object-relation involved. . . . In neuroses the object-relation, both internal and external, is well established. It is the instinctual and intrapsychic conflict in relation to it that constitutes the pathogenic problem. In psychoses the objective reality of the external object is in all essential dimensions negated by the omnipotence of the subjective intrapsychic processes and instinctual needs. In the perversions the object occupies an intermediary position: it is not-self and yet subjective; registered and accepted as separate and yet treated as subjectively created; it is needed as an actual existent not-self being and yet coerced into complying with the exigent subjective need to *invent* it. Spatially it is suspended half-way between external reality and inner psychic reality. (21)

We might remember Khan's distinction when, in chapter 4, we explore the relation between the fetish and the transitional object.

40. According to Kohut, "the ego part of this split-off sector of the psyche of the fetishist is under the influence of the id part with which it is in unbroken contact. . . . The manifest result . . . is therefore, not [usually] an openly held belief that women have penises. Instead, the fetishist experiences conscious desires which are in tune with the conviction of the existence of the female phallus which is held in the deeper (unconscious) layers of the split-off sector of the psyche" (*Analysis* 177). There is, then, an unusually fluid relation between conscious, preconscious, and unconscious fantasy in the fetishist. At each step from the unconscious toward the conscious some censorship occurs, but the censorship between the preconscious and the conscious "differs from censorship proper (that between the unconscious and the preconscious) in that it *distorts* less than it *selects*—its function consists essentially in preventing disturbing thoughts from reaching consciousness" (Laplanche and Pontalis 326).

Preconscious thought is characterized by its close tie to language and the ego. "Freud always put the difference between unconscious and preconscious down to the fact that preconscious ideas are bound to verbal language—to 'word-presentations'" (Laplanche and Pontalis 326). Thus what we might call Hemingway's *verbarium* (to borrow a term from Abraham and Torok)—his personal lexicon of "word-presentations" like "hair," "silk," and "ivory" which recur throughout his work and which evoke elaborate bodies of memory and fantasy—indicates the preconscious residence of many of his fetishistic ideas. This is important, because while the preconscious designates what is *implicit* in mental activity without being the object of conscious thought, it is nonetheless *accessible* to consciousness—particularly if that consciousness belongs to a relentlessly self-probing writer.

If preconscious ideas tend towards "secrecy" and "reticence," we might wonder how or why Hemingway ever wrote *The Garden of Eden*, but it is not clear that Hemingway ever intended to publish this posthumous novel. When Catherine and David discuss "the narrative" that David is writing about their sexual adventures—a work which presumably corresponds roughly to *The Garden of Eden* itself—Catherine asks, "Can you publish it or would it be bad to?" David explains that it's difficult enough simply trying to write it. In the Scribner's version, Catherine then exclaims, "I'm so proud of it already and we won't have any copies for sale and none for reviews and then . . . you'll never be self-conscious and we'll always have it just for us" (77). In the manuscript, however, she does plan a limited edition of five, one for each of the major characters (minus Marita who hasn't yet appeared on the scene). Nevertheless, this sort of secrecy is opposed by a compulsive exhibitionistic drive which moved but unsettled Hemingway. While Catherine and Marita love strolling through Madrid or Nice as "boys" or lovers, wondering if the public can somehow sense their transformation, these forays disturb David deeply. And in the manuscript, Barbara Sheldon explains her engagement in fetishistic practices as follows: "It was private but I made it public. That's the danger. The necessary danger. And I didn't know things took possession of you. That's when you've gone wrong of course" (K422.5 4.14).

41. Apropos of this, Aarons reports the case of a foot and shoe fetishist, also a creative writer, who was continually distracted by fantasies about *one-legged* women.

> The salient features of these fantasies were: (1) an exciting preoccupation with the girl's 'stump' which he would touch and caress; (2) an adventure of rescuing her from some hardship or danger; and (3) that in spite of her handicap she did not act as if she were incapacitated. These fantasies were often indulged to the accompaniment of detailed drawings of female amputees, together with the perusal of pictures of them in books and magazines. Never in his fantasies was there a double amputation, and he would avoid that condition whenever coming upon it in illustrations. (205)

(This perversion, in fact, is not uncommon, and I will return to it briefly in chapter 7.) Aarons further notes that "just prior to the onset of [his patient's] fantasies of one-legged girls in early adolescence, the patient had a repetitive dream in which he was peering expectantly at the genital area of a nude girl, and as he continued his scrutiny, a penis appeared. He then exclaimed in the dream with relief, 'that's the way it should be'" (206).

42. Unlike *The Garden of Eden*'s Catherine Bourne or "The Last Good Country"'s Littless, Renata in *Across the River* never declares any desire to be a "boy"; yet addressing a portrait of Renata that exaggerates her beautiful raven-black hair, Cantwell somehow sees something androgynous in the image: "'Portrait,' he said. '*Boy* or daughter or my one true love or whatever it is; you know what it is, portrait'" (my emphasis, 173). The image of Renata, in fact, seems like a photographic negative of Tadzio, the beautiful boy whose "ivory-white" skin is set off by the "golden darkness of his clustering locks," in Thomas Mann's *Death in Venice* (Mann 26). Given Hemingway's obvious allusion to this novella about an older man's love for an angelic youth in his own tale of an old soldier's love for a nineteen year-old girl and his subsequent death in Venice, we might say that Renata's relation to Tadzio is supplementary; thus, she retains an element of Tadzio's boyishness.

43. When Catherine Bourne cuts her hair in Biarritz, she significantly starts with an "Eton crop." This hairstyle enjoyed a brief vogue

with women in 1926, about a year before the events of *The Garden of Eden* take place. Hemingway's second wife, Pauline, one of the most immediate models for Catherine Bourne, was not only habitually "in vogue," she had once *worked* for *Vogue*. That a character based, however loosely, on her sports the latest fashion should, therefore, hardly surprise us. Yet Hemingway's Catherine Bourne clearly doesn't *follow* fashion; she *invents* it. The coiffeur obviously doesn't know what she has in mind, and she is plainly making it up as she goes. We can only assume, then, that within the novel she is the creator of a major, if short-lived, fashion trend. This re-endows the cut with psychological significance—as, of course, does David's reaction to it. The fact that the coif is a boy's cut named after a boy's school is suggestive enough, but this cut also went by two other significant names—"The *Garçon*," in France, and the "boyish bob" in America. "According to London hairdresser Gilbert Foan, it was worn during its short vogue in England chiefly by fashionable mannequins and their imitators as well as a few mannish women" (qtd. in Corson 613). Catherine, however, *starts* with this cut and then cuts it still shorter—emphasizing both its boyishness and its connection to castration.

44. Freud suggests that this happens when the fetishist identifies strongly with the father, since in Freud's view the child ascribes the mother's "castration" to him. Subsequent study, however, has revealed that this is not exactly the case. "The [primary] 'castrator' in the perverse structure is invariably the mother, not the father" (McDougall 65). Joyce McDougall has demonstrated that the fetishist typically splits the paternal imago into an idealized phallic masculinity (often based upon the maternal grandfather, idolized by the mother) and a symbolically "castrated" father (often based upon a remote or denigrated father who somehow fails to live up to the masculine ideal represented by the maternal grandfather). Hemingway's representations of his own family confirm this in spades. Thus the fetishist wants to identify not with the (Imaginary) father (who has been "castrated" by the mother) but with an idealized masculinity which is accessible only through the mother (the grandfatherly phallus) or in the realm of the Symbolic. The emphasis on castration in the fetish object is derived, then, not so much from an identification with the father-as-castrator as from a combination of forces: (1) the function of the fetish object at the moment of deployment; (2) the strength of the "reality sense" permitted to exist within the structure of the fetishist's disavowal of castration; and (3) the strength of the fetishist's aggression and revenge fantasies—his need to identify with the *mother*-as-castrator and his need to reverse roles and undo trauma by castrating the mother who symbolically castrated him and his father. An identification with the father as the mother's castrator can exist within this framework, but it is not the dominant, much less the sole, factor.

45. We can see this link between *cutting* and *bleaching* in the following conversation between Harry Morgan and his wife in *To Have and Have Not*:

> "Listen, are you letting your hair grow out?"
> "I thought I would. The girls have been after me."
> "The hell with them. You keep it like it is."
> "Do you really want me to?"
> "Yes," he said. "That's the way I like it."
> "You don't think I look too old?"
> "You look better than any of them."
> "I'll fix it up then. I can make it blonder if you like it." (116)

46. When his wife refused to participate in his perverse scenario, this patient would accuse her of trying to "emasculate" him. One night after his wife refused to allow him to cut her hair so close to the scalp, he spent the entire night in the bathroom shaving every bit of hair from his head and body. This, however, rendered him impotent, and he remained so until his hair grew back. This behavior may look extreme, but it would not be difficult to find parallel scenes from Hemingway's fiction—for instance, the progressively shorter haircuts of Catherine Bourne. Romm's patient resembled Hemingway in other ways. He had been kept in a girlish Dutch bob until he was twelve years old, and he had a strong bisexual identification. He had fantasies of fusing the masculine and feminine by possessing simultaneously a penis and female breasts.

Krafft-Ebing cites three cases of "hair-despoilers" in his *Psychopathia Sexualis*. In one case a young man was arrested at the Trocadero, in Paris, after forcibly cutting off a young girl's hair. "He was arrested with the hair in his hand and a pair of scissors in his pocket. He excused himself on the ground of momentary mental confusion and an unfortunate, irresistible passion; he confessed that he had ten times cut off hair, which he took great delight in keeping at home. On searching his home, sixty-five switches and tresses of hair were found, assorted in packets" (242). It seems this young man was in the habit of rubbing the stolen hair over his genitals and the rest of his body while masturbating. But the act of cutting the hair was itself also erotic. "When he touched the hair with the scissors he had erection, and, at the instant of cutting it off, ejaculation" (243).

47. "The fear of death should be regarded as analogous to the fear of castration. . ." (Freud, *SE* XX, 56). According to Carlos Baker, Catherine's little stick is based upon a historical swagger stick that belonged not to Catherine's prototype, Agnes von Kurowsky, but to another Red Cross nurse whom Ernest knew in Italy, Elsie Jessup. Nevertheless, Hemingway's memory of this stick, his transferal of it to his Agnes-substitute, the circumstances in which it is mentioned, and the story

he invents for its origin all imbue it with psychological significance. As I have said before, like all of us, the fetishist finds his symbols most easily in what is readily at hand. In the words of J.-B. Pontalis, "A text, like a dream, has its 'day's residues'" (39).

Chapter Three

1. Likewise, in *The Garden of Eden* manuscript, Marita, with her cropped hair, looks like "a close sheared beaver" (qtd. in Comley and Scholes 100). The *OED* lists "beaver" used for the female pubic hair dating back to 1927, and Joyce used the term in *Finnegans Wake* (1939).

2. In the published version of *At the Hemingways*, Marcelline's friend does the cutting, but Burwell has recently printed a comparatively unsanitized version of this story from an earlier draft of Marcelline's book, and in this version Marcelline does the cutting. In the draft, Marcelline tells the story as an example of the "psychological punishments" employed by her mother (and permitted reluctantly, but silently, by her father), and she exposes Grace as an extraordinarily manipulative mother, hell-bent on having identical twins even though Marcelline, then eight and a half years old, resented it thoroughly.

3. Marcelline claims that her mother made as much as $1000 a month through her voice lessons. Michael Reynolds suspects that Marcelline exaggerates, but he notes that Grace's earnings were "larger than Dr. Hemingway's income which between 1900 and 1920 grew from about $2000 a year to perhaps $5000 a year" (*Young Hemingway* 106).

4. Bak records the case of a fetishist (who also periodically behaved transvestically) with a strong maternal identification who "up to the age of four . . . was dressed like a girl and had long blond, silky hair. From early puberty he had a recurrent fantasy in which he was dancing naked with long hair in front of his father and the lower part of his body was indistinct" ("Fetishism" 294). Bak continues: "In his outward behavior this poor young man used all the accessories to appear like a man. The gait, the holding of the head, big mustache, pipe, rough clothing, way of speech, were superimposed on the fantasy of the long-haired, blond, little boy with indistinct genitals" (296). Needless to say, this sounds a bit like Hemingway.

5. To this, Greenacre adds, "These children hardly solve their oedipal problem at all; and even the subsequent feminine identification which follows seems to have had its origin earlier and been a way of bypassing the full intensity of the oedipal conflict rather than resulting greatly from the oedipal conflict itself" (27).

6. M. Masud R. Khan has called attention to precisely such mothering in the formation of the perversions: "From the intensive analytic treatment of some dozen cases of perversion over the past twenty years a distinct pattern of early mother-child relationship leading to choice of perverse sexual practices . . . has begun to crystallize. . . . The mother lavished intense body-care on the infant-child but in a rather impersonal way. The child was treated by the mother as her 'thing-creation' rather than as an emergent growing person in his or her own right" (12). Glasser concurs: "Frequently we have no objective information to corroborate the patients' depiction of their mothers, but one characteristic features so consistently in the accounts the true perverts give that one is safe to assume their veracity. This is that she has a markedly narcissistic character and relates to her child in narcissistic terms. To varying degrees . . . she is seen both to use her child as a means of gratification of her own needs and to fail to recognize his own emotional needs" ("Aggression" 292). As Jessica Benjamin argues in *The Bonds of Love*, such mothering involves a failure of the *mutual* recognition between mother and child necessary for the child to develop a secure and healthy sense of identity.

7. Here Stoller's ideas blend easily into those of Lacan. As Lacan explains in his fourth seminar, the fetishist's perversion is rooted in the preoedipal triangle of mother, infant, and phallus. Within this triangle, the fetishist establishes an identification that oscillates between his mother and the imaginary phallus that represents the object of her desire. If this is how the *mother* perceives her child (as in the case cited by Stoller), one can easily imagine how the child might arrive at an identical conclusion.

8. Fenichel calls attention to a similarly divided attitude in the parents of a transvestite patient who "was the recipient in his childhood of both phallic and feminine admiration, in that adults called his penis by pet names and also—because of his long hair—extolled him as a 'beautiful girl'" ("Symbolic" 4). The idea of the child as a replacement for the phallus, of course, originated with Freud.

9. Case studies of transvestism, from those recorded by Havelock Ellis in the twenties and thirties to those offered today, almost universally bear this out. Even *DSM-III-R*, a purely diagnostic tool that openly shuns any attempt to account for the etiology of mental disorders, cannot resist appending an etiological note in this case: "According to the folklore of people with this condition, 'petticoat punishment,' the punishment of humiliating a boy by dressing him in the clothes of a girl, is common in the history of those who later develop this disorder" (289). Yet Stoller is careful to note that a single episode of petticoat punishment does not necessarily produce a transvestite. He presumes that "only a boy who is already susceptible—

some special uneasiness of gender development in the first two or three years of life—will need the perversion structure in order to preserve identity" (*Observing* 28). In light of Hemingway's boyhood haircuts, it is also worth noting that in a recent survey of eighty-five cross-dressing males, twenty-one percent of the respondents "reported having had long hair as children—quite unusual for young boys in the 1940s and 1950s when most of the sample were growing up" (Schott 316).

10. In those cases where fetishism grows weaker with time, there is a concomitant growth of gender dysphoria as the transvestite becomes more comfortable with his feminine self. At the extreme end of a spectrum this eventually leads to secondary transsexualism and the desire for a sex change operation. My claims about transvestites and transvestism in this book pertain largely to those transvestites who are still erotically (fetishistically) aroused by wearing female clothes. It should be understood, however, that many of these claims would have to be qualified for those transvestites who are drifting toward secondary transsexualism.

11. On the other hand, this use of the term *transvestism* may dilute it beyond the point of usefulness. According to Fenichel, "The crucial difference in transvestism is that while other perverts identify with the mother and with the phallic woman, the transvestite *wears* her clothing" (Socarides 366). I use the term as I do, however, because I am trying to suggest a fundamental identity between *wearing fetishized female clothing* and *wearing the fetish object to negotiate a phallic-feminine identification* regardless of whether or not the fetish is an item of female clothing. Stoller's term for transvestism, "fetishistic cross-dressing," calls attention to this dynamic, and Stoller has shown that the wearing of a single fetish object by the fetishist often leads to the later wearing of a complete feminine costume.

12. Mahler defines separation and individuation as a two-track process: "One is the track of *individuation*, the evolution of intrapsychic autonomy, perception, memory, cognition, reality testing; the other is the intrapsychic developmental track of *separation* that runs along with differentiation, distancing, boundary formation, and disengagement from [a symbiotic relation with] the mother" (63). Both interrelated tracks eventually help the infant to distinguish between self-representations and object representations. (Mahler believed the infant's early symbiosis with the mother was absolute, but more recent research on infant behavior, surveyed by Milton Klein, suggests that this symbiosis is *relative* instead of absolute.) For the etiological relation between the perversions and a failure of separation-individuation, see the work of Aarons, Bach, Bak, Glasser, Greenacre, Khan, McDougall, Rosen, Socarides, Stoller, and Zavitzianos.

13. According to Mahler and her colleagues, to form a stable and enduring individuality the infant must first attain a sense of itself as a separate and individual entity; second, it must develop a *gender-defined self identity.* If the mother "respects and enjoys the boy's phallicity . . . especially in the second half of the third year," this can be done with comparatively little conflict; however, "in some cases in which the mother has been interfering with the little boy's autonomy, establishment of his early gender identity is threatened and disturbed, particularly if she is unable to relinquish her son's body and the ownership of his penis to him" (215).

14. It will inevitably strike some as odd that a man with such a colossal ego, in the *popular* sense of the term (what psychologists call "grandiosity," a characteristic of both narcissism and hypomania), could be described as having a "fragile ego," but I am using the term "ego" in a restricted sense. My assertion pertains to the ego in its role as what Laplanche and Pontalis call "the 'binding' factor in the psychical processes" (130). The radically divided subjects one encounters in Hemingway's fiction, as well as the subjects who merge together all too easily, can be taken as evidence of a weakness in this binding process.

15. Ernest's unwillingness to identify with his father undoubtedly owes much to the depression that during Ernest's adolescence increasingly distanced Clarence Hemingway from his family.

16. Sheldon Bach has also called attention to this sort of splitting and melancholia in a sadomasochistic patient: "He had a split-off part of his psyche so that he could remain close to his mother in her own omnipotent fantasy world, whereas another part of him was strongly connected to reality. Thus, like the pervert who behaves as if he both affirmed and denied the existence of the maternal phallus, he behaved as if he both affirmed and denied the existence of a loving and idealized mother, and so long as this dissociation persisted, his mourning could never be complete" (14).

17. Such a situation will remind readers of Lacan's *stade du miroir,* and one could say that the experience of being twinned for the first seven years of his life (and in subtle ways after that) was much like being lost in a funhouse of mirrors with no way beyond the mirror stage. Another approach to this theme would be Winnicott's notion of maternal mirroring. According to Winnicott, *the mother is the mirror* (her eyes in particular), and she helps her infant to form a stable ego by reacting to, and thereby "reflecting," *its* impulses and actions. Grace, on the other hand, forced Ernest to function as *her* reflection, as *her* "Dutch dolly"; to an abnormal degree she forced Ernest to play roles that she scripted, thus functioning as a "wrong-way mirror," further inhibiting her son's formation of a stable ego.

18. According to Greenacre, the fetish

> must satisfy the requirements to be stable, to be visible, to be tangible. It must be capable of symbolizing both the penis and its obverse. Further, it often includes the quality of being smelly, so that it can furnish a kind of material incorporation through being breathed in, without loss, i.e., without diminution of its size or change of its form. It must be capable of remaining intact outside the body so that it may at the same time be visually introjected and stabilize the sense of the own body. Gillespie has especially emphasized that the durability of the fetish withstands the fear of the sadistic annihilation impulses and that it generally is inanimate in order to be assuredly nonretaliative. (27)

19. "In Italy my husband sometimes whispered into various ears that he had married an heiress, and behind the curtain in a hairdressing shop I overheard one customer confiding to another that Signor Hemingway had married a childbride who was also an heiress" (Mary Hemingway 220). Just as "heiress" chimes with "hair," Barbara Sheldon's first name chimes with "barber."

Hemingway's unpublished manuscripts also abound with the name Harry. In "Philip Haines Was a Writer. . ." (K648), Philip's wife—an obvious surrogate for Hadley—is named Harriet, and he calls her Harry. And in "At that time of year. . . ," a long Thomas Hudson story at the Princeton Library, Hudson's World War II R.A.F. flying buddy is named Harry Blakely. (In this manuscript, a chapter from Hemingway's never-completed "Land, Sea, and Air Book," Hudson is a romanticized autobiographical portrait of Hemingway in London in 1944 when he flew a few missions as an observer with the R.A.F. Hudson introduces Blakely to two young women—a brunette and a blonde with a short haircut, whose hair had once been even shorter. It turns out that the blonde, with whom Hudson had once been intimate but whom he now considers a "bitch," is named Janet Rolfe—a name which suggests that she may be the same Jan that Hudson remembers in Kennedy Library manuscripts 112 and 113. We will consider these manuscripts in detail in chapter 7.)

20. Perhaps I should have begun this section with a different opening sentence—"There is something a little manic (i.e. 'counter-melancholic') about love at first sight." Yet, aside from the sheer awkwardness of such a sentence, I would like to suggest that there is an element of melancholia in perversion (though not necessarily the reverse)—a cannibalistic introjection of the lost narcissistic object which is identified with and held to be simultaneously present and absent. Freud noted that one sign of melancholia was the inability to love. Passionate love at first sight, then, becomes an obvious sign of a manic defense against melancholia. Even Shakespeare's Romeo is suffering from melancholia, due to the unavailability of the chaste Rosaline, when he first sees Juliet. In this context, I

might note that Joyce McDougall has recently referred to fetishism as "a manic defense against a deep depression" (Denzler 64).

21. This was Josephs's argument in "Hemingway's Poor Spanish," but he has recently expanded it. He notes, as I do below, that "Rabbit" was one of Ernest's nicknames for his third wife, Martha Gellhorn, and he suggests that Hemingway simply borrowed this nickname along with a number of Martha's other characteristics when creating the fictional Maria. He adds that rabbits symbolize the "natural, innocent and pure world of which María, whose name connotes innocence and purity, is a part" (*Undiscovered* 158). He still thinks that Hemingway was ignorant of the slang significance of Maria's nickname. His argument is persuasive, but I think Hemingway *was* aware of the slang significance of *conejo*, and I think the significance of Maria's nickname is a good deal more complex than Josephs suggests.

22. The Spanish word for rabbit warren, *conejera*, is a slang term for a brothel.

23. In "A Contribution on Fetishism," Michael Balint called attention to this ability of the fetish object to simultaneously represent the vagina and the illusory female phallus.

24. "Certainly, there is an increase in sadomasochistic behavior in all perversions and a tendency to show rather pointless anger to relieve anxiety, anger which is obviously displaced and serves a discharge function rather than one of effecting a remedy" (Greenacre 310). If this sounds rather like the often explosive Hemingway of later years, we must also recognize the importance of the irritable moods that often accompany manic or hypomanic episodes.

25. Hemingway's letters to his fourth wife, Mary, attest to this. In a number of letters Ernest urges Mary to dye her hair, but he repeatedly warns her to do nothing that might permanently damage it.

26. "But what about sadism?" some will surely ask. Sadism, however, is a game with very strict rules. Pain is to be inflicted, but only in carefully measured doses—for instance, until welts of a precise color and height are raised on the buttocks. Just as the fetishist takes great care to do no *permanent* damage to the fetish object, the sadist takes great care to do no permanent damage to his love object. When the game gets out of hand, sadism, too, can slip into psychosis.

27. In yet another unfinished manuscript at the Kennedy (K824), Hemingway recalls the shelling in Madrid and describes his quarrels with a woman named "rabbit" who is clearly based on Martha. After Martha returned to Cuba in 1940 after a long trip, Ernest wrote a mock contract obligating her to never again abandon him while he

was writing; this contract was witnessed by "Judge R. R. Rabbitt" and "Judge P. O. Pig" (Lynn 481). "Pig" was Martha's nickname for Ernest, and "Rabbit" was clearly Ernest's nickname for Martha.

Chapter Four

1. Maskin denies hearing any such story and thinks that Hemingway invented it from whole cloth. The story in fact comes from Colonel Lanham's unpublished memoir, but he must have heard it from Ernest, for it relies on information that Lanham could not have invented. Furthermore, there is a letter from Ernest to Mary, dated November 30, 1944, which seems to allude to the event: "Tonight we had very funny time with the Division Psychiatrist. He came in to study us all for his future works. Will tell you much funnier. . . . Willie and me going to write play. Div. Psych in as comic villain" [sic] (qtd. in Fuentes 371). Whether Hemingway actually told the tale to Maskin or not matters little for our purposes; told either to Maskin or Lanham, it is a mock-fantasy with overtones of genuine fantasy.

2. Boise was named after a battleship, but this matters little given the linguistic mechanism of Hemingway's fetishistic associations.

3. Hemingway demonstrates his negative oedipal revision of totemism most clearly in his treatment of the bullfight. In a classical Freudian ("positive" oedipal) reading of totemism, the bull represents the father, and the matador and *cuadrilla* represent the son and "brother horde" who castrate, cannibalize, and replace the father they must ceremonially kill. Yet, as Freud explains in *The Ego and the Id*, "the simple Oedipus complex," the "classical" Oedipus complex in which the child desires sexual union with the opposite-sex parent and regards the same-sex parent as a loved and hated rival, "is by no means its commonest form, but rather represents a *simplification*. . . ." Freud continues:

> Closer study usually discloses the more complete Oedipus complex, which is twofold, positive and negative. . .: that is to say, a boy has not merely an ambivalent attitude toward his father and an affectionate object choice toward his mother, but at the same time he also behaves like a girl and displays an affectionate feminine attitude to his father and a corresponding jealousy and hostility toward his mother. . . . In my opinion it is advisable in general . . . to assume the existence of the complete [bipolar] Oedipus complex. Analytical experience then shows that in a number of cases one or the other constituent disappears, except for barely distinguishable traces; so that the result is a series with the normal positive Oedipus complex at one end and the inverted nega-

tive one at the other, while its intermediate members exhibit the complete form with one or other of its two components preponderating.
(33–34)

This certainly complicates Freud's reading of totemism for those individuals, like Hemingway, with a largely negative or bipolar Oedipus
complex. The primary "castrator" in perverse fantasy is almost invariably the preoedipal and negative oedipal *mother*, not the positive oedipal father. The result, however, is not a simple negative oedipal reversal
of the positive Oedipus complex. Rather, the pervert splits both the maternal and paternal imagoes into "good" and "bad," and the result is a
strongly bipolar and unresolved Oedipus complex that is "altogether
more complicated than in the neuroses" (Greenacre 305). Intense castration anxiety and guilt suggest oedipal dynamics, but these dynamics
are driven by far more primitive and powerful preoedipal anxieties and
fixations. According to Greenacre:

> While the outlines of the more regular problems of the phallic phase
> and the Oedipus complex *appear* to be etched in uncommonly heavily,
> closer examination indicates that this is due to the attenuation of the
> object relationship, with a corresponding increase in the narcissisti-
> cally driven aggressive components. Envy, spite, possessiveness, and
> derogation of one or both parents may play a larger part than is true in
> the healthier object-related jealousy, which permits the boy a freer pos-
> toedipal identification with the father. (305)

In the perversions, "oedipal jealousy and the castration complex become a disorganizing experience rather than the reverse (i.e., the nodal
point for a new and more mature reorganization of the whole personality)" (McDougall 66).

Bullfighting was nothing if not an elastic metaphor for Hemingway.
Though Jake Barnes poses as a "bull," emasculated as he is, he remains
consistently a "steer." (Some will protest that Jake is missing his *penis*,
not his *testicles*; but while this was an important *conscious* distinction for
Hemingway, I think it matters little on the level of the *unconscious*. Furthermore, Hemingway didn't get around to making this distinction clearly
until the 1950s, although admittedly to protest precisely that Jake was
not a "steer" [Plimpton 230].) Robert Cohn, on the other hand, is at one
moment compared to a bull, an animal which fights with "a left and a
right just like a boxer" (*SAR* 139); and at other moments he acts like a
steer, following Brett around and being "gored" repeatedly by insults from
Mike and Jake; at still other moments he is, along with Mike, one of the
"two other matadors" who "did not count" (167). Brett, however is invariably a "bull." After first meeting Lady Ashley, that Circean embodiment of
the phallic woman, Robert Cohn remarks to Jake, "There's a certain quality about her, a certain fineness. . . . I don't know how to describe the
quality. . . . I suppose it's *breeding*" (my emphasis, 38); however, as Mike

asks later, "Who has breeding, anyway, except the bulls?" (141). Hemingway's homophobia equates homosexuals with "steers," and Brett enters the novel amidst a crowd of homosexuals, as a bull is traditionally released into a corral of calming steers. Her witty remark to Jake about being "safe" among these escorts has a double edge: true, she is in no sexual danger, but then neither are her companions. Brett, in fact, represents the most dangerous sort of bull—the animal which has fought repeatedly and knows how it feels to gore a man. Until she meets Pedro Romero, Brett emasculates, or "gores," nearly every heterosexual man she meets. She represents a genuine threat of castration for the young matador as well, but Romero handles her with skill and emerges virtually unscathed. As Jake knows, Brett only wants what she cannot have, and it would seem Pedro knows this as well: "Romero . . . dominated the bull by making him realize that he was unattainable" (168). Instead of being castrated by Brett, Romero forces her to come to terms with her status as a woman, telling her to grow her hair, and in a Freudian sense, forcing her to "recognize" her own "castration." (Gerry Brenner, in *Concealments in Hemingway's Works*, has called attention to the importance of the negative oedipal and offers a similar reading of the bullfight.)

4. Hadley purrs "like a cat" in *A Moveable Feast* and calls herself and Ernest "Rich feathercats with no money" (176). Hemingway, an accomplished inventor of nicknames, gave Hadley more than a half dozen—including "Bones," "Binney," "Hash," "Tiny," "Wicky Poo," and, most tellingly, "Mummy"—but "Feather Cat," "Feather Kitty," and "Katherine Kat" are the nicknames used most frequently in his letters to her. The connection between his "Feather Cat" and cats in general also remained quite strong in Ernest's mind. Thus in a letter to Sylvia Beach, written from Toronto in 1923, he complains that "the humane society kills 7,853 feather cats a year" (*SL* 98).

According to Jeffrey Meyers, Martha, at least on occasion, called Ernest "Pussy"—a feline variation that certainly recalls the double-edged meaning of *conejo* for Hemingway. Was this a pet name that Ernest shared with Martha? Their personal letters are not open to scholars, so for the moment this question must remain unanswered. Ernest and his wives often shared identical nicknames, a habit which while hardly unusual was probably related to Ernest's need to reproduce twin-like relationships with them that reproduced his boyhood relationship with his sister. It may also have allowed him to represent both parts, masculine and feminine, of his divided ego.

5. This feline passage is followed immediately by Catherine's description of her excitement at getting a haircut that starts out to be a boyish (phallic) Eton crop, but which eventually becomes, at her insistence, even shorter. In another scene, just before becoming a "boy" in bed, Catherine, cat-like, pushes her cropped head up against David's

chest and chin (K422.1 9.16); and when Andrew cautions David about taking care of Catherine, whose instability is obvious, David wonders if Andrew wants him to lock Catherine up in a cage with the "other lionesses" (K422.1 7.11.9).

6. Karkov's mistress, in *For Whom the Bell Tolls*, with her "reddish gold hair (sometimes more red; sometimes more gold, depending on the coiffeurs)," also has "cat-eyes" (232). From the description of her hair, one might think that Hemingway is trying to make her sound trashy, but Robert Jordan gives her his seal of approval: "Karkov had good taste in women" (232), and Hemingway paid her hair the ultimate compliment: In 1947 he dyed his own hair as bright red as a newly minted penny.

7. In his *African Journal* (from his 1953–54 safari) Hemingway writes remorsefully about having years before shot "cheetah to get hides for a coat . . . that turned out beautifully." Although his love of cats and fur met in this coat, it was ultimately not a success. "Any coat of that sort was regarded by nearly all women as an evasion of responsibility in that it was neither mink nor sable and was not an investment and without resale value. It was as bad as giving some substitute for jewels. After the good dark wild mink coat of proper length had been given, a man might be permitted some fantasies but not before. . ." (3.4). Hemingway concludes that he now prefers to see cheetah fur on cheetahs. Yet in the full manuscript of the *Journal*, at the Princeton University library, the passage continues. Hemingway reflects that a cheetah or leopard skin would look good on the shoulders of Debba, his African "fiancée," but he realizes that women cannot wear leopard in "our tribe" (the Wakamba) and so decides to start her out on a coat made of "spring *hare*" or "cerval cat." Thus Hemingway links cats, hair (hare), and fur to his fetishization of race.

8. Ernest claims here that he seldom drank beer at breakfast, but the manuscript he wrote about his 1953–54 safari suggests that he did so on a daily basis in Africa. In fact, he was often on his *third* drink by breakfast, he occasionally drank *gin* with breakfast, and he often took a flask to bed with him at night. According to Denis Zaphiro, Ernest's friend and a ranger with the Kenyan Game Department (Zaphiro's dog, Kibo, appears as David Bourne's dog in *The Garden of Eden*), Hemingway was almost always drunk, though he seldom showed it. With drink he just became "merrier, more lovable, more bullshitty." Without drink he was morose, silent, and depressed (Brian 303). Ernest's behavior on this safari was erratic long before his twin plane crashes in January. I suspect that his perpetual drunkenness facilitated his blurring of the boundaries between fantasy and reality.

9. One might suppose that Ernest's dream was nothing if not original, yet a creative writer and foot fetishist analyzed by Aarons ex-

perienced a somewhat similar dream: "The patient dreamed that he was
walking in a wooded area, then found himself in a cage with a lioness.
In the midst of a feeling of paralysis, he kept in mind that if he revealed
his fear, he would be done for. . . . Upon retelling the dream, he said he
had forgotten that the lion's face turned into that of his mother" (208).
Taylor describes yet another patient, a transvestite, fetishist, and 63-
year-old professional writer, who "consciously associated cats and furs
with his mother" (516). In a bizarre and compulsive ritual, this patient
would masturbate in front of the mirror while wearing his wife's furs
and homemade fur-covered animal masks. Hemingway's dream seems
healthy next to this, but it also implies an overtly erotic component
lacking in the dream of Aarons's patient, and we will soon see that the
face of Hemingway's lioness indeed turns into the face of his mother.

10. Nick Sheldon's "mane" and the bullfighter's *coleta* also function
as *homeovestic* objects—latently homoerotic tools to incorporate the *paternal* phallus. I will explore this subject at length in chapter 6.

11. When Grateau retired and moved to a country house in the
early twenties, the coiffeurs of Paris threw a two-day party in his honor,
which culminated in the unveiling of a statue dedicated to the inventor
of the marcel wave. This party was large enough to make the newspapers in the United States.

12. The shoe fetishist of Hamilton's study often used the term
"pussy" for the female genitalia, and as a child "he had wished repeatedly he were a cat" (331).

13. Sylvia Beach described Hadley at this time as "an attractive
boyishlooking girl" (qtd. in Fitch 116).

14. Hemingway tells a better-known version of this same tale in *A
Moveable Feast*. James Mellow, however, suggests that both of these accounts are decidedly fictional. According to Mellow, Hemingway did not
return to Paris himself to verify the loss of his manuscripts until some
six weeks after being told of their loss. Instead, he asked Lincoln Stef-
fens and Guy Hickock, who were returning to Paris, to inquire about
his luggage at the Gare de Lyon. Moreover, as Paul Smith notes, Hemingway's list of what the valise actually contained tended to grow ever
longer well into the 1950s ("1924" 41).

15. Interestingly, after this complaint in his letter to Mizener, Hemingway proceeds to tell a number of outrageous lies about having killed
in war "122 sures beside the possibles" (697). He seems to be both bol-
stering his masculinity through military posturing and acknowledging
that on some level his denial of his love for his mother is a flagrant lie.

16. In New York on his way to the First World War, Ernest wrote
home telling his parents a tall tale about being engaged to the film star

Mae Marsh, to which Grace responded, "It was only yesterday that you were Mother's little yellow-headed laddie, and used to hug me and call me Silkey Sockey" (qtd. in Comley and Scholes 26). The fact that the word "silky," in Hemingway's work, so often signifies the sensation of female hair against a man's face may further allude to Ernest's childhood cuddling games with his mother.

17. Winnicott is careful to note that the object's symbolic value is not initially its most important quality:

> It is true that the piece of blanket (or whatever it is) is symbolical of some part-object, such as the breast. Nevertheless, the point of it is not its symbolic value so much as its actuality. Its not being the breast (or the mother), although real, is as important as the fact that it stands for the breast (or mother).
> When symbolism [proper] is employed the infant is already clearly distinguishing between fantasy and fact, between inner objects and external objects, between primary creativity and perception. But the term transitional object . . . gives room for the process of *becoming able to accept difference and similarity.* (my emphasis, *Playing* 6)

Nevertheless, Winnicott argues that we find the *root* of all later symbolism in the child's relation to his or her transitional object; he also states that the transitional object generally eventually takes on the status of a symbol as the infant begins to distinguish between fantasy and fact.

18. "The transitional object may eventually develop into a fetish object and so persist as a characteristic of the adult sexual life" (Winnicott, *Playing* 9). While the transitional object "is the first *not-me* possession, it must also carry qualities that serve as a link to the *mother-me* state. There is a certain resemblance to this Janus-facedness in the fetish, but in a different setting. The fetish is conspicuously a bisexual symbol and also serves as a bridge which would both deny and affirm the sexual differences" (Greenacre 321).

Lacan, likewise, considered the transitional object "a key-point for the explanation of the genesis of fetishism" ("Direction" 251). Unfortunately, Lacan's most sustained explication of the relation between his theory of the phallus and Winnicott's theory of the transitional object is to be found in his as yet untranslated fourth seminar, *La relation d'objet*. In this same seminar, Lacan acknowledges the work on fetishism by Payne, Greenacre, and Gillespie.

19. "While the fetish function is limited to concern about the genitals, it too has a relation to the mother and sometimes there are indications of memories of her breast. But these seem to have been derived mostly from an early period of confusion between breast and penis" (Greenacre 333). This lends significant support to Brunswick's claim

that the infant's first sexual object is the breast, the penis being projected back onto the breast to create the imago of the phallic mother only as the little boy enters the phallic phase.

20. This passage in which Richard Gordon looks at the wife he has just lost deserves a closer look, for it demonstrates particularly clearly how the fetishized hair, breasts, and sweater substitute for the disavowed female genitalia: "'Good-by,' she said, and he saw her face he always loved so much, that crying never spoiled, and her *curly black hair, her small firm breasts under the sweater* forward against the edge of the table, and *he didn't see the rest of her that he'd loved so much and thought he had pleased, but evidently hadn't been any good to, that was all below the table. . .*" (my emphasis 192). The female genitalia are occluded from vision and replaced by the fetish.

For yet another example of Hemingway pairing fetishized hair with the movement of breasts beneath a sweater, we might look at *A Moveable Feast*. A drunken Jules Pascin strolls into the Dôme with two models, a blonde and a brunette. He sits down with Ernest and asks him if he would like to "bang" the brunette. "The dark girl was restless and she sat on display turning her profile and letting the light strike the concave places on her face and showing me her breasts under the hold of the black sweater. Her hair was cropped short and was sleek and dark as an oriental's." Pascin notices: "You've posed all day," Pascin said to her. "Do you have to model that sweater now at the café?" (103).

21. In his *African Journal* Hemingway writes (with a nod to T. S. Eliot's "Whispers of Immortality"): "Because I was awake now . . . I thought about another girl that I knew and, at that time, loved very much. She was a rangy-built American girl with the usual pneumatic bliss that is so admired by those who do not know a *small, hard, well-formed breast is better*" (my emphasis, 3.16).

22. Krebs's war record reveals that he was on the French front, not the Italian front of the Nick Adams stories. Krebs's father is in the real estate business, whereas Nick's father is a doctor. Yet aside from such trivial differences, the two protagonists share remarkably similar families and personalities.

23. Even in the 1950s, Ernest still had a "favorite light cashmere blanket" (Mary Hemingway 270).

Chapter Five

1. Lillian Ross called this Ernest's "joke Indian language," and she captured it wonderfully in her famous *New Yorker* profile (14).

Ernest's friend, William Walton, remembers that during his low periods Ernest would "talk in fake childish, or primitive terms, almost down to his accent," and Hotchner notes that Hemingway occasionally liked to "sound like an Ojibway Indian," because he claimed to *be* part Ojibway (qtd. in Brian 205). Given the argument I will make in this chapter, such cross-racial identification is significant.

2. Hemingway also told Hotchner that he had slept with Mata Hari, though Hotchner managed to recognize this as a tall tale (Mata Hari having been shot by the French in 1917, a year before Ernest first arrived in Europe). While I don't believe Ernest's story about Josephine Baker, I recognize that Baker and Hemingway were friends. Sorting out the exact nature of Hemingway's relationship with Baker, however, is difficult if not impossible, since Baker was even more prone to self-mythologization than was Hemingway. According to Phyllis Rose, Baker "tried on different pasts as though they were dresses, to see which suited her" (114).

3. Michael Reynolds suspects that, "after ten days of fever, night sweats and bug bites Hemingway was probably in no shape for sexual adventure" (*Paris Years* 77). James Mellow, however, is less inclined to dismiss Hemingway's story. He points out that Hemingway convinced his good friend Bill Smith "that during the early years of marriage he had been unfaithful to Hadley only once and that had been in Constantinople" (197). If the story was a fiction—a fiction that Hemingway told more than once—it nevertheless seems to occupy a position in his *psychological* autobiography.

4. Hemingway's fondness for the Shakespearean expression "sea change" was apparently linked to the sea's ability to naturally bleach hair. Hemingway calls attention to this in *To Have and Have Not, Islands in the Stream*, and *The Garden of Eden*. This bleaching, for Hemingway, signified a sexual metamorphosis.

5. As a demonstration of how, in editing the manuscripts, Tom Jenks muted Hemingway's concern with race, we might note how this line appears in the published version of the novel: "I'm your lazy naked wife" (43).

6. Hemingway told Hotchner that while in Aigues-Mortes he and *Hadley* had "stained themselves with walnut juice so they could crash a gypsy dance" (Hotchner 123).

7. In his African story, David writes, "The tusks of the elephant weighed two hundred pounds apiece. Ever since these tusks had grown beyond their normal size the elephant had been hunted for them. . ." (*GE* 173). A few pages later, after putting aside his story for the day, he looks at Catherine's "dark face and [at] the incredibly flat *ivory* color of

her hair" (my emphasis, 178). In the manuscript, Catherine's link to the elephant is even more obvious. At one point David realizes that he has tried to bring the elephant back to life in his story; he wonders, then, if perhaps he can make Catherine "whole" and "happy" again too. Yet he immediately and tragically realizes that this is impossible.

8. The loss of Eden is epistemophilic and narcissistic insofar as it evokes the child's first recognition of sexual difference. (The narcissist longs for a world anterior to such recognition, but such a world, like Eden, is always-already-lost.) The loss of Eden is oedipal insofar as it is the consequence of a transgression against God the Father.

9. We might notice a similar instance of repression when Catherine covers her hair with a scarf to gain the acceptance of the village priest. In doing so, she displaces its fetishistic value (which Hemingway clearly associated with *sin*, *remorse*, and *corruption*) onto a subtly disguised substitute—her furry "long-sleeved cashmere sweater." I would further argue that this displacement, insofar as it implies a denial or concealment of the (phallic) fetish, allows Catherine to sit among the women while David takes his place at the back of the church with the men (*GE* 6).

10. In her memoir, Marcelline recalls, "We had weird and wonderful nicknames in our family. Some evolved naturally, but most of them, the ones that stuck the longest were Ernest's creations. . . . Ernie called me "the Great Iverian" from a character in a Latin play in high school. Naturally this was soon shortened to Ivory. . ." (Sanford 127). Hemingway's habitual use of "ivory" to describe *skin* (though he also uses it to describe Catherine Bourne's *hair*) makes it the counterbalance in his field of fetishistic fantasy to the fetishization of deeply tanned skin. In fact, just as Catherine Bourne's ivory hair stands out against her dark skin, so Lil's olive skin creates a color contrast with her "lovely black hair" (*IITS* 273). It could be, in fact, that *hair* and *skin* (i.e., the body with and without hair) served as counterbalances for each other within Hemingway's field of fetishistic fantasy—an extreme variation of his fascination with *short* and *long* hair.

At another point in *The Garden of Eden*, Hemingway describes Catherine as "the same wonderful *dark* and beautiful girl as ever [with] the *ivory* white hair . . . like a *scar* across her forehead" (my emphasis, *GE* 156). Here, again, we find the color contrast, dark/ivory; moreover, the "scar" clearly alludes to the castrated aspect of the fetish. In another scene excised from the published version of the novel, David admires Catherine's "ivory" hair against her dark face and the dull white of the bed sheets (K422.1 19.1), and in still another passage Catherine enters a room "wearing a white linen dress. . . . Her hair across her dark forehead and her cheeks was a different *ivory* color than her dress" (K422.1 23.25).

11. *Méconnaissance* is Lacan's term for the misrecognition by which the ego constitutes itself during the mirror phase.

12. In describing the relation between separation-individuation and narcissism, Rothstein argues "that secondary narcissistic investment is motivated by feelings of separation anxiety implicit in the perception of a separate self. The perception of separateness stimulates separation anxiety and the experience of object loss. This anxiety stimulates an incorporative identification with the maternal object" (310). This illuminates Hemingway's taste for rabbit and lion.

13. In *Playing in the Dark*, Toni Morrison clearly states that Hemingway "fetishizes" race. It isn't clear from her text, however, if she means to use the term loosely (meaning merely that Hemingway "eroticizes" race) or if she means it in the strict psychoanalytic sense that I intend.

14. Ernest's sister Marcelline described her parents in exactly these terms: "Mother, having fair skin, never tanned; she only freckled and blistered. My dark-haired, bearded young father loved the sun and tanned to mahogany" (Sanford 74). The figure of the tanned woman can, thus, be seen not only as a "phallic woman" but also as what Melanie Klein would call a "combined parent figure."

15. Greenacre has noted the importance of exactly this sort of color-symbolism in the choice of a fetish object: "The color black may play an important part in the attractiveness of many fetishistic objects: black shoes, black underwear and stockings often being more stimulating than white or pastel shades. The contrast may enhance the visible dependability. . . . [Presuming that the fetishist is white], it may also add to the definite visible outline of the fetishistic object, causing it to stand out conspicuously against the background of the adjacent skin" (321).

16. "At the starting point in fetishism, the difference of the sexes ceases to be 'neglected.' It is admitted, but *only* perceived, and localized as an anatomical difference: it is recognized, but as a law of nature in which the subject refuses to recognize *himself*. At this point there is a clash between knowledge and belief, as expressed by Octave Mannoni's formula *Je sais bien, mais quand même. . .* [I know, but still. . .]. . . ." (Pontalis 74).

17. The following passage, from a case report of transvestism recorded by Havelock Ellis ("C.T.," age 25), bears an uncanny resemblance to the night-games of Catherine and David Bourne: "My wife tells me sometimes, and I think truly, that she often wishes she were a man, and could take a man's part in our love-life: not always, but as an alternative. And sometimes she lies upon my body and makes me almost forget my sex—an experience which gives me greater pleasure

than I can ever get from my virility. . . . One night I got my wife to dress in a suit of mine. The result was that I was almost mad with desire to be a girl and to love her as a boy" (2.2.66–7).

18. In the African Book at the Princeton Library, Hemingway records a scolding from Mary. When he was just playing at being Wakamba, Mary enjoyed it and could laugh at him, but she was disturbed that Ernest kept confusing his play with reality. Ernest tried to explain his erratic behavior, but all he could say was that all of his games during these weeks were somehow all intricately related. Exactly what this interrelation was, however, he couldn't say. He worked it all up into something that he called his "religion," one of the prime tenets of which was the fantasy that he and Mary were not white. In his fantasies, he reinterpreted the delicate scars on Mary's face, the legacy of a car crash, as tribal scars. This should remind us of David Bourne's similar fantasy in front of the mirror, and by linking David to Ernest's *wife*, it reveals the cross-gender identification that accompanies the wearing of the fetish.

19. Describing Masai and Kikuyu women in *Out of Africa*, Isak Dinesen writes: "Native women shave their heads, and it is a curious thing how quickly you come to feel that these little round neat skulls, which look like some kind of dusky nuts, are the sign of true womanliness, and that a crop of hair on the head of a woman is as unladylike as a beard" (144).

How can a *hair* fetish be symbolized by a *shaved* head? If hair functions as a fetish—an object which is simultaneously a substitute phallus and a memorial to castration—wouldn't a shaved head baldly represent unredeemed castration? Confronted with a similar problem (interpreting baldness within a context in which hair is phallicized), Parveen Adams notes that "the ratio between hair and baldness is complex. Shaving may stand in for the act of castration, but baldness need not" (186). Baldness, Adams asserts, may be even *more* phallic than the fetishized hair. In the instance of Hemingway, it might be fairer to say that the bald head represents an exaggerated form of the fetish—more castrated *and* more phallic—and this exaggeration helps Hemingway to identify with the phallic woman with a minimum of anxiety.

20. Mary describes this time at Torcello in the winter of 1948 as follows: "We had joyous late mornings in bed. . . . Small loving jokes, speculations on girl and boy love, with which Ernest was brimming in those days. The Kinsey people would not have believed us, I noted. Ernest taught me many new delights and I taught him some" (237).

21. My emphasis. Mary Hemingway's diaries, John F. Kennedy Library (206). This passage appears in Mary's memoir, *How It Was*, a little altered (370), so I have printed the version from her journal. Interest-

ingly, Hemingway's own account of his 1953 safari ends abruptly the day before Mary returns from Nairobi with her Christmas haircut.

In a previously unpublished letter (July 15, 1954), Ernest urges Mary to "get a good *boy safari hair-cut* the way you had in Nairobi and on the boat and *to please me* in Madrid" (my emphasis). He continues:

> I love it that way and you never look prettier and when we get really brown on the boat it will look so wonderful really platinum. . . . It certainly moves your kitten. . . . Mr. S. ["Mr. Scrooby" was Ernest's pet name for his penis] cannot wait until we are together again in the biggest and widest and loveliest of all beds. Mr. S. is at present arms as I write and I cannot wait to see my kitten. (©1998, Ernest Hemingway Foundation)

The fact that Mary had this "safari haircut" in *Madrid* may explain Madrid's mythic psychosexual status in *The Garden of Eden*. It is not so much a physical place as it is a psychological state; "going to Madrid," like "going to Africa," functions as a code phrase for undertaking some sort of transvestic transformation. Catherine's hair is at its shortest in Madrid, and her sexual games there bleed over into the day and leave her husband suffering from acute "remorse." Midway through the manuscript, Marita plans to replace David's boyhood African "fiancée" by getting an extremely short "African haircut," but her plans are forestalled by Catherine's decision (later revoked) that they should all return to Madrid. Marita reluctantly decides that in Spain one extremely short-haired blonde ("freak" is the term she uses) is enough.

22. I use the phrase "polymorphously perverse" here *metaphorically*. What I mean is that Hemingway's perversion contained elements of many perversions; it was *not*, however, truly polymorphously perverse. Infantile polymorphous perversity is *not* characterized by rigidity and compulsion; Hemingway's adult perversity *was* rigid and compulsive.

23. As for "tribal marks" and the "earring crisis," Fenichel notes a "particular preference for shoes or earrings" in the fetishistic trappings of transvestites ("Transvestitism" 167), and Havelock Ellis (1936) cites a case of transvestism (C.T.) that parallels remarkably Hemingway's desire for pierced ears and tribal marks: "Perhaps it is well to say a little more about two special peculiarities: my desire to be tattooed and to wear earrings." C.T. eventually tattooed most of his body, including his penis, after which he spontaneously experienced "the phenomena of erection and ejaculation accompanied by a feeling of physical exaltation so great that it almost prostrated [him]. . . ." (C.T. makes it very clear, his tattooing was a matter of *compulsion*, not taste; he even had to have tattoos removed from his face.) C.T. goes on to discuss at great length his interest in pierced ears, his compulsion to pierce his own ears, his forays to find prostitutes with pierced ears and tattoos, and his need to

convince his wife to pierce her ears. Five years after his initial interview with Havelock Ellis, C.T. mentioned in a note, "My desire for female clothing, jewelry, etc., is undiminished. I still wear earrings at times when alone, and very frequently sleep with them" (2.2.67–70).

24. In the African Book, Ernest wants to pierce his ears and Debba's at the same time, and he takes great pleasure in rubbing Debba's head.

25. Greenacre, in fact, has described the fetish object as "a materialized screen memory" (168).

Chapter Six

1. This sentence in brackets appears at this point in *The Garden of Eden* manuscript—not on the next page as it does in the Scribner's version (K422.1 15.13).

2. For the preoedipal origins of ego-splitting, see the work of Aarons, Bak, Greenacre, Khan, Kaplan, Socarides, Stoller, and Zavitzianos—a veritable consensus of experts in the field. This approach to ego-splitting does not imply the absolute unity and self-sufficiency of the "normal" ego. Entirely consistent with Lacan's notion that the ego is always an *effect* built up from narcissistic identifications and "structured exactly like a symptom" (*Seminar I* 16), this conceptualization of ego-splitting would only add that the formation of a *relatively* stable ego and sense of gender identity in boys (reciprocally reinforcing developments) also presupposes an eventual *dis*identification from the mother (or sister) and an identification with the father (or a male figure). (Lacan, in fact, seems to suggest something similar in his fourth seminar, *La relation d'objet*.) This process of *dis*identification from the maternal and identification with the paternal (described so clearly by Ralph Greenson) was seriously interfered with in Hemingway's youth.

3. *1926–1933 sources for the David/Catherine/Marita thread*: In 1926 Hemingway returned from writing in Madrid to summer next to the Fitzgeralds on the Riviera. Catherine's tan, blonde hair, "craziness," interest in women, and jealousy of David's work all clearly invoke aspects of Zelda. The love triangle in *The Garden of Eden* seems almost a gender-inverted version of Zelda's famous affair with the French naval aviator, but Ernest was also involved in his own love triangle:

> The Hemingways, with Pauline, rented two rooms at the Hôtel de la Pinède in Juan-les-Pins. It was near the beach and had a small garden where the *ménage à trois* took most of their meals. Each morning they spent on the beach, swimming and taking in the sun. . . . At the Hotel

> there were three of everything: breakfast trays, bicycles, bathing suits
> drying on the line—and worst of all two women in love with the same
> man. (Baker 171)

At Ernest's urging, Pauline and Hadley were both obsessed with tan-
ning and involved with tonsorial experiments. (Pauline also shared
Catherine Bourne's lesbian desires.) In 1927, after his divorce from
Hadley (a partial source for the profound sense of loss in *The Garden of
Eden*), Ernest and Pauline spent their honeymoon at the Grau du Roi
and then Madrid. In 1933 Hemingway and Pauline traveled to Africa.

   1947–1954 sources for the David/Catherine/Marita thread:
Throughout 1947–1954, Ernest spent a good deal of time urging Mary
to get deep tans and dye her closely-cropped hair various colors, one of
his favorites being a "smoky silver" or "ash blonde." And as we shall
soon see, Ernest dyed his own hair as well and involved himself in
transformations whereby Mary became "Pete" and he became (at night)
"Catherine," a transvestic alter-ego. Burwell speculates that Ernest
may have engaged in a *ménage à trois* with Mary and his second wife,
Pauline, in the summer of 1947, and in 1950 Ernest returned to Le
Grau du Roi with Mary. At this time Ernest, who was fond of saying "I
corrupt easily" (Baker 481), was also in love with the young Italian
noble-woman Adriana Ivancich. He claimed that it was "no sin to love
both Mary and Adriana" (Baker 484), but *The Garden of Eden* suggests
otherwise. In 1953, Ernest traveled first to Madrid and then to Africa,
where he was involved in all sorts of transvestic transformations and
tonsorial experiments. Again there was a sort of fantasy *ménage à trois*
with Debba replacing Adriana as the third party. Of course, the original
ménage à trois which serves as the template for all of these later relationships was Ernest's infantile love triangle with his sister and mother.

   4. Describing his 1951 visit to the Finca Vigía, A. E. Hotchner
noted that Ernest was suffering from "black-ass" at night, but he was
"always" cheerful in the morning (71).

   5. Soon after his break from Hadley (at the end of August 1926),
in a letter to Fitzgerald, Ernest complained that he had been "in hell"
since Christmas "with plenty of insomnia to light the way around" (*SL*
217). That same day, in a note to Sherwood Anderson, Hemingway
complained: "I've been living this side of bughouse with the old insomnia for about eight months now" (*SL* 218).

   6. In his article "The Phallic Woman: The Ubiquitous Fantasy in
Perversions," Bak offers the following explanation for the transvestite's
need to "pass" in public.

> [The] irrepressible urge of transvestites to pass in public as a woman is
> a fulfillment, a proof in the outside world, in *reality*, of the existence of

the female phallus. On the one hand, it is an attempt to rid the ego of the anxiety engendered by the "uncertainty"; on the other, the main thrill of the experience that must be repeated again and again lies in the achievement of unity and fusion with the phallic mother and sister. (26)

True, Catherine is not a transvestite male, but in her capacity as the split-off feminine half of Hemingway's ego, she seems to function much *like* a transvestite male.

7. The "remorse" that David suffers from after switching sexes with Catherine is not uncommon in transvestism. Take, for instance, the following passage from the monologue of a transvestite ("D.S."): "By the time I was 10 or 12 years old I had stolen a fair hoard of my sister's underwear, and borrowed her corsets on any available occasion. These I used to don and invariably had sexual sensations. I had a slight feeling of disgust and *remorse* afterwards, but nevertheless the fascination grew stronger" (my emphasis, Ellis 2.2.54). D.S. continues: "I was alarmed at my powerlessness to resist the fascination of ladies' wear and made a most determined and constant fight against it. I now admire the spirit I showed then, but I think it was unwise. Yet every time I gave way to self-abuse my determination increased; I was constantly losing yet always fighting, with brief reactionary fits of despair after each 'downfall'" (2.2.55). I think this, blended with a sense of "sin," is exactly what we see in David Bourne's "remorse."

8. If, as Hemingway claimed, it had been twenty-two days since he had last dyed Mary's hair, then he had last dyed it on April 14— three days after first noticing Patrick's unusual behavior—and right before Mary left for Chicago. On April 16, Ernest wrote to Mary that Patrick had been extremely violent and that Pauline had insisted on coming over from Key West to help take care of him. Thus, Rose Marie Burwell's theory that *The Garden of Eden* grew out of a *ménage à trois* between Ernest, Pauline, and Mary later in the spring and summer of 1947 cannot be correct. Ernest may well have projected his Edenic fantasies onto his relationship with Mary and Pauline, but these fantasies clearly predated Pauline's arrival at the Finca. Ernest had been involved in bleaching Mary's hair before Pauline arrived, and his references to Mary as "Pete" and to himself as "Catherine" in his letters from early May obviously rely on Edenic games with hair and gender-swapping that predate Pauline's arrival. If Pauline later became involved in Ernest's nocturnal sports with Mary—and this seems likely enough (see Burwell 210)—she was a late arrival, rather like *Eden's* Marita.

9. Note the attention to *Mary's* desire. Ernest waxed ecstatic in the letter because the morning *after* he dyed his hair he received a letter from Mary (not extant) which apparently asked him to do exactly

that. He was amazed by his foresight. No doubt, Mary played along with Ernest's games, and she remembered this incident fondly enough to preserve a momento of it—a full lock of bright red hair in a envolope dated August 1947 and labeled in Mary's distinctive handwriting "Papa's Hair." (Stephen Plotkin, curator of the Hemingway Collection at the John F. Kennedy Library, discovered this lock of hair while cataloging Mary Hemingway's papers in February 1998.) Nevertheless, Mary's existing letters suggest a good deal of detachment from her husband's fantasies, and we shouldn't be fooled about the source of fetishistic desire. *The pervert always projects his own desire onto the partner with whom he identifies.* McDougall's patient, Professor K, a fetishist, transvestite, and sadist, offers an excellent example:

> His insistence on the fact that the girl victim *ardently desired the beating* (this being a constant theme whether attached to K's masturbation fantasy or enacted with his girlfriends) reveals the importance attached to the partner's orgasm as a way of validating both his fantasy and the means by which satisfaction was achieved. The partner was thus required to prove that K had indeed stumbled upon the real secret of sexual intercourse. . . . K was overwhelmed to discover that he projected upon his girlfriends his *own* excitement at the idea of being whipped in order to identify with their supposed ecstasy. This reconstruction enabled K to say to me, for the first time, that he would sometimes flagellate himself before the mirror, watching excitedly for the whip marks, just as he did when he could play the scene out with a girlfriend. (29)

Ernest's need to project his desires onto his partners partially explains why fetishistic and transvestic plans in his fiction are most often hatched by his female characters.

10. My argument in this section implies that worry, sleep deprivation, depression, separation anxiety, and castration anxiety, all played a significant role in the genesis and fetishistic urgency of Ernest's behavior in May 1947; yet it is also clear from this particular letter that Ernest's transvestic games with Mary *predated* the unusually stressful circumstances of May 1947. Importantly, Hemingway knew *from experience* that hair like his own had to go through red before it could become blonde. In June 1933 Hemingway wrote to Pauline asking her how to get his own bleached hair from red to blonde. Pauline replied: "About your hair, don't know how to turn red to gold. What about strong peroxide—or better what's the matter with *red* hair. Red hair lovely on you and you lovely yourself, and it will be so nice to have you again. I was thinking at lunch sick of not having you here" (qtd. in Burwell 196). As Pauline's note implies, separation anxiety may have played as large a role in this round of hair-coloring as it did in 1947. Furthermore, other events not so unlike those of 1947 may have contributed to the flagrancy of Ernest's fetishistic/

transvestic outburst. On May 27, 1933, Jane Mason, with whom Ernest may have been having an affair, suffered back injuries when a car she was driving with Ernest's two eldest sons rolled down an embankment. (Patrick and Bumby were uninjured.) A few days later, in an apparent (and unsuccessful) suicide attempt, she jumped out of a second story window, breaking her back in the process. Thus, in June 1933, as in May 1947, Hemingway may have been under considerable stress.

Yet even in less stressful times, Hemingway wrote letters to Mary that bear a remarkable resemblance to the letters cited here. For instance, in a previously unpublished 1952 letter to Mary, Ernest writes: "Last night I had a dream you came back true copper pan coloured red-headed. That was fairly exhausting and then I went back to sleep again . . . and dreamed you came back silver-blonder than Ceezy" (October 2, 1952, ©1998, Ernest Hemingway Foundation). And in still another previously unpublished letter (July 29, 1955), Ernest writes:

> Last night I dreamed you were red headed color of French copper pans. You were very beautiful and a *devil* in the dream. I like to remember when you were such a devil in Africa, like when you first got to Tanganyika and always in Kimana and *your wonderful African haircuts* and making love in the tents in the daytime and at night and listen to the beasts. . . . I know, if I didn't know it for such a long time, again what a true and necessary INSPIRATION (there's that word) you are to me *beside being small brother and partners and bed devils.* . . . [sic] (my emphasis, ©1998, Ernest Hemingway Foundation)

Similar fetishistically-invested letters from Ernest to Mary date from August 1948, September and October 1949, October 1952, and July 1954.

11. The twin personalities of the transvestite should not be confused with those found in a multiple personality disorder. The transvestite is aware of both personalities and manages to integrate them more or less successfully within the self. Nevertheless, the dual personalities of the transvestite cannot be reduced to a simple matter of masquerade. In a study of 504 cases of transvestism, Prince and Bentler noted that "78% of the sample reported that they felt like a different personality when cross-dressed" (Langevin 216). Gosselin and Eysenck, moreover, have found that transvestites score quite differently on personality questionnaires depending on whether they are in their male or female roles.

12. A scene from *Across the River* calls attention to the sapphic signifying power of the fetish object. Drinking with Renata at Harry's Bar, Cantwell notices a woman at a table with three other women. The one who catches his eye has a "pleasant face" and "hair three times as white as hair can be." On this evidence alone, he asks Renata, "Are they les-

bians?" Renata doesn't know; she knows only that they are nice people. But Cantwell somehow understands something that Renata doesn't: "I should say they are lesbians" (86).

13. The childhood of Winnicott's patient bears a notable resemblance to Hemingway's own experience of childhood: "We have very good evidence from inside the analysis that in her early management of him the mother held him and dealt with him in all sorts of physical ways as if she failed to see him as a male" (*Playing* 74). Khan has also written about split-off other-sex halves, and we can see something of this phenomenon in a passage from the monologue of a transvestite ("R.L.," age 48), recorded by Havelock Ellis. Noting the tension during his marriage between his masculine and feminine identities, he explains, "I did . . . have a sort of wish that it would be nice to divide myself in two and have both individualities" (2.2.73).

14. Gillespie has made much the same point. After explaining that the perverse individual attempts to escape an intense castration complex by partially abandoning genital sexuality, regressing to earlier pregenital fixations, he continues:

> The relation to the castration complex accounts for the affinity to the neuroses, noted so early by Freud. The partial regression to oral and early anal levels corresponds to the clinical fact that perverts are not infrequently near to, or actually develop, psychosis. In so far as they do not actually do so, I wish to suggest that the reason is to be sought in their exploitation of the splitting mechanism, which permits them to remain in part at the phallic level, with a superficially normal relation to reality, whereas another part of the personality is virtually psychotic. It is the fact that the first part remains to act as liaison officer with reality that prevents clinical psychosis. ("Notes" 402)

15. The famous instability of Zelda Fitzgerald and Jane Mason needs no elaboration, but I should say a word about Pauline and Hadley. During Ernest's "100 Days" separation from Pauline, a condition imposed upon him by Hadley as a condition for granting him a divorce, Pauline suffered from "uncontrollable fits of weeping" and what she described as "madhouse depressions." Hadley suffered from a nervous breakdown in 1912 which forced her to drop out of Bryn Mawr (Kert 187; Diliberto vii); she also worried about her lesbian desires and "white nights" of anxiety and depression (Griffin 247).

16. One of the psychotic patients in Blacker and Wong's study of autocastrati heard male and female voices "planning to possess his genitalia for their own purposes" (173). Hamilton's patient, a shoe fetishist and transvestite who had shared a bed with his older sister until he was eleven years old, worried that people were trying "to get" his penis, and he nicknamed his girlfriend "Grabdick."

17. Though obvious in *A Moveable Feast* (which Hemingway worked on concurrently with his 1958 revisions of *Eden*), Hemingway's conviction that Zelda had tried to ruin Scott, however ill-founded, was of long-standing. In 1928 Hemingway complained to Max Perkins, "Instead of thinking Zelda a possible good influence . . . for Scott, I think 90% of all the trouble he has comes from her" (*SL* 289). The fact that Hemingway had seen Zelda, and noted her supposedly evil influence on Scott, while he was in the process of revising *A Farewell to Arms* (Baker 198), probably influenced Catherine Barkley's desire to "ruin" Frederic. The same must be said, however, for the December 1928 suicide of Ernest's father for which he unjustly blamed his mother.

18. David also thinks that the color of his hair is an impossible color for a *man's* hair; thus it must be the hair of a woman.

19. A slightly Bowdlerized version of this passage appears in the Scribner's version of the book:

> "Now see how dark we are together. We're just the way we planned. . . ."
> They looked at each other standing touching in the long mirror on the door.
> "Oh you like us," she said. "That's nice. So do I. Touch here and see." She stood very straight and he put his hand on her breasts.
> . . . . "Isn't it funny our hair hasn't any color at all when it's wet? It's pale as seaweed. (175)

20. "Such episodes," Bak adds, "were followed by intense castration anxiety—he feared that the shaft was broken, that the penis had become crooked, that the spermal duct was torn and he would be sterile" ("Phallic Woman" 25). In an earlier article ("Fetishism"), Bak relates two more cases of mirror masturbation. In the first case a fetishist/transvestite would identify with the phallic mother by periodically wearing fetishized boots or rubber raincoats while he masturbated in front of the mirror. (As a boy, he had often worn his mother's dresses and shoes; his mother, in fact, had encouraged this behavior.) In the second case, a young man with a fetish for riding pants would don a pair to masturbate before the mirror. Until the age of four, this patient had been dressed as a girl.

21. The transvestic impulse is fairly clear in David Bourne but quite subtle in the case of Jake Barnes. Jake is fetishistically attracted to Brett's boyish haircut, but he never wears the fetish himself or behaves transvestically. In fact, he gets angry at Cohn for obsessively preening before Brett arrives in Pamplona: "I was blind, unforgivingly jealous of what had happened to him. . . . I do not think I ever really hated him until he had that little spell of superiority at lunch—that and when he went through all that barbering" (99). Yet the bisexual split in Hemingway's ego is still detectable in Jake Barnes. It lies encoded in Jake's very name.

Kenneth Lynn has ingeniously interpreted Jake's name as an allusion, conscious or unconscious, to two of the most prominent lesbians
of the Left Bank—Natalie Barney, who hosted her legendary Friday sa-
lons at 20 Rue Jacob, and Djuna Barnes, who lived at the Hôtel Jacob.
But Hemingway offers us the most obvious hint about Jake's name in
the text itself. Early in *The Sun Also Rises*, in the *bal musette* scene in
which we first meet Lady Ashley, Brett escapes Cohn's dance invitation
by turning to Jake: "I've already promised this dance to Jacob. You've a
hell of a biblical name, Jake!" (22).

The manifold irony of the scene is obvious. Jake, as narrator, has
just compared Cohn to Moses, staring at Brett as his "compatriot must
have looked when he saw the promised land" (22). In a sense, Jake becomes Cohn's compatriot and double. Yet the irony is too bitter. Unlike
his biblical namesake, Jake will never be the "father of nations." But
there is something more than irony at work here. The circumstances of
the biblical Jacob's birth and youth point to the origins of Hemingway's
fetishism. Jacob, after all, had a *twin* brother, Esau, who was born covered with a "hairy mantle." Hair, or the absence of it, becomes the distinguishing mark between the twins, and when Jacob (mama's boy) cheats
Esau (papa's boy) out of his blind father's blessing he does so by wearing,
at his mother's direction, his brother's clothes and a hairy disguise.

22. According to Reynolds, Hemingway revised much of the novel
in Oak Park during the week after his father's funeral, writing in the
room that had once been his father's office.

23. Carlos Baker speculates that "the luxuriant beards [Heming-
way] grew in adulthood [might have been] motivated partly by the fact
that he had never known his father to be without one" (17). Yet Hemingway always maintained that his father's beard "hid some elemental
weakness" (Mellow 10). Given the phallic significance of hair (and
beards) for Hemingway, what "elemental weakness" could this be if not
his father's symbolically emasculated condition?

24. Zavitzianos associates homeovestism with "imposture" (494),
and Aarons has called attention to a similar inclination toward gender
masquerade in one of his patients who was a fetishist: "When among
people he played two roles: a deferential, shy caricature of the female;
or a blustering, crude display of himself which he characterized as
'fraudulently masculine.' A female man and a male woman were
equated in these pretenses. They both possessed a penis; the former in
actuality, the latter in fantasy" (208). Aarons continues: "I would speculate that the 'as if' characteristics of the patient were not only manifestations of confusion in self identity, due in large measure to his
identification with his mother, but, upon closer scrutiny, revealed the
'split in the ego' in the fetishist. The patient had both a female and a
male self image, with the former predominating" (210).

25. For another homeovestic uniform in Hemingway's work, see Francis Macomber's new safari suit, a parodic imitation of Wilson's otherwise identical outfit: "He was dressed in the same sort of safari clothes that Wilson wore except that his were new. . ." (*SS* 4). This suit allows Macomber to defend against his emasculation (signified as much by his crew cut as by his cowardice) by masquerading as a version of the identically-clad, macho, white hunter (based on the white hunter Philip Percival, whom Hemingway called "Pop").

26. The subject in Bradlow and Coen's essay on mirror masturbation used the mirror for both transvestic and homeovestic identifications.

27. Havelock Ellis derived the term *eonism*, which he used for both transvestism and secondary transsexualism, from the Chevalier d'Eon (Charles-Geneviève Éon de Beaumont, 1728–1810), a French political adventurer who intrigued all of Europe by cross-dressing and refusing to disclose his true sex. Cross-dressed by his mother until age seven, d'Eon became one of the best swordsmen of his time, fought courageously for the French against Prussia as a Captain of the Dragoons, served as a secret diplomatic agent, and periodically adopted feminine garb, much to the consternation of Louis XVI. While all of Europe speculated about d'Eon's true sex, Louis XVI decreed that d'Eon could only return unpunished to France if he stopped alternating between male and female clothes and remained permanently in women's dress. "Although he kept asking to wear his beloved dragoon uniform, permission was never granted" (Buhrich and McConaghy 421).

28. Hemingway's first complete sentence was "I don't know Buffalo Bill," uttered when he was taken to see Pawnee Bill's Wild West Show. Later, when his mother called him her "Dutch dolly" (a reference to his haircut) "he stamped his foot, saying, 'I not a Dutch dolly, I Pawnee Bill. Bang, I shoot Fweetee'" (Baker 4).

29. Hutton notes that Custer's long flowing locks were so notable in his own time because they were "long out of style" (3). But to this day, Custer's hair seems to be the most important signifier in his iconography, so much so that, via a reversal, Custer can also function as a signifier of hair. In his book on the Custer myth, Dippie recounts a joke from *Playboy* in which Custer snarls to one of his men as Indians swirl round them, "Who said that blondes have more fun?" The iconicity of Custer's uniform can perhaps best be appreciated in Raoul Walsh's 1941 film *They Died with Their Boots On*. Here Custer, played by Errol Flynn, shows up for his first day as a cadet at West Point wearing an outlandish comic-opera uniform so flamboyant that he is mistaken for a visiting foreign general.

30. There *were* other Custers at the Little Big Horn, most notably the General's brother, Tom, but the identical heads and hats of Steineg-

ger's Custers, and the use of poses which were already iconic of the General, suggest that both images are meant to represent George.

31. While no one doubts that most of Custer's men were scalped and mutilated, the status of Custer's body at the time of its discovery is a matter of contention among Custer buffs. According to Edward S. Godfrey, author of what is often considered to be the most reliable account of the battle by a white participant, "All the bodies, except a few, were stripped of their clothing, according to my recollection nearly all were scalped or mutilated, but there was one notable exception, that of General Custer, whose face and expression was natural; he had been shot in the temple and in the left side" (309). Native American accounts vary considerably. Black Elk describes the scalping and mutilation of Custer's soldiers by the Lakota and Cheyenne women and children, but he says he didn't see Pahuska, and he doesn't think anyone could tell him from the other soldiers. Others claim that Custer was indeed scalped or offer contradictory explanations for the fact that he was *not* scalped: He had already cut his long hair (true) and so his scalp was of no interest; he had committed suicide and was therefore considered contaminated; or his scalp was respected as a tribute to his bravery.

32. These letters are at the Harry Ransom Humanities Research Center at the University of Texas at Austin. In the early pages of the manuscript Renata's name is "Nicola"; thus Burwell interprets her as a feminine avatar of Nick Adams and of young Hemingway himself. If Renata, like Catherine Barkley and Catherine Bourne, represents on some level the split-off feminine half of Hemingway's ego, this may shed some light on the age disparity between Cantwell and Renata. According to Winnicott, "The split-off other-sex part of the personality tends to remain of one age, or to grow but slowly" (*Playing* 77). In spite of feeling terribly old as she loses her mind, Catherine Bourne is almost as young as Renata. In the *Eden* manuscript, Barbara Sheldon thinks Catherine looks like fourteen-year-old "jailbait" (K422.1 5.7.2). In fact, her oscillation between the extremes of youth and age may capture both halves of Hemingway's ego.

33. This need to disavow the role of the paternal phallus in the primal scene is obvious in a childhood fantasy of May Romm's patient— the man, mentioned in chapter 2, who needed to cut his wife's hair during intercourse. As a little boy, he wished that he were the Christ Child and his mother the Madonna. This would prove that his father had never had intercourse with his mother.

34. I hope it is clear that my understanding of Hemingway is almost entirely complementary to Boker's recent psychoanalytic reading of his work in *The Grief Taboo in American Literature*. It should be clear by now that fetishism and transvestism are both, among other things, forms of mourning—manic defenses meant to undo the pain of separa-

tion from objects of primary narcissistic identification. They are a sort
of obsessive fingering of a psychic wound. Boker's reading of Hemingway's relation to masculinity and the oedipal is quite similar to my own.
I would only stress one difference. She reads Hemingway as a *neurotic*
whose *repressed* femininity was the result of an unwillingness to identify with his disappointing father. I read Hemingway as a *pervert* who
disavowed his identification with his disappointing father because: (1)
Ernest's femininity and narcissistic bond to his mother was so intense
that it diluted any paternal identification that would separate him from
it; (2) Ernest needed to disavow his father's agency in the primal scene
in order to disavow sexual difference and avoid a narcissistic injury;
and (3) his mother denigrated his father and held up another man as a
model of masculinity; *she* thereby became for him, on some level, the
arbiter of masculinity and conduit for the idealized paternal phallus. I
have no doubt that Boker is right about Hemingway's use of neurotic
defenses, but I think it is vital to recognize that these neurotic defenses
were superimposed upon the more primitive and extreme perverse defenses of *disavowal* and *splitting*. Whereas Hemingway could partially
work through some of the neurotic conflicts that concern Boker, he was
never able to work through his perverse conflicts.

35. Westbrook rightly insists that Mrs. Adams is *not* Mrs. Hemingway. Given his argument, I should take a moment to clear up a misun-
derstanding that is all too common among those who traditionally
dislike psychoanalytic readings of Hemingway's work. I obviously don't
mean to imply that Mrs. Adams is a simple portrait of Ernest's mother.
All will admit, however, that she is a fictional character based *loosely* on
Hemingway's mother. As a fictional character she does reveal something about how Hemingway *imagined* his mother and the role she
played in his family. If a mother-figure appears in an analysand's
dream, the analyst doesn't worry about whether or not this figure is an
"accurate" reflection of the analysand's mother. What is important is
how the analysand *imagines* her. If the analysand imagines a toothless
mother when in fact she had a flawless smile, this alteration of reality
is not so much an "inaccuracy" as it is something to be interpreted. My
dream-analogy is, of course, problematic, but it applies to that aspect
of the creative process which is unconscious.

36. Lynn 30. According to Reynolds, Ernest regarded "his father
and his father's family as the victims of his mother's ego." Ernest was
not only named after his maternal grandfather; his middle name—
Miller—was a tribute to his mother's uncle and great grandfather. Likewise, his sister Carol "was named for Grace's mother Caroline Hancock
Hall," and his little brother, Leicester, was named after Grace's brother.
"Of the six children, only Leicester's middle name—Clarence—memorialized the Doctor and the Doctor's family" (*Young Hemingway* 104).

37. Hemingway began consciously growing his hair out in February 1940 and didn't cut it until July (Baker 349; Lynn 481). He wrote his account of El Sordo's battle during April.

38. In her psychoanalytic study of this novel, Boker argues that Jordan does come to terms with his father in order to establish in the novel's conclusion a more mature and realistic masculinity. However, I see little evidence of this in the text. Jordan has a choice between heroism (idealized grandfather) or suicide (denigrated father), and he does everything in his power to be like his grandfather.

Chapter Seven

1. Unlike Hemingway, T.S. deliberately wrote "from the feminine standpoint," and he boasted that his novels were accepted by the public as being written by a woman. "Long passages of these I drafted while dressed and made up as a woman, often before the glass" (2.2.62). His novels, thus, provided him with the opportunity to "pass" as a female in public. By contrast, most readers, particularly those most influenced by American literary myth, are struck by a sort of homeovestic hypermasculine posturing in Hemingway's texts. Yet I hope the previous chapter has demonstrated that Hemingway's fiction also allowed him to "pass" in public as a woman through those parts of himself that he projected into female characters who on some level functioned as the avatars and emissaries of the split-off feminine half of his ego.

2. In the *Eden* manuscript, Catherine and Marita both wonder how many people are turned on by the same things that move them. At times they suspect that *everyone* is secretly turned on by haircutting, tanning, and gender-swapping. At other moments they're much less certain. Catherine sometimes suspects that this is how other people are afraid of being. Marita can't believe that everyone feels the way she does, but she suspects that "many people" must feel this way.

3. I realize that I've posed a sort of conundrum here. To define pornography as *literature intended to produce erotic excitement* implies a rather old-fashioned theory of meaning based upon authorial intent. To say, on the other hand, that *not all pornography is pornographic for all people* offers a reader-response corrective that may seem at odds with the first definition. These positions, however, can be reconciled. Literature always means something *for someone*. For most readers and literary critics this "someone" hardly needs to be the author. Yet, as a psychoanalytic literary critic engaged in an argument about the psychology of *an author*, I am interested in what the work meant to him. This can help us to understand why he constructed the story as he did, but it may not tell us much about our own engagement with the novel.

If the pornographic kernel in *The Garden of Eden* fails to function for us *as pornography* (and, as I say, it *will* fail for the vast majority of us), the novel even ceases to function for us as erotica. Perhaps my claim in this chapter should be, then, that the novel was *for Hemingway* a work of transvestite erotica. I have retained the more abstract claim, however, precisely because Hemingway was *not* alone. The novel may fail as erotica for *most* of us, but it will not fail for *all* of us.

4. Stoller, *Observing* 50. Though Hemingway was a hair fetishist, not a foot fetishist, one of his six "true sentences," those five-finger exercises he wrote in 1922, would have greatly pleased Aarons's patient: "I have seen the one legged street walker who works the Boulevard Madelaine between the Rue Cambon and Bernheim Jeune's limping along the pavement through the crowd on a rainy night with a beefy red-faced Episcopal clergyman holding an umbrella over her" (qtd. in Baker 91). Given Hemingway's built-in radar for detecting fetishism in others this may be just an instance of him recognizing a fetishistic desire in the beefy red-faced clergyman. Yet, as we have seen, amputation also figured prominently in Hemingway's psychosexual symbolism, and the fact that this prostitute works the Boulevard *Madelaine* may be significant. Although Hemingway's fetishism most often alludes to his sister Marcelline, he also had a younger sister named "Madelaine." Thus, the allusion to a *sister* suggests that the fetishistic fantasy in this vignette might belong as much to Hemingway as to the clergyman.

5. Those familiar with Althusser's essay "Ideology and Ideological State Apparatuses" will recognize my allusion to his notion of interpellation. There are two reasons why this should not surprise: (1) Althusser arrives at his theory of ideology by cross-breeding Marx with Freud and Lacan (which implies a circularity in my reference to Althusser—it is his formulation of an essentially psychoanalytic dilemma which interests me); (2) pornography can usefully be conceptualized as a form of erotic ideology. An entire essay, however, would be necessary to explain this second contention, and Althusser's theory of interpellation would have to be updated using the recent work of Slavoj Žižek. Žižek posits interpellation as a "response to the real"—the assumption of a subject position within a narrative as a defense against a traumatic "pre-subjective" encounter with an absolute Other. This, more or less, is what the work of Stoller tells us—in much more direct language.

6. The reader might wonder, "So was Shakespeare a transvestite?" I think not. Cross-dressing in theater becomes inevitable when the only available actors are of a single gender. That it would then furnish material for sexual double entendres is only to be expected. This, however, doesn't prevent Shakespeare's cross-dressing plays from having a special appeal for the transvestite and homeovestite.

7. In their study of transvestite fiction, Buhrich and McConaghy cite a story by the Abbe de Choisy, a seventeenth-century transvestite, which is an excellent example of this fantasy of dual transvestism. In the story, a mother raises her son from birth as a "girl" named Marianne. Forced to wear an "iron bodice" to bring out "her" hips and heighten "her" bosom, Marianne is kept in ignorance of "her" true sex until age sixteen. By then, Marianne is a beautiful "girl," courted by the neighboring petty nobility, and "she" is not particularly upset to discover that "she" is really a man. Marianne eventually falls in love with and marries an effeminate marquis, only to discover on the wedding night that "he" is really a she. Overjoyed, the couple decides to continue their cross-dressing. Marianne will live as a woman and the marquis as a man.

8. See Rancour-Laferriere, *Signs of the Flesh*, 187–8; 315.

9. The following passage appears in Simon Karlinsky's *The Sexual Labyrinth of Nikolai Gogol*:

> When Gogol came to St. Petersburg in November of 1839, he stayed at Zhukovsky's apartment in the Winter Palace. He was surprised in his room there one morning by Zhukovsky and Sergei Aksakov, who entered quietly and without knocking. "There was Gogol in front of me, wearing the following fantastical costume," Askakov reported in his memoirs. "Instead of boots, he wore long woolen Russian stockings, reaching higher than the knee; instead of a jacket, a velvet spencer worn over a flannel camisole; around his neck was a large multicolored scarf and on his head was a crimson velvet woman's headdress (*kokoshnik*) embroidered in gold and very similar to the headdresses of Finish tribeswomen." Gogol did not seem to be particularly embarrassed at being caught in this outfit. He simply asked Aksakov what his business was and then dismissed him by pleading the need to go on writing. (206)

Karlinsky argues that Gogol was a latent homosexual, but I would suggest that a better "diagnosis" might be transvestite/homeovestite, with emphasis given to the homeovestic position. An element of latent homosexuality always plays a crucial role in transvestism and homeovestism, but a "diagnosis" of latent homosexuality isn't very meaningful. There are simply too many kinds of manifest and latent homosexuality, many of which are by no means perverse. Gogol's transvestism and homeovestism may, however, have been an organized perversion within the structure of a largely psychotic personality. His terror of women and marriage was far more pronounced than is typical among transvestites, as if he feared *real* instead of *symbolic* harm. As a child he often heard hallucinatory voices, and in his final years he had a good deal in common with Freud's Dr. Schreber.

10. Rancour-Laferriere has interpreted Akaky Akakievich's over-coat as a mother substitute (it becomes Akaky's "wife"), as a female phallus, and as a tool to identify with a paternal figure (the tailor, Petrovich). Here, then, the overcoat is both fetish (with a trace of the transitional object) and homeovestic object.

11. The two brothers seem to reflect what Henri Troyat calls Gogol's "divided soul." Gogol's identification with Andrei is obvious, but so is his identification with Ostap. Troyat notes that one of Gogol's ancestors, Ostap Gogol, was a noted seventeenth-century Cossack warrior.

12. For the fetishist, transvestite, and homeovestite, *both* the ma-ternal phallus and idealized paternal phallus function to shore up mas-culinity, but they do so differently. The maternal phallus allows for a feminine identification with the mother, but by disavowing sexual dif-ference it simultaneously reinforces masculinity by disavowing the sig-nificance and threat of castration. The idealized paternal phallus "acknowledges" castration and wards off an identification with the mother by representing an unassailable, monolithic, fraudulent mas-culinity. It can be obtained homeovestically (by impersonating the ide-alized paternal imago) or transvestically (by impersonating the mother and being penetrated by the idealized paternal phallus). Insofar as in perverse families the idealized paternal phallus belongs not to the real, denigrated father, but to the ideal model of masculinity held up by the mother, it could be said that on some level there is a rough equation be-tween the mother's phallus and the ideal paternal phallus.

13. Joyce McDougall's patient Professor K realized exactly this: "It is finally clear to me that I disguise myself as a woman in order to be-come a man! As though I don't possess my own penis or as though I need to get hold of a very special one" (30). By identifying with his mother, Professor K could internalize her phallus—a "very special one" which denied sexual difference and thereby warded off castration anxi-ety. Yet his disguise also enabled him to internalize an idealized pater-nal phallus that belonged not to his denigrated father but rather to his idealized maternal grandfather.

14. I should qualify Stoller's assertion about the role of transvestite fantasy in preserving masculinity. Stoller reserves the word *transvestite* for those who are fetishistically aroused by putting on the clothes of the opposite sex. There is, however, an important sub-genre of transvestite fiction that seems to be aimed primarily at older, more gender dys-phoric, and less fetishistic transvestites who are drifting toward sec-ondary transsexualism. These stories are much less concerned with restoring the transvestite's masculinity and often end with the protago-nist deciding to spend the rest of his life dressed as a woman. Humilia-tion and misogyny are relatively absent in these stories. The male

protagonists are still cross-dressed by women, but the women appear as helpful guides, not as humiliators. It would be safe to say, however, that the stronger the element of fetishism in the story the more certain we can be that the preservation of masculinity is high on the agenda.

15. According to McDougall, another crucial, although almost always hidden, member of the audience is the pervert's denigrated and emasculated father. This may illuminate a strange scene in *To Have and Have Not*. Richard Gordon is making adulterous love to Helène Bradley, "her bright hair . . . spread over the pillow," when he is startled by a bearded man peering at them from the doorway. Gordon stops in his tracks, much to the consternation of Helène who urges him to continue. "That's only Tommy. . . . He knows all about these things. Don't mind him. Come on, darling. Please do" (189). Gordon, however, will have none of it and receives a slap in the face from Helène, who is disappointed to find out that he isn't a "man of the world."

16. Taylor's case offers another excellent example of trauma transformed into triumph. The patient's mother had dressed him in girls' clothes until he was two-years-old, and "until the age of five he wore long, black, above-the-knee stockings and girls' buttoned shoes which he resented strongly. He wanted to wear boys' lace-up shoes and his mother finally relented when he refused to go to school" (513). The patient's adult mask-wearing ritual (which also involved wearing women's dresses, shoes, and furs) memorialized, among other things, a series of traumatic operations performed on him as a young boy. Then he had been terrified that he would suffocate under the mask used to deliver anesthesia. During his adult masturbation rituals, however, he often wore three masks at once, one on top of the other, and he preferred masks without holes for the mouth and nose so that he had to breathe through the slits for his eyes. It is also worth noting that, as a form of unconscious revenge against his parents, he almost always destroyed his masks after using them.

17. This line from the traditional Scottish ballad "The Twa Corbies" had haunted Hemingway for decades. He had considered using it as a title for *A Farewell to Arms*, and it was the provisional title for his aborted novel about Jimmy Crane. It is an odd line to find so haunting, but the poem from which it comes may say something about how Hemingway interpreted his experience in the First World War. In the poem, the new slain knight's "lady fair" has "taken another mate" before his body has even grown cold—much as Agnes von Kurowsky dumped the wounded Ernest for the dashing Italian Arditi officer, Domenico Caracciolo. The two crows in the poem plan to pick the knight's bones and thatch their nest with a lock of his "golden hair." For Hemingway, this symbolized castration and an annihilation of the ego; hence, Jan's pronouncement in the *Islands* manuscript.

Bibliography

Aarons, Alexander Z. "Fetish, Fact and Fantasy: A Clinical Study of the Problems of Fetishism." *International Review of Psycho-Analysis* 2 (1972): 199–230.

Abraham, Nicolas and Maria Torok. *The Wolf Man's Magic Word.* Trans. Nicholas Rand. Theory and History of Literature 37. Minneapolis: U of Minnesota P, 1986.

Adams, Parveen. "The Bald Truth." *Diacritics* 24.2–3 (1994): 184–189.

Althusser, Louis. "Ideology and Ideological State Apparatuses: Notes Toward an Investigation." *Lenin and Philosophy and Other Essays.* New York: Monthly Review Press, 1971.

American Psychiatric Association. *Diagnostic and Statistical Manual of Mental Disorders. DSM-III-R.* Washington, D.C.: American Psychiatric Association, 1987.

———. *Diagnostic and Statistical Manual of Mental Disorders. DSM-IV.* Washington, D.C.: American Psychiatric Association, 1994.

Apter, Emily. *Feminizing the Fetish: Psychoanalysis and Narrative Obsession in Turn-of-the-Century France.* Ithaca: Cornell UP, 1991.

Bach, Sheldon. *The Language of Perversion and the Language of Love.* London: Aronson, 1994.

Bak, Robert C. "Aggression and Perversion." *Perversions: Psychodynamics and Therapy.* Ed. Sandor Lorand & Michael Balint. New York: Random House, 1956. 231–240.

———. "Distortions of the Concept of Fetishism." *Psychoanalytic Study of the Child* 29 (1974): 191–214.

———. "Fetishism." *Journal of the American Psychoanalytic Association* 1 (1953): 285–298.

336   *Bibliography*

———. "The Phallic Woman: The Ubiquitous Fantasy in Perversions." *Psychoanalytic Study of the Child* 23 (1968): 15–36.

Baker, Carlos. *Ernest Hemingway: A Life Story.* New York: Macmillan, 1969.

Balint, Michael. "A Contribution on Fetishism." *International Journal of Psycho-Analysis* 16 (1935): 481–483.

———. "Perversions and Genitality." *Perversions: Psychodynamics and Therapy.* Ed. Sandor Lorand and Michael Balint. New York: Gramercy, 1956. 16–27.

Barea, Arturo. "Not Spain but Hemingway." *Horizon* 3 (May 1941): 350–361.

Beigel, H. G. and R. Feldman. "The Male Transvestite's Motivation in Fiction, Research and Reality." *Advances in Sex Research.* Ed. Beigel. New York: Harper and Row, 1963.

Benjamin, Jessica. *The Bonds of Love: Psychoanalysis, Feminism, and the Problem of Domination.* New York: Pantheon, 1988.

Benson, Jackson. *Hemingway: The Writer's Art of Self-Defense.* Minneapolis: U of Minnesota P, 1969.

Blacker, K. H. and Normund Wong. "Four Cases of Autocastration." *Archives of General Psychiatry* 8 (1963): 169–176.

Bloom, Harold. "Introduction." *Modern Critical Interpretations: Ernest Hemingway's* The Sun Also Rises. *Modern Critical Interpretations.* Ed. Harold Bloom. New York: Chelsea House, 1987. 1–8.

Boker, Pamela A. *The Grief Taboo in American Literature: Loss and Prolonged Adolescence in Twain, Melville, and Hemingway.* New York: New York UP, 1996.

Bollas, Christopher. "The Aesthetic Moment and the Search for Transformation." *Transitional Objects and Potential Spaces: Literary Uses of D. W. Winnicott.* Ed. Peter L. Rudnytsky. New York: Columbia, 1993. 40–49.

Bradlow, Paul A. and Stanley J. Coen. "Mirror Masturbation." *Psychoanalytic Quarterly* 53 (1984): 267–285.

Brenner, Gerry. *Concealments in Hemingway's Works.* Columbus: Ohio State UP, 1983.

Brian, Denis. *The True Gen: An Intimate Portrait of Hemingway by Those Who Knew Him.* New York: Delta, 1988.

Brierley, Harry. *Transvestism: A Handbook with Case Studies for Psychologists, Psychiatrists and Counselors.* New York: Pergamon, 1979.

Bruccoli, Matthew J. "Introduction." *The Sun Also Rises: A Facsimile Edition.* Archive of Literary Documents. Ed. Matthew J. Bruccoli. Ann Arbor, MI: Omnigraphics, 1990.

Brunswick, Ruth Mack. "The Preoedipal Phase of the Libido Development." *Psychoanalytic Quarterly* 9 (1940): 293–319.

Buhrich, Neil and Neil McConaghy. "Transvestite Fiction." *The Journal of Nervous and Mental Disease* 163.6 (1976): 420–427.

Bullough, Vern. *Sexual Variance in Society and History.* Chicago: Chicago UP, 1980.

Bullough, Vern and Bonnie Bullough. *Cross Dressing, Sex, and Gender.* U of Pennsylvania P, 1993.

— Burwell, Rose Marie. *Hemingway: The Postwar Years and the Posthumous Novels.* New York: Cambridge UP, 1996.

Chasseguet-Smirgel, Janine. *Creativity and Perversion.* London: Free Association Books, 1985.

Chodorow, Nancy. "Gender as a Personal and Cultural Construction." *Signs* 20.3 (1995): 516–544.

— Comley, Nancy R. and Robert Scholes. *Hemingway's Genders: Rereading the Hemingway Text.* New Haven: Yale UP, 1994.

Corson, Richard. *Fashions in Hair: The First Five Thousand Years.* New York: Hastings House, 1965.

De Lauretis, Teresa. *The Practice of Love: Lesbian Sexuality and Perverse Desire.* Indianapolis: Indiana UP, 1994.

Denzler, Betty. "Panel Report: Psychic Reality and Perversions." Henry Smith, Chair. *International Journal of Psycho-Analysis* 77 (1996): 61–66.

Desnoyers, Megan Floyd and Stephen Plotkin. "News from the Hemingway Collection." *Hemingway Review* 13.1 (1993): 120.

Devereux, George. *From Anxiety to Method in the Behavioral Sciences.* The Hague: Mouton, 1967.

Diliberto, Gioia. *Hadley.* New York: Ticknor & Fields, 1992.

Dinesen, Isak. *Out of Africa and Shadows on the Grass.* New York: Vintage, 1985.

Dippie, Brian W. *Custer's Last Stand: The Anatomy of an American Myth.* Lincoln: U of Nebraska P, 1976.

Eastman, Max. "Bull in the Afternoon." *The New Republic* 75 (June 7, 1933): 94–97.

Eby, Carl. "'Come Back to the Beach Ag'in, David Honey!': Hemingway's Fetishization of Race in *The Garden of Eden* Manuscripts." *Hemingway Review* 14.2 (1995): 98–117.

Ellis, Havelock. *Studies in the Psychology of Sex.* 2 vols. New York: Random House, 1936.

Farnell, Lewis Richard. *The Cults of The Greek States.* Vol 2. New Rochelle, NY: Caratzas Brothers. 5 vols. 1977.

Feigelson, C. "The Mirror Dream." Psychoanalytic Study of the Child 30 (1975): 341–355.

Fenichel, Otto. *The Psychoanalytic Theory of Neurosis.* New York: Norton, 1945.

———. "The Psychology of Transvestitism." *The Collected Works of Otto Fenichel.* Vol. 1. New York: Norton, 1953. 167–180. 2 vols. 1953–1954.

———. "The Symbolic Equation: Girl = Phallus." *The Collected Works of Otto Fenichel.* Vol. 2. New York: Norton, 1954. 3–18. 2 vols. 1953–1954.

Fetterley, Judith. *The Resisting Reader: A Feminist Approach to American Fiction.* Bloomington: Indiana UP, 1978.

Fiedler, Leslie. *Love and Death in the American Novel.* 3rd ed. New York: Anchor, 1992.

Fine, Reuben. *A History of Psychoanalysis.* New York: Columbia UP, 1979.

Fitch, Noel Riley. *Sylvia Beach and the Lost Generation.* New York: Norton, 1983.

Fleming, Robert. "The Endings of Hemingway's *Garden of Eden.*" *American Literature* 61:2 (1989): 261–270.

———. *The Face in the Mirror: Hemingway's Writers.* Tuscaloosa: U of Alabama P, 1994.

Frazer, James George, Sir. *The Golden Bough.* New York: Macmillan, 1922.

Freud, Sigmund. *The Ego and the Id. The Standard Edition of the Complete Psychological Works of Sigmund Freud.* Trans. James Strachey. Vol. 19. London: Hogarth, 1961. 3–68. 24 vols. 1953–1974.

——. "Fetishism." *The Standard Edition*. Vol. 21. London: Hogarth, 1963. 147–158.

——. *From the History of an Infantile Neurosis*. *The Standard Edition*. Vol. 17. London: Hogarth, 1955. 3–124.

——. *The Interpretation of Dreams*. *The Standard Edition*. Vol. 4. London: Hogarth, 1953.

——. *Jokes and their Relation to the Unconscious*. *The Standard Edition*. Vol. 8. London: Hogarth, 1960.

——. *Leonardo da Vinci and a Memory of His Childhood*. *The Standard Edition*. Vol. 11. London: Hogarth, 1957. 59–137.

——. "Medusa's Head." *The Standard Edition*. Vol. 18. London: Hogarth, 1960. 273–274.

——. "Mourning and Melancholia." *The Standard Edition*. Vol. 14. London: Hogarth, 243–258.

——. "On the Sexual Theories of Children." *The Standard Edition*. Vol. 9. London: Hogarth, 1959. 205–226.

——. *An Outline of Psycho-Analysis*. *The Standard Edition*. Vol. 23. London: Hogarth, 1964. 141–207.

——. "Splitting of the Ego in the Defensive Process." *The Standard Edition*. Vol. 23. London: Hogarth, 1964. 271–278.

——. *Three Essays on the Theory of Sexuality*. *The Standard Edition*. Vol. 7. London: Hogarth, 1953. 123–243.

——. *Totem and Taboo*. *The Standard Edition*. Vol. 13. London: Hogarth, 1955.

Fuentes, Norberto. *Hemingway in Cuba*. Trans. Consuelo E. Corwin. Secaucus, N.J.: Lyle Stuart, 1984.

Gamman, Lorraine and Merja Makinen. *Female Fetishism*. New York: New York UP, 1994.

Garber, Marjorie. *Vested Interests: Cross-Dressing and Cultural Anxiety*. New York: HarperPerennial, 1992.

Gautier, Théophile. *Mademoiselle de Maupin*. Trans. Joanna Richardson. New York: Penguin, 1981.

Gillespie, W. H. "A Contribution to the Study of Fetishism." *International Journal of Psycho-Analysis* 21 (1940): 401–415.

——. "Notes on the Analysis of Sexual Perversions." *International Journal of Psycho-Analysis* 33 (1952): 397–402.

Glasser, Mervin. "From the Analysis of a Transvestite." *International Review of Psycho-Analysis* 6 (1979): 163–173.

———. "Some Aspects of the Role of Aggression in the Perversions." *Sexual Deviation.* Second Edition. Ed. Ismond Rosen. New York: Oxford UP, 1979. 278–305.

Godfrey, Edward S. "Custer's Last Battle." *The Custer Reader.* Ed. Paul Andrew Hutton. Lincoln: U of Nebraska P, 1992. 257–318.

Gogol, Nikolai. "Taras Bulba." *The Complete Tales of Nikolai Gogol.* Ed. Leonard J. Kent. Trans. Constance Garnett. 2 vols. Chicago: U of Chicago P, 1985. Vol. 2. 22–132.

Gosselin, Chris C. and S. B. G. Eysenck. "The Transvestite 'Double Image'": A Preliminary Report." *Personality and Individual Differences* 1.2 (1980): 172–173.

Gosselin, Chris C. and Glenn Wilson. *Sexual Variations: Fetishism, Sadomasochism, and Transvestism.* London: Faber and Faber, 1980.

Gould, Thomas E. "'A Tiny Operation with Great Effect': Authorial Revision and Editorial Emasculation in the Manuscript of Hemingway's *For Whom the Bell Tolls.*" *Blowing the Bridge: Essays on Hemingway and For Whom the Bell Tolls.* Ed. Rena Sanderson. New York: Greenwood, 1992. 67–81.

Green, André. *On Private Madness.* London: Hogarth, 1986.

Greenacre, Phyllis. *Emotional Growth: Psychoanalytic Studies of the Gifted and a Great Variety of Other Individuals.* 2 vols. New York: International Universities Press, 1971.

Greenson, Ralph R. "Dis-Identifying from Mother: Its Special Importance for the Boy." *International Journal of Psycho-Analysis* 49 (1968): 370–373.

Griffin, Peter. *Along with Youth: Hemingway, The Early Years.* New York: Oxford UP, 1985.

Grosz, Elizabeth. "Lesbian Fetishism?" *Fetishism as Cultural Discourse.* Eds. Emily Apter and William Pietz. Ithaca: Cornell UP, 1993: 101–115.

Hagopian, John V. "Symmetry in 'Cat in the Rain.'" *College English* 24 (1962): 220–222.

Hamilton, James. "The Evaluation of a Shoe Fetish." *International Journal of Psychoanalytic Psychotherapy* 6 (1977): 323–337.

Hammond, Bryan and Patrick O'Connor. *Josephine Baker.* London: Jonathan Cape, 1988.

Haney, Lynn. *Naked at the Feast: A Biography of Josephine Baker*. New York: Dodd, 1981.

Hays, Peter L. "Catullus and *The Sun Also Rises*." *Hemingway Review* 12 (1993): 15–23.

———. "Hemingway's Clinical Depression: A Speculation." *Hemingway Review* 14.2 (1995): 50–63.

———. *The Limping Hero: Grotesques in Literature*. New York: New York UP, 1971.

Hemingway, Ernest. *Across the River and Into the Trees*. New York: Scribner's, 1950.

———. *African Journal*. *Sports Illustrated* (December 20 and 27, 1971; January 2, 1972).

———. *African Journal* Manuscript. Princeton University, Firestone Library. Archives of Charles Scribner's Sons.

———. "The Christmas Gift." *Look*. 18.8 (April 20, 1954): 29–37 and 18.9 (May 4, 1954): 79–89.

———. *The Complete Short Stories of Ernest Hemingway. Finca Vigía Ed.* New York: Scribner's, 1987.

———. *Dateline: Toronto: Hemingway's Complete Dispatches for* The Toronto Star, *1920–1924*. New York: Scribner's, 1985.

———. *Death in the Afternoon*. New York: Scribner's, 1932.

———. *A Farewell to Arms*. New York: Scribner's, 1929.

———. *The Fifth Column. The Short Stories of Ernest Hemingway: The First Forty-Nine Stories and the Play* The Fifth Column. New York: Modern Library, 1938: 3–101.

———. *For Whom the Bell Tolls*. New York: Scribner's, 1940.

———. *The Garden of Eden*. Ed. Tom Jenks. New York: Scribner's, 1986.

———. *The Garden of Eden* Manuscript. Hemingway Collection, John F. Kennedy Library, Boston.

———. *Islands in the Stream*. New York: Scribner's, 1970.

———. *Islands in the Stream* Manuscript. Hemingway Collection, John F. Kennedy Library, Boston.

———. *A Moveable Feast*. New York: Scribner's, 1964.

———. *The Old Man and the Sea*. New York: Scribner's, 1952.

————. "Philip Haines Was a Writer." Ed. Donald Junkins. *Hemingway Review* 9 (1990): 2–9.

————. *Selected Letters: 1917–1961.* Ed. Carlos Baker. New York: Scribner's, 1981.

————. *The Short Stories of Ernest Hemingway.* New York: Scribner's, 1987.

————. *The Sun Also Rises.* New York: Scribner's, 1926.

————. *The Sun Also Rises: A Facsimile Edition.* Archive of Literary Documents. Ed. Matthew J. Bruccoli. Ann Arbor, MI: Omnigraphics, 1990.

————. *To Have and Have Not.* New York: Scribner's, 1937.

————. *The Torrents of Spring.* New York: Scribner's, 1972.

————. Unpublished Letters. Hemingway Collection, John F. Kennedy Library, Boston, and the Harry Ransom Humanities Research Center, University of Texas at Austin.

Hemingway, Gregory H. *Papa: A Personal Memoir.* New York: Paragon, 1988.

Hemingway, Mary Welsh. *How It Was.* New York: Knopf, 1976.

————. Journals and Papers. Hemingway Collection, John F. Kennedy Library, Boston.

Hotchner, A. E. *Papa Hemingway: A Personal Memoir.* New York: Random, 1966.

Hovey, Richard B. *Hemingway: The Inward Terrain.* Seattle: U of Washington P, 1968.

Hutton, Paul Andrew. "Introduction." *The Custer Reader.* Ed. Hutton. Lincoln" U of Nebraska P, 1992. 3–6 & 229–238.

Jamison, Kay R. *Touched with Fire: Manic-Depressive Illness and the Artistic Temperament.* New York: Macmillan, 1993.

————. *An Unquiet Mind: A Memoir of Moods and Madness.* New York: Knopf, 1995.

Johnston, Kenneth G. "Hemingway and Freud: The Tip of the Iceberg." *Journal of Narrative Technique* 14.1 (1984): 68–73.

Josephs, Allen. For Whom the Bell Tolls: *Ernest Hemingway's Undiscovered Country.* Twayne's Masterwork Studies. New York: Twayne, 1994.

————. "Hemingway's Poor Spanish: Chauvinism and Loss of Credibility in *For Whom the Bell Tolls.*" *Hemingway: A Revaluation.* Troy, NY: Whitson, 1983: 205–223.

Jucovy, Milton E. "Initiation Fantasies and Transvestism." *Journal of the American Psychoanalytic Association* 24.3 (1976): 525–546.

Kaplan, Louise J. *Female Perversions: The Temptations of Emma Bovary.* New York: Anchor, 1991.

Karlinsky, Simon. *The Sexual Labyrinth of Nikolai Gogol.* Cambridge: Harvard UP, 1976.

Kennedy, J. Gerald. *Imagining Paris: Exile, Writing, and American Identity.* New Haven: Yale UP, 1993.

Kernberg, Otto F. *Aggression in Personality Disorders and Perversions.* New Haven: Yale UP, 1992.

Kert, Bernice. *The Hemingway Women.* New York: Norton, 1983.

Khan, M. Masud R. *Alienation in Perversions.* London: Hogarth, 1979.

Klein, Milton. "On Mahler's Autistic and Symbiotic Phases: An Exposition and Evaluation." *Psychoanalysis and Contemporary Thought* 4 (1981): 69–105.

Klerman, Gerald L. "Depression and Related Disorders of Mood (Affective Disorders)." *The New Harvard Guide to Psychiatry.* Ed. Armand M. Nicholi, Jr. Cambridge, MA: Harvard UP, 1988: 309–336.

Kohon, Gregorio. "Fetishism Revisited." *International Journal of Psycho-Analysis* 68 (1987): 213–228.

Kohut, Heinz. *The Analysis of the Self.* Madison, CT: International Universities Press, 1971.

———. "Forms and Transformations of Narcissism." *Essential Papers on Narcissism.* Ed. Andrew P. Morrison. New York: New York UP, 1986. 61–87.

Krafft-Ebing, Richard von. *Psychopathia Sexualis.* Trans. F. J. Rebman. New York: Physicians and Surgeons Book Co., 1930.

Lacan, Jacques and Wladimir Granoff. "Fetishism: The Symbolic, the Imaginary and the Real." *Perversions: Psychodynamics and Therapy.* Ed. Sandor Lorand. New York: Gramercy, 1956. 265–276.

Lacan, Jacques. *Freud's Papers on Technique, 1953–1954. The Seminar of Jacques Lacan: Book I.* Ed. Jacques-Alain Miller. Trans. John Forrester. New York: Norton, 1988.

———. "The Direction of the Treatment and the Principles of Its Power." *Écrits: A Selection.* New York: Norton, 1977. 226–280.

———. *La relation d'objet. Le séminaire de Jacques Lacan: livre IV.* Ed. Jacques-Alain Miller. Paris: Éditions du Seuil, 1994.

Langevin, Ron. *Sexual Strands: Understanding and Treating Sexual Anomalies in Men.* Hillsdale, N.J.: Lawrence Erlbaum Associates, 1983.

Laplanche, J. and J.-B. Pontalis. *The Language of Psycho-Analysis.* New York: Norton, 1973.

Latham, Aaron. "A Farewell to Machismo." *New York Times Magazine* 16 Oct. 1977: 52–53, 55, 80, 82, 90, 92, 94, 96, 98–99.

Lewis, Murray D. "A Case of Transvestism with Multiple Body-Phallus Identification." *International Journal of Psycho-Analysis* 44 (1963): 345–351.

Lewis, Robert W. *Hemingway on Love.* Austin: U of Texas P, 1965.

Lihn, Henry. "Fetishism: A Case Report." *International Journal of Psycho-Analysis* 51 (1970): 351–358.

Lorand, Sandor. "Fetishism in *Statu Nascendi.*" *International Journal of Psycho-Analysis* 11 (1930): 419–427.

———. "Role of the Female Penis Phantasy in Male Character Formation." *International Journal of Psycho-Analysis* 20 (1939): 171–182.

Lynn, Kenneth S. *Hemingway.* New York: Simon and Schuster, 1987.

Mahler, Margaret S., and Fred Pine, and Anni Bergman. *The Psychological Birth of the Human Infant: Symbiosis and Individuation.* New York: Basic Books, 1975.

Mann, Thomas. *Death in Venice and Seven Other Stories.* New York: Vintage, 1936.

McAlmon, Robert. *Being Geniuses Together: 1920–1930. Revised with Supplementary Chapters and an Afterword by Kay Boyle.* San Francisco: North Point Press, 1984.

McDougall, Joyce. *Plea for a Measure of Abnormality.* New York: International Universities Press, 1980.

Mellow, James. *Hemingway: A Life Without Consequences.* New York: Addison-Wesley, 1992.

Meredith, Major James H. "The Rapido River and Hürtgen Forest in *Across the River and Into the Trees.*" *Hemingway Review* 14.1 (1994): 60–66.

Messent, Peter. *Ernest Hemingway.* Modern Novelists. New York: St. Martin's, 1992.

Meyers, Jeffrey. *Hemingway: A Biography.* New York: Harper, 1985.

Money, J. "Two Names, Two Wardrobes, Two Personalities." *Journal of Homosexuality* 1 (1974): 65–70.

Moorjani, Angela. "Fetishism, Gender Masquerade, and the Mother-Father Fantasy." *Psychoanalysis, Feminism, and the Future of Gender.* Ed. Joseph H. Smith and Afaf Mahfouz. Baltimore: Johns Hopkins UP, 1994. 22–41.

Morrison, Toni. *Playing in the Dark: Whiteness and the Literary Imagination.* New York: Vintage, 1993.

Neihardt, John G. *Black Elk Speaks.* New York: Pocket, 1959.

Ostow, Mortimer. *Sexual Deviations: Psycho-Analytic Insights.* New York: Quadrangle/New York Times Book Co., 1974.

Pausanias. *Description of Greece.* Trans. W. H. S. Jones. Cambridge, MA: Harvard UP, 1979.

Payne, Sylvia M. "Some Observations on the Ego Development of the Fetishist." *International Journal of Psycho-Analysis.* 20 (1939): 161–170.

Plimpton, George. "Ernest Hemingway." *Writers at Work. The Paris Review Interviews.* 2nd Series. Ed. George Plimpton. New York: Penguin, 1977. 215–239.

Pontalis, J.-B., *Frontiers in Psychoanalysis: Between the Dream and Psychic Pain.* Trans. Catherine Cullen and Philip Cullen. London: Hogarth, 1981.

Raeburn, John. *Fame Became of Him: Hemingway as Public Writer.* Bloomington: Indiana UP, 1984.

Rancour-Laferriere, Daniel. *Out from Under Gogol's Overcoat: A Psychoanalytic Study.* Ann Arbor, MI: Ardis, 1982.

———. *Signs of the Flesh: An Essay on the Evolution of Hominid Sexuality.* Indianapolis: Indiana UP, 1985.

———. "Some Semiotic Aspects of the Human Penis." *Versus* 24 (1979): 37–82.

Rehberger, Dean. "'I Don't Know Buffalo Bill'; or, Hemingway and the Rhetoric of the Western." *Blowing the Bridge: Essays on Hemingway and For Whom the Bell Tolls.* Ed. Rena Sanderson. New York: Greenwood, 1992. 159–184.

Reynolds, Michael. "The Agnes Tapes." *Fitzgerald/Hemingway Annual* (1979): 251–277.

———. "Hemingway's Home: Depression and Suicide." *Ernest Hemingway: Six Decades of Criticism.* Ed. Linda W. Wagner. East Lansing: Michigan State UP, 1987. 9–17.

———. *Hemingway's Reading, 1910–1940: An Inventory.* New Jersey: Princeton UP, 1981.

———. *Hemingway: The 1930s.* New York: Norton, 1997.

———. *Hemingway: The American Homecoming.* Cambridge, MA: Basil Blackwell, 1992.

———. *Hemingway: The Paris Years.* Cambridge, MA: Basil Blackwell, 1989.

———. "A Supplement to *Hemingway's Reading: 1910–1940.*" *Studies in American Fiction* 13 (1985): 99–108.

———. *The Young Hemingway.* Cambridge, MA: Basil Blackwell, 1986.

Róheim, Géza. "Aphrodite, Or the Woman with a Penis." *Psychoanalytic Quarterly* 14 (1945): 350–390.

Roiphe, Herman and Eleanor Galenson. *Infantile Origins of Sexual Identity.* New York: International Universities Press, 1981.

Romm, May E. "Some Dynamics of Fetishism." *Psychoanalytic Quarterly* 18 (1949): 137–153.

Rose, Phyllis. *Jazz Cleopatra: Josephine Baker in Her Time.* New York: Doubleday, 1989.

Rosen, Ismond. "The General Psychoanalytical Theory of Perversion: A Critical and Clinical Review." *Sexual Deviation.* Second Edition. Ed. Ismond Rosen. New York: Oxford UP, 1979. 29–64.

Ross, Lillian. *Portrait of Hemingway.* New York: Simon and Schuster, 1961.

Rothstein, Arnold. "The Theory of Narcissism: An Object-Relations Perspective." *Essential Papers on Narcissism.* Ed. Andrew P. Morrison. New York: New York UP, 1986: 308–320.

Rudat, Wolfgang E. H. "Hemingway's Rabbit: Slips of the Tongue and Other Linguistic Games in *For Whom the Bell Tolls.*" *Hemingway Review* 10.1 (1990): 34–51.

Russo, John Paul. "To Die is Not Enough: Hemingway's Venetian Novel." *Hemingway in Italy and Other Essays.* Ed. Robert W. Lewis. New York: Praeger, 1990. 153–180.

Sanford, Marcelline Hemingway. *At the Hemingways: A Family Portrait.* Boston: Little, Brown, 1962.

Schor, Naomi. "Female Fetishism: The Case of George Sand." *Poetics Today* 6 (1985): 301–310.

———. "Fetishism and Its Ironies." *Fetishism as Cultural Discourse*. Eds. Emily Apter and William Pietz. Ithaca: Cornell UP, 1993: 92–100.

Schott, Richard L. "The Childhood and Family Dynamics of Transvestites." *Archives of Sexual Behavior* 24.3 (1995): 309–327.

Segal, Morey M. "Transvestism as an Impulse and as a Defence." *International Journal of Psycho-Analysis* 46 (1965): 209–217.

Slotkin, Richard. *Fatal Environment: The Myth of the Frontier in the Age of Industrialization, 1800–1890*. New York: Atheneum, 1985.

Smith, Paul. *A Reader's Guide to the Short Stories of Ernest Hemingway*. Boston: G. K. Hall, 1989.

———. "1924: Hemingway's Luggage and the Miraculous Year." *The Cambridge Companion to Ernest Hemingway*. Ed. Scott Donaldson. New York: Cambridge UP, 1996. 36–54.

Socarides, Charles W. *The Preoedipal Origin and Psychoanalytic Therapy of Sexual Perversions*. Madison, CT: International Universities Press, 1988.

Sperling, Melitta. "The Analysis of a Boy with Transvestite Tendencies." *Psychoanalytic Study of the Child* 19 (1964): 470–493.

Spilka, Mark. *Hemingway's Quarrel with Androgyny*. Lincoln: U of Nebraska P, 1990.

Stein, Gertrude and Sherwood, Anderson. *Sherwood Anderson/Gertrude Stein: Correspondence and Personal Essays*. Ed. Ray Lewis White. Chapel Hill: U of North Carolina P, 1972.

Stoller, Robert. "The Gender Disorders." *Sexual Deviation*. Second Edition. Ed. Ismond Rosen. New York: Oxford UP, 1979. 109–138.

———. "The Mother's Contribution to Infantile Transvestic Behaviour." *International Journal of Psycho-Analysis* 47 (1966): 384–395.

———. *Observing the Erotic Imagination*. New Haven: Yale UP, 1985.

———. *Perversion: The Erotic Form of Hatred*. New York: Pantheon, 1975.

———. *Presentations of Gender*. New Haven: Yale UP, 1985.

———. *Sex and Gender*. New York: Aronson, 1968–1975. 2 vols.

Stolorow, Robert D. "Toward a Functional Definition of Narcissism." *Essential Papers on Narcissism*. Ed. Andrew P. Morrison. New York: New York UP, 1986: 197–209.

Styron, William. *Darkness Visible: A Memoir of Madness*. New York: Random, 1990.

Suslick, Alvin, "The Phallic Representation of the Voice." *Journal of the American Psychoanalytic Association* 11 (1963): 345–359.

Taylor, Graeme J. "Splitting of the Ego in Transvestism and Mask Wearing." *International Review of Psycho-Analysis* 7 (1980): 511–520.

Tintner, Adeline R. "The Significance of D'Annunzio in *Across the River and Into the Trees*." *Hemingway Review* 5.1 (1985): 9–13.

Torgovnick, Marianna. *Gone Primitive: Savage Intellects, Modern Lives*. Chicago: U of Chicago P, 1990.

Troyat, Henri. *Divided Soul: The Life of Gogol*. Trans. Nancy Amphoux. Garden City, NY: Doubleday, 1973.

Urwin, Gregory J. W. "Custer: The Civil War Years." *The Custer Reader*. Ed. Paul Andrew Hutton. Lincoln: U of Nebraska P, 1992. 7–32.

Van De Water, Frederic F. *Glory Hunter: A Life of General Custer*. New York: Argosy, 1963.

Villard, Henry Serrano and James Nagel. *Hemingway in Love and War: The Lost Diary of Agnes von Kurowsky, Her Letters, and Correspondence of Ernest Hemingway*. Boston: Northeastern UP, 1989.

Westbrook, Max. "Grace Under Pressure: Hemingway and the Summer of 1920." *Ernest Hemingway: Six Decades of Criticism*. Ed. Linda W. Martin. Michigan State UP, 1987. 19–40.

Whitebook, Joel. *Perversion and Utopia: A Study in Psychoanalysis and Critical Theory*. Cambridge, MA: MIT Press, 1995.

Whittaker, Frederick. *A Complete Life of General George A. Custer*. New York: Sheldon, 1876.

Winnicott, D. W. *Playing and Reality*. 1971. New York: Routledge, 1993.

———. *Psycho-Analytic Explorations*. Ed. Clare Winnicott, Ray Shepherd, and Madeleine Davis. Cambridge, MA: Harvard UP, 1989.

Yalom, Irvin D., and Marilyn Yalom. "Ernest Hemingway—A Psychiatric View." *Archives of General Psychiatry* 24.6 (1971): 485–494.

Zavitzianos, George. "Homeovestism: Perverse Form of Behaviour Involving Wearing Clothes of the Same Sex." *International Journal of Psycho-Analysis* 53 (1972): 471–477.

———. "The Object in Fetishism, Homeovestism and Transvestism." *International Journal of Psycho-Analysis* 58 (1977): 487–495.

———. "The Perversion of Fetishism in Women." *Psychoanalytic Quarterly* 51 (1982): 405–425.

Index

fetish words in, (Hare) 109, 150,
(silk) 149–50, 152; Krebs's affinity to Nick Adams, 147, 313; and
loss, 12; names in, (Hare) 109;
Oklahoma as substitute for Oak
Park in, 147, 188; and World
War I, as sexual trauma, 148–49
"Strange Country, The": and breasts,
phallic, 144; fetish objects in,
(hair) 76, 144; fetish words in,
(silk) 76; haircuts in, ("boyish"
on women) 74–76, (gender transforming) 76; and loss, 137;
names in, (Harris) 110
"Summer People, The," 42, 166, 283
[There is a girl selling stockings under
a canvas shelter . . . .], 141
"Undefeated, The," 64–65
"Up in Michigan," 283
"Very Short Story, A," 62, 193
"Way You'll Never Be, A," 148, 195

Hemingway, Grace Hall (mother): am-
bivalence about EH's gender, 89,
95, 96–100, 102, 205; ambiva-
lence about own gender, 50,
97–99, 233; androgynous, EH's
opinion of her as, 48–50, 102;
childhood, 98–99; cross-dressing
of EH, 89–100, 102, 105, 213;

disciplinarian, 68; EH's aggression directed toward, 93, 139–40;
EH's "first love," 139–40; and EH's
feline associations, 137–38; EH's
petnames for, (Mama Mink) 138,
(Mama Kitty) 137–38, (Silkey
Sockey) 140–41, 182, 312; encoded in EH's fetish objects, 138,
140–41, 152–53, 182, 312; hair
color, preferences, 36, 89; haircutting, 48, 88–92, 150; humiliation
of children, 92, 100, 102, 301;
identification with EH, 11, 50, 98,
102–4; identification with father,
50, 98, 102, 233–34; introjected
by EH, 103–4, 203; as lost object
for EH, 104, 137; as model for
Mrs. Adams, 329; as model for
Pilar in *For Whom the Bell Tolls*,
46–49; narcissistic personality,
98, 304; as nurse figure, 139; as
phallic woman, in EH's imagination, 50, 102, 213; possible lesbian relationship, 47–48; primary
breadwinner in Hemingway
household, 301; primary castrator
in EH's family romance, 103, 109,
202, 233; and tanning, 316;
twinning of EH and Marcelline,
11, 48, 88–93, 95–99, 104–8, 150,
167, 301, 304; use of Ernest as
doll or "thing-creation," 98, 150,
304; use of Ernest as feminized
phallus, 102, 233–34; voice, 47,
49–50
Hemingway, Gregory (son, Gigi), 36,
88, 94, 117, 123, 291
Hemingway, John (son, Bumby,
Jack), 94, 132, 136, 323
Hemingway, Leicester (brother), 291
Hemingway, Lorian (granddaughter),
291
Hemingway, Marcelline, see Sanford,
Marcelline Hemingway
Hemingway, Margeaux (granddaughter), 291
Hemingway, Martha Gellhorn (third
wife, Marty): EH's aggression
directed toward, 117–18; EH's
pets names for, (Pussy) 309,